COMMUNICATION
AN INTRODUCTION TO SPEECH

COMMUNICATION
AN INTRODUCTION TO SPEECH

P. Judson Newcombe

Professor of Communication
University of South Florida
Tampa, Florida

Allyn and Bacon, Inc.
Newton, Massachusetts

About the Author

P. Judson Newcombe (Ph.D. Northwestern University) began his teaching career in high schools in Michigan. He is Professor of Communication at the University of South Florida, Tampa, Florida.

Text and photo acknowledgments appear on pages 531–532.

Supplementary Materials:

A *Teacher's Resource Book* is available for use with this text. The *TRB* includes the following materials:

> Chapter-by-chapter teacher's guides
> Chapter and unit tests
> An audio-cassette tape and copymasters

COMMUNICATION: An Introduction to Speech

The publisher would like to thank the following people for manuscript review and/or consultation for this text.

Jennifer Albritton
T.R. Robinson High School
Tampa, Florida

Rita C. Harlien
Burges High School
El Paso, Texas

Jerí Johnston
Richardson Junior High School
Richardson, Texas

Donna Webster
Will Rogers Junior High School
Miami, Oklahoma

EDP 480304-3

ISBN 0-205-10304-9

Printed in the United States of America

6 7 8 9   93

CONTENTS

UNIT 4 PUBLIC SPEAKING 189

UNIT 1

SPEECH AND YOU

CHAPTER 1 What Is Communication?

Tony and his friends are listening to Lee describe one of his latest adventures. As he listens, Tony thinks . . .

"Lee can really tell a story.

He doesn't just use words.

He uses his face, hands, and his whole body!

I wonder if I tell a story that well."

How well do *you* communicate? How can you learn to communicate better?

In this chapter, you will read about:

- a simple model of the process of communication
- the three kinds of messages
- five kinds of communication
- the importance of communication in society

You are constantly exposed to words. You hear them, write them, read them, speak them. For example, you find a note on your desk. You read it, then write a response. Or you hear a friend shout your name from across the street. Then you cross the street and talk with your friend. If you are like most people your age, you probably listen to many hours of radio and television every day.

The words from these and other sources form **messages.** Messages are ideas, feelings, thoughts, and statements sent from one person and received by another person. This process of sending and receiving messages is called **communication.**

THE ELEMENTS OF COMMUNICATION

For many years you have studied written communication, that is, communication that uses words on paper to convey a message. But communication is more than just words. A smile can communicate. A frown can communicate. The wave of a hand or the wink of an eye can communicate. Also, a mutter, a gasp, a sigh, or a moan can communicate. Words, actions, and sounds are the basis of oral communication. This book is about oral communication—the use of spoken words, gestures, facial expressions, and vocal inflections to send messages.

The Four Parts of Communication

Pam and Thor are pen pals. Although they have never met, they have been writing to each other for five years. They have shared pictures of themselves, their homes, and their friends. Recently, Pam sent Thor a cassette recording of her voice. Pam is using the cassette to communicate orally with Thor.

This situation has all of the four elements of communication. Here is a model that shows how communication works.

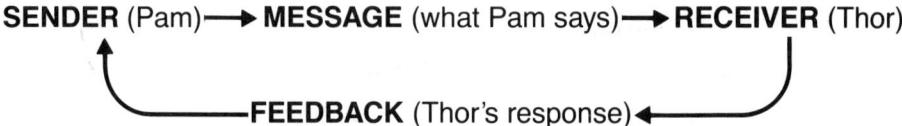

The **sender** wants someone to understand his or her message. The message, of course, is what is sent, or said. The **receiver** gets the message and interprets what it means. The receiver then answers the message through some form of feedback. The **feedback** is the receiver's response to the message. In this form, communication rotates in a pattern like a circle. You will learn more about the communication process in the next unit.

Three Types of Messages

A sender sends different kinds of messages. One kind of message is the **verbal message.** These messages are the actual words a sender uses. They can be single words like *yes* or *stop,* or they can be many words strung together. The words in verbal messages communicate the dictionary meaning of the words. For example, a receiver would not mistake the word *cat* for the word *cow.* If a sender described a green wooden house, a receiver would picture a green wooden house, not a red brick house. Specific words set limits to what is received.

Another kind of message is the **vocal message.** These messages are voice sounds. They include cries, whistles, grunts, moans, and so on. They also include the ways in which words are said. The voice can do many things. It can speed up, slow down, or add emphasis. Vocal messages, therefore, can add additional meaning to words—beyond the dictionary meanings. For example, the sentence "Who's at the door?" can be said in different ways. It might suggest concern, happiness, excitement, or surprise. Most of the emotional content of words is supplied by *how* they are said.

A third kind of message is the **nonverbal message.** These messages have no words or sounds. They are made up of clues like facial expressions and body movements. Nonverbal messages can tell a receiver many things. For example, they can tell a receiver that you are sincere. Or, they might tell a receiver—with the wink of an eye—that you really don't mean what you are saying.

During a conversation, both the speaker and the listener may send all three kinds of messages. Understanding these different kinds of messages is very important. If you understand all three kinds of messages, you can say more precisely what you intend to say. You can also better understand what someone else is saying. You will learn more about the three kinds of messages in the next unit.

THE FIVE KINDS OF COMMUNICATION

Oral communication always involves a speaker and an audience. That audience can be one person or many people. Who that audience is determines what kind of communication is taking place.

Talking Alone or One-to-One

Two of the most common types of communication occur when you are alone or with only one other person. You use both these kinds of communication everyday from the time you are a very small child.

Intrapersonal communication is communication with yourself. Many people talk aloud to themselves. They find that voicing ideas to themselves helps clear up problems or provides them with insight into a complex situation. Most often however, intrapersonal communication consists of personal, unvoiced thoughts.

Interpersonal communication is on a one-to-one basis. You are talking to another person. This form may range from a friendly chat to a serious conversation. It may occur face-to-face or in a telephone conversation.

Talking with More Than One Person

Three other kinds of communication involve multiple listeners and may include multiple speakers.

Group communication involves three or more people. People in a group often share the same purpose or goal. The group may have a leader, who directs discussion, but everyone in the group talks. The purpose of such communication is usually to solve a problem. The group often sets a time limit on the discussion.

Public communication involves one or more speakers who present a message to a group of inactive listeners. Public speaking is one example of public communication. It can be done in person, or it can be recorded and presented later. A public speaker often informs or persuades an audience. You will read more about public speaking in Unit 4.

This public speaker is communicating not only with those who can hear but also with those who are hearing-impaired. The man on the speaker's right is giving the message in sign language.

Oral interpretation and drama are forms of public communication that are known as performing arts. Oral interpretation involves one or more people reading aloud and interpreting a literary selection for an audience. Drama uses verbal and vocal messages, as well as nonverbal communication, to present a story to an audience. You will read more about the performing arts in Units 5 and 6.

In **mass communication** one or more people communicate with a large audience. Usually, the senders and receivers are not together when mass communication occurs. Radio, television, newspapers, and magazines are examples of mass communication media. Chapter 21 in Unit 6 offers a more detailed examination of mass media.

YOUR TURN

1. Study each of the two following communication situations. Then identify the *sender,* the *message,* the *receiver,* and the *feedback* in each situation. Be prepared to discuss and explain your answers in class.

    a. Tim has been walking along a section of street for twenty minutes. He has a confused look on his face. He notices a police officer walk onto the same section of the street. He approaches the officer and asks, "Could you tell me where the Exeter Building is?" The officer points to a building only ten feet away. "Wow," says Tim. "I've been very close for quite a while."

    b. Ms. Osorio places three packages on the post office counter and says, "First class, please." The postal clerk picks up one, places it on the scale, and weighs it. Then he says, "That one will be a dollar and 65 cents."

2. Often verbal, vocal, and nonverbal messages are sent at the same time. Describe what each of these messages is in the following situation.

    The waitress brings a menu and a glass of ice water to a man in a three-piece suit. He looks up from his newspaper and says, "I don't need the menu. Please bring me black coffee, whole wheat toast, scrambled eggs, and a glass of grapefruit juice." The waitress makes a quick note and says, "Thank you, sir. I'll bring your coffee right away." She smiles, takes the menu, and goes into the kitchen.

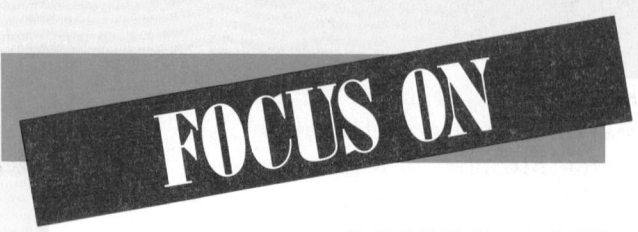

SONGS AND SPEECHES
The Same Language

What does your favorite singer have in common with a public speaker? Performing at a concert, your favorite singer communicates in much the same way as a public speaker. Those characteristics that make a singer's performance successful are very similar to the characteristics that make a public speech successful.

When you deliver a speech, you use many of the same techniques that a concert performer uses. The concert performer describes ideas and feelings through lyrics. As a speaker, you deliver your message through carefully chosen words. The concert performer stresses important feelings and meanings in the chorus, which occurs at regular intervals throughout the song. In a speech you repeat the important words and phrases that you want to stress.

A good speaker uses the voice in the same way as a concert performer does. As a speaker, you can raise or lower the pitch of your voice for emphasis. You can also control the volume of your voice to change the mood or intensity of your message. Just as a singer does, you can use pauses and stops to change the tempo and direction of your speech.

As a singer uses gesture and movements to highlight the lyrics, you, as a speaker, can use similar movements. You can add emphasis to parts of your speech by leaning toward the audience or by establishing eye contact with individual members of the audience. You can draw attention to an important detail in your speech with a gesture.

Concert performers and speakers do use the same language. When you deliver a speech, you use the same communication devices that your favorite singer uses. All of these elements together help convey your message to your audience.

THE IMPORTANCE OF COMMUNICATION

Written communication certainly plays an important role in our everyday lives. Newspapers, books, and magazines are all examples of written communication. Some forms of oral communication depend on written communication. For example, actors usually learn their roles by reading scripts; public speakers often write out their speeches before presenting them orally; the topic of many day-to-day conversations is often something that one of the participants has read.

Oral communication, too, is very important. Talking is a quick, immediate way to communicate. In certain situations talking is more effective than writing.

- *Talking is faster.* In the time it would take you to read a page, you can say the ideas and get a response.

- *Talking takes less concentration.* Often you can do other things while you have a conversation.

- *Talking can be more meaningful.* You can use your voice to add extra meaning to your words.

- *Talking is more immediate.* You can deal with problems right at the moment. You don't need to wait for a written response.

- *Talking is more convenient.* You don't need any special materials like paper and pencils.

You probably make the decision whether to write or speak several times each day. For example, you decide to speak each time you pick up the phone to *call* a friend instead of writing a letter. Usually the decision is a simple one; you know instinctively whether to use written or oral communication. In any case, it is important to be sure that the message you convey is clear.

Reasons to Study Speech

Why should you take a speech course? The following are some reasons other students have given. Maybe some of them are the same as your reasons.

- Even though I have some good ideas, I'm scared to speak out in public. I would like to feel confident enough to speak without being afraid.

- Every time I want to say something in class, I get "tongue-tied." Things don't come out the way I want them to. I get things all mixed up. I'd like to be able to say things right the first time and not have to repeat myself.

- Sometimes I think people judge me on how I say things. I want people to see me as a friendly person. Instead, I think they see me as a shy person. I'd like to change this image people have of me.

- It seems that many interesting people speak well. I see famous people speaking perfectly on TV. I'd like to be able to talk the way they do.

- I enjoy watching TV shows and movies. Sometimes I think I'd like to be an actor. I'd like to have the chance to see if I would be a good actor.

- I often have to read stories to my younger sisters and brothers. I'd like to be able to read the stories in an exciting way.

- I have trouble arguing a point. I usually get too angry. I would like to know how to present my side of a disagreement well.

In general, a speech class should help you:

1. Understand how communication takes place.
2. Know more about yourself and how to communicate with others.
3. Understand better what people are saying to you.
4. Feel comfortable in social situations.
5. Gain speaking and listening experiences that will be useful now and in the future.

Communication in the Work Place

Speaking and listening consume much of each day of your life. Therefore, it is not surprising that good speaking and listening skills are needed in most jobs. The following is a list of some jobs that require good communication skills. Of course, some jobs require more

"I often read stories to my brother and sister. I try to read the stories in an exciting way to capture their interest."

communication than others, but all jobs require a certain degree of communication: for example, talking with co-workers, listening to or giving instructions, and asking questions.

Sales   Whether you're selling a product, a service, or your own skills, you must depend on your speaking ability. Customers will want information about what you are selling. They will want to know the features, the advantages, and the cost. How well you can present this information will determine your success.

Customer Service   Many companies have customer service departments. If you work in one of these departments, you will have to answer customers' questions. Sometimes you might even have to deal with their complaints and problems. Listening carefully and speaking calmly to customers is the most important skill in this kind of job.

Health, Welfare, and Other Helping Professions   This field includes nurses, doctors, welfare agents, guidance counselors, and parole officers. All of these people work with the public every day. If you choose one of these professions, you will need to be a good listener and a good speaker. You will have to listen and understand people's problems. Then you will have to be able to communicate information to your clients effectively.

Religious Professions   The main goal of most religious leaders is to help people. If you enter this field, your words will be very

Police officers are members of a helping profession in which communication skills play an important role.

important. Often you will have to say just the right words that will bring hope to people in distress. Also, you probably will have to give public speeches on a regular basis.

Construction Workers   People who work at construction sites must be able to ask questions that are clear and to the point, so they can be certain they are carrying out instructions properly. They must be able to communicate effectively with a variety of people, including architects, engineers, plumbers, electricians, and sometimes even public relations workers or newspaper reporters.

Mass Communication   The people you hear on radio and TV usually have had formal speech education and considerable experience. There are, however, many others who work behind the scenes. These people include script writers, directors, make-up artists, and many others. If you become a member of such a team, you will have to listen carefully for directions. You will also have to speak clearly and concisely when you are working with others. Seldom is there any extra time when producing a show.

Education   When you think of education, you probably think of teachers in public or private schools. Education, however, includes much more. It includes the people who run training sessions for employees and who produce programs on educational television. If you become an educator, you will have to be a good speaker. You will constantly have to find easy ways to explain difficult ideas. You will also have to be a good listener. You will need to listen to your students to find out whether they are learning.

Politics, Government, and Law As a part of any level of government, you will be speaking for the people you represent. In addition, you will need to know the rules for formal hearings and court procedures. Debate will often become a necessary part of your life.

Transportation Workers Bus drivers, train conductors, porters, airline representatives and flight attendants, taxicab drivers, and ticket sellers are examples of transportation workers who must communicate not only with the general public, but with other employees as well. The skills of effective communication play an important part in their daily work lives.

These are just some of the professions that require good listening and speaking skills. Think of others that haven't been mentioned. How important is communication in them? If you want one of these jobs, formal speech education can give you an advantage.

YOUR TURN ////////////

1. Some reasons that other students have given for taking speech are listed on page 10. Your teacher will assign you to a group of five or six people. For five or ten minutes, brainstorm with your group to see how many other reasons you can come up with to explain why someone might want to take speech. Compare your group's list with those of other groups in the class. Which reasons were duplicated in each group? Were any reasons only listed by one group?

2. As a class, brainstorm a list of other jobs and professions that require communication skills. Identify as many day-to-day situations of each job as you can think of in which communication plays a critical role.

1 CHAPTER REVIEW

 ## Chapter Summary

Communication is sending and receiving messages through words and actions. All communication consists of four elements: a sender, a message, a receiver, and feedback.

There are three kinds of messages. Verbal messages are words and their actual meanings. Vocal messages are the way in which words are said. These messages can add meaning or emphasis to verbal messages. Nonverbal messages include facial expressions and body movements, and can support or contradict the verbal message.

Oral communication always involves a speaker and an audience. Who the audience is determines what kind of communication occurs. Intrapersonal communication is one person talking or thinking to himself or herself. Interpersonal communication is communication on a one-to-one basis. Group communication involves three or more people. Public communication, which usually involves a main speaker and a group of inactive listeners, includes public speaking, oral interpretation, and drama. Mass communication involves one or more speakers and a large audience.

There are many reasons why a speech course is helpful. For example, it can help you learn more about yourself and others. It can also help you communicate better with others. Good communication skills are also important for your future because most jobs require good speaking and listening skills.

 ## Checklist

Effective Communication Skills

1. Remember that all communication involves a sender who sends messages and a receiver who receives them. When the receiver gets the message, he or she usually responds with some sort of feedback.

2. Carefully select verbal messages, which are your words and their meanings.

3. Add emphasis and special meaning by using vocal messages.

4. Remember that nonverbal messages can support *or* contradict the verbal message.

5. Use intrapersonal communication to help you clarify your own thoughts and feelings.

6. Recognize the difference between interpersonal and group communication.

7. Be aware that good communication skills can help you not only now, but also in the future.

 ## Vocabulary

Define each term in a complete sentence.

communication	nonverbal messages
feedback	public communication
group communication	receiver
interpersonal communication	sender
intrapersonal communication	verbal messages
mass communication	vocal messages
messages	

 ## Review Questions

1. Briefly define the word *message*.

2. Draw a simple model of the communication process.

3. List some forms that *feedback* can take.

4. Identify the three kinds of messages.

5. In the 1800s, men tipped their hats to women as a sign of courtesy. Identify this kind of message.

6. Give an example of a vocal message.

7. List five kinds of communication.

8. Identify the kind of communication that involves people on a one-to-one basis.

9. Explain why speech is sometimes preferable to writing.

10. Name four advantages of taking a speech course.

Discuss with Your Classmates

1. Describe ways in which junior high and high school students use intrapersonal, interpersonal, and group communication at school.

2. Explain how a course in speech communication might benefit an exchange student from a foreign country.

3. Discuss ways in which oral communication plays an important role in local government.

4. Compare an attorney's need for good communication skills with a physician's need for those same skills. How does their need differ? How is it alike?

Critical Thinking

1. **Comprehension:** Describe the model of the communication process presented in this chapter. Then give two examples of the communication process.

2. **Analysis:** Analyze the role that nonverbal messages play in everyday interpersonal communication situations. Describe common nonverbal messages.

 **Activities**

In-Class

1. Use the model on page 4 to diagram the following:
   a. Louise places a telephone call to Robert. Robert is not home, but his answering machine answers the telephone. Louise leaves a recorded message, asking Robert to call her when he returns. When Robert gets home, he listens to the recorded messages. Then he calls Louise.
   b. Kim and Patty are at the zoo. Kim talks to a child. The child responds, but Kim doesn't understand the response. Patty explains to Kim what the child said. Kim understands and responds to the child.

2. Two people are putting on a pantomime. They can use only nonverbal messages. Select one of the situations below and describe some things that the two people could do to communicate without using words. Compare your ideas with others in the class.
   a. One person is excited about leaving to go on an ocean voyage around the world. The other person is sad that the friend is leaving.
   b. Two friends have an argument because of a misunderstanding. When the misunderstanding is explained, they apologize to each other.
   c. Two people are building a dog house. One of the people is conscientious and quite good with tools; the other is impatient and a bit clumsy.

3. Some people show lots of expressions on their faces. You can *see* emotions on their faces before you can hear it in their voices. What emotions are the easiest to see? How are these emotions expressed? With one or two other people, act out some of these emotions.

4. Think of how various foods, flowers, or perfumes smell. Choose one aroma. Describe it to the class, without telling what it is. How long did it take for the class to identify it? What other verbal, vocal, or nonverbal clues could you have given?

Out-of-Class

NOTE: You will be keeping a speech notebook throughout this course. This will help you organize your thoughts and keep track of what you learn. You will complete many of these activities in your speech notebook.

1. Watch a situation comedy on TV. Watch for vocal and nonverbal messages that enhance the humor of the verbal messages. Watch for situations in which vocal and nonverbal messages communicate the *opposite* of the verbal messages. Write a brief report in your notebook describing how the three different kinds of messages were used during the show.

2. Talk with a parent, other relative, or an older friend about his or her job. Find out how much of that person's job involves communication. Is the communication mostly interpersonal, group, or public? Does the communication occur basically with the same people or with many different people? How does the person think a speech course might help on the job? Take notes during the conversation for your notebook and be prepared to discuss what you learned.

3. Make four columns on a sheet of paper. Label the columns *Job, Verbal, Vocal,* and *Nonverbal.* Under the first column, list at least ten jobs that you have observed people doing. Then check the column that identifies the type of communication most used by people who do that job. For example, a writer would deal mostly with verbal communication. A traffic officer would deal mostly with nonverbal communication.

▨ Chapter Project

Your teacher will assign you to a group of four to six people. Each group will be given one of the situations described below. The group will then imagine traveling in a foreign country. With your group, you will decide how to communicate the situation to a native of the country who does not speak English. Each group will then select one person to act out the situation using only nonverbal and vocal messages.

1. I have a headache. Where can I find a drug store? I need to buy some aspirin.

2. I am lost. Can you tell me how to get to the train station?

3. Someone stole my wallet! I need to find the police station!

4. I am tired and hungry. Can you tell me where the closest hotel is?

5. Can you tell me when the parade will begin?

6. I would like to buy food for a picnic lunch. Can you tell me where a grocery store is?

7. My tour bus left without me. Can you tell me how to get to the town that is just north of here?

CHAPTER 2 Self and Others

These are some of Rita's thoughts as she talks with her friend Sharon.

"Sharon always seems so confident.

She doesn't seem to worry about talking to other people.

I wonder if I seem that sure of myself."

How confident do *you* feel? How can you build your self confidence?

In this chapter, you will read about:

- using intrapersonal communication to develop a clearer self-concept
- how greater self-confidence can improve self-esteem
- how snap judgments and stereotyping can prevent people from getting to know each other
- basic needs that all people have
- the importance of being supportive during stressful events in other people's lives
- the importance of feedback

If you were asked to draw a picture of yourself, what would you do? Would you draw only your face? If so, would you be smiling or frowning? If you drew a full-length picture, would you change anything about yourself? Would you be taller or thinner?

Drawing yourself as you see yourself is easier than drawing yourself as others see you. You see yourself at your best and worst. Your friends usually see you only at your best. After seeing your self-portrait, would your friends say, "That looks just like you"? If so, you would have successfully captured the outward features that others see.

Unfortunately, few people can draw realistic pictures of themselves. Instead, most people probably would describe themselves with words. Even then, they would have many decisions to make. Should they describe only their best features? Should they also describe their personalities? What words would best describe them?

FINDING THE "YOU" IN YOURSELF

In the first chapter you learned that intrapersonal communication is communication with, or within, yourself. You learned that it could include thinking as well as talking aloud to yourself. Probably you spend little time actually talking aloud to yourself. However, like most people, you probably think a lot about your relationships with others. How do you look today? Why did you get angry at your best friend? What will your friends think if you try out for the play? These things that you see and think about yourself form your **self-concept.**

Many artists, such as Cézanne, painted self-portraits that give us a glimpse of the artist's personality and self-concept.

Becoming Aware of Your Self-Concept

How well do you actually know yourself? Imagine that you are trying to describe yourself to someone who has never seen you. How would you answer the following questions?

Things other people can see:
1. How tall are you?
2. What is the color and length of your hair? How curly or straight is your hair?
3. What is the basic color of your eyes? Are any other colors noticeable?
4. Is the basic shape of your face round, oval, square, or triangular?

Facts others may not know about you:

1. What is your full name? Were you named after anyone? Do you have a nickname? What is it? How did you get the nickname?
2. In what city, state, and/or country were you born? On what date? How old are you in years and months?
3. How many relatives or friends do you have?

Traits and preferences others may not know:

1. What one thing irritates you most about members of your own sex? About members of the opposite sex?
2. What time of the day do you like most of all? Why do you like this time? If you could decide for yourself, what time would you get up and go to bed each day?
3. What is your favorite meat? Vegetable? Salad? Beverage? Dessert?
4. Use a scale of one to ten—with ten being the best or highest. Rate your interest in each of the following areas.
   a. animals/pets   f. parties/social events
   b. art   g. farming
   c. computers   h. cooking
   d. sports   i. traveling
   e. movies   j. fishing

Through intrapersonal communication, you just made certain things about yourself clearer to yourself. Probably some of the answers were easy. Others may have taken you some time to decide. However, all of your answers should have helped you to take a closer look at yourself.

Once you have a greater self-awareness, intrapersonal communication can help you even more. It then can help you decide which things you believe in and which things you don't believe in. It can help you decide which things you value and want, and which things you don't value and don't want. The more you know about yourself, the easier it will be to set goals for yourself. Then you can find out what you have to do to reach those goals.

Being Aware of Your Perceptions

Perception is the process of taking in information from your surroundings through the five senses (sight, hearing, touch, taste, and smell). Most people experience the world through all of these senses so their basic perceptions are about the same.

Your total perceptions and self-concept come from a combination of three general sources:

1. *Physical senses.* Your world is very different if you can't see or hear, for example.
2. *Responses and reactions of other people.* Your family, friends, and acquaintances influence your view of the world and of yourself.

Their friendly reactions improve your self-concept.

3. *Your total experience.* Each new experience expands your perceptions of the world and of yourself. Your daily surroundings affect this. For example, if you live in an isolated, lonely area, your experiences with other people will be limited. You may feel that you are not capable of communicating well with others because of your lack of experience. Also, your view of the world will tend to be narrow rather than broad. Many different life experiences open up more possibilities. You can make more educated choices based on first-hand knowledge.

During the process of intrapersonal communication, you are developing greater self-awareness. You decide the things you believe and don't believe, value and don't value, want or don't want. By knowing more about yourself, you become better able to set realistic goals for yourself. You see how your current skills and beliefs limit you. You also may see what you need to do to expand them.

Building Self-Confidence and Self-Esteem

One of the goals of intrapersonal communication is to help you build **self-confidence.** Self-confidence is the belief that you have the ability to do things and to do them right. The first step toward self-confidence is to find out what you already can do. Then you can try new things. Each new success lets you say to yourself, "Since I can do this, maybe I can do *this* also." You won't always succeed the first time at a new task. Still, you should feel good about all the things you have already done. Part of becoming an adult is understanding this important fact.

As your self-confidence grows, so will your **self-esteem.** Your self-esteem is the value that you place on yourself. Improving your self-esteem is not always easy. However, by trying new things and succeeding, you will feel better about yourself. Furthermore, you will gain the courage you need to try other things.

You can ask yourself the following four questions as you begin to work on your self-esteem.

1. *What is one thing I want to change about myself right now?* See if you can find where and when this problem started.

2. *How can I break up a big task into smaller ones?* Solving a big problem may seem too hard. However, if you can deal with small parts of a big problem, you may succeed.

Often family members can help you reach your goal. If you trust family members your relationships with them will become stronger.

3. *Who can help me reach my goal?* Can any family members or friends help you? Let them know you want their help. By doing this, you also are telling them that you trust them. Mutual trust always makes relationships stronger.

4. *Is this the best time to work on this problem?* Timing is very important. Perhaps you want to concentrate on changing some aspect of your speech or behavior patterns, but you have several important school assignments that are due in the next week. You may want to wait until you have fewer school pressures before you embark on a self-improvement project.

When you like and accept yourself, you will find it easier to communicate with others. You also will be able to accept others without being too critical. As a result, you will be able to build stronger, happier relationships with people.

SELF-CONCEPT AND SPEECH COMMUNICATION

What does your self-concept have to do with a speech course? Most things that you say and the way in which you say them are a direct result of your thoughts. This speech course can help you in two ways.

Expressing Yourself

If you are a shy person, you probably feel awkward or uneasy in new situations. You may not know what to talk about, how to introduce yourself, or how to show that you are interested.

Or you may think that people are not interested in what you have to say. You may feel that you often express yourself in a way that causes people to misunderstand you.

Your self-concept affects the way you express your thoughts. This speech course will help you develop effective tools for improving the way in which you express yourself—and improving the way that you respond to other people can help you improve your self-concept.

Overcoming Stage Fright

Stage fright is a type of fear that affects you emotionally and physically. A quickened pulse, sweaty palms, a dry mouth (symptoms of stage fright), are not limited to people who appear on stage.

Have you ever gone to a party where most of the people were strangers to you? Or have you ever been asked to make a telephone call to someone you didn't know? Situations such as these can produce the symptoms of stage fright. Taking a speech course can help you learn to overcome excessive stage fright and, perhaps more importantly, to use the emotional excitement to your advantage.

YOUR TURN

1. Intrapersonal communication helps you decide your values and goals. In your speech notebook, answer the following questions.

   a. Whom do you trust the most? If you had a big decision to make, would you go to this person for advice? Explain.

   b. If you could change one aspect of your personality, what would you change? Why would you make this change? Do you think peer pressure is influencing you at all? Explain.

   c. What do you think is your most important accomplishment so far? Why was it so important? How did you feel when you did it?

2. In your notebook, make two columns. Label one *Wonderful Things About Me*. Label the other *Things About Me That Could Be Improved*. Then write as many entries as you can.

FORMING RELATIONSHIPS

Friendships are a wonderful source of learning, entertainment, affection, and support. The people who are our friends help make good times better, and they help us get through difficult times in our lives. But friendships don't simply happen. People must work at a relationship to help it develop from mere acquaintanceship to full-grown friendship.

Meeting New Friends

Read the following case study of two people meeting each other.

Cindy is at the city airport. She is waiting for Carla, an exchange student from Peru. She looks again at a picture of Carla. Cindy wants to be sure that she'll recognize her. Carla's large brown eyes and long black hair should be easy to spot. Cindy reads again the description that Carla sent her.

Height: 5 feet 3 inches
Weight: 102 pounds
Age: 13
Hobbies: horseback riding, swimming, and reading
Home: Lima, Peru
Goal: to become a doctor
Parents: Professor Juanita Cordova-Viella (mother)
Doctor Pedro Viella (father)

That is all Cindy knows about Carla. Still, she feels sure she'll like her. They both like swimming, and Cindy always wanted to ride a horse. They both will be in the same science class, and they both want to be doctors.

Will Carla like the United States? Will she mind staying with a family that has three boys and only one girl? Will she be afraid of Cato, their Saint Bernard? Will she have a good sense of humor and be able to put up with the boys' teasing? Will they be able to speak together easily in English?

Cindy feels the same way most people feel when they first meet someone. They guess what the person will be like, based on what they know about the person. In Cindy's case, she is quite sure she will like Carla. However, she is worried about Carla's reaction to her brothers and their huge dog. Cindy has some mixed feelings.

Making friends is just the first step in a long-term relationship. You must work to keep a friendship.

Most interpersonal communication, communication on a one-to-one basis, begins with some shyness. This is especially true if people are meeting for the first time. Most people tend to accept others little by little. They allow for some doubt so that they can "escape" easily if things don't work out well.

Your attitude toward meeting people could affect new relationships. For example, you can take a positive attitude. You can look at meeting people as a good learning experience. Each person you meet can teach you something new about all people in general. You probably will learn something about each new person, and yourself.

On the other hand, you might not gain anything if you have a negative attitude. ("I won't be accepted." "It'll be a dull evening.") If you think you won't have a good time, you probably won't. Other attitude problems can prevent a first meeting from being positive. These problems include making snap judgments and stereotyping.

Making Snap Judgments   Too often people make snap judgments about others. Based on very little information, some people decide to be friendly or unfriendly. Snap judgments may result from:

- *Verbal messages:* "He gave such a dull speech, he must be dull himself."

- *Vocal messages:* "She laughs all the time. She must be a silly person."

- *Nonverbal messages:* "He always wears the latest styles. He must be a terrific person."

Stereotyping **Stereotypes** are false generalizations or conclusions that are made from a few, quick facts. For example, people sometimes give certain traits to groups of people. ("All sixth graders are childish." "All parents are mean.") Of course, most stereotypes are negative statements. If you stereotype someone, you'll never have a chance to look for anything good in that person. Stereotyping may result from:

- *Verbal messages:* "She uses big words. She must be so smart that she's no fun."

- *Vocal messages:* "Their voices on the record were so high-pitched, they must have been children."

- *Nonverbal messages:* "Because they're red-headed, they must have really bad tempers."

Too often first impressions are lasting ones. If they are negative, they can prevent any future communication. Because of this, avoid making snap judgments and stereotyping. Never form opinions of people after only one meeting. Also, instead of looking for negative traits in people, look for their unique qualities. Search for ideas or experiences you have in common. Look for interests you both enjoy. In other words, give new relationships some time to grow.

BUILDING LASTING RELATIONSHIPS

Making friends is just the first step in a long-term relationship. Once you have a good friend, you must work to keep that friendship. Why do some friendships last a lifetime and some for only a few months? Interpersonal communication—or the lack of it—is often a major factor. When people are talking to each other, relationships usually last. A breakdown in communication, however, often signals the end of a relationship. The following pages contain some suggestions for keeping friendships strong.

Recognize Needs

Everyone has certain needs. What are your needs? Do you know what your friends' needs are? Basically, all people need to be needed. However, that is only one need. People also share needs, as you will see in the list on page 30.

Friends are supportive of each other. This means learning to give sincere compliments when they are deserved.

- the need to satisfy physical necessities
- the need to remain healthy and active
- the need to feel safe and secure
- the need to set and reach personal goals
- the need to communicate
- the need to have hope and trust in the future
- the need to experience beauty

Good relationships can satisfy many of these needs. In fact, many people believe they gain something from continuing certain relationships. When they believe this, they usually will make an effort to make those relationships last.

Although all people share the same basic needs, your needs may be greater in some areas, and your friends' in other areas. By recognizing these different needs, you may be better able to help yourself and others.

Be Supportive

Interpersonal communication will improve if you learn to be supportive of others. This means learning to give sincere compliments when they are deserved. It also means that criticism of others should be positive, not negative. Avoid comments that will hurt others or damage their self-concept.

EXTROVERTS AND INTROVERTS
The Great Balancing Act

Can different personalities be classified into types? Some experts identify two opposite personality types: *extroverts* and *introverts.* An extrovert looks toward the external world and is happiest when surrounded by people and activity. An introvert, on the other hand, enjoys thinking and wondering, solitude, and the inner life.

We can observe introverted and extroverted behavior even in newborns. Extroverted babies are likely to cry when awake. They need the external stimulus of being rocked or talked to. Introverted babies are likely to be quiet while they are awake. Although they love attention, they are happy to spend time alone.

Later, we continue these behavior patterns, although we show them differently. Julie, 13, and Gregg, 16, are sister and brother. Gregg's extroverted personality motivates him to join school activities, and at home he organizes his sisters and brothers in basketball games. Sometimes he has trouble getting Julie to participate. She would rather read a book, practice her guitar, or talk to a friend.

In time, both Gregg and Julie will move toward what the experts call "psychic equilibrium." This describes how a definite extrovert or introvert tries to balance his or her particular personality type. Gregg, though not comfortable with constant soul-searching, will discover the value of an occasional serious talk with a friend. Julie will learn to enjoy leading songs around the campfire with her guitar.

The search for psychic equilibrium is aided by the fact that every personality contains elements of both the "outer-directed" and the "inner-directed." Now we understand why introverted writer Karen, who used to work at home, has rented an office. Working alone, she nevertheless likes to feel life around her. And we understand why extroverted salesman Doug enjoys an occasional solo weekend of fishing.

Be Sensitive

From time to time, everyone must deal with stressful events. A good friend is always sensitive about how these events affect their friends. These events might include the following:

- suffering physical illness or injury
- suffering a personal loss, such as experiencing the death of a loved one or breaking up with a special friend
- failing to reach a personal goal, such as winning a contest or passing a test
- failing to meet others' expectations, such as getting home late or letting a friend down

During stressful times, people usually need extra help and understanding. That is why being sensitive to another person's stressful times is important. It is especially important if you want your relationship to last.

Building Lasting Relationships

Be supportive and sensitive.

Give Feedback

"I know my friends like what I'm doing. I only wish they would say it sometimes." Have you ever said that? Have you ever heard someone else say that? You know how important it is to be praised for a good job. Everyone likes to hear positive feedback. Even if you know you did a good job, you feel better if someone else notices and tells you. Remember this with your friends and family. Just like you, they also like to hear praise.

Many people think that everyone knows how to give praise and offer sympathy. This isn't true. Some people have never learned how to give—or receive—a compliment graciously. Other people purposely avoid someone who is experiencing a personal sorrow because they don't know how to express concern.

The following statements are examples of things you might say to indicate praise or sympathy.

To compliment or show personal recognition:

- "You seem to know exactly what to say to put people at ease."
- "Congratulations on winning the race."
- "Your poster for the dance was terrific!"
- "You are one of the nicest people I know."
- "That was a great shot! Absolutely great!"
- "Thanks so much for all your help. I really appreciate it."

To show understanding or personal concern:

- "I was sorry to hear about your uncle being so sick."
- "We're all thinking about you. Hope you feel better soon."
- "If there's something I can do to help, please let me know."
- "I miss you. I can't wait till you get back to school."

Develop Mutual Respect

Successful interpersonal communication also requires that the people involved develop **mutual respect,** which is an understanding and acceptance of each other's views. This may mean respecting someone's beliefs, accomplishments, knowledge, skills, or appearance. One way to help establish mutual respect is to avoid deciding why someone did or said a particular thing. The reason people say or do something is known only to them. You should also avoid interpreting other people's actions in terms of what you would have done in the same situation. Judging people on what you would have done is unfair to them and to you.

IMPROVING RELATIONSHIPS

Most habits are unconscious. We do certain things without even thinking about them. These unconscious habits can hurt our communication with friends. Becoming aware of our actions can improve our relationships. The following are some common habits to avoid.

Taking Over Conversations Three people are sitting at a table in the cafeteria. One person is doing all the talking. This person may be talking so loudly or incessantly that no one else feels free to speak. The other people look bored. Has this ever happened to you? Make sure that all your conversations include everyone. You can bring others into a conversation in two ways. You can ask them questions or ask for their opinions. Including others in a conversation is being sensitive to them and their needs.

Glancing Away You're talking to someone. Suddenly that person isn't looking at you. He or she is looking over your shoulder at something or someone behind you. What should you do? Obviously, that person isn't listening to you anymore. When you are talking to people, look directly at them. This will show them that you are interested in them and in what they are saying.

When you talk to people, look directly at them.

Constantly Interrupting   Some people constantly interrupt others. Interruptions are usually made for one of two reasons: Either the other person wants to disagree with what is being said, or the other person is impatient, wanting to finish the speaker's sentence faster. Neither reason is acceptable. If you start to interrupt someone, stop and say, "Excuse me. Go on with what you were saying." Then wait for that person to finish.

Using Excessive Small Talk   Small talk is useful for getting conversations started, particularly among strangers. It offers an opening for interpersonal communication. But small talk alone doesn't advance a relationship. Try to find out the other person's interests and talk about those things. You should also realize that you don't have to fill every moment of silence with words. Silence doesn't necessarily signal the end of communication.

Speaking Too Loudly   Be considerate of people in and around your conversation. Loud talking or laughter, particularly in public places, clearly says, "Look at me!" Controlling the volume and pitch of your voice is not only courteous to bystanders, but it assures that the people with whom you are talking are not embarrassed by unwanted attention.

YOUR TURN ////////////////

1.   Your teacher will divide the class into small groups. One by one, all students should tell about one of their first good friends. Each student should explain how the friendship came about. Then each group should compare and discuss the reasons that its members gave. Each group should come up with its own list of things to do to build lasting relationships and share this list with the class as a whole.

2.   Ads often include stereotyped characters. Search through some magazines and bring to class as many of these ads as you can. Discuss what aspects in the ads stereotype the characters. Why do you think stereotypes are used?

2 CHAPTER REVIEW

 ## Chapter Summary

You can get to know yourself better through intrapersonal communication, or communication with yourself. The things you see and think about yourself form your self-concept. Intrapersonal communication can also help you be aware of your perceptions and build your self-confidence. Greater self-confidence will increase your self-esteem, the value you place on yourself. As your self-esteem grows, you will be able to communicate better with others. This speech course will help you understand and build your self-concept. It will help you express yourself and understand stage fright.

Meeting new people is sometimes difficult. However, meeting new people can have many positive results. To have positive results, though, you must start out with a positive attitude. Making snap judgments and stereotyping people can prevent relationships from developing. To avoid this, give relationships time to grow. To build lasting relationships, you should recognize other people's needs. Be sensitive and supportive to other people during stressful times. Give feedback and develop mutual respect. Make sure everyone is included in conversation. During conversations, look directly at others and do not interrupt someone who is talking. Avoid indulging in excessive small talk and talking too loudly.

 ## Checklist

Intrapersonal and Interpersonal Skills

1. Use communication with yourself to help enhance your self-concept and to build your self-confidence.
2. Build your self-confidence in order to increase your self-esteem.
3. Avoid making snap judgments about people.

4. Remember that stereotyping people can prevent relationships from developing.

5. Be sensitive and supportive of other people.

6. Remember the value of positive feedback; everyone likes to feel appreciated.

7. Look directly at someone who is speaking, and do not interrupt the person.

8. Avoid excessive small talk.

9. Be aware of how loudly you are talking.

 ## Vocabulary

Define each term in a complete sentence.

mutual respect   self-esteem

self-concept   stereotypes

self-confidence

 ## Review Questions

1. Define *self-concept*.

2. Explain how intrapersonal communication can change your self-concept.

3. Explain how you can build your self-confidence.

4. Explain the difference between intrapersonal communication and interpersonal communication.

5. Explain how your attitude toward meeting people will affect your relationship with them.

6. Identify two mistakes that people sometimes make when they first meet someone. What can you do to avoid these mistakes?

7. Name five basic needs of all people. Why is it important for you to know about these needs?

8. Identify three stressful times in a person's life.

9. Explain why it is important that you give your friends and family positive feedback. Why do you think some people find it difficult to express sympathy?

10. Identify three habits that could hurt a growing relationship.

 ## Discuss with Your Classmates

1. Describe the three general sources from which you develop your perceptions and self-concept. Give three or four examples for each source. Discuss ways in which these specific examples affect your perceptions and self-concept.

2. Discuss the importance of timing in a decision to develop self-esteem. Are there situations when delaying the decision might be appropriate? Are there situations when delay might not be advisable?

3. Define stage fright. Discuss instances when you or someone you know has suffered from stage fright.

 ## Critical Thinking

1. Comprehension: Distinguish between someone who is supportive of a friend and someone who never disagrees or expresses a personal opinion.

2. Analysis: Think of a time when you judged someone too quickly and later changed your judgment of the person. List the evidence that your initial conclusion was based upon. List the evidence that you gathered later that caused you to change your conclusion about the person.

 **Activities**

In-Class

1. In small groups, design an ad that includes one stereotyped character. Then for the same product, create an ad that does not have a stereotyped character. Be prepared to explain your ads to the class.

2. Think of one friendship you have had. Then write answers to the following questions:
    a. What did you gain from the friendship?
    b. What did you contribute to the friendship?
    c. What did you do to keep the lines of communication open?
    d. Does the friendship still exist? Why or why not?

Compare your answers with those of classmates to get ideas for strengthening and maintaining friendships.

3. Write down the five traits you value most in your friends. When everyone has finished, fold your paper and pass it to your teacher. Your teacher will choose four folded lists at random, and then write the traits on the board. The class will discuss these traits. Which ones were repeated most often? How many of the most common traits were on your list?

4. People often do nice things that go unnoticed. For each of the following situations, develop a list of things that you could say to show that you truly appreciate the kindness and consideration shown to you.
    a. A brother or sister cleans your room so that you can take a babysitting job.
    b. Your parents give up their vacation so that you can go to summer camp with your friends.
    c. Cafeteria workers bake fresh cookies, even though buying them would be easier.
    d. Your older sister offers to pick you up after school when you are using crutches because of a broken ankle.

Out-of-Class

1. Using a scale of one to ten, with ten being the highest or best, rate your self-esteem in your speech notebook. Then list some ways that you think you can increase your self-esteem. Can you break up a large task into smaller ones? Can people you know help you achieve any of the goals? When is the best time to pursue each task?

2. Did you ever make a snap judgment about someone? Did it almost prevent a friendship from developing? In your speech notebook, write two paragraphs. Explain your first impressions of the person in the first paragraph. Then tell how time changed that opinion in the second paragraph.

3. In a magazine or newspaper, find a cartoon of a character who has low self-esteem. Paste the cartoon in your speech notebook. Beneath it, list as many reasons as you can for the character's low self-esteem. Then write four or five suggestions the character might follow to develop better self-esteem.

4. In your next conversation with a friend, find an opportunity to compliment or show personal concern. Make a mental note of your friend's response. Did he or she seem more at ease? Was this a difficult thing for you to do? Record this in your notebook. Describe how being concerned for others made you feel.

5. Think of something that you would really like to do, but for which you lack confidence. Perhaps you would like a part in the school play. Perhaps you would like to sing a solo in a school concert. List in your notebook all the positive things about yourself that make your ambition reasonable. If you have convinced yourself that you are capable of carrying out your wish, act on it.

 **Chapter Project**

Bring to class at least two ads from different magazines. Each ad should be for a product designed to meet one of the basic needs that people have, which are listed on page 30. Your teacher will select one or more ads for each need.

The teacher will then divide the class into groups of five or six people and give two ads to each group. For each ad, discuss what self-concept is displayed by the characters in it, and the ways in which the ad appeals to people's self-esteem. Do the ads contain stereotypes? If so, are the stereotypes positive, or negative?

After each group has analyzed the ads assigned to them, they should present their information to the rest of the class. The class should then develop a list of general conclusions about the ads that were analyzed.

UNIT 2

THE COMMUNICATION PROCESS

CHAPTER 3 The Elements of Communication

As Jeff slides into home plate, he thinks . . .

"Oh no! The umpire is signaling me out!

I thought I was safe.

The team sure looks upset.

They're all shouting."

Have *you* ever been in a situation like this? What kinds of messages and feedback did you notice?

In this chapter, you will read about:

- how people, animals, and machines can be senders and receivers of messages
- how messages can be verbal, vocal, and nonverbal
- how feedback can be positive, neutral, or negative
- how noise can cause a breakdown in communication

Communication seems so simple. You communicate every day without ever stopping to think about it. If someone understands you, you have communicated. You have shared your message.

But what if someone doesn't understand you? What happened? Maybe the listener wasn't paying attention. Maybe the message was too confusing to understand. Maybe you were to blame. Maybe you spoke too fast or too quietly.

Most people don't think about the process of communication until it's too late. Suddenly they are faced with a breakdown in communication, and they don't know what happened. They don't know what the problem is or how to solve it.

EXPANDING THE MODEL OF COMMUNICATION

This chapter will help you understand more about how communication works. It will expand on the simple model of communication that you learned in Chapter 1. You also will learn the reasons for communication.

In Chapter 1, you studied the following model of communication.

Notice how the following examples are all simple forms of this model.

1. Your father (sender) says, "Remember to take out the trash this morning." (message) You (receiver) say, "I will on my way to school." (feedback)

2. You are on your way home from school. Your best friend (sender) whistles (message) to you (receiver) from across the street. You turn around and shout, "Meet me at Tony's in five minutes." (feedback)

As long as the sender and receiver keep responding, communication will continue. However, sometimes a communication is more complicated than a simple sender-receiver-feedback model.

SENDER

Communication begins when someone or something sends a message. People, of course, are the main senders. From birth, people say—in one way or another—that they are alive and should be heard. Since many messages are spoken, the term *speaker* can often be used in place of *sender*. All speakers are senders of messages. However, all senders of messages are *not* speakers.

Animals can also be senders of messages. Through certain actions or sounds, your pet tells you it wants to eat or to go outdoors. Although an animal cannot speak, it *does* communicate. Many animals can also learn to respond to simple, spoken messages.

Machines can also be senders of messages. For example, you can dial the telephone for the correct time. When you do, you may get one of two responses. One is a recorded voice with a prerecorded message.

Although an animal cannot speak, it *does* communicate. Many dogs learn to respond to simple, spoken messages.

The other is an artificial, or synthesized, voice. In this case, a computer makes sounds that create words and phrases mechanically. The study of machines that send messages is called **cybernetics.** These machines include lasers, computers, and microwave transmitters.

RECEIVER

A receiver may be a person, an animal, or a machine. Often a receiver is called a "listener." All listeners are receivers. However, all receivers are not listeners. For example, machines such as computers receive messages as electrical impulses. However, they don't listen actively to sounds.

To expand the model of communication, you now can add the three types of senders and receivers.

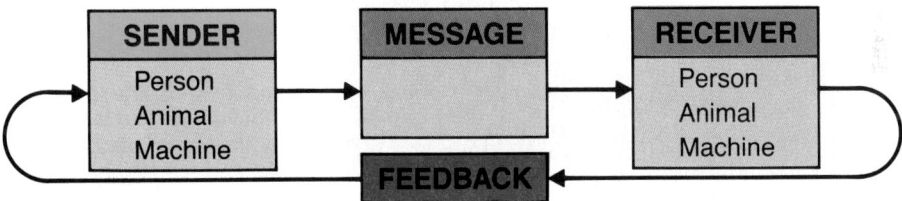

YOUR TURN

1. Can you identify any machines that
   a. are senders of messages to other machines?
   b. use English to communicate with people?
   c. are no longer used to communicate because newer machines have replaced them?

Be prepared to explain and discuss your answers in class.

2. Find an example of each of the following:
   a. A human sender communicates with a machine, and the machine responds.
   b. An animal sends a message to a person.
   c. An animal sends a message to a machine, and the machine responds.

Share your examples with your classmates.

By means of Braille, people who have impaired vision can enjoy the verbal messages of books and magazines.

MESSAGES

Messages can be ideas, emotions, or factual information. Senders want to share these thoughts, feelings, or facts with receivers. In Chapter 1, you learned that messages can also be verbal, vocal, or nonverbal.

Verbal Messages

As you will remember, verbal messages are made up of words. Senders, of course, can send words to receivers in many different ways. For example, if you wanted to advertise a new fruit drink named Sunrise, you could say or sing the name. You could print it in a newspaper or on a bumper sticker. You could even have a skywriter write it in the sky. The purpose of all these forms of advertising would be the same. You want people to see the name, remember it, and buy the fruit drink.

Verbal messages are only useful if the receiver understands them. Verbal messages, therefore, must meet certain requirements.

1. If written, verbal messages must be legible. A person might write you a wonderful letter. However, if you can't read the handwriting, you will never receive the message.

2. If spoken, verbal messages must be heard. If a friend speaks quietly on a noisy train, you will never receive the message.

3. The language of verbal messages must be understood. If you don't read Chinese, you won't understand messages written in Chinese. If you have never taken a computer course, you probably won't understand computer language.

4. Verbal messages must be correct. You see a mongoose for the first time but think it is a large rat. Later your verbal message about the mongoose will be incorrect. Others will not "see" in their minds what you saw with your eyes.

Sometimes people from different countries have trouble communicating. Many of their messages lack the last two requirements listed above. As a result, a breakdown in communication can occur. For example, the British call a subway a *tube*. This term could confuse Americans. Most Americans think of a tube as a type of container.

Vocal Messages

Vocal messages are voiced sounds. They include the ways words are said, such as changes in rate, vocal quality, pitch, and inflection. Some researchers think vocal messages are often more important than the actual words used.

A change in inflection can sometimes change the meaning of a vocal message. For example, the simple statement "Sure you tried hard" is positive and conveys confidence. The same sentence, however, said with a rising and falling pitch on "sure" and with exaggerated emphasis on that one word, conveys sarcasm or doubt: "*S-U-R-E* you tried hard." Changes in inflection that change the meaning of a vocal message are called **paralanguage.**

Vocal messages often emphasize what is being said. On the other hand, they can also deny what is being said. For example, actors can say they are not nervous. But if their voices are shaking, receivers will know the truth.

When you read, you can't hear any vocal messages. However, authors often describe vocal messages. You might read, for example, "he screamed" or "she said excitedly."

TALKING TO COMPUTERS

"I know you! You're the boy who lives down the street!" Imagine how many different meanings those words could have. By changing the vocal quality, pitch, inflection, and rate of speech, you could dramatically change the *vocal* message of the words. "I know you" can sound friendly, teasing, or threatening. Humans would not have difficulty understanding the vocal message. But programming a computer to understand the vocal message is a difficult problem.

Human speech communication is a complex activity involving several parts of the brain. Understanding the literal meaning of the words—the verbal message—is only one part of the process. In many ways computers are like the human brain. Like the brain, computers process and store information using electrical impulses. Computers can "learn" a vocabulary, parts of speech, and rules of grammar. They can, for example, be programmed to distinguish between the sentences "The dog bit the man" and "The man bit the dog." Even though the words in the two sentences are the same, computers can learn that word order affects sentence meaning.

Much of our understanding of messages is based on our experiences. Computers cannot duplicate those experiences. Unlike computers, we can interpret what something *really* means even though the verbal message may not contain that meaning. For example, the following announcement was made in a subway station: "Dogs must be carried on the subway." Any English-speaking person would understand the meaning. A computer, however, might think everyone boarding the subway must carry a dog.

Computers can communicate with people through a keyboard using a written language. But human speech is not just vocabulary and grammar processed through electrical impulses. Although some machines respond to sound, a real R2D2 has not yet been designed.

Vocal Message

If your friends all talk to you at once, you won't receive any of their messages.

Nonverbal Messages

Nonverbal messages are all other messages that do not depend on either voice or words. They include such things as facial expressions, body movements, and gestures. They also could be clothing, music, dance, or any other form of personal expression. Nonverbal messages usually include the things you are doing while you are speaking.

Suppose you are talking with your older sister. She tells you that she is not worried about her job interview the next day. As she talks, she bites her nails. She also jumps slightly when the telephone rings. Her nonverbal messages are not the same as her words. In fact, her nonverbal messages are "speaking" much louder than her words. She really is worried. Nonverbal messages, therefore, are important for total understanding.

People often send all three types of messages at the same time. If all three support one another, the communication is unified and clear. However, sometimes one message will say something different from the other messages. In such a case, the receiver must decide which is the strongest message. When the receiver doesn't guess correctly, a breakdown in communication occurs.

Nonverbal messages do not depend on either voice or words. Dance is a beautiful and expressive form of nonverbal communication.

To expand the model of communication further, you now can add the three types of messages.

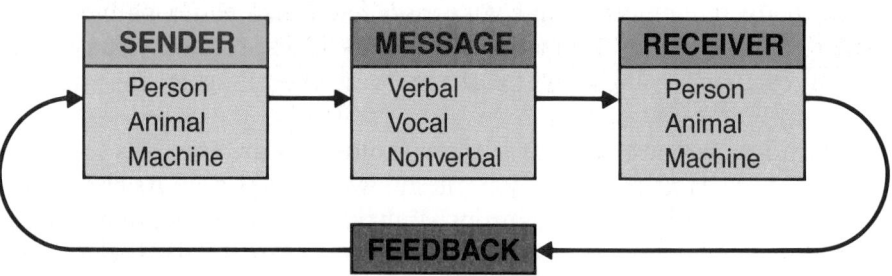

SENDER	MESSAGE	RECEIVER
Person	Verbal	Person
Animal	Vocal	Animal
Machine	Nonverbal	Machine

FEEDBACK

FEEDBACK

Feedback is the receiver's response to the sender's message. It may be verbal, vocal, or nonverbal. True feedback can influence the sender's message. For example, as you give your book report, you notice that some students are not listening. Since you want their attention, you change what you were going to say. Or, you talk louder or show a picture on the cover of the book. The feedback that students were bored made you change the delivery of your book report.

There are four kinds of feedback—positive, negative, neutral, and mixed. The four different types can be illustrated by responses to a public speech. Loud and lengthy applause would be **positive feedback.** A total lack of applause—especially if applause were expected—would be **negative feedback.** Light or polite applause would be **neutral feedback. Mixed feedback** would occur if various people in the audience responded in ways that were obviously different. Some would applaud loudly, some politely, and some not at all.

You can now add the three methods of feedback to the model of communication.

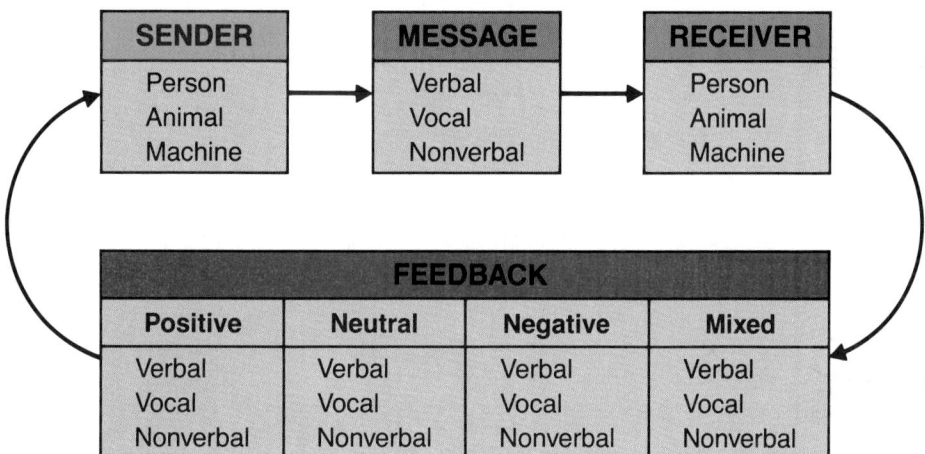

NOISE

The last element in the model of communication may be called **noise,** or **interference.** Noise is anything that takes attention away from the message or the feedback. It may be physical, such as a ringing bell or a toothache. It may also be mental, such as nervousness or sadness.

Noise may be clear to both the sender and the receiver. On the other hand, neither may be aware of it, or only one may be aware of it. For example, suppose you are talking to your cousin on the telephone. Because of static, your cousin cannot hear you clearly. You are unaware of the static, and your cousin doesn't mention it. As a result, your cousin hears only part of your message. Noise may occur at any point during the communication process.

In the final expanded model of communication, the element of noise surrounds every other element. To show this, the word surrounds the model.

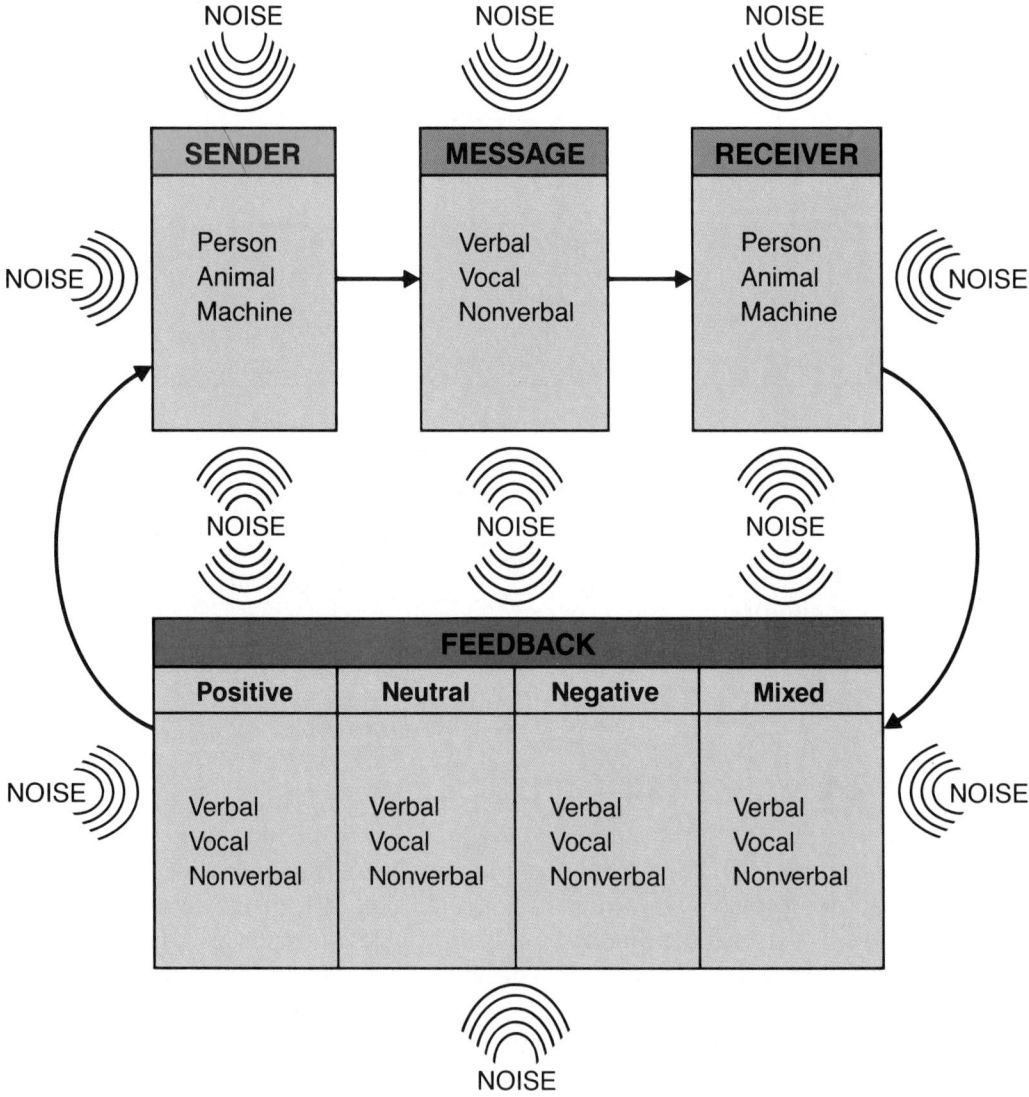

Noise is anything that takes attention away from a message. Noise can interfere with the enjoyment of an outdoor concert.

YOUR TURN

1. Make up a communication situation that includes the following elements. Then draw a communication model for the situation.

    a. Names for senders and receivers (Lee, David)

    b. The different messages being sent at the same time (verbal only or verbal and vocal)

    c. The type of feedback (negative overall)

    d. Specific noises (barking dog)

Be ready to explain in class how your model works. Compare your model with those of your classmates.

2. Which type of feedback would you expect in the following situations?

    a. People at a wrestling match see their hero thrown out of the ring.

    b. Faye's dog sits up and begs for some of her dinner.

    c. Two children are watching a funny movie on TV.

    d. At a team meeting, the coach announces the names of those who will be cut from the team.

    e. A public speaker at a town meeting presents an opinion that some people agree with, while others do not.

Be prepared to explain and discuss your answers in class.

 # CHAPTER REVIEW

 ## Chapter Summary

An expanded model of communication begins with a *sender,* who may be a person, an animal, or a machine. The sender delivers a *message.* The message may be verbal, vocal, or nonverbal—or a combination of these. To be effective, the message must meet certain requirements. If written, it must be legible. If spoken, it must be audible. The language must be understood. Finally, the message must be accurate. The message is sent to a *receiver,* who also may be a person, an animal, or a machine. The receiver provides feedback which may be positive, neutral, negative, or mixed. Often, however, *noise* causes a breakdown in communication. Noise includes anything that interferes with the communication process.

 ## Checklist

Basic Communication Skills

1. When sending a verbal message, be sure your listeners can hear you. When sending a written message, make it legible.
2. Use language that can be understood when you send any kind of verbal message.
3. Make all your messages accurate.
4. Changes in inflection can alter verbal meanings.
5. Recognize nonverbal messages.
6. Aim to present a unified and clear message through your verbal, nonverbal, and vocal communication.
7. Watch for feedback to your communication.
8. Try to avoid interfering noise when you are involved in the process of communication.

 **Vocabulary**

Define each term in a complete sentence.

cybernetics   neutral feedback

interference   noise

mixed feedback   paralanguage

negative feedback   positive feedback

 **Review Questions**

1. Name three kinds of senders and receivers.

2. Give an example of a situation in which a sender is not a speaker.

3. Give an example of a situation in which a receiver is not a listener.

4. Give examples of how animals communicate with people.

5. Explain how a machine can be a receiver of messages.

6. Identify the three types of messages.

7. Identify the following type of message: Your friend gives you a "thumbs up" sign from across the field.

8. Define *feedback*.

9. Give an example of positive feedback, negative feedback, neutral feedback, and mixed feedback.

10. Identify the kinds of noises that are affecting you now. Explain how some or all of these noises could interfere with communication.

Discuss with Your Classmates

1. List as many ways as you can think of for someone to send a *nonverbal* message. What does each of these messages mean?

2. How important is feedback to us? What kinds of feedback do you get every day in school? How would school be different if you got no feedback about your progress there?

3. Explain how noise can cause a breakdown in communication. Identify situations that you have been in where noise interfered with the communication process.

4. Identify ways in which animals can communicate nonverbal messages. Discuss as many examples from your own experience as possible.

 # Critical Thinking

1. **Analysis:** Think of two communication situations that you have been in recently where two different kinds of feedback occurred. Summarize each incident and explain the kind of feedback that took place.

2. **Evaluation:** Discuss what impact "intelligent" computers will have in our society and in our communication habits. Will the communication model change when computers can speak and understand speech? Will society benefit from this technology or not?

 # Activities

In-Class

1. In small groups, think about the communication model developed in this chapter. Brainstorm together other ways to diagram the model. Present your diagram to the class.

2. In small groups, think of one sentence that can be said in several different ways. Then, each person in the group should demonstrate to the class a version of this sentence using inflection, pitch, rate, etc. When all individuals in each group have finished, the members of the class should comment on the various versions.

3. In small groups, discuss ways in which people could show positive feedback in a one-to-one communication situation. Then discuss ways in which people could show negative feedback. Role-play two examples to illustrate your group's findings.

4. Pair off and have a "conversation" with a classmate nonverbally. Then talk about how the conversation worked.

Out-of-Class

1. Watch a situation comedy or movie on TV. In your notebook, describe all the noises or things that distract characters. Be ready to share your findings with the class.

2. During the coming week, keep track of the breakdowns in communication that occur between you and other people. Be ready to describe some of these situations to the class.

3. Keep track for a week of all the *feedback* you get from people at home. How does feedback affect your life?

Chapter Project

Analyze a communication. Choose a very short conversation that you hear, either among friends, family members, or on television. Write the conversation down. Then write all your impressions about the communication. Include the following information:

> Who was the sender? The receiver?
> What was the message? Was it delivered?
> How was the message delivered?
> Was there feedback?
> How effective was this communication?
> Did the sender or receiver send any nonverbal messages?
> Did any noise intrude upon the message?

Diagram your information. Your diagram should illustrate clearly what happened in the communication exchange. Be prepared to discuss your diagram in class.

CHAPTER 4 Listening

David and Ellen are learning to use a jigsaw in their wood-working class. As Mr. Barton begins, Ellen thinks . . .

"This is really going to be fun.

I think I'll make a shelf for my stereo.

I guess I'd better pay attention and listen or I won't know what to do."

How well do *you* listen? How can you learn to improve as a listener?

In this chapter, you will read about:

- the difference between hearing and listening
- the different purposes for listening
- the difference between fact and opinion
- generalizations, half-truths, misleading comparisons, personal attacks, and faulty cause-effect relationships
- ways to become a better listener

Ms. Davis, an English teacher, is explaining linking verbs at the board. She notices that Bill is not paying attention. To get Bill's attention, she taps a piece of chalk against the board. Then she quietly says, "Board, Bill, board." Bill looks up surprised. He sits up and replies, "Yes, Ms. Davis, very bored!"

Have you ever found yourself in a similar situation? You have not been listening, but you should know what has just been said. People in such situations can do several things. They can apologize for not listening. They can pretend they heard—even if they didn't. Or they can try to make sense out of the few pieces of the message they did hear.

Hearing words is not listening. Listening is an active process. It requires that the eyes and ears work with the brain. When an incomplete or inaccurate message is received, there is usually a breakdown in communication.

REASONS FOR BEING POOR LISTENERS

On the average, people spend about 63 percent of each waking day just listening. With all this practice, why aren't people better listeners? Why do most people remember only about 25 percent of what they hear? There are several possible reasons.

One reason could be distractions, either the distraction of a listener's own thoughts or an outside distraction. Usually listening doesn't offer a second chance. Unless a spoken message is recorded, it is said and then disappears.

Another reason for poor listening might be a lack of patience. Some people lose patience with things they don't understand easily.

Listening is an active process, even when it involves listening to someone play the piano.

If they don't understand something they stop listening and think, "Why listen? I haven't understood anything so far."

A third reason might be the need to be entertained. Some people are used to being constantly entertained by television. If they aren't entertained, they may think, "If this isn't interesting, why should I listen at all?"

WHY LISTEN?

Listening is a little like eating. You have been doing both for a long, long time. In fact, you don't even stop to think about how or why you do either of them any more. They are both second nature to you now. However, thinking about listening is important. By understanding the reasons for listening, you could learn what you are missing if you don't listen carefully.

Listening for Information

This is the kind of listening that you do most during your life. You listen to learn. You listen for facts and ideas. You might want to know what a new product does. You might want to know the facts behind a news story. You might need directions to a new park. You might need advice to help you solve a problem. The list is endless. Over a period of time, you do not remember all the facts you hear. However, you *do* remember some of them. As a result, you are constantly becoming more knowledgeable. You know more than you knew before.

Listening to Analyze or Compare

You have heard your favorite singer sing one song hundreds of times. Then you hear another singer sing the same song. Without realizing it, you start to compare the two versions. You listen for any differences. In such a case, you are more interested in comparing parts of the message than you are in the message itself. Those parts may be such things as emphasis, rhythm, or inflection. In other situations, you might compare verbal messages.

Reasons for Listening

For Information

To Analyze

To Judge

For Relaxation

Listening to Judge or Evaluate

Was the story you just heard funny or serious? Was the conclusion happy or sad? Did a reporter present both sides or just one side of a story? You make judgments every time you meet a person for the first time or every time you go somewhere new. You also make judgments when you hear anything new or different.

All new people, new situations, and new ideas, however, demand caution. Wait before you decide an idea is worthless. First, listen to the entire story or speech. Don't stop listening just because some ideas, opinions, or facts disagree with your own. If you stop listening, you will never hear the "proof" of the new ideas. You will never learn anything new.

Listening for Relaxation and Enjoyment

Sometimes you can take an hour's "vacation" by listening. After a whole day at school and several hours of homework, you probably want to relax. To do this, you could turn on the TV and watch a western. You and your friends could go to a concert or listen to tapes or records at someone's home. All of these situations involve listening. They also offer relaxation and enjoyment.

LISTENING FOR CORRECT MEANING

Communication only occurs when correct meanings are received. However, some things that you hear are easily misunderstood. These things are either unclear or misleading. Some of them, in fact, are simply not true. It's important, therefore, that you are aware of the following speech "traps."

Distinguish Between Fact and Opinion

"The basketball team lost every game this season." This statement is a **fact.** It can be proved. On the other hand, "The team didn't try very hard this season" is an **opinion.** Opinions are statements that have not been proved true or false. The problem comes when people state their opinions as if they were facts. As you listen, you must always be deciding whether a statement is a fact or an opinion. Then you must decide whether you want to believe it or not.

Facts and opinions are tricky by themselves. But sometimes they appear in the same statement at the same time. You can sort out some of the double statements if you look for certain words. *Said, said that, suggested,* or *thinks* are all qualifying words. These words can signal that an opinion is coming up.

For example, "Sam said that UFO's come from outer space." It is a fact that Sam made a statement. That part can be proved. What Sam said, however, is an opinion. The qualifying words, of course,

Is it a fact or an opinion that people who ride bicycles are fighting air pollution?

were *said that*. Those words made the whole statement seem like a fact, even though it contained an opinion. See if you can tell the difference between the following facts and opinions.

- Elvis Presley was the most popular singer of the 1960s.
- My mother thinks that Elvis Presley was the greatest singer in the world.
- People who ride bicycles are fighting air pollution.
- More people are riding bicycles today than ever before.

Recognize Generalizations

Have you ever heard anyone say, "Teenagers today are lazy"? This statement is a generalization. A **generalization** is a statement that lumps a whole group of people or things together. Then it condemns all for the qualities of some. Obviously, generalizations are misleading. Nevertheless, people make them all the time. The bad part is that generalizations have a way of sounding like the truth. Here are some other examples of generalizations.

- Teenagers are unreliable.
- All men like football.
- All college students have rich families.

Catch Half-Truths

Half-truths are statements that tell only half the story. They are correct as far as they go, but they don't go far enough. Imagine, for example, that there is a house paint called "Forever." A TV commercial says that houses painted with "Forever" have gone ten years without needing repainting. On the other hand, houses without "Forever" needed repainting every five years. Although the facts are true, the commercial is misleading. The "Forever" houses had surfaces made to hold paint. Also, these houses were less exposed to sun and rain. *Any* paint on those houses would have lasted longer. Here are other examples of half-truths.

- A student tells everyone that her drawing of a horse came in third in a state-wide contest. She doesn't say, however, that there were only three entries in that category.

- A movie critic states that a certain movie "was totally enjoyable at the beginning. The ending, however, was boring." Later an ad for the movie quotes the critic. It says only that the movie was "totally enjoyable."

Beware of Misleading Comparisons

Some statements are misleading because they don't compare equal things. They compare the best thing in one group with the worst thing in another group. Such statements are called **misleading comparisons.** People make misleading comparisons to try to prove that the first thing is better. They sometimes even compare a current situation with a past one. Of course, they do not point out any changes that have occurred in the meantime.

For example, Ken asks his older brother for some money. His brother says, "When I was your age, I got along on 25 cents a week." Ken's brother made a misleading comparison. He set one time period against another. He overlooked the fact that inflation has made a quarter almost worthless today. Here are other misleading comparisons.

- Everyone in my day walked to school. Why can't you?

- My cousin in Minnesota is the same age as I am. He has a snowmobile. Why can't I have one?

WHEN SEEING IS HEARING

When you get home today, turn on your television but keep the sound off. See if you can understand anything that is being said. Some people, particularly those with hearing impairments, could tell you much of what is being said by lipreading, or speechreading, as it is more often called. Speech-reading is the ability to understand words by interpreting the visual cues of a speaker, including lip, mouth, and jaw movements, facial expressions, and gestures.

If you try to understand what is being said on a silent television, you'll quickly see that speech-reading is very hard to learn. For example, about 60 percent of sounds in English are either very hard to see or not visible at all. Other sounds, like *bit, mit,* and *pit,* look the same when they are said, but they sound different. Also, people normally say about 13 speech sounds per second, but the eye can see only about 10 sounds per second.

Alexander Graham Bell, who is best known for his invention of the telephone, was a teacher and a great promoter of speechreading during most of his life. He felt that speechreading would free the deaf from the isolation they often feel by allowing them to communicate with everyone.

Mr. Bell's devotion to the deaf was easy to understand. His mother and his wife both became deaf at an early age. In fact, his invention of the telephone grew out of his experiments in developing sound amplification for the hearing handicapped. When he was 70, Alexander Graham Bell wrote, "The recognition of my work for and interest in the education of the deaf has always been more pleasing to me than even recognition of my work with the telephone."

Of course, hearing-impaired people are not the only ones who use speechreading. Think about that the next time you are talking to someone when an airplane flies overhead or when a friend is trying to talk to you in a crowded, noisy school cafeteria.

Recognize Personal Attacks

Bart and Tina are running for Student Council president. Bart can't find anything wrong with Tina's ideas or plans for the school. Therefore, Bart personally attacks Tina instead. Personal attacks like these are called **ad hominem arguments.** These remarks try to discredit a person's ideas by attacking the person who holds them. Here are some examples of *ad hominem* arguments.

- He's so young, he doesn't know what he's talking about.

- She's lived in this state for only a month. How would she know anything about the people running for governor?

Recognize Faulty Reasoning

Part of your responsibility as a listener is to analyze what you hear. You may need to make decisions based on what people say. So be a thinking listener. Don't just believe everything you are told.

Be especially alert when listening to messages that are meant to persuade you. Clever speakers can sometimes seem to be giving you facts when they are actually presenting their own opinions or misleading you with faulty reasoning.

There are many methods of persuasion that try to convince listeners of arguments that lack a solid basis in good reasoning. The following examples are among the most common.

Card Stacking   A speaker who is stacking the cards seems to be presenting all the evidence, but really tells only those facts that support the point he or she is trying to make. Suspect card stacking if a speaker is strongly in favor of something and mentions no drawbacks at all to the idea and makes no positive points about the alternative.

Bandwagon   In this technique, a speaker asks you to "get on the bandwagon" by joining an overwhelmingly large group of people already in favor of the idea. When a television commercial tries to convince you that you should use a certain kind of shampoo because all the loveliest actresses do, it is using the bandwagon technique.

Glittering Generality   This is an idea so broad and all-encompassing that everybody agrees on its value, but no one is really sure what it means. A politician says she is in favor of "law and

Be alert when listening to messages that are meant to persuade you.

order." You have to agree with that, right? No one but a criminal is in favor of crime! But you may discover that the politician's interpretation of "law and order" is very different from your own. A good listener looks beyond the broadly stated idea to try to find out what a speaker really means.

Non Sequitur This is a Latin term meaning "it does not follow." Suppose a speaker is running for class president. He tells you that you should vote for him because he did a fabulous job coaching the track team last year. It does not follow that just because someone is a good coach, he will also make a good class president.

Recognize Cause-Effect Relationships

Read these two sentences.

1. I drop the vase.
2. The vase smashes into pieces on the floor.

The vase was broken *because* I dropped it on the floor. Therefore, the fact that I dropped the vase and the fact that it broke are in a **cause-effect relationship.**

But sometimes events are presented as cause and effect when a little thought will show that they are not really related in that way.

Look at these two sentences.

1. Bob started reading *Newsline*.
2. Bob made the honor roll.

These two events—Bob reading *Newsline* and Bob making the honor roll—are related in time, but they are not necessarily a cause and effect. Bob might have begun studying harder at the same time he began reading *Newsline*. Just because one event closely follows another does not mean that the first event caused the second one.

Listen carefully for faulty cause-effect statements. They can sound true if you don't think through what is being said.

YOUR TURN

1. What do you think will happen in each of the following situations? Explain how listening is involved in each one.

   a. A mother is talking to her son. She is telling him what he must do before he plays softball. While the mother is talking, the boy sees his younger sister in the next room. She is trying to make him laugh by making faces at him.

   b. The woodshop teacher is talking about safety rules. One of the students worked for her father in his furniture factory for two summers. She is familiar with most of the machinery in the shop.

2. Name the speech "traps" in the following statements.

   a. "Your sister should be able to do this work easily since my sister didn't have any trouble with it."

   b. "Everyone in Hawaii knows how to do the hula."

   c. "Last week the Hendersons pulled into their driveway with a sailboat attached to their car. They must have won a contest."

   d. "I should have received an *A* for my work. I put a lot of effort into it."

   e. "My friend says that the Cougars are the best team in the state."

   f. "Maria isn't qualified to be the leading actress. I think her hair is too short."

   g. "Mr. Robertson's new book is . . . stunning."

   h. "I don't see why you don't join like everyone else in the club."

BECOMING A BETTER LISTENER

Breaking old habits and starting new ones take time. You will not become a better listener overnight. However, you should start by working on one thing each day. Then you will gradually—but permanently—improve your listening skills. The following are some suggestions that might help you.

Prepare to Listen

If you want to hear and understand everything a speaker has to say, you should prepare ahead of time. For example, if you are going to talk over something important with a friend, it would be helpful to prepare by arranging a place to meet that is quiet with no distractions. Or, if you want to hear everything a teacher has to say, preparation could be as simple as planning to be in class on time.

Another preparation to consider for good listening is the amount of time you will have to spend sitting and understanding the speaker. If you know that you will be doing a lot of listening, you can prepare yourself by getting enough rest the night before. Also, eating lightly before a long lecture can really improve your attention.

These hints on preparation for listening can help you see how important listening is, and, at the same time, how distractions and lack of preparation really interfere with understanding what is said. The preparations are fairly simple, but good concentration for listening is hard enough without making it more difficult by trying it when you are hungry, upset, or tired.

Further preparations for a lecture, play, or some other formal event, will make listening easier if you take a seat where you can see and hear the speaker easily and clearly. When you sit down, put away anything that could distract you. Don't look around the room. Also, don't look at people who will take your mind off what is being said. Then concentrate on what is being said. Work extra hard if you are not interested in the topic. Sometimes you will have to answer questions at the end. If this is the case, have paper and a pencil ready to take notes.

Listen for the Main Idea

Active listeners understand more of what is said than passive listeners. As you listen, think about what the person speaking is really trying to say. The **main idea** is the central thought a speaker

Active listeners understand more of what is said than passive listeners. As you listen, concentrate on what the speaker is really trying to say.

wants to express. In conversations and informal speaking situations, the main idea is sometimes difficult to find, but active listening will help you pick it out.

In formal speaking, the main idea is often included in the introduction. In the very first sentence, a speaker may tell you what will be done and how it will be done. Don't miss it. Understanding the main idea will help you understand the rest of the speech.

Main ideas can be stated in different ways. Here are some examples.

- *A topic sentence.* "I believe that solar power soon will be the world's main source of energy."

- *An axiom.* "Honey will draw more flies than vinegar."

- *A quotation.* "H.G. Wells once said, 'The past is but the beginning of a beginning'."

- *A question.* "Do you enjoy scary movies?"

- *An analogy.* "Young children are like tennis shoes. They are always underfoot, constantly dirty, but very comfortable when you want them."

- *A personal example.* "This morning I saw five cans, three bottles, and four candy wrappers on the school grounds."

To be an active listener, try to keep track of the main idea by listening for instances when the speaker seems to be "talking off the point." Also, be alert for times when a speaker seems never to "get to the point." Listening actively will help you to grasp the main idea.

Listen for Supporting Details

Listen first for the main idea. Then listen for points that further explain that main idea. These are the **supporting details.** Supporting details can be anything from facts to beliefs. Transitional words such as *moreover, yet,* and *furthermore* can help you spot a new idea. Some speakers also may use *for example* or *for instance* when they are going to support an idea with an example. Other speakers will use words such as *first, second, third,* and *finally* to signal supporting points. Listen carefully for any or all of these "hints." They can help you easily recognize supporting points.

Link Introductions with Conclusions

In conversations and any informal listening situations, you may have to ask questions or restate what a person has said to be sure you understand what the conclusion is. For example, if a friend explains that he has failed math, you may have to ask what this means and what its effects will be. Does it mean he will have to repeat a grade? Does it mean he will be unable to go with you to summer camp? Does it mean he will have to go to summer school? You can ask questions to follow a main point through to its conclusion.

In formal speaking situations, the main idea of a speech is often repeated or rephrased at the end. By doing this, a speaker emphasizes his or her main point. For example, a speaker might begin with a question and end with the answer to that question. A speaker first might ask, "Have you ever wondered what causes . . .?" Then in the conclusion, he or she might say, "The things that cause . . . are . . ." It is important to listen for the concluding statement. It should be the same or similar to the main idea. If they are the same, you will know that you understood the main idea of the speech.

Recognize Context Clues

Have you ever heard anyone say, "My words were taken out of context. That wasn't what I meant at all"? **Context clues** include anything that comes before, during, or after a verbal message. They also include verbal, vocal, and nonverbal messages. As you have seen in past chapters, something as simple as a gesture can change the meaning of a verbal message. Therefore, when an idea is taken out of context, it is changed in some way by the person repeating it. For example, notice how the meaning changes when the following statement is taken out of context.

> *Out of Context:* He said he wouldn't help you with your homework.
>
> *In Context:* He said he wouldn't help you with your homework because he has the mumps and is contagious.

Context clues can be very helpful. They can help you understand words you don't know. For example, suppose you heard someone say, "At the outdoor market today, people selling apples, pineapples, mangosteens, and bananas were all in the same area." Even though you may not know what *mangosteens* are, you could take a good guess that they are some kind of fruit. Context clues can help you understand more fully what you are listening to.

Take Notes

When appropriate, taking notes can help you concentrate. Taking notes can also help you spot main ideas and supporting details. For example, a speaker may say that there are three reasons for something. In your notes you should use Roman numerals (I, II, III) for each of the three reasons. Then you can write any supporting points under each of these main points. Your notes, therefore, would look like an outline.

Some people are not good note-takers because they do not write down important facts like names and dates. Other people, however, are not good note-takers for the opposite reason. They write down too much. You should write down only those facts that are necessary for you to remember accurately. Your notes can't include everything. They should have just enough information to trigger your memory.

The next time you miss hearing something important, stop and think about it. What happened? Why did you stop listening? What were you thinking about at the time? Did some word make you remember something else? Did a noise or some movement distract you? If you can discover the cause, you can take steps to correct it. If you correct it, you are on your way to becoming a better listener.

Taking notes can help you concentrate. It can also help you to identify main ideas and supporting details.

YOUR TURN

1. Most people have played the game called "Rumor" or "Gossip." The game begins when someone whispers something to the next person. That person tells the next person what he or she heard. The message passes throughout the group. Finally, the last person repeats the message out loud. Then the sender of the original message tells what had been said at the beginning. Play this game in class. Discuss what happens to the message. Did the main idea of the message change? Did any supporting details change?

2. Select a partner. One of you will research a word in the dictionary that you do not know. Then use this word as you talk conversationally with your partner. Give as many context clues as possible. When you have finished, ask a question to see if your partner listened well enough to understand the meaning of the new word from the dictionary.

4 CHAPTER REVIEW

 ## Chapter Summary

This chapter discusses listening, an important part of good communication. The purposes for listening are to gather information, to analyze or compare, to judge or evaluate, and to relax or enjoy.

You are a better listener when you are attentive enough to notice speech errors, such as opinions presented as facts, generalizations, half-truths, misleading comparisons, personal attacks, and faulty cause-effect statements. Finally, you can become a better listener if you prepare, listen for the main idea and supporting details, link introductions with conclusions, recognize context clues, and take notes.

 ## Checklist

Effective Listening Skills

1. Distinguish between fact and opinion.
2. Recognize generalizations.
3. Catch any half-truths in what a speaker says.
4. Beware of misleading comparisons.
5. Recognize personal attacks for what they are.
6. Listen for faulty reasoning, especially when a speaker is trying to persuade you about something.
7. Be on the lookout for faulty cause-effect statements.
8. Prepare yourself for listening by getting rid of distractions and arranging for a situation in which you can concentrate.
9. Listen for the main idea in what someone is saying.

10. After you have understood the main idea, listen for supporting details and link what is being said to the conclusions the speaker would like you to draw.

11. When you are unfamiliar with a word or phrase, use context clues to help figure it out.

Vocabulary

Define each term in a complete sentence.

ad hominem arguments	half truths
cause-effect relationships	main idea
context clues	misleading comparisons
fact	opinion
generalization	supporting detail

Review Questions

1. Identify and explain one reason why some people are poor listeners.

2. List four reasons for listening.

3. Identify the kind of listening that you do the most. Explain why.

4. Give an example of a fact and an opinion.

5. Define *generalization*. Give an example of one.

6. Define an *ad hominem* argument. Give an example of one.

7. Identify some things you can do to prepare for listening.

8. Describe some of the ways in which the main idea of a speech can be presented.

9. Name six things you can do to become a better listener.

Discuss with Your Classmates

1. What sorts of distractions might affect your ability to listen in the following situations? How might you get rid of such distractions?

> In a classroom.
> At a play.
> At home.

2. Identify from your own experience at least two communication situations in which listening proved to be especially difficult. Discuss techniques you could have used to make listening more successful in each case.

3. Identify the listening purpose in each of the following situations. Be ready to discuss your reasons in class.

> **a.** A play director asks a stagehand to go to the lobby during intermission. He should listen to what people in the audience are saying about the play.
> **b.** Tim is taking care of his three-year-old sister. She is outside, playing in the backyard. After a while, she comes in. She says to Tim, "There's a frumpin out there making noises." Tim asks her what a *frumpin* is. She begins to describe it.
> **c.** As Margie walks in the front door, she hears her brothers arguing. She goes into the kitchen and asks them what they are arguing about. They each give her a different explanation of the argument.

4. Which of the following is a true cause-effect statement? Be prepared to discuss and explain your answers in class.

> **a.** Marty must not like me. He didn't come to the party.
> **b.** Jeff started guitar lessons last month, and a lot more kids sit with him at lunch now.
> **c.** I just had a tooth pulled, so I can't eat anything chewy.
> **d.** This camera was very expensive, so it must take perfect pictures.

Critical Thinking

1. Comprehension: Distinguish between someone who listens carefully to a political debate and someone who merely hears it. Offer examples of how each person is likely to react to the candidates and their messages.

2. Analysis: The ability to listen carefully is very important in many jobs. Identify two jobs in which listening is an important skill. Analyze the role that listening plays in each job.

Activities

In-Class

1. Think of something fairly simple that you know how to do that not everyone in the class will be familiar with. (Examples might be changing a tire, making homemade bread, adjusting the brakes on your bike, cooking something in the microwave, etc.) Make sure the process has at least four steps. When called on, tell the class your directions. After you have finished, choose someone to repeat each step. If someone cannot repeat a step, try to find out why. Were the directions too long? Too complicated? Out of order or unorganized? Was the listener distracted?

2. People are able to think almost five times faster than they can talk. Because of this, a person can sometimes predict what someone else will say next. To test this, play parts of recordings of speakers or singers to your class. Stop the recording at a certain point and ask others to write down what they think will be said or sung next. After some students have read their predictions, play the next part. Were the predictions correct? What clues led to their answers?

3. Learn how a speaker might respond to an audience of good listeners and an audience of bad listeners by reading a short passage to the class. This should be done twice. The first time it is read, the audience is to act as though they are not interested in the passage or the speaker. The second time it is read, the audience should act very interested in the passage and show they feel friendly toward the speaker. After the passage has been read twice, tell how you felt about the audience in both cases. Finally, the audience should discuss how you responded to them.

Out-of-Class

1. Listen to commercials on television and radio. Also, look at advertisements in newspapers and magazines. Try to find examples of all four kinds of faulty reasoning listed in this chapter. Keep a record of your research in your speech notebook.

2. Assume that your English teacher will be giving a talk tomorrow on mystery stories. List all the ways in which you might prepare for the talk. Using your list, prepare for the teacher's talk.

3. Write an ad or a speech trying to persuade people to your point of view on a particular subject. Use at least two faulty reasoning techniques.

4. Go to the quietest place you know. Listen to all the sounds. Observe the many different ones that you never really noticed before. List them in your speech notebook.

 **Chapter Project**

Pair up with one or more partners for this project. Together, discover who your representatives are in local or state government. Then choose one representative and an issue you would like to get his or her views on. The issue should be an important one in your community. Write or call your representative and ask for information about this issue. Also, ask if the person has issued statements or white papers about other issues that affect your city or state. Ask for a copy of one or more statements.

When you receive the information, one partner should read it carefully to the others. Can you identify any instances of faulty reasoning? Is it easier to find them listening or reading? Why? Write a report on your findings and present it to the class.

CHAPTER 5 Speaking: Vocal Messages

Lisa is hearing impaired. A speech therapist helps Lisa learn to speak clearly. These are Lisa's thoughts as she practices making sounds.

"To make the *s* sound, I must put my teeth together.

My tongue should be flat, and then I should smile.

If I hold my finger up, I will feel the air moving out from the center of my mouth."

Do *you* know how sounds are made?

In this chapter, you will read about:

- the parts of the body responsible for producing sound
- using pitch and inflection to improve speaking
- controlling resonators to create a pleasant voice
- improving the articulation of words

The telephone rings. Beth answers, and the voice on the other end says, "I've been trying to think of the name of that funny song we learned in the second grade." I thought you might remember."

"Jim!" Beth screams. "I haven't heard from you since you moved away two years ago! How are you? Are you back in town?"

Jim didn't give his name, but Beth still recognized him. She remembered his voice even though she hadn't heard it for two years. How was she able to do that? Since she couldn't see him, she had to rely on vocal messages.

As you learned in Chapter 1, vocal messages depend on the sound of the voice and changes in the voice to communicate. Vocal messages also include such things as yawns, moans, and cries. They are totally separate from words. Most vocal messages, nevertheless, usually go along with verbal messages. Of course, vocal messages and verbal messages do not always say the same thing. Sometimes they say opposite things at the same time.

SHOULD YOU CHANGE?

You have spoken for many years now. You no longer have to think about how you make sounds. You speak without thinking about it. Over the years you have also formed certain speech patterns. And, right or wrong, family and friends accept the way you talk. They are used to it.

However, most people can recognize those who speak clearly and effectively to large groups of people. This kind of clear and forceful communication often comes from making some changes in our speaking habits. Those who speak effectively to audiences have made changes by careful study and practice. They recognize that speaking informally at home or with friends is different from communicating formally. You might want to make some changes in your speaking habits in order to become a better public speaker.

Good public speakers have studied and practiced so that they communicate well with an audience. Formal speaking to an audience involves more skill than speaking informally with friends or family.

Following is some basic information which can help you improve your vocal skills. Just remember one important thing. To change comfortable habits, you must be willing to exert some effort. You must also be patient. Change takes time.

THE GENERATORS OF SOUND

Breathing is automatic. You don't have to think about it. Its main purpose, of course, is to supply the body with oxygen. Breathing, however, has a second purpose. It produces the air you need to make sounds.

To make sounds, you must use the sources of power for volume. These sources of sound include the lungs, rib cage, diaphragm, and related muscles. The lungs are large sacs. They are surrounded by the rib cage and the diaphragm. The **diaphragm** is a powerful muscle that separates the chest from the stomach area. The diaphragm goes from the front of the ribs to the spine.

As air enters the lungs, the diaphragm is pushed downward. Then the muscles between the ribs are expanded. Breathing in air is called **inhaling.** As the muscles between the ribs contract, the diaphragm relaxes. Then air is forced out of the lungs. Breathing out air is called **exhaling.** The air goes through the bronchial tubes and the trachea to the larynx, where sound is actually made.

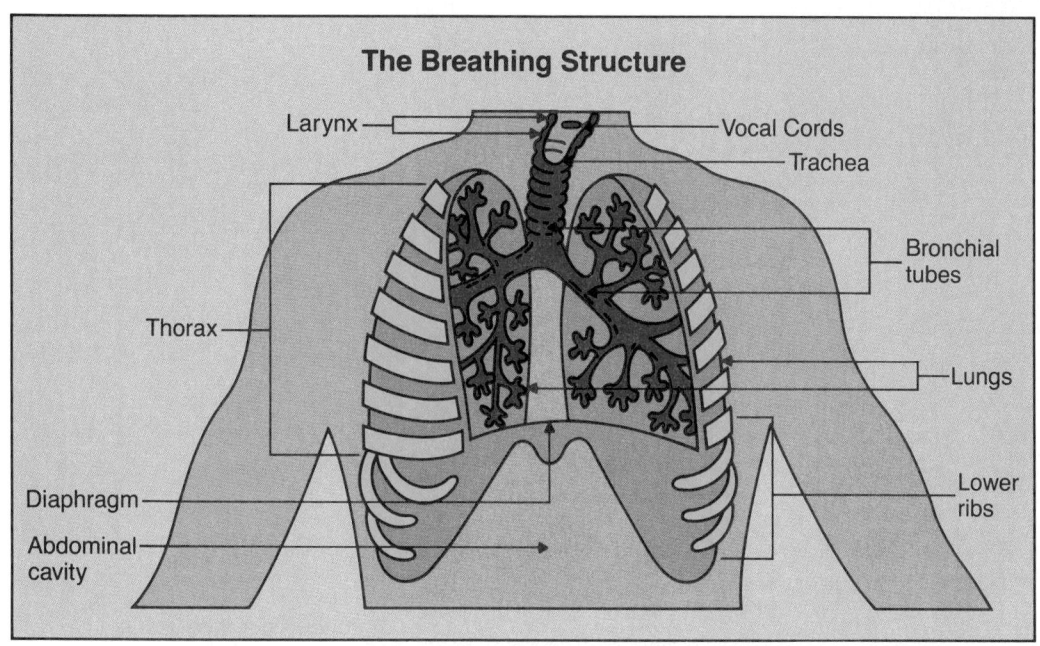

The Breathing Structure

Larynx

Vocal Cords

Trachea

Bronchial tubes

Thorax

Lungs

Diaphragm

Lower ribs

Abdominal cavity

THE VIBRATORS OF SOUND

John was uneasy about being in the cottage. Sometimes at night he would hear strange, moaning noises in the attic. After one noisy night, he decided to investigate. As he climbed the stairs and flicked on a small light, he heard two sighs. One came from one side of the attic, and the other came from the opposite side. John looked closely at those two places. He discovered two small broken windows at either end of the attic. Both had several thin wires fastened tightly over the openings. The wires were to prevent squirrels or birds from getting in. John was greatly relieved. He realized that there wasn't anything to worry about. As wind blew across the wires, they vibrated slightly, creating the eerie sounds.

The Larynx and the Vocal Cords

In the example above, wind passed through tight wires and made sounds. The **larynx,** or voice box, works the same way. Air passes through the larynx, across the vocal cords, and makes sounds. The tightness of the vocal cords affects the sound. The sound is high if the cords are very tense. The sound is low if the cords are relaxed.

A good singer is skilled in breathing properly and in projecting the sound of her voice.

Therefore, air from the lungs makes very little sound until the vocal cords begin to vibrate. This process is called **phonation.** Once the cords are moving, you can raise or lower your pitch. You can do this by increasing or decreasing the tension of the vocal cords.

The same thing happens when you blow up a balloon and let the air out. If you just hold the balloon, the air will make a low-pitched sound. However, something else happens if you hold the opening of the balloon loosely with your fingers and let the air escape very slowly. You can raise or lower the sound as you change the opening's width.

The vocal cords are in the larynx. The larynx is in your neck—about where your Adam's apple is. The larynx has one main purpose. It is used as a valve at the opening to the **trachea** or windpipe. It prevents food, water, or objects from getting into the lungs through the trachea. If an object tries to enter, the cords close tightly. If something does enter the larynx, there is an instant reflex reaction. The cords and the stomach muscles contract. This builds up pressure in the chest, and the object is forced out.

THE RESONATORS OF SOUND

The vocal cords create sound. That sound, however, is weak and does not sound very nice. The voice gains quality, or **resonance,** from solid bodies and partially enclosed spaces; the pharynx and oral cavity. These vibrate in response to sound from the larynx. Then the sound is directed upward and outward through the nose and mouth.

A simple comparison might help you understand the idea of resonance better. You could compare your resonators with various sizes, shapes, and types of radio speakers. Small, inexpensive plastic radios produce fair sound at a normal volume. Turn the volume up, however, and something happens. Some of the high and low notes are shaky or less clear.

Larger, more expensive plastic radios are different. They have good quality resonance. High and low notes have good sound. In fact, the overall quality is pleasant—even at a high volume.

Large wooden console speakers have even better sound. Depending on the size of each speaker, the sound may be almost as real as an actual live performance.

Radios with large speakers can convey a sound that is almost as real as what you might hear at a live performance.

The Oral Cavity and Pharynx

The oral cavity encloses, or connects, the teeth, tongue, lips, and the hard and soft palates. The throat, or pharynx, extends this oral cavity.

You can change the size and shape of your oral cavity when producing sound by doing three things. First, you drop your lower jaw. Second, you open your lips. Third, you raise the soft palate or move your tongue. All of these things happen when you make the different sounds of the English language.

Some people hardly drop their jaws or open their lips when they speak. As a result, they get a "squeezed" quality for many sounds. Their voices could be described as sickly or fuzzy. These people need to practice dropping their jaws and tongues. Then they need to open their mouths wider and direct their sounds toward the front of their mouths and their upper gum ridges.

Other people have tense face muscles. These people don't drop their jaws either. They usually develop throaty or guttural voices. This quality is sometimes described as harsh or muffled. These people must learn to relax their muscles when they're talking. They also need to do the things mentioned above to prevent squeezed sounds.

The Nasal Cavity

The oral cavity and the throat must work together all the time. On the other hand, the soft palate can completely close off the nasal cavity from other resonators. Usually, people who have nasal voices are not controlling the soft palate well. They allow air to get into the nasal cavity and through the nose. When this happens, a nasal quality results. It is the same sound that many country-western singers have.

Three sounds in English are made in the nasal cavity. They are *m, n,* and *ng.* Since these are common sounds, you need to make them correctly. You need to control the movement of the soft palate so that it will move quickly up and down. In so doing, it will close the nasal cavity.

How much nasal quality do you have in your voice? You can find out easily. All you need is a lit candle or a small piece of paper. Place one of these objects below your nostrils. Then speak at a medium volume. Watch the flame or the paper carefully when you make non-nasal sounds. If it flutters often, your voice is probably too nasal.

You can check the nasal quality of your voice by means of a lit candle.

1. Keep your lips as close together as possible while saying the following sentences. Then, open your mouth, drop your jaw, and say the same things. How do the vocal messages change?

    a. Call my accountant.   **d.** Pack up my cowboy boots.

    b. San Antonio was fun.   **e.** My name comes last.

    c. How can we find her?   **f.** I hope so!

2. Close your nostrils with two fingers. Say the vowel sounds slowly. Do you hear extreme nasal sounds? Do you feel any vibration in your nose? If you do, you are allowing the soft palate to relax. This means that air is getting into your nasal cavity.

THE ARTICULATORS OF SOUND

As you just learned, the resonators create a full, pleasant voice. However, once that's done, that sound must still be changed to produce precise sounds. **Articulation** is the process of starting and stopping consonant sounds clearly. Without good articulation, sounds are slurred. In fact, different sounds can even sound the same. As a result, people don't understand what is being said, and communication breaks down.

The articulators include the jaw, lips, teeth, and the gum ridge. They also include the hard and soft palates and the tongue. These things can make sounds clear. Clear speech, however, also involves the correct blending of sounds. For example, the word *situation* should be said "SITCHooAshun." It should not be said "SITyouAshun." How to say a word correctly, of course, can always be found in the dictionary.

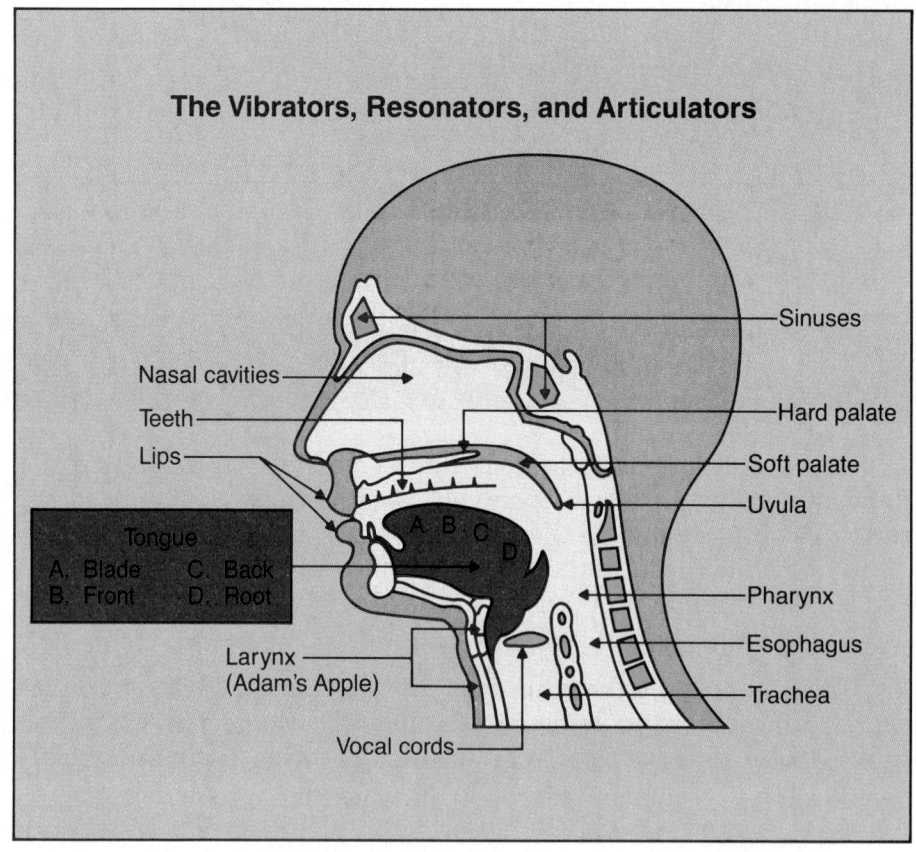

The Vibrators, Resonators, and Articulators

Sinuses

Nasal cavities

Teeth

Lips

Hard palate

Soft palate

Uvula

Tongue
A. Blade   C. Back
B. Front   D. Root

A B C
D

Pharynx

Esophagus

Larynx
(Adam's Apple)

Trachea

Vocal cords

BECOMING A BETTER SPEAKER

Your larynx, throat, and the other parts of your head and chest are very important. Without them, you could not speak. On the other hand, they are nothing more than tools. You must do something with them. You must use them. But how will you use them? Will you speak only well enough to get by and be understood? Or, will you take these tools and use them to their greatest potential? The following sections will show you how to do the latter.

Finding Your Optimum Pitch

Everybody has an **optimum pitch.** This is the pitch at which a person speaks with the least effort. You can easily find your optimum pitch. Simply sing "ah" up and down the musical scale. Go as high and as low as you can. If you use a piano, you can find out the total notes you can reach. Count up one-fourth of the total number of notes. Then press the piano key that represents that note. This should be very close to your optimum pitch. Once you have found your pitch, relax your throat. Then speak at that level. "Normal" pitch, of course, changes in all people as they grow older.

Pitch Changes and Meaning   Most people have a wide range of pitch. Different pitches can express emotion or change of attitude. Using different pitches when you read is important. You should understand that written punctuation is a substitute for what the voice does. For example, read the following sentences.

They're my closest friends
I'm the winner
I'm next

Notice that there are no end marks. How, then, do you know what each sentence means? Are they questions, statements, or exclamations? To be sure these written sentences make sense, you need to add end marks. To be sure these spoken sentences make sense, you need to change your pitch.

Say each of the sentences above as a question and then as an exclamation. Finally, say each one as a statement. Pitch and stress, you will notice, are both important. Changes in pitch show changes in meaning. In addition, gradual glides in pitch create inflections. All of these patterns, in turn, convey meaning.

SPEECH—A HUMAN TREASURE

In 1947, Keith and Katherine Hayes brought a newborn female chimpanzee into their home. Viki stayed with them for six years. The Hayeses were conducting an experiment to see if and how chimps could use language.

For years Viki was taught the basics of talking. The Hayeses would move Viki's lips and mouth to get her to produce certain sounds. When she made a sound close to the desired sound, she was given a reward. Gradually, Viki moved her mouth and lips.

But Viki could never say the sounds easily and rarely used her lips to produce the sounds. Her voice was also hoarse and unclear. After much hard teaching, the Hayeses' student could say only four words—*papa, mama, cup,* and *up.* She seemed to understand the language that was spoken around her, but she did not use it well herself.

Several studies show that, no matter how hard Viki might have tried, she would never have been able to master speech. The chimpanzee vocal tract can't produce the range of sounds of humans. There are similarities and differences between the vocal structures of humans and chimpanzees. One difference is the position of the larynx. Another is the ability to stretch out a vocalization long enough to form the recognizable sounds of letters. Still another is the variable pharynx region needed to produce vowel sounds.

The Hayeses and others watching Viki recognized that she used her hands and arms in gestures that clearly expressed her ideas. When she wanted to go for a ride, for example, she would point out the window to the car. These observations led to the theory that chimps could learn language even if they couldn't learn speech. Their solution? Teach chimps sign language.

Scientists still debate whether or not chimps actually use language when they use signs. But most agree that speech is unique to humans.

Inflections Changes of pitch within a single breath are called **inflections.** They may occur in a sound, a word, or a group of words. There are three kinds of inflections: rising, falling, and medial.

Rising inflections begin at one note on the musical scale and glide to a higher note. These are used to ask a question. They are also used to show an unfinished thought, doubt, or suspense. **Falling inflections** begin at one note on the musical scale and glide to a lower note. They are used for stating facts and making commands. Usually they show self-assurance, finality, and certainty. **Medial inflections** begin at one note on the musical scale and glide either up or down to another note. Then they move back close to the original note. Often they express suspicion, unhappiness, or irritation.

Say the following statements with the proper inflection.

rising: Shall we go?

falling: Let's go!

medial: Are we going or staying?

Steps Inflections are gradual pitch changes. *Steps* are a special kind of inflection. They are abrupt pitch changes which show a change in thought, feeling, or mood. For example, the following sentences show how steps can explain time. Imagine someone saying, "Long, long ago . . ." and moving down the musical scale for each word. Imagine someone else saying, "At two we left school (step up), but at three (step up) we were *still* waiting for a ride."

Sometimes steps are also used to emphasize certain words or groups of words. They would be equal to underlined or italicized words on a printed page.

Read the following sentences. Be sure you don't glide up and down the scale as you speak. Make clear breaks in your pitch.

rising: Did we *win?*

falling: We lost.

medial: Do you *know* them?

Some people never learn to use inflections and steps. Others use the same patterns regardless of what they are saying. You should learn to use inflections and steps to express different meanings. If you do, you will improve your speaking ability in all situations.

Improving Articulation

After many years of speaking carelessly, some people have developed some bad speech habits. Basically these speech errors fall into several broad groups. They are listed below. As you read them, see if any of them apply to you.

Careful articulation was an essential qualification of those who applied for a job as the town crier.

Substitutions   The most common error is a substitution. A different sound replaces a standard one in a word. The following are some common substitutions.

Sounds	Examples of Words
d for th (voiced)	the, with, that
t for th (voiceless)	north, thought, anything

f for th (voiceless)	truth, teeth, both
v for th (voiced)	with, mother, rather
in for ing	doing, going, being
s for z	coaches, dreams, Kathy's
tch/tsh for j	college, lodging, language
sh for s	administration, it's true
e for short i	which, is, did
ōō for ŏŏ	push, bush, cushion
ah for ŭ	us, up, some
short i for eh	any, get, many
er for or	or, for, your
eh for short a	ask, planted, can
w for r	wrong, carry, cross
gz for ks	extra, exercise, excuse
t for d	end*ed,* head*ed,* floo*ded*

Omissions Another error is leaving out sounds. Sometimes this happens when people talk too fast. Sounds are also omitted when people articulate too slowly. In such a case, the tongue is not moved from one position to another fast enough to say all the sounds in a word. Here are some common omissions.

Sounds	**Examples of Words**
d	in many contractions such as *wouldn't, couldn't, didn't,* and in such words as *told, friend, hand*
t	most, just
h	him, her (especially after words ending in *ve* such as in *have*)
y	re*g*ular, po*p*ular, partic*u*lar
g	reco*g*nize
uh	fi*n*ally, fa*m*ily, pro*b*ably
be	*be*cause
v	*o*f (especially when used after words ending in *t, p,* or *d* such as *kind, sort, brand, cup, heard*)
r	lib*r*ary

Additions   A third error is the addition of sounds to words, either by adding an entirely new sound or by pronouncing a sound that should be silent in a word. The following are a few examples.

Sounds	Examples of Words
t	is added to *often* (the *t* should remain silent as it is in *soften*)
e	is added to *grievous, mischievous* (not *ious*)
uh	is added to *film* (fil *uh* m), *athletic* (ath *uh* let ic), *athlete* (ath *uh* lete)

If you want to improve your speaking, look for a good model. Imitate national radio and TV news reporters. For the most part, they have accurate articulation. Just remember one important thing. It is easier for you to change any bad habits now than it will be 20 years from now!

Poor articulation often causes a breakdown in communication.

YOUR TURN

1. Which inflections or steps should you use to say the following?
   a. *Determined:* "I will not go!"
   b. *Coyly:* "Could you put up with me for a little while?"
   c. *Defiantly:* "If we can't work, we won't give to your campaign!"
   d. *Unsure:* "We could ask our parents."

2. Read aloud the following stanzas from a poem by Edgar Allan Poe. What kinds of vocal changes are needed at the end of the lines? At the end of each stanza?

ANNABEL LEE

It was many and many a year ago,
   In a kingdom by the sea
That a maiden there lived whom you may know
   By the name of ANNABEL LEE;
And this maiden she lived with no other thought
   Than to love and be loved by me.

I was a child and *she* was a child,
   In the kingdom by the sea,
But we loved with a love that was more than love—
   I and my ANNABEL LEE—
With a love that the winged seraphs of heaven
   Coveted her and me.

5 CHAPTER REVIEW

 ## Chapter Summary

Vocal messages involve the sound of the voice and changes in the voice to communicate meaning. These messages include such things as yawns and cries. They also include pitch, rhythm, and volume in the spoken word.

The sources of sound in the body include the lungs, rib cage, diaphragm, and related muscles, which make air flow through the vibrators of sound. These vibrators consist of the vocal cords in the larynx. Vocal cords can increase and decrease tension. As a result, they determine the pitch of the voice. Changes in pitch are called inflections and steps. These changes suggest changes in meaning.

The vocal cords create sound, but the quality of that sound comes from the resonators and articulators. The main resonators include the mouth, the throat, and the nasal cavity. First the resonators amplifly and condition sound. Then the articulators mold it into precise sounds. The articulators consist of the jaws, lips, teeth, gum ridge, hard and soft palates, and tongue. The three main problems of articulation are substitutions, omissions, and additions.

 ## Checklist

Improving Vocal Skills

1. To avoid sounding "squeezed" when you speak, drop your jaw, open your lips, and raise your soft palate or move your tongue.

2. To keep from sounding harsh or guttural, relax your facial muscles while talking.

3. To prevent a nasal tone in your voice, close off your nasal cavities by raising your soft palate.

4. Use pitch to express emotion or change of attitude.

5. To speak with excellent articulation, avoid substitutions, omissions, and additions to word sounds.

 **Vocabulary**

Define each term in a complete sentence.

articulation	larynx
diaphragm	optimum pitch
exhaling	phonation
inflection	resonance
inhaling	trachea

Review Questions

1. Explain what a vocal message is.

2. Identify the technical name for the voice box. Explain where it is located.

3. Describe the quality of sound that is made by the vibrators.

4. Define optimum pitch. Explain how it can be found.

5. Identify the part of the body that is most responsible for deciding a person's pitch.

6. Explain the difference between inflections and steps.

7. Define the term *resonance*.

8. Identify some of the resonators of the human voice.

9. Explain the difference between sound additions and omissions.

10. Define sound substitutions. Give an example of a common one.

Discuss with Your Classmates

1. Listen as one of your classmates reads the following passage aloud. Discuss how pitch and changing inflections can be used to make the reading interesting and to emphasize the most important or emotional points.

> We are prisoners on a planet that is hurtling through space to an unknown destination. We must provide for each other. At the same time, we must prepare for whatever the future brings. We are running out of fuel, food, good water, and clean air. Must we run out of patience too? Who can tell? The very people we seek to destroy may be the ones who can find answers to our problems. We must work together.

2. Think about television and radio reporters and announcers who are well-known in your community. Discuss how effectively each delivers vocal messages. If one of these personalities has a particularly distinctive or unusual style, discuss what makes it distinctive or unusual.

3. Identify someone—a radio or television personality, a movie actor or actress, a sports figure, a political leader—who you believe possesses a pleasing voice. Discuss the qualities that make that person's voice pleasing.

4. Study each of the following vocal messages, and then identify what the speakers are doing incorrectly to produce such messages. Discuss what steps could be taken to correct each problem.
    a. I taught de bus was goin nort.
    b. Harry wou'n't go cause 'e was tired.
    c. I've oftten said she's a great ath-uh-lete.

Critical Thinking

1. Analysis: Watch a news program on television that is broadcast by one of the national networks. Analyze the vocal messages of the various reporters who appear on the program. Explain your findings.

2. Evaluation: Choose a passage or a poem or use a passage in this text. Read it aloud and record it. Then listen to the recording several times. Evaluate the quality of your own vocal messages, using the information gained in this chapter.

Activities

In-Class

1. Tongue twisters have been used to teach people to articulate quickly and clearly. Read each one. Begin slowly and then gradually increase your speed. Be sure that each sound is pronounced.

  a. Theophilus Thistle, the thistle thruster, thrust three thousand thistles through the thick of his thumb.
  b. She sells seashells by the seashore.
  c. Peter Piper picked a peck of pickled peppers.
  d. How much wood could a woodchuck chuck if a woodchuck could chuck wood?
  e. Around the rough and rugged rock the ragged rascal ran.
  f. He that sows thistles shall reap pickles.

2. Read the following sentences aloud to a partner. Feel how your tongue and lips move as you say each distinct sound. Have your partner help you identify any articulation problems you are having.

  a. Time and tide wait for no man.
  b. Meat is much; manners are more.
  c. When caught by a tempest, wherever it be
       If it lightens or thunders, beware of a tree.
  d. Virtue could not go far if a little vanity walked not with it.
  e. A tale twice told is a cabbage twice sold.
  f. A thousand possibilities do not make a truth.
  g. Half the world knows not how; the other half lives.
  h. He who laughs last laughs best.

3. Read the following poem aloud. Based on the words, what is its general mood? Can you change the mood by changing your rate, inflections, overall pitch, and voice quality? Explain how.

> A hurry of hoofs in the village street,
> A shape in the moonlight, a bulk in the dark,
> And beneath, from the pebbles, in passing, a spark
> Struck out by the steed flying fearless and fleet;
> That was all! And yet, through the gloom and the light,
> The fate of the nation was riding that night;
> And the spark struck out by that steed in his flight,
> Kindled the land into flame with its heat.

> *from* PAUL REVERE'S RIDE *by Henry Wadsworth Longfellow*

 Out-of-Class

1. Close your nose with two fingers and say the vowel sounds slowly. If you feel vibration in your nose, air is entering your nasal cavity, and you need to practice lifting your soft palate. As you yawn a few times, feel the soft palate pull to the top and rear of your nasal cavity. Now yawn and immediately say the vowel sounds. Your soft palate should remain high enough for you to say some of them correctly. Practice this until you can say the vowel sounds several times with one breath. Make sure you say them without dropping your soft palate. Record your observations in your speech notebook.

2. Read the following sentences—first slowly and then quickly. None of them have any nasal sounds. Hold your nostrils shut while you read them through the first few times. This will show you whether air is escaping through your nose. Record your observations.
    a. I thought she was your sister.
    b. If you take this road, you will get to Carterville.
    c. What is the first idea you suggested at breakfast?
    d. Call your brother to see if he has a crosscut saw.
    e. Which flower will grow best with little light or water?

3. Choose a well-known singer, actor, or politician. Practice mimicking the person's voice. What changes do you have to make in pitch and articulation? Record your observations in your speech notebook.

Chapter Project

Choose a favorite piece of writing at least one page long for a dramatic reading. Copy it on a sheet of paper. Use the inflection diagrams presented in this chapter to mark the places where the inflection should change, either a little or dramatically. Show how the inflection should go up or down. Be prepared to discuss why you chose to emphasize the words or phrases that you did.

Next, think about the articulation needed to read the passage clearly. Circle the letters or words that might be lost or changed with imprecise or incorrect articulation. Prepare for reading the passage in class.

6 Verbal and Nonverbal Messages

Luis and Anne are riding the bus to school. As Luis hears snatches of different conversations, he thinks . . .

"The bus isn't crowded this morning.

Everyone has a different way of dressing, acting, and talking.

I wonder if Anne notices all the differences."

What differences do *you* notice in the way people communicate?

In this chapter, you will read about:

- verbal and nonverbal communication
- the difference between standard and nonstandard usage
- the levels of formal and informal communication
- ways to improve verbal messages
- ways of expressing nonverbal messages

When Stephanie opened the front door, the first thing she saw was Bill's new cowboy hat. "Oh, I love it!" she exclaimed. Bill smiled as he pulled the brim down over one eye. With his thumb, he pointed over his shoulder to a bicycle in the driveway. Stephanie's face lit up. "You finally got your ten-speed racer! I don't believe it." Bill nodded and laughed.

In this short exchange, Stephanie used verbal messages. Although Bill did not say a word, he did communicate. His hat, gestures, smile, and laugh all communicated things that Stephanie understood. Even Bill's silence may have told her something—if he was not usually quiet. Bill communicated nonverbally.

In this chapter, you will learn more about both verbal and nonverbal messages.

VERBAL MESSAGES

Have you ever stopped to think about the effect words can have? They can calm riots, end friendships, and create superstars. Or, think of the millions of dollars that international businesses spend each year finding product names that will not offend people in any country. How many words have no negative or double meanings throughout the whole world? For example, would a small Japanese car called *Pain* or a Russian radio called *Nogoodnik* appeal to Americans? What images would an Italian drink called *Rotten* create for people in the United States?

Words have always been important. Before writing was invented, a person's "word" was a form of trust. It was a bond between two people. In courts of law, a person's word was a form of oath. When writing was created, people began to place more and more faith in the written word. Written contracts, signed by both parties, replaced a person's word. People who could not read or write could sign

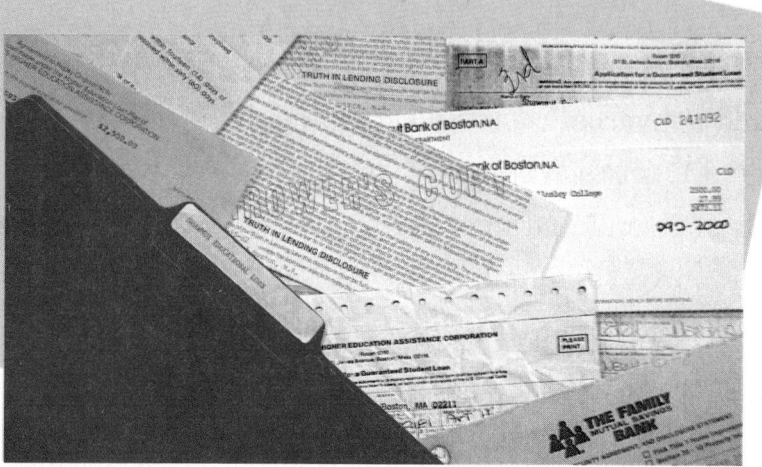

Written contracts have replaced a person's word.

important papers with an "X" if others witnessed it. That "X" became the person's sign or word.

As you learned in Chapter 1, verbal messages are the words you send out to receivers, or listeners, around you. Verbal messages include words and groups of words. If the words in a verbal message mean about the same thing to the sender and the receiver, communication is correct. However, a speaker may use words that a receiver does not understand. In such a case, communication will be incorrect or will not happen at all.

Standard and Nonstandard Messages

The terms standard and nonstandard are often used to describe verbal messages. **Standard English** refers to the set of grammar rules taught in English classes. These rules include such things as agreement of subject and verb and correct use of verb tenses.

Nonstandard English refers to messages that do not follow formal rules of grammar. For example, the statement, "It don't make no difference," is nonstandard English. It contains a double negative and an error in subject-verb agreement. In standard English, the statement would be "It doesn't make any difference."

Formal and Informal Usage

People must make decisions about the kinds of verbal messages they give. To make these decisions, a person must think about the formality of a speaking situation. Speech can range from very informal to very formal. **Formal usage** refers to careful, controlled communication. Senders and receivers choose their words carefully. They judge one another's statements. A job interview, for example, is a formal situation. In such a situation, a person should speak carefully and correctly.

Informal usage refers to more relaxed communication. In very informal situations, senders and receivers do not worry so much about rules and correctness. For example, going to a basketball game with friends is an informal situation. In this kind of situation, a person would probably use informal language. However, as the following chart shows, there are different degrees of formal and informal usage. People must adapt their messages to fit the situation.

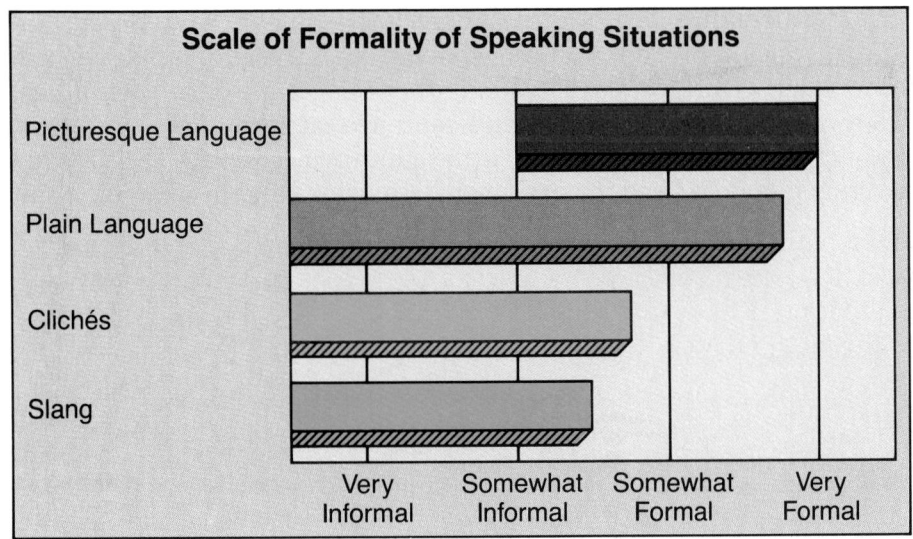

Slang is informal language that uses words and phrases in many different contexts. Because of this, slang really has very little meaning. Every generation has its own slang fads. Sometimes a slang expression is accepted by most people. This happened, for example, with the term "okay." However, slang is usually meaningful only for a short time, and then it disappears.

Clichés such as "white as a ghost" and "cold as ice" are expressions that have been used very often. At first, these expressions were interesting and descriptive. But when they became overused, they lost their meaning. For this reason, you should avoid clichés. Following are some other clichés and worn-out expressions.

pretty as a picture
busy as a bee
stiff as a board
as honest as the day is long

sly as a fox
happy as a lark
put your best foot forward
doing your own thing

If you want to use descriptive expressions, try to find fresh, new ones. These kinds of expressions make a conversation or speech more interesting.

Plain language is simple, straightforward language that is direct and understandable. Sentences usually follow a set pattern —subject and verb; or subject, verb, and object are used. Plain language is usually accepted in formal and informal situations. (For an example of plain language, see Susan B. Anthony's speech in the back of this book.)

Picturesque language is descriptive, clear, and exact language. Speakers and writers who use picturesque language are concerned with how words sound when placed next to each other. They use a variety of words and sentence patterns. By doing this, they create a certain effect or atmosphere with words. Picturesque language may be used in very formal situations and in some informal

Busy as a bee

Putting your best foot forward

Taking the bull by the horns

situations. A good dictionary or thesaurus can help you come up with synonyms. However, it is not a good idea to use too many difficult words and sentences in an informal situation.

Improving Your Verbal Messages

Following are some steps you can take to improve your verbal messages.

- Use words that: 1. fit the receivers of your message; 2. fit your topic; 3. fit the situation you are in.

- Use variety in your ideas, vocabulary, and sentence structure.

- Use personal pronouns (I, we, you, they, etc.) when they are useful.

- Use questions occasionally. (In speeches, these questions are often called **rhetorical questions** because a speaker does not expect listeners to answer aloud.)

- Use short, simple clauses or phrases.

- Use commands when they fit your presentation. (For example, "Take time to vote. Do it today!")

Speaking is not merely words and sentences. It is also *how* you say these words and sentences. However, by building a larger vocabulary, you can improve your speaking range.

One way to do this is to write a few new words each week in a notebook. Include the word meanings, pronunciations, and some synonyms. Then watch for these words in your reading, conversations, television watching, and class discussions. Try to use the words at least once a day. At the end of the week, these words should be part of your vocabulary. Then you can begin working on other words.

As you write down new words, remember that many words have two meanings. **Denotation** is the direct, specific dictionary meaning of a word. For example, *thin* is defined as "slim; slender." **Connotation** is the emotional, subjective, implied meaning of a word. It is based on people's experiences with those words. For example, *skinny* has the same denotative meaning as *thin*. However, it can also have a more negative connotative meaning. Just remember when you use words like *skinny,* that they may suggest different meanings to your listeners.

As you begin to study words, you also will begin to find a difference in *abstract* words, which name concepts (faith, brotherhood, beauty), and *concrete* words, which name things or people (Kim Jones, Florida oranges, speckled trout). Abstract words bring more varied emotional responses from listeners than concrete words do. If you want your listeners to understand what you're saying, use concrete words.

YOUR TURN

1. Following are some "old" slang expressions. What do you think each one means? How many of these expressions have you heard before?

a. Kiddo	**d.** He's the most.	**g.** Let's blast off.
b. Scram!	**e.** That's keen.	**h.** Get the picture?
c. What cheek!	**f.** He's square.	**i.** Bug off.

Can you think of any slang expressions used today that mean about the same thing as the expressions in this exercise?

2. How many of the following clichés or worn-out expressions can you finish?

a. As good as _____.	**e.** It's as obvious as _____.
b. Thin as _____.	**f.** It's bigger than _____.
c. As tough as _____.	**g.** She turned as red as ___.
d. As sour as _____.	**h.** As slow as _____.

Now create new figures of speech for the clichés in this exercise.

NONVERBAL MESSAGES

Nonverbal communication is communication without words. It includes delivery, gestures, and facial expressions. Each of these labels describes what people do and how they look when they speak.

Nonverbal and verbal messages usually occur at the same time. They are often accompanied by other vocal sounds such as groans or laughter. Because of this, you will not see or hear all of them at once. However, you should realize that they are present, and they are *all* important in person-to-person communication.

Public speakers such as Senator Gary Hart are aware of the importance of nonverbal messages. They are at ease in a formal setting or in an informal one. They communicate this ease to the audience.

You might be surprised to learn that there are ways to express nonverbal messages. You use them everyday. For example, you may slouch down in your chair in class. By doing this, you may give a very clear nonverbal message to your teacher. The message may be that you are not prepared. You have probably become so used to sending certain nonverbal messages that you are not even aware of them. Following are some sources of nonverbal messages. Reading about them will help you become more aware of them.

Dress and General Appearance

Dress and grooming carry important nonverbal messages. Imagine, for example, that you have an interview for an after-school job. You wear an old pair of shorts and a faded shirt. What might your dress say to an employer? The employer may think you are careless in your dress and, therefore, may be careless in your work. On the other hand, suppose you wear neat, clean, suitable clothing. The employer may quickly notice your appearance and assume that you will be responsible and careful in your work.

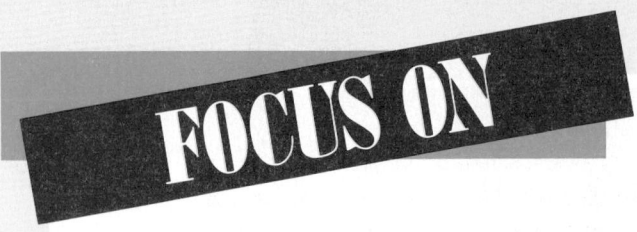

A MATTER OF SPACE

Almost everyone has watched a dog or a cat enter a room, walk deliberately to a certain spot, and then lie down. Usually this "spot" will be one of several fixed places to which the dog or cat returns time after time, depending on the occasion or time of day. These animals are exhibiting territorial behavior. They are all laying claim to—and sometimes defending—a non-physical set of boundaries.

Like these and other animals, human beings also have territorial instincts. Some are easy to see. For example, everyone in your family knows which chair in your grandparents' living room is your grandfather's chair and wouldn't think of sitting in it. Other territorial instincts are not quite so easy to see. Have you accidently brushed up against someone in the checkout line of a grocery store? Did you notice that person stiffen and step away?

Understanding these human territorial instincts can be very difficult. They can even be confusing from culture to culture because "enough space" is thought of differently in each culture. When people say that some foreigners are "pushy," for instance, what they really mean is that the foreigners' handling of space is different from theirs.

For example, people in Latin America generally stand closer together when they talk than people from the United States do. Americans set up a "safe" distance of about 21 to 24 inches, and they will then avoid touching strangers. When people are first introduced in Chile, however, they usually kiss each other on the right cheek.

The next time you are talking with your best friend or an exchange student from Peru, remember your dog or cat. Remember that people have a need for a certain amount of space and distance, and that this fact is an important part of communication.

Posture and Large Body Movements

Many people notice how others stand and walk or move. In fact, you can learn a lot about people from their posture and body movements. A nonverbal message may be as general as "I'm tired." Or, it may be as specific as "My knee is hurting again." Following are some examples.

The Speed of Movement Fast movement suggests that a person is tense or in a hurry. Slow movement may suggest sadness, illness, thoughtfulness, or injury.

Control of the Shoulders Sagging shoulders suggests defeat, tiredness, or poor health. Shoulders that are pulled back and up (or squared) suggest readiness for action, control, or confidence.

The Tilt of the Head When the head tilts forward during movement, it suggests concentration, purpose, or hurry. If the head tilts forward when standing or sitting and speaking, it suggests interest or concentration. When it tilts to one side, it usually suggests that the person is listening carefully or concentrating. When the head tilts backward, confidence or resistance is suggested. When the chin is tilted back and up, it suggests overconfidence.

The Tension of the Spine A person slouches when he or she relaxes the spinal column, shifts the pelvis to one side, and leans on one foot. This position suggests a casual or uncaring attitude. When a person moves with the spine relaxed, it suggests laziness or disinterest. When the spine is very straight, it suggests an attitude of fear or stiffness. When the spine is comfortably straight, confidence or readiness for action is suggested.

Control of the Pelvis During movement, the pelvis either leads or follows the rest of the body. When the pelvis leads, it suggests confidence or purpose. When the pelvis follows or "drags," caution or fear is suggested.

Weight Distribution and the Feet In normal movement, people move from the heel, to the ball of the foot, to the toes. However, when a person moves mostly on the heels, it suggests insecurity or shyness. When a person moves mostly on the front part of the feet, it suggests tension or hurry.

Gestures

Gestures are descriptive movements of parts of the body. Hand gestures, are the most common. However, gestures can also be made with the head, shoulders, elbows, legs, and feet. Gestures help speakers to be more descriptive. They can show actions, shapes, or sizes. They can be very formal such as a salute, or very informal such as a wave goodbye. Usually gestures are only meaningful within cultures or national groups. For example, in Western cultures nodding up and down means "yes." But in some Eastern cultures "yes" is shown by tilting the head from shoulder to shoulder.

Basically, there are two types of gestures: descriptive gestures and figurative gestures. **Descriptive gestures** give visual pictures of size, shape, or action. For example, a speaker is describing the causes of whiplash. To show what happens on impact, the speaker may throw his or her head back quickly. **Figurative gestures,** on the other hand, suggest ideas and emotions. For example, a speaker wants to show the need to separate junior and senior high school students. To do this, the speaker may use one hand to show the junior high school students and the other hand to show the senior high school students. He or she might start with the gesture of hands together. Then, by separating the hands, the speaker makes the point of keeping the two groups apart.

Sometimes people use gestures that have no meaning. These movements, such as playing with the hair, may be habits or may be caused by nervousness. They can draw attention away from the speaker's message. Following are three gestures that are the most often overused by beginning speakers.

- The "flipper" motion is made with one or both hands held waist-high, palms up. The hands are flipped outward or upward from the wrist. The upper arms do not move.

- Another gesture is made with one or both hands cutting vertically through the air. Speakers use this gesture to emphasize ideas or words.

- The third gesture is made by pointing the index finger. The speaker may point up, down, sideways, or at the listeners.

These gestures may be acceptable if they are not the only ones used.

Meaningful descriptive gestures can add to a speech. For example, they might show *length* by the distance between two hands (The fish I caught was about this long). They might show *size* by the

Gestures help speakers to be descriptive. Gestures can indicate actions, shapes, or sizes.

distance between the finger and thumb (About this much water was in the beaker). The *shape* of something may be shown with the hands and fingers (The round gear sits on top of the rod at about this angle). Or, *action* can be shown by moving the hands (One wheel turns this way; the other one, this way).

Meaningful figurative gestures can also be made with one or both hands. Following are some examples.

- Hands with palms down (We can meet our goal just as fast if we just *keep calm*.) (Please *sit down*.)

- Hands with palms up (We have *asked* you twice for help.) (Let me *give you* an example.)

- Hands with palms toward the listener (Just *listen* one minute more, please!) (They cannot *stop* us now.)

- Hands with palms facing each other (In one year, we have moved from *this* point to *this* point.) (Imagine that we are dividing the class into three sections—*here, here,* and *here.*)

- Using one or more fingers (There are *three* simple things we have to do.) (I want to make *one* point!)

The way in which you use space and distance can be a strong nonverbal message.

Facial Expression and Eye Contact

Another way to give nonverbal messages is by changing facial expressions and by looking—or not looking—at people. If you are talking with friends, you usually look right at them. This lets them know you are interested in them and in what they are saying. You should do the same thing when you give a speech. In good communication situations, the sender of messages should be aware of the receiver's responses.

On the other hand, listeners are also watching the speaker. They are trying to see whether facial expressions support or deny what is being said. Following are some facial changes that can influence meaning.

- smiling
- frowning
- raising the eyebrows in surprise or doubt
- squinting slightly as if questioning or concentrating
- staring without smiling

- clenching the teeth

- opening the mouth as if surprised or amazed

- drawing the corners of the mouth down to pout or grimace

Use of Space and Distance

All people have an idea of what amount of space belongs to them. Have you ever noticed people protect the space around them? They may place books, packages, or purses on chairs next to them so that no one will sit too close. People also carry large purses, newspapers, or umbrellas to act as "bumpers" in crowded places. Even in elevators, some people read newspapers or put their hands on their hips to avoid being closed in too much. If you are not aware of this, you may accidentally intrude into someone else's space.

Furniture and seating arrangements can also affect communication. In a meeting, for example, chairs placed in a circle encourage people to share ideas with one another. In a home, a close grouping of couch and chairs adds to a warm, friendly mood. Such an arrangement encourages conversation. The use of space and distance become strong nonverbal messages if you are aware of them.

YOUR TURN //////////////

1. A student play will be followed by an awards dinner, honoring students who have served both the school and the community. The mayor has been invited and will attend. One student arrives wearing faded jeans and a torn T-shirt. What nonverbal message is the student sending to:
    a. fellow students?   **b.** invited guests?

2. How might posture, large body movements, and gestures express the following moods and attitudes?
    a. nervousness   **f.** laziness
    b. tiredness   **g.** fear
    c. concentration   **h.** formality
    d. begging   **i.** dislike
    e. anger   **j.** defeat

6 CHAPTER REVIEW

 ## Chapter Summary

Verbal messages are the words and groups of words you send out to receivers. *Standard* describes verbal messages that follow formal grammar rules. *Nonstandard* describes verbal messages that do not follow these rules. Verbal messages may range from formal to informal, depending on the speaking situation. The scale of formality includes the use of slang, clichés, plain language, and picturesque language.

You can improve your verbal messages by choosing words that fit your listeners, your topic, and the situation. Your messages should be short, simple, and varied. Use personal pronouns when useful. Use questions occasionally and commands when appropriate. You should also build your vocabulary by learning new words each week.

Communication without words is called *nonverbal communication*. You express nonverbal messages by your dress and appearance, posture and large body movements, gestures, facial expressions and eye contact, and use of space and distance.

Checklist

Improving Verbal and Nonverbal Skills

1. Decide whether the speaking situation is formal or informal and choose your language accordingly.

2. For the more formal speaking occasions, use only picturesque or plain language.

3. Use variety in your ideas, vocabulary, and sentence structure.

4. Use personal pronouns such as *I* or *we* when appropriate.

5. To vary the pace, use questions occasionally.

6. To make a strong statement, use a command.

Vocabulary

Define each term in a complete sentence.

clichés

connotation

denotation

descriptive gestures

figurative gestures

formal usage

informal usage

nonstandard English

picturesque language

plain language

rhetorical question

slang

Standard English

Review Questions

1. Define a verbal message.
2. Define a nonstandard verbal message. Give an example.
3. Describe the scale of formal and informal usage.
4. Briefly describe plain and picturesque language.
5. Explain the difference between denotation and connotation.
6. Briefly define nonverbal communication.
7. Name two ways in which you might send nonverbal messages without being aware that you are doing so.
8. Explain the difference between descriptive and figurative gestures.
9. Explain why speakers should avoid expressionless faces when they are talking to other people.
10. Describe a situation in which space and distance could send a verbal message.

 Discuss with Your Classmates

1. As a class, list as many situations as you can think of when it is acceptable to use slang. Then list situations in which formal language is appropriate. Is there ever a situation in which formal language is inappropriate? Discuss your opinions as a class.

2. As a class, examine the following list of plain terms. For each term, suggest as many synonyms as possible that would express the idea in a more picturesque manner. Discuss the more picturesque words. Are there any that are perhaps too picturesque or too formal?

a. angry	**d.** car	**g.** old	**j.** house
b. hot	**e.** blue	**h.** tree	**k.** gem
c. walking	**f.** dog	**i.** thought	**l.** bird

3. Study each of the following situations. Discuss whether formal or informal language would most likely be appropriate in each.
    - **a.** a conversation between a player and a coach
    - **b.** a newspaper reporter interviewing the governor of a state
    - **c.** a discussion between a baseball manager and an umpire
    - **d.** a meeting of a school's basketball team
    - **e.** a conversation between the principal and the president of the student council

4. Discuss how an audience is likely to react to someone who speaks nonstandard English. What are listeners likely to think about the person? Are listeners likely to respond in the same way to a speaker of informal English? Explain and offer examples.

Critical Thinking

1. **Comprehension:** Read Martin Luther King's speech "I have a Dream" in the back of this book. You should be able to find at least ten examples of descriptive words and expressions. Which ones do you think are most effective? Why?

2. Evaluation: Watch a public speech on television or watch a performer or an entertainer for at least five minutes. Pay careful attention to the speaker's use of gestures. Keep track of all gestures, not just the use of the hands. How effective was the speaker's use of gestures? Why or why not?

 Activities

In-Class

1. Your teacher will divide the class into groups of from three to five students. Discuss expressions used by your peers that are nonstandard. What rules are broken by these expressions? Each group should keep a list of broken rules and then report to the class as a whole. The class should discuss how to avoid these nonstandard features.

2. As a group, write a short paragraph on the chalkboard that describes an event in your home, school, or community. Use plain language and avoid complex sentences. Then rewrite the same paragraph using picturesque language. Which paragraph do you prefer? Why?

3. One person might say, "Why don't you assert your authority?" Someone else might say, "Why don't you show them you're the boss?" In the first case, the person was using picturesque language. In the second case, plain words were used. Tell which of the following words are plain or colorful. Then, find an easier word for each colorful term.

a. assembly	**d.** property	**g.** speak
b. devoted	**e.** good	**h.** cathedral
c. help	**f.** fashionable	**i.** rock

Out-of-Class

1. Make a list of five slang words and five clichés which are not in this book. Rewrite each of them in a more descriptive way. Keep your work in your speech notebook.

2. Watch a television game show or talk show that involves several people. In your speech notebook, keep a written record of all the different ways that the people on the show send nonverbal messages. Does one participant use more nonverbal messages than another? Does the host or hostess use as many nonverbal messages as the contestants or guests? Discuss your results in class.

3. Go to a busy mall or store. Notice the differences in dress among the clerks and customers. Pick a few different styles and write a short paragraph describing them in your speech notebook. Then tell what each of these different styles suggested to you about that particular person.

4. Restaurants place people close together in a small place. Go to any restaurant, including a fast food chain, and notice the space and distance between people. Can you tell by the space people put between them whether or not they are friends? Note other observations about space and distance. Discuss your results in class.

Chapter Project

People communicate both verbally and nonverbally every day, in their normal relationships with others.

Role-play with a partner the characters of employee and boss in a department store. Have the person who plays the employee use the gestures that might communicate the following nonverbal messages to his or her boss. The boss should write down on a sheet of paper exactly what the gestures seem to be conveying.

I just don't understand.

I will think seriously about that suggestion.

I don't feel very relaxed talking to you.

I'm in a hurry right now.

Now have the boss decide exactly what words he or she would use to express the following messages verbally to the employee. Each boss should use imagination to create the situation surrounding each message.

I'm thinking about firing you if you don't improve.

You're doing a good job.

You are rude to customers on the phone.

I'm going to give you a raise, but only a small one.

INTERPERSONAL AND GROUP COMMUNICATION

125

CHAPTER 7 Informal Talk: Conversation

These are some of Billy's thoughts as he talks with his grandfather.

"Grandpa is really interesting.

He remembers what this street looked like 50 years ago.

I'll have to talk with him more often."

Whom do *you* like to talk with? What can you learn from talking with other people?

In this chapter, you will read about:

- the most common purposes of conversation
- common traits of good conversationalists
- ways to improve conversational abilities
- telephone techniques
- practical suggestions for conversationalists

The word *chatterbox* describes a person who talks rapidly, without stopping, about a trivial subject. Have you ever heard someone say "That was the most boring conversation. Mr. Y chattered so I couldn't squeeze a word in edgewise"? When someone chatters, it is difficult —if not impossible—for others to talk. They can only listen. And when one person does all the talking and another does all the listening, they are not having a conversation.

Conversation is a process in which two or more people exchange verbal, vocal, and nonverbal messages. Through these messages, they share ideas, experiences, information, and feelings. Think about it. Without conversations, there would be no friendships or relationships. Friends talk directly *with* one another about common interests. In fact, during your life you will probably use conversation more than any other form of communication.

PURPOSES OF CONVERSATION

Although conversations are always different, they do have some common purposes. Sometimes these purposes overlap; you might not be able to tell where one ends and another begins. Following are some of the most common purposes of conversation.

Gaining Pleasure and Companionship

Conversation was once the way people received most of their information. It was also a major source of pleasure and enjoyment. Today, however, many people get a majority of their information from listening to the radio, watching television, and reading. Nevertheless, conversations still play a major role in most friendships, and are a great source of pleasure.

Conversation was once the way people received most of their information. Conversation with friends was also a major source of pleasure and enjoyment.

Sharing Ideas and Experiences

When people talk with one another, they often test out new ideas. Seeing someone else's reactions and insights can help people clarify their own thoughts. At other times, people may discuss their own experiences in an effort to understand them better. Sharing ideas and experiences helps people grow and learn. Through conversations, people improve their ability to talk with others about many different subjects.

Influencing Others

You may have heard someone say, "I wish you'd talk with him. He listens to you." As this statement shows, one purpose of conversations is to persuade people. A conversation might convince someone to do a particular thing, to alter certain behavior, or to change his or her point of view. This is why conversations are used to sell things in many businesses and professions. Such conversations are often informal. They may take place on a golf course, at a restaurant, or on the telephone. Little or nothing may be said directly about the product, service, or idea being sold. However, as a result of a conversation the people involved might reach mutual understanding and respect.

Developing Speaking Skills

Some people claim that they are not very good speakers because they have never had much training in speaking. Usually they mean they have had little *formal* training in *public speaking*. But people can develop better speaking and listening skills through informal conversation. By engaging in conversations with different people, a person has the opportunity to model his or her speaking—and listening—patterns after good conversationalists.

QUALITIES OF GOOD CONVERSATIONALISTS

What are some qualities of good conversationalists? If you observed many such people, you would notice that they have many of the following **traits,** or characteristics.

Sincerity

Good conversationalists try to be themselves. They do not pretend to be more than they actually are or to know more than they actually do. For example, they admit when they do not know the answer to a question. They do not use difficult words if simple ones are just as effective. As speakers and listeners, good conversationalists are genuine.

Adaptability

Good conversationalists are flexible. They can change their vocal, verbal, and nonverbal messages to suit people and situations. They can change topics, for example, when new people enter a conversation. They take each person in a conversation seriously. Good conversationalists try to understand how each person feels about a topic—even if they do not agree with each opinion.

Tact and Courtesy

Good conversationalists have **tact,** or the ability to know the right time to say or do something. They try not to make others feel uncomfortable. They are considerate of their listeners. For example, imagine that someone new has entered a conversation after it has already started. A good conversationalist would tell that person what has been said so that he or she could join in easily. Good conversationalists are also thoughtful of those people they are talking about. Also, when subjects become too boring or too personal, they change the topic tactfully.

Interest

Good conversationalists try to find topics that will be interesting to everyone. They do not think only of their *own* interests. They make their conversations more interesting by adding stories or personal experiences. Good conversationalists are also good readers, thinkers, listeners, and observers. As a result, they always have fresh information to add to conversations.

Ability to Be Good Listeners

Part of being a good conversationalist is being a good listener. Good listeners keep eye contact with the speaker. They show that they have been listening by commenting on what someone else has just said. They do not do all the talking, and they do not interrupt others. Even when topics are hard to understand, they listen carefully. Good listeners ask questions that help everyone understand the topic better.

YOUR TURN ////////////

1. What part does conversation play in the work of the following people?
   a. road crew workers
   b. department store clerks
   c. telephone operators
   d. nursery school teachers
   e. newspaper reporters
   f. farmers
   g. nurses
   h. television repairers

Discuss your answers with your classmates.

2. Using a scale of 1 to 10 (with 10 as the highest rating), rate your conversational abilities. Consider each of the items given in the last section. Be prepared to explain why you ranked low or high in certain areas. Compare your ratings with those of your classmates.

Good conversationalists know when to speak and when to listen.

IMPROVING YOUR CONVERSATIONS

Knowing the qualities of a good conversationalist gives you a good place to start to improve your conversations. However, knowing what to do in a conversation will not make you a better conversationalist. *Talking about* good conversations is not the same as *having* good conversations. You must put what you know into practice. Following are some practical things you can do to improve your conversations.

Develop a Storehouse of Information

Craig and Liz had to be at the tennis tournament at 5 P.M. They put their rackets in the car, climbed in, fastened their safety belts, and closed the doors. "We'll be there five minutes early," said Craig as he turned the key. The engine turned over, but the car didn't start. Craig tried again to start the car. Nothing happened. Then his face fell, as he looked at the gas gauge. "Oh, no!" he said. "We're out of gas!"

Conversations are like cars; they don't work without fuel. The fuel of conversations is the information shared by each person. It includes the knowledge, experiences, and ideas of all members of a

Good conversationalists are also good listeners. This rule applies to telephone conversations as well as to face-to-face conversations.

group. Without this fuel, conversations can be boring or meaningless. In other words, they don't go anywhere. For this reason, good conversationalists are always adding words and ideas to their storehouse of information.

Develop an Interest in a Variety of People

Another practical way to improve your conversation is to develop an interest in people. You can learn much from different kinds of people. If you talk only with people exactly like you, you will miss out on a lot. You will never understand the differences that age, racial, ethnic, religious, national, and political influences have on people. Good conversation flourishes when it includes members of other groups. For example, students should talk with younger people and adults—as well as with their peers.

By broadening the range of people with whom you have conversations, you can learn about unusual opinions and experiences, original ideas, and just plain facts and information. By listening to others, you will also develop the ability to give and take in many different situations.

ARE YOU TOO SHY TO TALK?

Maryann dropped her eyes. She felt her cheeks burn. The palms of her hands were sweaty, and her heart was beating faster. Jerry, the new boy in school, had just asked her a question. Maryann was so shy that she was having trouble answering.

A lot of people have periods of shyness, especially when they are growing up and experiencing changes. For the very shy, the simplest conversations can be painful. But excessive shyness can be overcome. Here are some tips to help you feel more confident in conversations.

Make up imaginary conversations that you might have with people at school. Imagine conversations with a variety of people—a friend, a casual acquaintance, a teacher, or a coach. Try to be realistic, and think of things you could actually say to people. Remember, most people are not likely to analyze or criticize your every word. They will usually respond in a friendly manner.

Practice these imaginary conversations aloud. Listen to the sound of your voice. People who are shy often speak too softly. Practice projecting your voice while enunciating properly. Don't

mutter or mumble. Try to control any shakiness in your voice. Use a tape recorder to practice making your voice sound more confident.

Practice these conversations before a mirror. Make eye contact with yourself. Practicing eye contact with yourself as you speak aloud will help you make eye contact during real conversations.

Before beginning a real conversation, take several deep breaths and practice breath control. Taking deep breaths and deliberately slowing down breathing decreases nervousness.

Begin a conversation with something that interests the other person. Ask questions that require more than a one-word answer and that will lead to further comments. Get the other person talking, then really listen. A genuine interest in others can cure shyness.

Use Personal Diplomacy

A diplomat must handle difficult situations calmly and correctly. **Personal diplomacy** is the ability to deal with people in a tactful way. To develop your own personal diplomacy, be open-minded about different ideas. In other words, look for things that you agree with in conversations. To do this, look for negative nonverbal cues from listeners such as frowns, head shakes, tone changes, and muscle tension. These cues show that people are becoming upset about something that is being said. By noticing these signs, you can change the topic of conversation.

Practice Being a Good Conversationalist

Most of the suggestions in this chapter take time and patience. However, the following are a few things you can do *now* for some instant success.

- When you start a conversation, ask questions that cannot be answered with a simple "yes" or "no." Opinion questions (What do you think about ____?) will help get other people talking.

- As you talk, appeal to your listener's senses (smell, taste, touch, sight, hearing). Mental pictures help people understand the things you are describing.

- Use direct, personal pronouns (*I, we, you, they,* etc.). However, if you find yourself using "I" a great deal, you may be talking too much about yourself.

- Use humor when it helps to explain an idea. However, don't tell a joke just to "top" someone else's joke. Jokes on yourself are fine, but personal jokes about others are not really funny.

- Don't talk too much. Give others a chance to talk.

TELEPHONE TECHNIQUES

In today's world, telephone conversations are one of the most common forms of communication. You probably spend a lot of time on the telephone because it is an easy way to get information and to enjoy friendships. In fact, talking on the telephone has become one of the easiest ways to keep in touch with other people.

Because you probably use the telephone a lot, you should understand telephone etiquette. **Etiquette** refers to accepted ways of behaving in certain situations. Following are some pointers that will help you make your telephone conversations more effective.

Making Telephone Calls

Let the Phone Ring The telephone should ring at least eight times before you hang up. The person you are calling may not be near the telephone. Give him or her enough time to answer it. People become upset when they rush to the telephone—only to find nothing but the dial tone at the other end.

Wrong Numbers Sometimes you may accidentally dial a wrong number. To avoid this, check the number and then dial it carefully. However, you may still get a wrong number. If the person who answers does not sound familiar, do not say "Who is this?" Some people do not like to give that information to a stranger. Instead, give the number you are calling and ask if you have reached that number. If you think you reached a wrong number, don't just hang up. Apologize for your mistake before you hang up.

Identify Yourself   When someone answers the telephone, do not ask "Who is this?" If the person you want to speak with does not answer, say, "Hello, this is _____. May I please speak with _____?" If the person you are calling is not there, you can do either of two things. You can ask whether you may leave a message, or you can tell the person who answered when you will call back.

Be Courteous   Make your calls at times that will not interfere with meals, bedtime, or other activities. For example, if you know when a friend watches a favorite television program, do not call at that time. Also, if you make calls to other time zones, make them at times that are convenient for the receiver. You also might ask the person you are calling whether it is a convenient time to talk.

You should also avoid tying up the line for long periods of time. As long as you are on the phone other people cannot use the phone to make or receive phone calls—at either household. The person who made the call is responsible for bringing the conversation to a polite close.

Control Vocal Qualities   When talking on the telephone, speak in a strong—but not loud—voice. Speak clearly and distinctly. Remember, nonverbal messages cannot be seen by the person on the other end. Therefore, your vocal changes must convey the total message. You should also realize that mechanical equipment amplifies unpleasant vocal qualities.

Receiving Telephone Calls

You also have rights and responsibilities when you receive a telephone call.

Receiving Inconvenient Calls   If you are busy when someone calls, simply say, "I'm sorry but I'm right in the middle of something. May I call you back?" Or, give the caller a time when you will be free and ask him or her to call you back then. If you are uncertain about when you will be free, you might offer to call the other person back.

Be courteous and helpful when you take a phone message for someone else.

Taking Messages   If a call is for someone else, do not say "Who is this?" or "What do you want?" Instead say, "May I tell _____ who is calling?"

When a person is not there, ask whether it is all right for that person to return the call. If the caller says "yes," ask for his or her telephone number. Check the spelling of the caller's name and repeat the telephone number.

Sharing the Responsibility   When you talk on the telephone, be considerate. Don't interrupt the other person or become impatient. Accept your share of the responsibility for a conversation.

YOUR TURN ////////////////

1. Discuss in class some of the things you dislike most about telephone conversations. Can you think of any solutions to these problems? You might role-play one or more of the things you dislike.

2. Nonverbal messages cannot be seen during telephone conversations. How, then, can receivers recognize the following emotions? Offer examples and discuss.

a. irritation	**c.** defensiveness	**e.** disinterest
b. happiness	**d.** boredom	**f.** enthusiasm

7 CHAPTER REVIEW

 ## Chapter Summary

Conversation is one of the most important forms of informal speech communication. The main purposes of conversation are to gain pleasure and companionship, to share ideas and experiences, to influence others, and to develop speaking skills.

Good conversationalists are sincere, adaptable, tactful and courteous, interesting, and good listeners.

To improve your conversational abilities, you should develop a storehouse of information and a real interest in different kinds of people. You should also practice personal diplomacy.

To be more successful in conversations, ask questions, appeal to your listener's senses, use personal pronouns, and use humor. Remember not to talk too much.

Because you spend a lot of time on the phone, you should know and apply good telephone techniques. When making telephone calls, you should let the phone ring at least eight times, long enough for someone to answer it. You should also identify yourself, be courteous, control your vocal qualities, and handle wrong numbers politely.

When receiving telephone calls, accept inconvenient calls politely, take messages, and share the responsibility for having meaningful conversations. Do not tie up the telephone.

 ## Checklist

Improving Conversation Skills

1. Develop an awareness of the purposes of conversation.

2. Remember that a good conversationalist is sincere, adaptable, tactful, courteous, and interesting.

3. Learn to be a good listener.

4. Develop a storehouse of information.

5. Develop a real interest in different kinds of people.

6. Practice personal diplomacy in your conversations.

7. Remember the importance of telephone etiquette.

8. Learn to ask questions that show you are interested in other people.

9. Appeal to your listener's senses.

10. Use direct, personal pronouns when you talk to someone.

11. Use humor when it helps to explain an idea.

12. Don't talk too much.

 ## Vocabulary

Define each term in a complete sentence.

conversation   tact

etiquette   traits

personal diplomacy

 ## Review Questions

1. Identify the most common purposes of conversation.

2. List some of the things you can do to make your conversations more interesting.

3. Name at least five characteristics of a good conversationalist.

4. Identify four characteristics of a good listener.

5. Explain why it is important for people to talk with others in different age groups.

6. Explain the ways in which you should be diplomatic in your conversations.

7. Explain what you should do if you dial a wrong number.

8. Name the kind of message that is not apparent in telephone communication. What can be done to make up for it?

9. Explain what you should do if you get an inconvenient call.

10. Name three ways to have instant success in improving your conversational abilities.

Discuss with Your Classmates

1. Discuss different sources of information that could provide background for interesting conversations. They should be sources that members of the class have found useful. Make a list of the sources on the board. Are these sources difficult to find or use? Are there any other sources that might be added to the list?

2. As a class, make a list of ten general topics that could be used for conversations. Then develop two questions for each topic that would get a conversation started.

3. Explain the importance of personal diplomacy in conversations. What are some instances when personal diplomacy might prevent an unpleasant situation? What are some specific examples of personal diplomacy?

4. Compare the responsibilities of people who make phone calls and of people who receive phone calls. How do these responsibilities differ? How are they similar?

Critical Thinking

1. Evaluation: Describe someone you know, other than a classmate, who is a good conversationalist. Consider what specific characteristics make this person enjoyable to talk with. Discuss differences and similarities between this person and others whom classmates consider good conversationalists.

2. Analysis: Think of a good conversation that you took part in recently. Analyze the conversation to discover what made it interesting. What was the topic and why was it a good one? What other factors helped to make the conversation an enjoyable experience?

 Activities

In-Class

1. Give an example of an occasion in which you were persuaded —through conversation—to change your mind about something. Explain what you originally believed. Then tell what was said to change your mind. What does this tell you about the power of conversation? Discuss your example with your classmates. As a class, try to identify the features that make persuasive conversations successful.

2. Your teacher will divide the class into groups of five to seven students. First, each group should review the five practical suggestions for conversations on page 134. One person in each group will be the recorder. He or she will list the topics that are discussed during the fifteen-minute period. At the end of this time, each recorder will read the conversation topics covered in the group. How many different topics were covered? How many were the same?

3. With a partner, role-play the following situations.
   a. reaching a wrong number
   b. leaving a message for a friend who is not home
   c. asking to speak to a friend when a parent answers the phone
   d. asking for information about a product in a store
   e. making an appointment for an after-school job interview

Out-of-Class

1. Make a list of some of your experiences, hobbies, or interests. Which of these topics could help to make a conversation more interesting? Recall the conversations you had this week. Were any of these topics discussed? If they weren't, do you think you could have added to any of the conversations by including some of them? Put your list and your observations in your speech notebook.

2. Over the next few days, have a conversation with at least two people outside your peer group. You might talk with an elderly neighbor, a young child, or a friend's mother or father. These should be people with whom you do not normally have a conversation. Then consider the differences between talking with these people and talking with your friends. What did you do differently to carry on a good conversation? Record your findings in your speech notebook.

3. Make a list of topics that would make good conversations among teenagers and adults together. Find interesting topics, not just small talk. Then ask an adult what topics he or she would include on such a list. Which topics are similar? Which are different? Which topics do you both agree would be interesting? Record your list in your speech notebook. Be prepared to discuss your list in class.

Chapter Project

Your teacher will divide the class into groups of five to seven students. Each group should imagine that it is stranded on a desert island. Since you do not know how long you will be there, you want to write down what people know so you will have a storehouse of interesting topics for conversation.

One person will be the recorder. For 15 to 20 minutes, brainstorm about different topics that people in your group are familiar with. Then, select *one* topic from this list. For example, your topic could be one of these: *American inventors and their inventions; famous musical groups;* or, *Olympic gold medal winners.*

Write down all that your group knows about the topic you have selected. Include only information that the group as a whole agrees is correct.

Within your group, carry on a conversation on the topic selected. Remember to apply the techniques for good conversation that you have read about in this chapter. Watch for nonverbal clues that indicate negative reaction. Try to include everyone in the conversation. Be a good listener.

CHAPTER 8

Introductions, Directions, and Interviews

Carol and her family are moving into a new house. As Carol looks around, she thinks . . .

"I miss my old house already.

I miss my friends too.

I guess I'll have to make new friends.

When I start school on Monday, I'll just introduce myself to the first person I see."

Do *you* enjoy meeting new people? How should you introduce yourself to others?

In this chapter, you will read about:

- introducing yourself to someone else
- introducing one person to another
- giving simple and clear directions
- conducting an informational interview
- participating in a job interview

How do rules for social behavior begin? Some are traditions that go so far back that no one knows where they came from. The handshake probably began as proof that two people were *not* carrying weapons. In some cultures today, men hug when they meet. This tradition probably began as a way to show that the men had no weapons hidden in their clothing. Your great-grandparents would be shocked at our "crude" social behavior. They followed strict rules of social behavior that you would think are stiff and artificial. But your great-grandchildren may think the social rules of today are just as strange.

MEETING AND GREETING PEOPLE

Today people are on the move! It is not unusual for families to pack up everything they own and move to another part of the country. On vacations or business, people are traveling to many parts of the country and the entire world as easily as their grandparents visited friends across town. Meeting new people and learning to get around in new places have become everyday happenings.

Often you are in situations where you do not know the person who is near you. A new student might sit next to you in math class. Someone you don't know might sit beside you on a bus. In situations like these, you should first decide whether you want to talk to the other person. If you do, how do you introduce yourself?

Basically, you can do one of two things. First, you can introduce yourself by saying, "Hello, my name is _____." If the other person doesn't give his or her name in return, he or she simply may not want to talk. If the person just says "Hello," you may say something else about yourself. You might say where you're going or where you're from. Avoid saying anything too personal. If the person doesn't respond, you should stop trying to start a conversation.

Beginning with small talk is a good way to introduce yourself informally.

A second way to introduce yourself is to begin with small talk. **Small talk** is casual conversation about impersonal topics, such as the weather or the news. The purpose of small talk is to let another person know that you want to be friendly, without being too personal. Sometimes the other person will join in the small talk or introduce himself or herself. If that happens, you can continue the conversation.

At other times, you may be in a group where you know very few people. At a party, for example, you may know only the host or hostess. In such a case, you will have to introduce yourself to others. If many guests are standing, you should stand also. Then you will be able to move around, and other people will easily see you. Look around to find people whom you might join. When you introduce yourself, make the greeting simple but sincere.

Many other situations require an introduction. You may be attending a club meeting, or you may be new in school. In both cases, you may not know anyone who can introduce you to other people. If you are a new student, introduce yourself to at least one person in each class. Let these people know that you are new. If you do this, you will greatly improve your chances of making new friends quickly. People who introduce themselves feel at home more quickly than people who wait for introductions.

Introducing People to Other People

At times, you may want to introduce friends to other friends. There are certain traditions for introducing strangers. The easiest way to remember them is to classify them in two categories:

- rank or position (principal, doctor)
- age (old, middle-aged, young)

Rank or Position Most people in the United States don't have such titles as "Countess" or "Duke." But many have important jobs or high positions. In such a case, *give the name of the person with the higher position first in an introduction.* For example:

- Representative Chang, this is my sister Melissa.
- Mr. Cohen (principal), may I present my father, Mr. Webster.
- Judge Greeley, this is my friend Mary Jane Delaney.
- Governor Ruiz, this is Rudy Springer, president of our computer club.

When two people have about the same position, *give the name of the person you know less well first.* For example:

- Dr. Sidney, this is my father, Dr. Carlson.
- Ms. Michaels (assembly speaker), I'd like you to meet Ms. Hildreth (principal of your school).

A less formal way of introducing people of the same position is with **inflection,** or alteration of pitch or tone. Use a rising inflection on the first person's name. Use a falling inflection on the second person's name. For example:

- Professor Selby ⌒ . . . Professor Bracken ⌄
- David Welbourne ⌒ . . . Robert Perkins ⌄

Age Sometimes you will introduce two people of very different ages. In such cases, *give the older person's name first if position is not a concern.* For example:

- Ms. Casey, this is my friend, Marcia Crescent.
- Mr. Greene, I'd like you to meet my younger sister, Phyllis.

Sometimes you may not be able to tell which person is older. At those times, don't worry about who is named first. Just use common sense and show respect for people's feelings.

Making introductions easily and correctly takes practice. Try to make correct introductions even in casual situations. Then you won't have to think about how to make them in formal situations.

Following General Guidelines

Personal advice columns in newspapers sometimes include questions about introductions. The following are some commonly asked questions.

Should someone stand when he or she is introduced? In formal situations, a person should stand for an introduction. However, problems caused by getting up must be considered. For example, if standing would bother others or block someone's view, a person should not get up. Standing is still accepted as a sign of respect, but common sense should be used.

Should people shake hands during introductions? Shaking hands is a custom in the United States. If a person holds out his or her hand, it is polite to shake hands. In some situations, however, shaking hands is not easily done. Reaching across someone's lunch, for example, does not show common sense. Looking at the other person, nodding, and saying "Hello" is acceptable.

How can you remember someone's name? Forgetting a person's name after an introduction is a common problem. Probably the most helpful thing is to repeat the person's name right after you hear it. If you didn't hear the name or if it is unusual, you may say, "I'm sorry, but I didn't get your name. Would you mind repeating it?" Then use the person's name as soon as possible. Knowing a person's name is important in beginning a good relationship.

Should young people call older people by their first names? Younger people should use an older person's last name in formal situations. The older person will usually tell you if you may call him or her by first name.

Shaking hands with a new acquaintance is a custom in the United States.

After an introduction, how is conversation started? If you introduce strangers, you should help start a conversation between them. You can do this by giving **cues,** or hints, about both people. These cues should be simple statements about interests, hobbies, or skills. For example:

- Mary Freeman, I'd like you to meet my brother Tom, who attends Queens College. Tom, Mary was a finalist in the national diving competitions last year.

- Ms. Tillson, I'd like you to meet my cousin Leroy Davis, who is a reporter for the *St. Louis Post-Dispatch.* Leroy, Ms. Tillson sponsors the school newspaper.

- Hello, Mary. This is Carlos Diaz, my new neighbor from Tennessee. Carlos, Mary is the best singer in our school dance band.

In these examples, the person making the introduction gave each person a fact that could be used to start a conversation. Try to make such information interesting to both people. It then becomes the responsibility of the people being introduced to use these facts to keep the conversation going.

Although there are rules for introductions and responses, the most important thing is to be sincere and friendly. People will not look for mistakes if you are sincerely trying to communicate.

GIVING AND RECEIVING DIRECTIONS

You are sitting on your front porch when a car drives up. A young woman calls out to you, "Excuse me, I wonder if you could tell me where 32 Evergreen Avenue is? I've been riding around so long that I'm late for my meeting." You know that the address is about ten blocks away on the other side of the river. There is a short way to get there, but it is hard to explain. The longer way is simpler. Which set of directions do you give? How do you explain clearly? You don't want to make her even later than she already is.

Giving Directions

Getting lost or confused is common when people travel. If it happens to you, you'll want someone to give you simple, clear directions. The following hints will help you give good directions.

Draw a Map or Name the Streets Sometimes the greatest help is to draw a map. However, even maps can be confusing if they lack enough detail or if the proportions are wrong. The next best thing is to name the streets where the person should turn. Also explain how many blocks or miles are involved.

Use *Right* and *Left* Use *right* and *left* instead of *north, south, east,* and *west. Right* and *left* are two choices, not four! You might say, for example, "Go straight for one mile and turn right on Oak Street." Most people could follow those directions more easily than "Go west one mile and turn north on Oak Street."

Mention Landmarks Most people can spot landmarks easily. Include some landmarks in your directions. A helpful landmark is unique and large enough to be seen clearly from the road. A brown cabin hidden by trees would *not* be a good landmark.

If you have not recently traveled the route, do not mention things that may have changed. That bright yellow house, for example, may now be gray.

Avoid Difficult Shortcuts Sometimes you may know a shortcut. However, if it is harder to explain, don't mention it. The longer, but simpler, route will be better for strangers. Directions with many

"Summer Street? Sure. I know a great shortcut."

"Go straight for 3.8 miles. Then make four lefts. You'll come to a blinking light. Go through that and . . . ."

"That will save you plenty of time."

turns can be confusing. One wrong turn could get the people lost a second time.

Give Only Some of the Directions; Then Repeat Them   If the directions are long and difficult, don't give all of them. Give directions only to a middle point. At the middle point, the people can ask for more directions. For example, you might direct people to a gas station about halfway to where they want to go. Someone at the gas station could then give directions for the rest of the route.

Another good practice is to repeat your directions. Or, have the travelers repeat them to be sure that they have understood.

If You Don't Know, Say So   What should you do when you don't know the directions to a place? Ask someone else or tell the people that you are not sure. Then direct them to a place where they can get directions.

Asking for Directions

When you are asking for directions, be as specific as possible. If you need directions to two places, ask about each place separately. For example, don't ask such double questions as, "Can you tell me how to find the expressway and the nearest gas station?" Instead, ask, "Can you tell me how to get to the nearest gas station? Also, I'd like to know how to get to the expressway from here."

The time needed to give and receive directions is often brief. It may not seem very important, but it is.

1. Imagine that you are involved in the following situations. Role-play with a partner the conversation that you might have.

a. You are going to visit a friend. You will be traveling on a full bus for the next three hours. An elderly man asks if he may sit next to you. You nod "yes," and the man sits down. He is wearing a Red Cross pin on his jacket.

b. A local service club invites some teenagers to a lunch meeting. You do not know the other students who are going. When you arrive, you see a boy from your school. However, you have never spoken to him. He seems to be looking for someone.

c. You are at a local high school football game. The person sitting next to you is wearing a school jacket with a letter from the opposing team. The person has a cast on his leg.

d. During registration day, you notice a new student in the hallway carrying her enrollment papers. She looks unfamiliar to you. The new student appears confused and a little frightened.

2. Give directions for getting from your school to another school at night. What landmarks that are helpful during the day probably will not be useful at night? Would highway numbers or street names be more or less useful? Why?

PURPOSES OF INTERVIEWS

An **interview** is a special type of communication that is planned and structured. Every interview has a definite purpose. The following are three general purposes of interviews.

Getting Information

A reporter interviews the head of the school board. The purpose is to find out how the board hires and fires employees. After gathering the information, the reporter will write a newspaper article.

Be brief and exact when you give people directions. Remember that those who ask directions are usually unfamiliar with the area.

Motivating or Persuading

Sally, the president of the Student Council, interviews each class president. She wants them to cooperate with one another in building school spirit.

Solving Problems

The principal of the junior high knows the school has a problem with student absenteeism. The principal interviews each teacher, asking for suggestions for solving the problem.

KINDS OF INTERVIEWS

There are many kinds of interviews. Some interviews are very formal and serious. Others can be casual and fun. Interviews, for example, would be used in all of the following activities.

- collecting information (census and public opinion interviews)

- counseling (psychological help or therapy)

- consulting (gathering legal or medical information)

There are many kinds of interviews. News reporters often use interviews as a means of gathering information.

- finding a job
- introducing policies (explaining a company's vacation policy)
- selling ideas, products, or services
- handling complaints (unfair hiring practices)
- reviewing job performance (yearly reviews of workers)
- exiting (people leaving school or jobs)

Conducting an Informational Interview

Steve Clifford is writing an article about a high school track star for his newspaper. Steve wants to tell about how the athlete prepared for last week's cross country track meet. He also wants to describe her personality and her ideas about high school athletics. To collect the information he needs, Steve must carefully plan the interview.

The following is a list of points for conducting an informational interview.

Make an Appointment Set up the date and time for an interview in advance. Both the interviewer and the **interviewee,** the person being interviewed, need time to prepare. When making the appointment, explain the purpose of the interview. Also tell about how long it will last so the interviewee can set aside enough time.

FOCUS ON

THE INTERVIEW
More than 20 Questions

by Carol Porter

Carol Porter is a free-lance writer who has won several awards. As editor of a medical publication, she regularly interviews people. In this article, she discusses how she prepares and conducts an interview.

Journalism, by popular opinion, is fascinating work. I agree. Of the elements of journalism—research, interviewing, and writing—none challenges me more than interviewing. This skill requires investigation, tact, intuition, and stage presence. It demands thorough preparation as well.

Suppose, for example, that I am doing a personality profile on Mr. Karsch, who is retiring from the school district after 40 years as choral music director. First, I call the school district's director of community relations for information about Mr. Karsch: his date of birth; where he attended college; whether he served in the armed forces; his outside interests; and the articles published in professional journals. These tell me his areas of expertise. Equally important, I speak with someone who knows him.

When I've gathered enough information, I write out my interview questions exactly as I will ask them, much like a script. I avoid questions with potential "yes" or "no" answers.

When I start the interview, I ask Mr. Karsch to verify basic data: "Before we begin, I'd like to make sure that I have your full name. . . ." We are at ease, and I am getting the facts.

Feeling at ease is all-important, and that's where stage presence comes in. It is my job to make Mr. Karsch feel comfortable. Soon, we both relax. We're having fun.

Always too soon, the interview is over. Much of the work has been done. The information has been gathered. Only the writing remains.

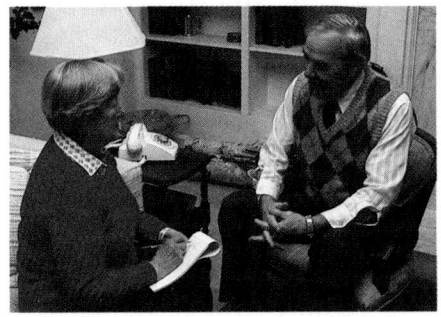

Write Your Questions   What do you want to know? Make a list of specific questions. Ask about the person's accomplishments and goals. You also might ask about the interviewee's personal likes and dislikes. However, avoid questions that are too personal.

Arrive Promptly   Always arrive on time for an interview. If you will be late for any reason, call the person. If necessary, set up another interview at a later date.

Record Notes Carefully   Accurate information is very important. Write careful notes, or use a tape recorder. Include all the major points in your notes. Take your time. Listen closely, and never interrupt.

Follow-Up   Always thank the person for his or her time and help. After writing the article, send the person a copy. Take the time to thank him or her once again.

Preparing for a Job Interview

In some cases you will not be the interviewer. Instead, you will be the interviewee. Most interviews are held for important purposes. People are interviewed for jobs, scholarships, or acceptance at a school or camp. Because such interviews can mean so much, people often get nervous or frightened.

In the near future, you may be interviewing for a job. If you remember that interviews are not trials, you will not worry so much. Think of them as conversations between two people.

Suppose you are looking for a summer job baby-sitting. The following points will help you prepare for an interview for such a job.

Think About the Job Beforehand   Show your interest in the job by being prepared to ask questions. For a baby-sitting job, for example, you might ask the following questions.

"What games do the children like to play?"

"What do they usually eat for lunch?"

"Is it all right to take them to the park?"

"What rules must the children follow?"

"How do you discipline the children?"

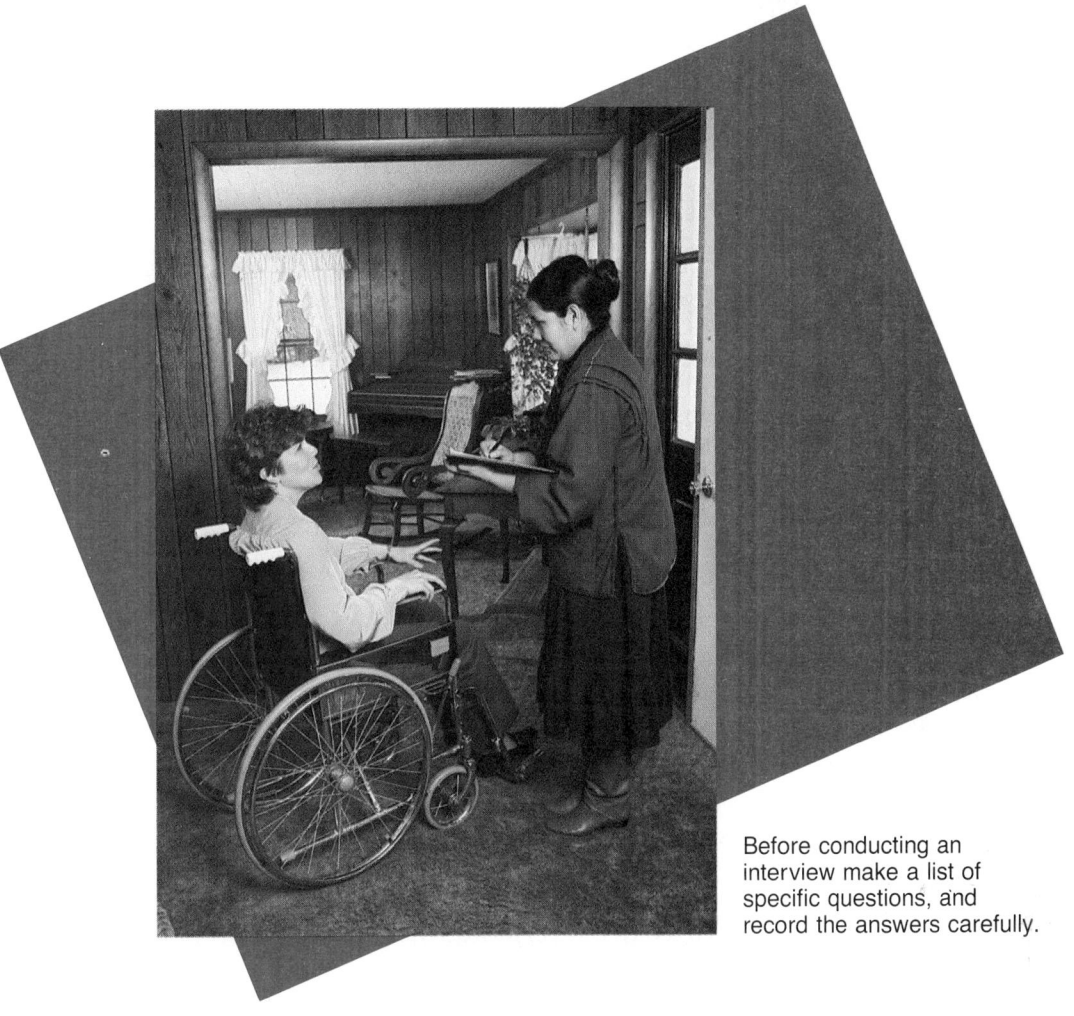

Before conducting an interview make a list of specific questions, and record the answers carefully.

Organize Your Answers to Questions Think about questions you might be asked. For example, you could be asked the following questions.

"Do you have any experience?"

"Why would you like to do this kind of work?"

"How much do you expect to earn per hour?"

Make an Appointment Call ahead and make an appointment for the interview. If you are answering a newspaper ad, give your name. Then explain that you are answering the ad and want to schedule an interview. Have several possible times in mind. When the date and time are set, repeat them. Then write them down so you will remember. Ask for directions to the address if you need them. Then thank the person you are talking to.

THE INTERVIEW ITSELF

The day of the interview arrives. What should you be thinking about and doing? How should you act during the interview?

Physical Appearance

Dress appropriately and make sure your clothes are neat and clean. A shirt and slacks or blouse and skirt would be appropriate; shorts and a T-shirt would not. Also, remember that people notice clean hands and fingernails and carefully combed hair immediately. You want to make a good first impression, so you should be well groomed.

Promptness

Leave for your interview in plenty of time. Give yourself extra time in case you are delayed by traffic. You don't want to be late for your appointment. It is better to arrive a few minutes early than to be late.

Communication

An interview is basically a conversation between two people. Your conversational skills can help make the interview pleasant for both you and the interviewer—and may help you get the job.

Meeting the Interviewer People will start to form impressions of you from the moment they meet you. Introduce yourself to the interviewer and follow his or her lead. If the person extends a hand, shake it. If not, don't worry about shaking hands, either before or after the interview. Smile, and be friendly but courteous. Present your résumé and wait for the person to ask you questions.

Listening and Answering Questions When the interviewer talks, listen carefully. An interview is a two-way conversation. Both people must talk and share information. The interviewer will describe the job to you. He or she will explain the duties, the working hours, and the wages.

The interviewer will ask about your past work experiences. Answer all questions as directly and honestly as possible. If you do not know the answer to a question, just say so. The interviewer primarily wants to find out if you are mature and responsible. He or she wants someone who will be dependable. That means coming to work on time every day, fulfilling all of the duties of the job, and showing good judgment in handling problems. For a baby-sitting job, for example, the interviewer may ask questions similar to the following.

"Do you have any younger brothers or sisters?"

"What ages were the children that you have taken care of?"

"What would you do if one of the children became sick?"

"I need someone who can work every Tuesday and Thursday from 10 to 2. Will you always be available during those hours?"

Leaving the Interview   At the end of the interview, the person may ask if you have any questions. Then the interviewer may tell you when he or she will make a decision. If the interviewer does not tell you this, feel free to ask. Simply say, "When may I expect to hear from you?"

As you leave the interview, smile. Thank the interviewer for meeting with you. Act as though you enjoyed the meeting.

Following-up After the Interview   The interview is over. You know you want the job. Is there anything else you can do to increase your chances of getting it? You may want to write a simple thank-you note. It should *not* be a long, formal letter. A few carefully written lines are enough.

YOUR TURN ///////////////

1.   With a partner, role-play an interview for one of the following jobs. Your classmates will discuss your interview.
   a. usher at a movie theater
   b. lifeguard
   c. assistant at a plant nursery
   d. dishwasher at a restaurant
   e. worker at a car wash

2.   Suppose you are going to interview your school's principal. Determine with your classmates a purpose for the interview. Then as a group make a list of questions you would ask.

8 CHAPTER REVIEW

Chapter Summary

You may sometimes need to introduce yourself to new people. People who introduce themselves feel at home more quickly than people who wait to be introduced. The rules for introductions and responses are based on tradition. You follow these rules when introducing one person to another. Two things to consider are *position* and *age.* Give the name of the person with the higher position first. Likewise, give the name of an older person first. However, the most important consideration when making an introduction is to be sincere, friendly, and courteous. Always use common sense.

In giving directions, be brief and clear. It is helpful to use street names, *right* and *left,* and landmarks. Avoid trying to explain difficult shortcuts. If the route is long and difficult, give directions to a middle point. Repeat the directions or have the person repeat them to you.

An interview is a structured type of communication. It has one of three general purposes: to get information, to motivate or persuade, or to solve problems.

When conducting an informational interview, always make an appointment. Prepare for the interview by writing your questions. Arrive promptly and take notes or tape-record the interview. When the interview is over, thank the person; then send the interviewee a thank-you note and a copy of your article.

In preparing to be interviewed, think about the job and the questions you want to ask. Prepare answers to likely questions. Schedule an appointment. Dress appropriately and neatly for the interview, and be prompt. Thank the person for the interview. You may also want to send a short thank-you note.

 ## Checklist

Developing Skills in Making Introductions, Giving Directions, and Interviewing

1. Make it a point to introduce yourself when you are with a group of new people.

2. Give the name of the person of higher rank first when introducing one person to another.

3. Introduce an older person by giving his or her name to the younger.

4. Be sincere, friendly, and courteous when making introductions; and use your common sense.

5. Give brief, clear directions, using precise language.

6. Always make an appointment for an interview, whether you are the interviewer or the interviewee.

7. Dress neatly and appropriately.

8. Arrive promptly for an interview.

9. Thank the person after the interview.

 ## Vocabulary

Define each term in a complete sentence.

cues	interviewee
inflection	small talk
interview	

 # Review Questions

1. Describe how you might introduce yourself to a stranger during a long bus ride.

2. Identify what standing up during an introduction shows. What determines whether one should stand up?

3. Describe what you can do to start a conversation between two people. Give an example.

4. Explain why you should not always describe the shortest route when giving directions.

5. Explain when it is best to give partial directions.

6. Identify the three general purposes of interviews.

7. Describe the process you would follow in conducting an informational interview.

8. Describe what you should do to prepare for a job interview.

9. Identify the kinds of information you can expect an interviewer to tell you about a job.

10. Describe what you should do at the close of a job interview and after the interview.

 # Discuss with Your Classmates

1. Discuss in class the correct way to introduce the following people to each other.
   a. your grandfather to the principal of your school
   c. your best friend to your cousin, who is about the same age
   d. a retired scientist to the president of your speech club

2. New students frequently get lost if direct routes to classrooms are not evident. Using your classroom as a starting point. Give someone directions to each of the following places.
   a. the gymnasium   d. the principal's office
   b. the teachers' lounge   e. the art room
   c. the cafeteria   f. the library

3. With a partner, role-play a scene in which the interviewer is conducting a survey on an important local issue. He knocks at the door of a house and must carry on a conversation with a person who answers and says one of the following:

    a. "Why do you want to interview me? My opinions aren't worth much."

    b. "I'm busy. Go away."

    c. "Who are you and what do you want?"

    d. "If you are trying to sell me something, I don't want any."

Discuss in class how well the interviewer does in each situation.

4. Have you or other members of your class ever been interviewed? If so, discuss your experiences in class. What was the purpose of the interview? What did you do to prepare? What questions were you asked?

Critical Thinking

1. Application: Explain how the communication skills you acquire in a speech course can help you when introducing yourself to new people. How can those skills help you during a job interview?

2. Evaluation: Think of situations in which you had to introduce people. Describe at least three such experiences. How successful were the introductions? Did they follow the guidelines presented in this chapter?

Activities

In-Class

1. Your teacher will divide the class into groups of three. Each person in the group will take turns introducing the other two people to each other as if they were strangers. The person making the introduction should think of cues to help start a conversation between the strangers. The other two people should then start a conversation based on these cues.

2. As a class, decide on a place in town that everyone knows. Each class member will write directions to that place from school, then read the directions aloud. Were any of the directions exactly alike? Which directions were easiest to follow? What made these directions easier?

3. Your teacher will pair you with a classmate. With your partner, choose a job from the classified ads in your newspaper and role-play an interview. Each of you should prepare for the interview. The interviewer will write questions that he or she wants to ask, and the interviewee will write answers to possible questions. Other members of the class will observe and discuss the interviews. What was good about each one? How could each one have been better?

4. Think of a place in your community that is somewhat difficult to get to from your school. Write out the directions that you would give. Your teacher will select a class member to listen as you read the directions aloud. After you have finished, that person will draw a diagram on the board. If the diagram is incorrect, give the directions again. Continue to give the directions until the person understands them.

Out-of-Class

1. Choose a location in your area that you are quite familiar with and that is at least three miles from your school. In your speech notebook, write a set of directions to the area. Show the set of directions to someone who knows how to get to the area from your school. Does the person agree that your directions are accurate? If not, make whatever changes are necessary.

2. Interview two people who are over sixty years old. Ask them to think about when they were young. Were introductions made differently than they are now? Have customs changed much since then?

Which customs have changed most dramatically? What probably caused the changes? Take notes during the interviews. Summarize the results of the interviews in your speech notebook. Present the results in class.

3. Suggestions for starting conversations between people who have just been introduced are mentioned in this chapter. What conversation starters would you use to introduce people you know to each other? Think of six people that you know who do not know each other. Decide which person to introduce to another. In your speech notebook, write cues that you would use to introduce each pair, and to get conversation started between each pair.

4. Think of a job you would like to have. Prepare ten questions that an interviewer might ask you. Write the answers you would give in your speech notebook.

Chapter Project

Your teacher will divide the class into groups of four or five. Each group will participate in two role-playing exercises.

The first will involve introductions at a party. Each group should choose one person who will role-play an individual arriving at a party. This person will introduce himself or herself to the others. The group should also select one person who will introduce two people to each other. The group should continue to role-play an informal conversation among these people.

The second role-play will involve interviewing. One person will be selected to conduct the interview. The other people in the group will be the interviewees. Each group should decide collectively on a topic for an informational interview. You might role-play, for example, an interview with the homecoming committee or with the members of the soccer team. Group members should prepare for the interview based on their roles.

CHAPTER 9 Group Discussion

These are some of Mike's thoughts as he prepares to act as the leader in a group discussion.

> **"My goal is to solve this problem.**
>
> **How do I get everyone in the group to take part in the discussion?**
>
> **I hope this circular seating makes everyone feel equally important.**
>
> **How do I keep the discussion on the right track?"**

Have *you* ever led a group discussion? Can you describe your experience?

In this chapter, you will read about:

- the purposes of group discussions
- the different kinds of group discussions
- John Dewey's Steps of Reflective Thinking
- ways to improve group discussions
- traits of the three most common styles of leadership
- how to evaluate group discussions

What is a discussion? It can be many things. It can be as simple as talking with friends about what movie to see. But it can also be as complex as a special meeting in the Senate. A **discussion** is an exchange of information or ideas about one subject. The main purpose of all discussions is to find an answer to a problem or a question.

Sometimes people have a problem, and they don't know how to solve it. When this happens, they often get together a group of people to sort through information and arrive at a solution. Bringing together different people assures a variety of experiences, knowledge, and insight. This variety can be very important in trying to reach creative and effective solutions.

PURPOSES OF GROUP DISCUSSIONS

The overall purpose of any discussion is to find solutions to problems. However, that general purpose can be divided into the following more specific purposes.

To Find Information

These discussions are primarily concerned with facts. People in the discussion group try to determine which pieces of information are true and which are false. Such discussions are usually called fact-finding sessions.

For example, a group might consider the following question: *Why are fewer students using the library this year than used it last year?* Group members could ask students and teachers for their opinions and ideas, talk with the town's librarian, or interview teachers and

A fact-finding session to determine true and false information may take place in your classroom.

librarians at other nearby schools. They would gather pertinent facts from as many sources as possible.

Then they would discuss what they learned, analyze the information, and try to identify the real cause. Once the cause of a problem is identified, it is easier to find a workable solution.

To Evaluate

The purpose of these discussions is to evaluate different ideas, to compare the worth of one idea with that of another, and then to decide which one is better.

For example, a discussion group might ask the following question: *Which high school courses are of most value to students who go on to college?* Group members must decide which courses to keep, which to drop, and whether new courses should be added to the curriculum. They would probably compare and contrast the benefits of different courses.

To Decide Policy

The purpose of policy discussions is to decide if something should or should not be done. If everyone agrees that something should be done, then the group discusses *how* it should be done.

For example, a discussion group might consider the following question. *When is the best time to add another week's vacation to the current school year?* Group members would probably first list the advantages of adding a week. Then they would list the disadvantages. If the group agreed that adding a week's vacation was advisable, they would make a policy decision about *when* to add the week.

KINDS OF GROUP DISCUSSIONS

Following are descriptions of the five most common kinds of group discussions. Some will be familiar to you, and some won't. Right now, you probably only get involved in panel discussions. However, as you get older, you will probably get involved in other kinds of group discussions.

Panel Discussion

A **panel discussion** is the most popular kind of discussion. It has four to eight members. One of the members is usually the leader. No prepared speeches are given, and there is no set order of speakers. Instead, members follow certain steps to find a solution to a problem. These steps could be John Dewey's Steps of Reflective Thinking. (These steps are discussed in the next section of this chapter.)

An **open forum** is a question and answer period that often follows a panel discussion. People in the audience ask panel members questions about statements the panel members made.

Symposium

A **symposium** is a more structured kind of discussion. During a symposium members do one of two things. They discuss one area of the topic, or they present their opinions about the topic. Usually the members talk about the topic. They do not give formal speeches. Each member is given a time limit.

A leader usually introduces each speaker before he or she speaks. Then when that speaker has finished, the leader makes a brief statement. These statements usually tie together what the different speakers have said. At the end, the leader summarizes the presentations and draws conclusions from them.

Many business meetings follow the format of a panel discussion.

Round-Table Discussion

A **round-table discussion** is usually held around a conference table. That is how it got its name. There may be people in the audience, but they cannot join in. The leader begins this kind of discussion by stating the problem. Then experts give short reports. Finally, these experts talk among themselves. Most of the President's cabinet meetings are round table discussions.

Lecture-Discussion

A **lecture-discussion** is a very formal discussion. During this kind of discussion the leader gives several prepared lectures. Before the discussion, members get assignments. Then during a lecture, the leader calls on the members to answer certain questions or give certain information. Sometimes the members can stop the leader to ask a question. When the members understand one issue, the leader goes on to another short lecture. This kind of discussion is often used by college instructors.

Progressive Discussion

In a **progressive discussion,** several small groups discuss different parts of a topic at the same time. For example, one group might discuss the causes of a problem. Another group would discuss the current status of the problem, and a third group would discuss solutions to the problem.

Before the discussion, all members study the whole topic. On the day of the discussion, the leader tells the members the part they will discuss. Then when the group time is up, members from all the groups meet together. Each group leader then reports the findings and decisions of his or her group.

STEPS FOR CONDUCTING A DISCUSSION

A good conversation often jumps from one topic to another. A good discussion never does. Good discussions follow a logical order. They do this so that everyone will know two things: First, what has already been done. Second, what must still be done before a solution can be found.

John Dewey, an American educator, came up with five rules to help groups follow a logical order during a discussion. These rules are known as Dewey's Steps of Reflective Thinking. When everyone in a discussion group understand Dewey's five steps, the discussion runs more smoothly.

Step 1: Define the Problem

The first task of a discussion group is to define the topic. If the topic is a problem, it needs to be stated clearly. Everyone in the group must understand it. To do this, certain terms may have to be explained. This will prevent misunderstandings later.

The topic, or problem, must also be limited. The problem, for example, might be about after-school activities. But is the problem about all after-school activities, or just some of them? If the problem is only about clubs, that should be stated. Limiting a subject will save lots of time during the discussion.

Step 2: Study the Problem

The next step is to gather information about the problem. What are its causes? What is happening now? If nothing is done, what might happen in the future? For example, the problem might be how

John Dewey developed five rules to help groups follow a logical order during a discussion. These rules are known as Dewey's Steps of Reflective Thinking.

to get local businesses to donate money for new band uniforms. Areas of discussion would include the following: Have businesses always refused to donate money? Do all businesses refuse to help? Do only some businesses refuse to help? Does the band need help from the businesses? Is there any other way to fund the uniforms? At the end of this step, everyone should know three things: (1) exactly what the problem is, (2) how long it has existed, and (3) the extent to which the problem has grown.

Step 3: Evaluate Possible Solutions

In this step, members suggest possible solutions to the problem. The group then discusses the advantages and disadvantages of each one.

Step 4: Select the Best Solution

The purpose of this step is to compare and contrast all the solutions. The advantages and disadvantages of each one are weighed. Then the best one is selected.

Sometimes, however, two or three solutions may seem equally as good. If this happens, group members might be asked which one they prefer and why. It's possible that everyone may not agree. Remember that the purpose of a discussion is to find answers or solutions. This does not mean that there will always be just *one* answer or solution. If everyone does not agree on a solution, members might debate the advantages and disadvantages of each solution that comes to light.

Step 5: Suggest Ways to Carry Out the Solution

Sometimes the purpose of a discussion is only to find a solution. In such a case, Step 4 would be the last step. However, many discussions often go on to include Step 5. In this step, members look for ways to carry out the solution. They can do this in several ways. They can make suggestions themselves. They can get the advice of experts outside the group, or ask the audience for suggestions.

IMPROVING DISCUSSIONS

How many discussions have you already been a part of? Would you guess hundreds or thousands? For just a moment, however, think of a few recent discussions. What part did you take in those discussions? Were you able to add to the discussion? Following are some suggestions for future discussions. They can help you become a valuable member of a group discussion.

Find Information

You don't have to prepare for a conversation. The information you have is generally enough. Discussions, however, are different. Most of the time, you will need new facts and figures. You can find needed information in the following places.

You and Your Experiences   Determine what you know about the topic. Look for things in your life that you could use in a discussion. For example, what have you done or seen that would be valuable? Reviewing what you know also saves time. You won't waste time hunting for facts you already have.

Other People and Places   Think of people you know. Would any of these people know something about the topic? Ask them; get their facts and opinions. Other people might also direct you to additional sources of information. What places do you know? Would a visit to the city hall or the local fire department be helpful? Could people in places like those help you?

Published Information   The card catalog in your library is a great source of information. You also might look in the *Readers' Guide to Periodical Literature* for recent information in magazines. Filmstrips and videotapes on the topic might also be available in the library.

As you find information, keep a list of the sources. Take notes so that you can remember the facts accurately. Keep the notes on 3- by 5-inch pieces of paper or note cards. (There is more material on gathering and organizing information in Chapter 12.) Here is an example of an information card.

Topic of card
Facts
Author, name of source, page number

Listen Carefully

A discussion is a sharing of ideas and information. If a discussion is going to work, you will need to listen as well as speak. What are the other people saying? Do you agree or disagree with them? Why? If you don't listen carefully, you won't know what other people are saying. Sometimes, conflicts occur because one member of a group misunderstands what someone else has said. Careful listening can help prevent this problem.

GATEKEEPERS, HARMONIZERS, BLOCKERS:
Roles People Play in Groups

Whenever several people come together to form a group, the group seems to take on a life of its own. Some people may seem to dominate the group while others hold back. At times the group will work together. At other times the group will seem divided. *Group dynamics,* the study of interactions of groups, can show why some groups succeed and others fail.

One group member takes on the special role of *leader* and brings purpose and direction to the group. Besides the role of leader, however, group members can take on a variety of different roles. The following are a few of the roles identified by Walter Lifton in his book *Working with Groups.*

- *Information Giver.* Offers facts and statistics about the group's goals.
- *Elaborator.* Expands on the information given, clarifies confusing points, often explains how a proposed idea will work.
- *Energizer.* Pushes a group to take action: to take a vote, to be more productive, or better organized.
- *Recorder.* Writes down ideas and is the group's memory.
- *Harmonizer.* Relieves tensions, is the group's referee.
- *Gatekeeper.* Limits dominating members and encourages all others.
- *Blocker.* Stands in the way of agreement.
- *Playboy.* Distracts the group by fooling around.
- *Dominator.* Interrupts and sets himself or herself above the others.

Do any of the above roles describe you?

Watch out for partial listening, or hearing words that are spoken without really absorbing their meaning. This might happen because you are thinking about what you are going to say next, or because your attention has wandered.

Here is a simple test to use to see whether you are listening carefully. Can you summarize the main points that were just made by someone else? If you can, you are probably listening carefully.

YOUR TURN

1. As a class, think of ways that a discussion could be used to solve the following problems.

   a. A flood-control project will destroy the farms of twenty families in a valley. Some of the families have lived there for four generations. The project will take three years to finish. However, when it is finished, it will supply water to a large city 200 miles away. It will also prevent yearly flooding of many small towns.

   b. The city has a strong leash law for dogs. Any stray dogs are picked up. They are held for a week and then destroyed unless the owner pays a $50 fine. Dog owners are angry because the law does not apply to cats.

2. You learned the three different purposes for discussions. As a class, list some topics, or problems, that could be included under each purpose. State each topic in the form of a question. Use the examples in the text as models.

Be a Good Speaker

Do you have something important to say? If so, speak clearly so everyone can understand you. Make sure your facts and examples are accurate and that they apply to the topic. Say just what you have to say and then stop. Don't talk just for the sake of talking.

Be a Good Discussion Member

If you have an opinion or information about the topic, say what you know. Then ask for the opinions and findings of others. When you

When taking part in a group discussion, share your own opinions and listen to those of other members of the group.

seek information from others, you help keep the discussion going by encouraging others to join in. Be prepared to hear opinions you don't agree with. Remember, one purpose of a discussion is to learn and gather information from others. Listen and be polite.

LEADING A DISCUSSION

All formal discussions have a leader. Anyone can become a good leader because leadership qualities can be learned and practiced.

Types of Leadership

All good discussion leaders have some abilities in common. They are organized and tactful. They keep the discussion on track. However, not all good discussion leaders use the same leadership style.

Three of the most common leadership styles are nondirective, directive, and supportive.

A **nondirective leader** is part of the discussion group. This person allows the group to make most of its own decisions. The group decides what it will do and how to do it. A nondirective leader gives very few directions.

A **directive leader** is the opposite. This person takes charge: gives orders, assigns tasks, and sets guidelines for the discussion. Often a directive leader also tells the members what they need to do to reach their goals.

Types of Discussion Leaders

Nondirective   Directive   Supportive

A **supportive leader** is somewhere in between the two previous kinds of leaders. This person makes suggestions but doesn't give orders. He or she supports the group's decisions but doesn't try to control them.

At one time or another, all three styles of leadership are used. The decision about which style to use may be based on the topic, the members of the group, the situation, or the time limit.

Responsibilities of a Leader

Just as all good discussion leaders have certain abilities in common, they also have certain responsibilities. They must ensure that the discussions are productive and effective.

Open and Close the Discussion   Leaders open discussions by introducing the topic and the other members of the group. They may also make an opening statement. They might explain, for example, why the topic is important. Then they begin the actual discussion by asking someone a question.

Leaders also close discussions when the time limit is reached. They usually give a short summary of the discussion. Then they restate the best solution. If there is time, the group may discuss ways to carry out the solution. Finally, leaders restate the original problem and its solution.

Be Well Prepared   Like the other members of a discussion group, leaders must be well prepared. They must find information to add to the discussion. Leaders also have other duties. For example, before a discussion, they should outline the topic and list the questions that need to be answered during the discussion.

Keep the Group on Track   Sometimes a discussion gets off the topic. One big responsibility of leaders is to keep everyone on track. They do this by reminding the group what has already been discussed. Then they explain what else must be done. Leaders may also have to do the following: summarize what has been covered, ask important questions, point out issues that need to be covered, encourage people to join in, and move to the next step in problem solving.

EVALUATING DISCUSSIONS

Each discussion you are in should be better than the one before it. There is a way to help ensure that this will happen. People in the audience can evaluate the discussion. From these evaluations, you can learn your strong points. You also can learn in what areas you need to improve. Following are two ways to evaluate classroom discussions.

Discussion Critiques

At the end of a discussion, people in the audience fill out critique forms. On these forms, they rate each member of the discussion group, usually with a scale. The most common one is a scale of 1 (poor) to 10 (superior). Of course, different people might rate the

Discussion Critique

Date: _____ Topic: _____

Name of Person	Quality of Messages Sent			Problem Solving Ability				Other	Score
	Verbal	Vocal	Nonverbal	Knowledge of Problem	Analysis of Problem	Solution of Problem	Tact and Cooperation		

All areas are judged on a scale of 1 (poor) to 10 (superior). Group total _____

same group member differently. Above is a sample critique form. Observers use this form to rate each person in the discussion in seven different areas.

Using this form, observers can rate each person in the discussion. They can give each one a total of 70 points in 7 different areas.

Observers may also evaluate a group as a whole. They add together the scores of each member. They can then compare the totals of different groups.

Interaction and Participation Diagrams

These diagrams record how many times each person speaks and to whom they speak. If you are making the diagram, draw a box for each member of the discussion group. Arrange the boxes in a circle. Put each person's initials in a lower corner of a box. Then draw lines to connect all the boxes. Each line between two boxes represents any direct communication between those two people.

During the discussion, draw a slash on these lines when two people talk. (Place the slash close to the box of the person who made the statement.) If a person makes a statement to the whole group, place a slash next to that person's box. Place it in the open space, rather than through the line.

The results are easy to see at the end of the discussion. Just count the number of times each person spoke. Here is an example of such a diagram.

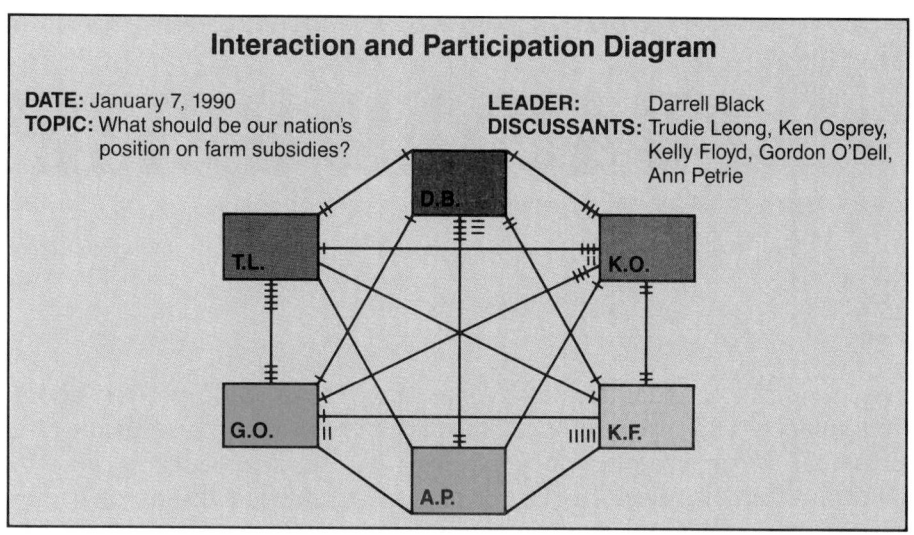

Interaction and Participation Diagram

DATE: January 7, 1990
TOPIC: What should be our nation's position on farm subsidies?

LEADER: Darrell Black
DISCUSSANTS: Trudie Leong, Ken Osprey, Kelly Floyd, Gordon O'Dell, Ann Petrie

YOUR TURN

1. Your teacher will divide the class into groups of five or six students. One person in each group will be a recorder. This person will keep an interaction and participation diagram. The other members of each group should discuss the following question: *What kind of person makes a good class president?* After 15 minutes, end the discussion and analyze the recorder's results.

2. Group members must keep the discussion going. If you were the leader what might you do if the following things happened in a discussion? Remember to be tactful. As a class, discuss what the leader should do.

a. One person hasn't done any research. Nevertheless, that person criticizes statements made by others.

b. Two members sit and whisper to each other. One has added a little to the discussion. The other is obviously bored.

c. One person takes over the discussion. That person is doing most of the talking. However, that person has done a lot of research and is saying important things.

d. A person is taking notes and isn't saying anything.

9 CHAPTER REVIEW

 ## Chapter Summary

Discussion is an exchange of information, ideas, and opinions about one subject. The purpose of all discussions is to find a solution to a problem. More specific purposes can be to find information, to evaluate, and to decide. Five of the most common kinds of group discussions are panel discussions, symposiums, round-table discussions, lecture-discussions, and progressive discussions.

A good discussion usually follows John Dewey's Steps of Reflective Thinking. The steps are: define the problem, study the problem, evaluate possible solutions, select the best solution, and suggest ways to carry out the solution. Ways to improve discussions include finding information, listening carefully, and being a good speaker and discussion member. Three of the most common types of leadership are nondirective, directive, and supportive. Leaders must open and close discussions, be well prepared, and keep the group on track. Discussions can be evaluated with critiques and interaction and participation diagrams.

 ## Checklist

Improving Discussion Skills

1. Remember that discussion is an exchange of information, ideas, and opinions about one subject.

2. Remember that the general purpose of all discussions is to find a solution to a problem. Recognize that three more specific purposes are to find information, to evaluate, and to decide.

3. Understand the differences between the five most common group discussions: panel discussions, symposiums, round-table discussions, lecture-discussions, and progressive discussions.

4. Apply Dewey's Steps of Reflective Thinking to group discussions.

5. Use different sources to locate information for a discussion.

6. Listen carefully during a discussion.

7. Speak clearly and remember not to talk too much during a discussion.

8. Recognize the three most common styles of leadership: nondirective, directive, and supportive.

9. Develop the ability to evaluate discussions with critiques and with interaction and participation diagrams.

 Vocabulary

Define each term in a complete sentence.

directive leader	panel discussion
discussion	progressive discussion
lecture-discussion	round-table discussion
nondirective leader	supportive leader
open forum	symposium

Review Questions

1. Identify the main purpose of all discussions. What are three more specific purposes?

2. Distinguish between a panel discussion and a symposium.

3. Name the contribution that John Dewey made to the process of group discussion.

4. List the five steps of reflective thinking.

5. Identify some things you can do as a group member to improve discussions.

6. Name three sources of information for a discussion.

7. Identify the three most common styles of leadership in discussions. What are the basic qualities of each one?

8. List the responsibilities of a discussion leader.

9. Describe two ways to evaluate members of a discussion.

10. Explain how a group interaction and participation diagram can help members of a discussion.

 Discuss with Your Classmates

1. Discuss the importance of a group leader's being well-prepared for a discussion. What might happen if the discussion leader is disorganized? What might group members do in this situation?

2. Review Dewey's Steps of Reflective Thinking. Then discuss why each step is important and what happens if any of the steps are omitted.

3. Discuss three different discussion groups in which one or more class members have participated in the last six months. What was the primary purpose of each group? What was the leadership style in each group? What was the outcome of the group discussion? What might have been the result if a different leadership style had been used?

4. Using John Dewey's Steps for Reflective Thinking, discuss how a discussion should be set up for each of the following topics.
    a. What type of grading system is best: letter grades, pass/fail, or comments only?
    b. Should a town have curfew hours for people under 18?
    c. What subjects should all students have to pass before graduating?

 # Critical Thinking

1. **Synthesis:** This chapter has presented principles and practical advice for conducting good discussion groups. Devise ways in which to apply this information in a classroom situation and during family discussions.

2. **Application:** Choose a topic that would be suitable for a class discussion. Select the type of group discussion that would be most appropriate for the topic. Decide what kind of information you would need in order to discuss the topic if you were a member of the group. Sketch out a plan for the gathering of the needed information.

 # Activities

In-Class

1. Participate in a brainstorming session to determine three interesting discussion topics that are appropriate for an in-class discussion. One of the topics should be on a national or international issue and one should be about your school.

2. In groups of four or five, select one of the topics determined above. Consider the most appropriate forum for a discussion on that topic. What sort of leadership would probably be most effective? Use this topic for a class discussion.

3. Your teacher will divide your class into two or three groups. With the members of your group, make arrangements to attend a session of a local school board meeting, a lecture-discussion at a local college or university, or an open meeting of your town government. Later, discuss the ways in which the discussions varied.

Out-of-Class

1. Imagine that someone in your community has suggested that senior high school be shortened to three years but that students go to school for twelve months a year. Imagine also that you will be a member of a group that will discuss this proposal. Decide whether you are for it or against it. In your speech notebook, prepare a set of notes that you could use during the discussion.

2. Watch a television discussion or listen to a discussion on the radio. Write a critique about the discussion leader.

3. Be aware of the next three situations during which you are talking with one or more people. Consider whether you participated in a conversation or discussion. In your speech notebook, write a brief explanation of your decision about each situation.

4. Think about five topics that would be interesting for class discussions. Write a discussion question about each topic. Be sure that you word your question carefully. Turn them in to your teacher for possible use in class discussions.

 # Chapter Project

Your teacher will assign you to a group of five or six students. Each group will choose a group leader and decide on a discussion topic. Using as many sources of information as possible, each group member should research the topic and be prepared to join in a 10- to 15-minute discussion.

Consult the interaction and participation diagram on page 181. Be certain that you understand its format and know how to use it in your group.

One person in each group will complete an interaction and participation diagram. During each discussion, other class members will fill out critiques. After each discussion, the class will analyze the results of the critiques and of the interaction and participation diagram.

UNIT 4

PUBLIC SPEAKING

10 Purposes and Types of Public Speaking

Chris's teacher has just given him a topic for an impromptu speech. As he gets up to speak he thinks . . .

"I feel kind of nervous.

I guess everyone else did too.

What do I know about the topic?

What would my classmates want to know?"

Have *you* ever given a speech on the spur of the moment? How did you use the few minutes you had to prepare?

In this chapter, you will read about:

- the four general purposes of a speech
- appropriate general and specific purposes for speeches
- the difference between an impromptu and an extemporaneous speech
- special occasion speeches

Public Speaking: These two words—public speaking—mean different things to different people.

"It's terrible giving a talk in front of people."

"It's giving a speech from notes to a large group."

"It's scary saying things in front of strangers. They just stare at me."

Most people remember only the unpleasant things about giving a speech. Some remember giving book reports to bored classmates. Others think about reciting poems before a group. But these same people have also made good speeches. They just didn't know they were making speeches. Some might have told their friends about a funny movie. Others might have told their families about something they did at school. In each case, a speaker delivered a message in a public place. The listeners did not do or say much during the speech. This is really all there is to public speaking!

FINDING A PURPOSE FOR YOUR SPEECH

Like every good story, every public speech has a purpose. It is often called the **thesis,** or main idea. The speaker states the main idea as a sentence or a question.

The purpose controls the development of a speech. A speaker may even repeat or rephrase the purpose to make it clear. A clear purpose does two things:

- It helps the listeners understand all the information.
- It helps the speaker stay on the topic.

Every speech must have a specific purpose. Some speeches, such as the one these people are listening to, are meant to entertain.

The first step in creating a speech is to decide on its purpose. A speech has one of four general purposes: to inform, to persuade, to entertain, or to inspire.

To Inform

You want your listeners to understand something. If they already know something about your subject, you may help them understand it better. You want your listeners to learn from the information you give them. You may want them to learn about a particular person, place, or thing. Or, you may want them to learn how to do something.

Suppose, for example, that you have a special talent for taking pictures of pets. You decide to give a speech that will teach this skill to others. The purpose of your speech, then, is to *inform*. Through the facts, examples, and methods that you describe, your listeners will learn about taking pictures of pets. You will learn more about the informative speech in Chapter 14.

To Persuade

You want to change your listener's minds. You want them to agree with you, or you may want to prove something. You may even want to get them to take some action.

Imagine, for example, that your school does not open the gym in the morning before classes start. You would like the gym opened an hour before the first class. You feel you have several good reasons for changing this policy. You decide to give a speech to convince your classmates to agree with you. You also want them to help you convince the principal to change the policy. The purpose of your speech is to *persuade*. You will learn more about the persuasive speech in Chapter 15.

To Entertain

You want your listeners to enjoy themselves. You want them to relax and forget their problems. You may even want them to see a funnier, lighter side of an issue or event.

Suppose you decide to give a speech about the first time you rode a horse. You remember several funny things that happened. When you describe this experience, you want your listeners to be amused. To *entertain*, then, is your purpose.

To Inspire

You want your listeners to share a belief or value, such as courage, justice, or love of country. You want them, through your speech, to feel encouraged or moved.

Imagine that two students in your school have done a very brave thing. You decide to give a speech about it. You want other students to be moved by the bravery of these two people. Your purpose, therefore, is to *inspire* your listeners.

Multiple Purposes

Public speeches have one main purpose. But they may include several secondary purposes. For instance, your main purpose may be to *persuade* your classmates to vote for Ann for Student Council. To do this, you may also have to *inform* them about Ann. Or you may want to *entertain* your classmates to get their attention. They may then listen more carefully as you try to *persuade* them. This speech, however, still has only one *main* purpose—to persuade. In any speech you give, you must decide what your main purpose is. This purpose must be very clear so that your audience will understand.

Before the days of television, public speeches were often major social and educational events. This public speaker, William Jennings Bryan, was as popular as one of today's movie stars.

YOUR TURN

1. Review the general purposes of speeches. Then identify the main purpose of each of the following speeches.

   a. A local reporter took a survey. She reported that most people think dogs are the best pets. You, however, prefer cats. Your topic is *Some of my best friends are cats.*

   b. Everyone in town knows Daniel. He's the blind man who has sold newspapers at a corner stand for 20 years. However, few people know that he taught himself to play the piano. He even made two children's records on how to play the piano. He and his wife put their three children through college. Then they adopted a 12-year-old girl. Your topic is *Who is handicapped?*

   c. Recently you toured a car plant. You learned many things about assembly lines. Your topic is *Seven steps in making a car.*

   d. A picnic is planned for some foreign students who have been here for a year. You are giving a short speech. You have just read some funny stories by American writers. Your topic is *Understanding American humor.*

2. Work in groups of two or three. Identify two topics for each of the four speaking purposes.

SPECIFIC PURPOSES OF SPEECHES

Deciding on the general purpose of your speech is the first step. The next step is deciding on the *specific* purpose. To do this, you have to zero in on a small part of a larger topic. Suppose, for example, that someone asked you: *Where would you like to spend your next vacation?* You could give them a general reply, a more specific one, or a very specific one.

General	More Specific	Very Specific
At a beach	At an ocean beach	At Miami beach
At a farm	At a Midwestern farm	At my uncle's farm near Kokomo, Indiana

You can use this method to choose a specific purpose for a speech.

General	More Specific	Very Specific
To inform	To inform about royal children	To inform about royal children who became rulers before their tenth birthday
To persuade	To persuade friends to join in school activities	To persuade friends to support the library by helping at the car wash
To entertain	To entertain with a funny personal experience	To entertain by telling about the mistakes you made as the cook's helper at camp
To inspire	To inspire by making the listeners grateful	To inspire by showing how fortunate Americans are to have freedom of speech

Keep in mind several things when thinking about a specific purpose for a speech. The purpose should *not* be:

Too Broad	To inform about interesting hobbies
Too Personal	To persuade by telling a friend's secret
Too Complex	To inform about advances in computers
Too Trivial	To inform about the uses of a flashlight

You should also think about yourself and your listeners, or audience. *What do you know?* If you know a lot about your subject, you can easily make your purpose quite specific. *What does your audience know about the subject?* If your listeners already know certain things, you can change your purpose to suit them. For example, suppose you are going to give a speech on the dangers of smoking. Your listeners will be other teenagers. You know that most teenagers know the hazards of smoking. Therefore, you decide to tell true stories of teenagers who suffer from ailments caused by smoking. These stories will mean more to your audience than a list of the hazards of smoking.

Time limits also affect the specific purpose of a speech. *The advantages of space travel* would not be a good topic for a five-minute speech. In five minutes, you could not cover even the major points.

TYPES OF SPEECHES

Before radio and television were common, public speeches were often major social and educational events. Public speakers like Edward Everett, William Jennings Bryan, and Russell Conwell were as popular as today's movie stars. These speakers planned their speeches very carefully and were known for their unique styles. They produced a "flow of sound" as they spoke to large crowds without the help of loudspeakers. Audiences enjoyed their long and formal speeches. Today, however, most Americans no longer enjoy this kind of public speaking. They like shorter, less formal speeches.

In spite of this change, public speeches are still grouped according to the amount of preparation time required. Speeches that involve little preparation time are called **impromptu speeches.** Speeches that take much time to prepare are called **extemporaneous speeches.**

TOASTING THE ART OF PUBLIC SPEAKING

Public speaking looks easy when a confident speaker has the podium. But many people—including many adults—lack confidence in their speaking ability. They know that good public speaking skills will help them, yet they have trouble finding time to polish their skills.

Toastmasters International, an organization founded in 1924, is there to help. (The name comes from the title of the person in charge of introducing after-dinner speakers at formal banquets.) Toastmasters International, with more than 100,000 members from 47 different countries, is made up of people who want to improve their communication skills. The organization works with clubs, businesses, and government agencies, offering training in public speaking and leadership skills. It also has youth leadership programs in junior and senior high schools. Publications, including the monthly "Toastmaster" and bimonthly newsletter, round out the educational programs offered by the organization.

In addition to helping speakers improve, Toastmasters International also recognizes skilled speakers. Every year the organization sponsors a World Championship of Public Speaking and chooses a winner from the highly qualified entrants.

A similar organization, International Toastmistress Clubs, was started in 1938. About 30,000 members belong to this organization, all of them interested in speech improvement and other aspects of communication and self-development. Like Toastmasters, this group provides educational programs for adults and youths and holds yearly contests.

If you would like one of these clubs to set up a program at your school, you can write for more information. Your teacher will give you the addresses.

The Impromptu Speech

To give an impromptu speech, you need to organize your ideas quickly and speak spontaneously. In other words, you must "think on your feet." The audience understands this and does not expect a polished speech.

Most impromptu speeches are short and are organized simply. For example, suppose your topic is *My favorite hobbies*. In a short speech, you could talk about only two or three hobbies. You might organize the speech as follows:

   I. I have three hobbies that I enjoy.
      A. First . . . (describe it and tell why you enjoy it)
      B. Second . . . (describe it and tell why you enjoy it)
      C. Third . . . (describe it and tell why you enjoy it)
  II. Summary or conclusion: These are my three favorite hobbies.

Suppose your topic is *What current event have teenagers been discussing the most and why?* You should think quickly about which events you and your friends have discussed recently. Choose just one and then answer the question *Why?* Your organizational plan might be:

   I. The current event that teenagers have been discussing the most is . . .
  II. The reasons they are interested in this topic are
      A. _____
      B. _____
      C. _____
 III. Conclusion: As you can see, teenagers have good reason for being concerned about this event.

The impromptu speech is often a first assignment in speech classes. Your teacher might give such topics as:

- Do you think schools should be open year-round? Why or why not?

- What is your idea of a perfect vacation?

- Describe the most beautiful thing you have ever seen.

- How would you improve school lunches?

- What does it mean to be honorable?

When you are assigned a topic, first read it carefully. Then decide what you should do. Should you take a stand on an issue or develop a specific idea? Make this decision as you walk to the front of the room. State your topic before you begin. Then tell how you feel and give your reasons. No one will expect you to have specific facts at your fingertips. But you should tell as much as you know and keep talking until your time is up. While you talk, look at your audience and do the best you can. This is all you will be expected to do for an impromptu speech.

Outside the classroom, impromptu speaking usually occurs among friends and family. At a family get-together, for example, an aunt might ask you to tell everyone what you did last summer. Guests at dinners are sometimes asked to give short speeches on the spur of the moment. A football coach might ask the captain to talk to the team about trying harder. All these situations call for impromptu speeches. Any past experience in giving speeches will help speakers at times like these.

President Theodore Roosevelt was particularly skilled at giving extemporaneous speeches.

The Extemporaneous Speech

The extemporaneous speech allows speakers time to prepare in advance. The speaker knows when, where, and to whom the speech will be given. In some cases, the speaker chooses his or her own topic. In other cases, the speaker is given a topic. But in most cases, the speaker must decide the specific purpose of the speech.

Once the purpose is clear, the speaker can begin to prepare the speech. A speaker may write an outline or notes. The speaker may give the speech with or without the aid of the outline or notes. In rare cases, a speaker might write out the whole speech. This type of speech is called a manuscript speech. Some speakers read this type of speech. Others memorize it and refer to it only once in a while. Manuscript speeches are very hard to present well. Students should avoid manuscript speeches because they usually sound stiff.

TYPES OF SPECIAL OCCASION SPEECHES

Some impromptu and extemporaneous speeches are so popular that they are called *special occasion speeches*. Audiences expect these speeches to take specific forms. Each kind of special occasion speech serves one of the four general purposes of speeches.

Introductions and Responses

An *introduction* is a short speech that introduces a guest speaker. It states the speaker's qualifications to talk about the topic. It may also give the speaker some facts about the audience or the place. An introduction is always complimentary and respectful. It does not discuss the speaker's topic at length.

A *response* is not part of the planned speech. The guest speaker usually thanks the person who gave the introduction. Then the speaker says how happy he or she is to be with the audience or at the event.

After-dinner Speeches

After-dinner speeches are given after banquets or luncheons. They are usually meant to entertain—even though serious points are made. For this reason, humor is often an important part of these speeches. Speakers include funny stories, jokes, and quotations. A speaker may refer to people in the audience or town to "personalize" the stories. The speaker talks directly to the audience and so uses few notes.

Presentation and Acceptance Speeches

A *presentation speech* is made when an award, gift, or honor is given. The speaker usually explains what the award is for and why the person deserves the award. All compliments and remarks should be honest and sincere. Sometimes, the receiver of an award is unknown. In such cases, the speaker may keep the receiver's name a secret until the end of the speech.

The person who gets the honor usually gives a short *acceptance speech*. The receiver thanks the donor and the presenter and explains the personal meaning of the award. Both presentation and acceptance speeches should be brief.

Commemorative Speeches

Commemorative speeches are given to remember people or events. They honor past accomplishments, which may have resulted

Abraham Lincoln's Gettysburg Address is one of the most famous American commemorative speeches.

from great sacrifices in lives, time, or money. These speeches are often given at dedications, anniversaries, or retirements.

Some commemorative speeches are given at funerals or memorial services. These speeches are called **eulogies.** One of the most famous commemorative speeches is Lincoln's Gettysburg Address, which is in the back of this book.

Graduation Speeches

Three different speeches are usually given at graduations. A guest speaker often gives the main speech. The purpose of this speech is to inspire the graduates. The **valedictorian speech** is given by the top student in the class. The second ranked student gives the **salutatorian speech.** These speakers may talk about past experiences or hopes for the future. They may review the accomplishments of the class and express their gratitude to the teachers and community. Both speakers talk for the whole class, though they may mention personal experiences.

The valedictorian speech is given by the top student in the graduating class.

YOUR TURN

1. Write a more specific topic for each broad topic below. Assume that you have only one week to prepare your speech.
    a. What It Takes To Be a Good Athlete
    b. Vacations at the Ocean
    c. We Must Conserve Energy!
    d. Fishing
    e. Hunger in the United States

2. Here is a list of students' topics for speeches. Work in groups of two or three. Decide which ones are too broad, too personal, too complex, or too trivial. Assume each speech is 15-minutes long. Suggest a good substitute for any inappropriate topic. Report your findings to the class as a whole.
    a. To inform about good grooming habits
    b. To entertain by showing how to draw
    c. To persuade the class not to judge people too quickly
    d. To inform about the three basic rhythms used in modern jazz
    e. To inform about raising rabbits
    f. To inspire by telling about great deeds

10 CHAPTER REVIEW

 ## Chapter Summary

Public speaking involves a speaker giving a message to others in a public place. Every public speech has a purpose called the *thesis,* or *main idea.* The four general purposes of speeches are to inform, to persuade, to entertain, and to inspire.

Once you have a general purpose for a speech, you must decide on a specific purpose. The specific purpose should not be too broad, too personal, too complex, or too trivial. The purpose of a speech should suit the speaker and the audience. It must also fit within a time limit.

Speeches that involve little preparation time are called *impromptu speeches.* These speeches must be organized quickly and given spontaneously. Speeches that take much time to prepare are called *extemporaneous speeches.* There are several types of special occasion speeches. They include introductions and responses, after-dinner speeches, presentation and acceptance speeches, commemorative speeches, and graduation speeches.

 ## Checklist

Improving Your Public Speaking Skills

1. Define a general thesis for your speech.

2. Refine your thesis into a more specific topic.

3. Decide whether you are speaking to persuade, entertain, or inform.

4. Beware of making your speech topic too broad, personal, complex, or trivial.

5. Fit the speech to the occasion and the audience.

 Vocabulary

Define each term in a complete sentence.

eulogy   salutatorian speech

extemporaneous speech   thesis

impromptu speech   valedictorian speech

Review Questions

1. Define the word "public" in the term *public speaking*.
2. Supply another name for the "purpose" of a public speech.
3. Explain what a clearly stated purpose will do for an audience.
4. Explain what a clearly stated purpose will do for a speaker.
5. List the four general purposes of speeches.
6. Explain the difference between a speech that informs and a speech that persuades.
7. Explain the difference between the general purpose and the specific purpose of a speech.
8. Give an example of a trivial purpose for a speech.
9. Define an impromptu speech. How does it differ from an extemporaneous speech?
10. Name three types of special occasion speeches.

Discuss with Your Classmates

1. Have you ever heard someone give a speech that was inappropriate for the time and place? What was the problem?

2. What would be appropriate topics for speeches in each of the following situations?

    a. a football awards banquet   **c.** a town meeting

    b. a PTA meeting   **d.** graduation

3. Discuss each of the following speech topics. How appropriate is each topic for a 15-minute speech?

    a. Telecommunication systems of the future

    b. How to use a screwdriver

    c. Fascinating cities

    d. My best friend's shortcomings

    e. Islands of the world

 # Critical Thinking

1. Comprehension: Speeches with the general purpose of persuading an audience are quite common. Think of a persuasive speech that you have heard. In addition to persuasion, what other purposes did the speaker have?

2. Application: Assume that you have been asked to deliver an impromptu speech on the topic "The Ideal Summer Job." You have one minute to plan your speech. How would you go about it?

Activities

In-Class

1. You know more about some things than about others. You have lived in certain places and know special people. You have unique interests and hobbies. You belong to certain clubs and teams. You may not be an authority on any of these topics. Still, you could speak about them at a moment's notice. On slips of paper, write five topics you know well. When your teacher calls on you, draw one slip of paper. Then give a two-minute impromptu speech on that subject.

2. Your teacher will give you a topic for an impromptu speech. Since you do not know what the topic will be, you cannot prepare for it. Think of a specific purpose as you walk to the front of the room. Try to talk on the topic for two or three minutes.

3. Give a short speech to inform in which you tell the audience how to draw a map locating your home or a specific building. Have the class draw as you talk. When you have finished, collect the maps and see how well you gave simple instructions.

Out-of-Class

1. Read Susan B. Anthony's speech in the back of this book. Write answers to the following questions in your speech notebook.
   a. What is the general purpose of her speech?
   b. How far did you have to read before you knew the purpose?
   c. Did the title give you any clue?
   d. What is the specific purpose of the speech?
   e. How much further did you have to read to discover it?

2. Your teacher will pair you with a partner. Meet with your partner and discuss each other's interests and backgrounds. Use this information to prepare a one-minute introduction of your partner. Write the notes for the introduction in your speech notebook. At the next class, present your introduction.

3. Imagine that your speech class is having an informal luncheon. Prepare a humorous two-minute speech for after the luncheon. In the speech, refer to at least two other members of your class. Include personal experiences, jokes, or funny stories that relate to your topic. Write the notes for your speech in your speech notebook.

 ## Chapter Project

Team up with a classmate to plan two speeches. One should be a presentation speech, the other an acceptance speech. Decide together what the occasion for the presentation is and what is being presented. Be sure to include enough information for the class to be able to see why the presentation is being made. Practice giving the speeches, and be ready to give them in front of the class.

CHAPTER 11 Choosing Topics

These are some of Maria's thoughts as she skims the newspaper for a speech topic.

"I want to find an interesting topic.

I'd like to give a speech about a problem in the neighborhood.

Maybe I can find something in the newspaper."

Where can *you* look for ideas for speech topics? How do you choose a topic?

In this chapter, you will read about:

- factors that influence the selection of a speech topic
- sources for a speech topic
- how to choose an appropriate, interesting speech topic
- how to select a good title for a speech

Three students are invited to give short speeches at a service club meeting. They are given one week to prepare. Jim is given the topic *Three things this club should do for local teenagers*. Janet is asked to talk about *Courage*. Corey is told that she may choose her own topic. Which student will have the easiest job?

Imagine that the tasks of preparing a speech are placed on a yardstick. The yardstick covers one week. It might look like the following.

Yardstick of Speech Preparation

Choosing a Subject or Topic	Deciding on General and Specific Purposes	Gathering Information	Organizing Information	Practicing Aloud

Jim was given a topic with both general and specific purposes. In his speech, he would persuade the club to do three things for teenagers. He was ready to begin the third step on the yardstick. Janet had only a topic with no general or specific purpose. Only one step of her yardstick was covered. Corey was at the very first step of the yardstick. She had to complete *all* the tasks of preparing a speech. Compared to Jim and Janet, she had more things to do. Because of this, she had less time to do each of them. The biggest problem comes when you are in Corey's position—having to choose your own topic. Read the following suggestions.

PRIMARY FACTORS IN CHOOSING TOPICS

Even before you begin thinking about a possible speech topic, you should think about the following factors.

Time Limits

How much time do you have to prepare your speech? How much time do you have to give it? If a topic will take too long to research, it may be too broad or complex. You might have to narrow it down or make it simpler. If a topic can't be presented within the time limit, you may have to shorten it. If you cannot do these things, you will have to find a new topic. Even if a topic is very interesting, you must be able to present it within the time limit. You should *never* end a speech by saying, "There is so much more, but my time is up."

The Audience

Will your audience like everything you like? Probably not. That's why you must think carefully about your audience before you choose a topic. If you know your audience will not be interested in a certain topic, choose a different one. For example, teenagers probably

How would you narrow your topic in a speech about the Concorde so that your audience would understand you and be interested?

would not be interested in a speech about social security benefits. They would, however, like to hear about ways to earn money during summer vacations.

When you choose a topic, take advantage of people's natural curiosity. People like to know how things are done or why they happen. Find topics that have *universal* appeal, or that will interest everyone. As you do this, think about the following basic needs and wants of all people.

- the need to satisfy physical needs (food, water, rest)
- the need to stay healthy and active
- the need to feel secure and safe
- the need to set and meet goals
- the need to communicate
- the need to have hope for and trust in the future
- the need to experience beauty

The Occasion

You may think that speaking to a speech class will always be the same. The same people are in the same room with the same teacher. However, this does not mean that the situation will also be the same. Every day is different. For example, a class on Monday morning is probably very different from a class on Friday afternoon.

When you think about a speech topic, look ahead to the day of your speech. Is the day near a holiday? Are there any special activities scheduled that day? How will these activities affect the mood of the class? For example, if everyone has just returned from an assembly, you may have trouble getting their attention. If you think about the situation ahead of time, your task of choosing a topic will be easier.

Variety

Finally, your topics should change from speech to speech— especially if you have the same audience. People get tired of hearing the same person talk about the same thing again and again. Choose topics with different general and specific purposes. More variety in your topics will create more interest in your audience.

MENTAL HEADSTANDS
And Other Means of Stalking Ideas

Brainstorming is a variation on the "let's put our heads together" approach. Anyone who has taken part in an intense brainstorming session knows about the creative energy generated. One person's suggestions spark an idea in someone else, and before the group knows how it happened, they have developed a strategy for a class treasurer campaign, worked out a plan to help needy families, or designed a set for a musical.

Brainstorming in a group is productive and fun. Sometimes, however, group participation isn't possible or practical. Fortunately, there are good ways to brainstorm alone when you need to explore an idea. All you need is a pen, a pad of paper, no distractions, and half an hour of concentration.

The basic method of brainstorming an idea is to list everything you can think of that is connected to the idea. Suppose you plan to give a speech about working in your older sister's restaurant over the summer. You begin listing thoughts, in no particular order, as they occur to you: tasting sauces —wasted food—impressions of customers. You find yourself gathering momentum as the list grows;

eventually these thoughts form into categories.

Sometimes it's more difficult to think of ideas. What if you are assigned a topic that challenges your creativity? Suppose you are asked to give a speech about earmuffs. You can think of little to say about earmuffs. This is the time to use the brainstorming technique of turning an idea on its head. Ask yourself questions like the following and write down what the answers suggest: Can earmuffs be expanded? Compressed? Reshaped? Reversed? Vaporized? Pulverized? Elasticized? Electrified? This technique is a powerful, creative stimulus.

Brainstorming, whether used by a group or an individual, is an excellent process for generating ideas. Try brainstorming. You will be pleased with the results.

1. By knowing something about the audience, you can choose speech topics that will interest them. Think of two topics that would interest the following audiences. Brainstorm in a group to find likely topics.

    a. A speech class of eighth and ninth grade students.

    b. A parent-teacher banquet at the beginning of the year for parents of teenagers

    c. A local wilderness club

2. Review the basic needs and wants of people on page 211. Which ones apply to the following general speech topics? Discuss your answers.

    a. Buying a home

    b. Visiting the dentist

    c. Taking canoeing lessons

    d. Learning to make soap

    e. Taking leadership training classes

    f. Buying the right kind of door locks

SECONDARY FACTORS IN CHOOSING TOPICS

There are several other factors to think about when choosing interesting speech topics. The *importance* of certain ideas to most people is one such factor. For example, people must breathe air to live. The quality of the air may affect the length of people's lives. Obviously, then, the topic of air pollution would be important to everyone. Another factor to think about is *self-improvement*. Everyone is interested in ways to help themselves—from becoming healthier to becoming more popular.

Events that include *suspense, mystery,* and *conflict* usually get people's attention quickly. People want to know how a story will end or who will win a conflict. These elements can make many topics fascinating. Also, most people are interested in the *rare, unusual,* and *exotic.* Topics that include people, places, or events that are far away or that happened long ago will often intrigue many people.

Most people like to have something they don't understand explained simply and clearly. *Simplification* and *clarification* are other factors to think about when choosing a topic. Some topics lend themselves to concrete examples or explanations. Often speech teachers hear students say, "Lots of people have tried to explain that to me. This speech really made it clear. For the first time, I understand!"

On the other hand, you should not choose topics that include difficult and complicated processes. For example, explaining an advanced math formula would be too technical for most people. You should also avoid topics that are too personal.

SOURCES OF TOPICS FOR SPEECHES

There are many different sources of speech topics. Ideas for speeches may come to you at any time. You might get an idea from reading something, seeing a movie or a play, or listening to music. An idea may just "pop" into your mind. For this reason, you should keep a notebook of ideas. If you think of something, write it down. Then you will remember it, and you can develop it later. Other sources of speech topics follow.

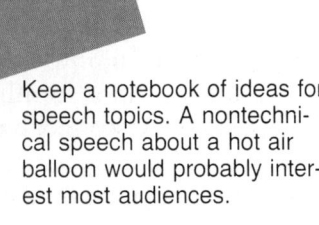

Keep a notebook of ideas for speech topics. A nontechnical speech about a hot air balloon would probably interest most audiences.

Personal Experiences

When you are looking for good speech topics, begin with your own experiences. Think about clubs, hobbies, special interests, or activities you enjoy. Think about places you have visited and people you have met. Consider your opinions and the reasons for them. Your family and friends can be sources of speech topics, too. Your own experiences can be very interesting to others. It may be the next best thing to having done something themselves.

Personal Experiences Make Good Speech Topics

"Nothing unusual ever happens on these backpacking trips."

Current Issues and Events

What events are happening in the world, your state, and your community today? What issues are people talking about in the newspapers and on television? These current events and issues can be good sources of speech topics.

As you think about these topics, look for a new or different angle to a story. Do not just repeat what a reporter has said. Show how an event or issue affects people and places. You might even show how your own life has been influenced. Remember, however, that national and international events and issues are usually more complicated than state and local ones. Your listeners may be more familiar with issues and events that are closer to them.

The current events and issues of today can often cause even greater problems in the future unless someone takes action. Think about these possibilities as you choose a speech topic. You may be able to include ways that your listeners can take some action or do something about a problem to prevent it from getting worse.

Timeless Issues and Questions

Some issues and questions are called *timeless*. They have existed for so long that most people don't know when or where they began. People still search for their answers—or for ways to live with them. Following are some of those issues and questions.

- What is the best way to learn?
- How can crime be reduced?
- How can world peace be achieved?
- How can prejudice be stopped?
- How can poverty be ended?

If you choose such a topic, show how it is a never-ending problem. Then make suggestions for solving it. Just remember, however, that there are no simple answers to these problems.

Historic Events and People

History is another good source of interesting speech topics. Think about the following people of the past: Napoleon, Joan of Arc, John F. Kennedy, Abraham Lincoln, George Washington Carver, Helen Keller, Dr. Martin Luther King, Jr., and Marie Curie. Think about these past events: the discovery of America, the first landing on the moon, the invention of the printing press, and the signing of the Declaration of Independence. What *actually* happened? What made these people and events and others like them so important? How did they change the lives of those who came after them? How can these people and events help people now and in the future? Thinking about these things can spark an idea for a good speech.

History is a good source of interesting speech topics. A speech about Napoleon might describe his coronation ceremony, at which he placed the crown on his own head.

Places

You may have visited other places or read a lot about them. Therefore, you could use these experiences and information as speech topics. For example, suppose you describe the dark, cold nights in Alaska or a steep climb up a Colorado mountain. You should describe them so clearly that your listeners *feel* as if they are there. If you can do this, your topic is a good one.

Interesting facts about the historical backgrounds of places can also make good speech topics. For example, suppose you visited Lexington, Massachusetts. There you learned that Paul Revere never made it through Concord to warn the people about the British. Actually, Paul Revere was captured by the British and held for a few hours. Two other men, Dr. Prescott and Billy Dawes, were really the ones who spread the warning. These facts would make an interesting speech topic.

Concrete and Tangible Things

Another category for speech topics is things. This category includes **concrete** and **tangible** objects—things that you can see, hear, smell, taste, or touch. For example, suppose you wanted to use a home computer for a speech topic. You might discuss its invention, uses, or strengths and weaknesses. Or, you might want to demonstrate how it is used. If you use things as speech topics, you can also compare and contrast them. Or you can suggest ways to make them better or more useful.

Abstract Ideas and Concepts

Abstract ideas and **concepts,** such as freedom, beauty, and courage, can also be sources for speech topics. You cannot see, hear, smell, taste, or touch these ideas and concepts. They mean different things to different people. If you choose such an idea or concept as a topic, you will have to define it with examples and illustrations. For example, suppose you choose the topic *What it means to be free.* You would have to use examples of freedom to explain what it means. Speeches about abstract ideas and concepts are often given to inspire the audience.

Processes and Procedures

Today, bookstores and libraries have many "How to . . ." and "How things work" books. People are naturally curious about such things. Because of this, processes and procedures make good speech topics. You might explain, for example, how a computer game works, how to use a pottery wheel, or how to make candles. If you think about it, you probably know how to do many different things and how many things work. Use this knowledge to select a speech topic.

Jobs and Professions

Finally, jobs and professions can be good sources for speech topics. As a student, you have probably been asked, "What are you going to be?" You are probably still thinking of many different career choices. Because of this, jobs and professions make interesting speech topics for students. What jobs pay well? How much education do certain jobs require? What are the requirements for particular jobs? How happy are people in certain kinds of jobs? Are many of these jobs available? Whether a speaker talks about part-time or full-time jobs, this subject is a good source of speech topics. It helps people in the audience think about their futures.

SELECTING TITLES FOR SPEECHES

A speech title should capture the audience's attention. It should be brief and give the subject of the speech—without being too specific. A title may be indirect. For example, a speech about the benefits of exercise might be called, "A Secret Road to Power." Notice how this title hints at the topic and sparks curiousity. You can use informal phrases in titles if they serve a purpose. For example, you might call a talk on home burglaries, "Safe and Sound at Home: Want to Bet?"

The best time to select a title is after you have practiced your speech aloud. If you choose your title first, you may write your speech to fit the title. You may pass up new ideas or material. Instead, develop your speech completely. Then select an interesting, attention-getting title.

YOUR TURN //////////

1. As a class, review the secondary factors for choosing speech topics on page 213. Decide which ones might apply to the following topics. Then think of two topics for each factor.
   a. A week of mountain climbing in Nepal.
   b. Jogging and swimming can make you healthier.
   c. The true story of the battle of the Alamo.
   d. Medic Alert can save your life if you have a serious allergy.
   e. An easy way to restore an old car.
   f. A tropical bird few people have seen.
   g. How to take tests successfully.
   h. Traitors who lived to regret their acts.

2. For each of the following general purposes, think of topics for all of the sources listed in this section. Work together in small groups. Then share your topics with the class as a whole.
   a. to inform   c. to inspire
   b. to persuade   d. to entertain

CHAPTER REVIEW

 ## Chapter Summary

The selection of a suitable speech topic is very important. There are four factors that you should think about before doing anything else. The first factor is *time*. How much time do you have to prepare a speech? How much time do you have to give the speech? The second factor is the *audience*. You should take advantage of people's natural curiosity. Find topics that have universal appeal. To do this, think about the basic needs and wants of all people. The occasion is the third factor. All speeches can be affected by the events surrounding them. Finally, you should think about *variety*. Your topics should vary from speech to speech. You should look for different topic ideas that have different purposes.

In addition, there are some secondary factors to think about when selecting a speech topic. These include *importance* of ideas, *self-improvement,* and people's interest in *suspense, mystery,* and *conflict.* You should also consider people's interest in the *rare, unusual,* and *exotic.* Finally, people like *simplification* and *clarification* of things they do not understand.

Some common sources for speech topics include personal experiences, current issues and events, continuing questions and issues, past events and people, concrete things, abstract ideas, processess and procedures, and jobs and professions.

 ## Checklist

Developing Topic-Choosing Skills

1. Match your topic to the amount of preparation time you have.
2. Keep in mind the interests of your audience.
3. Talk on a variety of topics.

4. To give variety to your speech topics, don't forget the many sources of speech ideas, including personal experience, history, current events, timeless issues, places, things, and abstract ideas.

 ## Vocabulary

Define each term in a complete sentence.

abstract ideas   concrete

concepts   tangible

 ## Review Questions

1. Explain why time is a factor in choosing a speech topic.

2. List some factors to consider in analyzing your audience before choosing a speech topic.

3. List some needs of people that could be the basis for a topic.

4. Name some secondary factors to think about when choosing a topic for a speech.

5. Name five sources of topics for speeches.

6. Explain why personal experience is often a good speech topic.

7. Explain how your approach in a speech on a current issue or event could be different from a television reporter's.

8. Tell why jobs and professions make good speech topics.

9. Explain the purpose of a speech title.

 ## Discuss with Your Classmates

1. People have been making speeches about abstract concepts like beauty and freedom for hundreds of years. Do you think there is anything new to be said on such topics? Why or why not?

2. Historical events and people are good sources of speech topics. Think about your own area of the country. Discuss with your classmates what historical people or events connected with your area might make good topics for speeches.

3. As you know, people are always interested in learning more about jobs and professions. Discuss with your classmates which jobs and professions people in your class would like to learn more about. Also, discuss how you might gather information about the jobs and professions that you identify.

Critical Thinking

1. Interpretation: Think of all of the speeches you have heard during the last year, in person or on radio and television. Select the three that you felt were most interesting. What were the topics of those speeches? Why were the topics good choices? Did each speech have something to do with the basic needs and wants of all people?

2. Synthesis: Knowing your audience is important when you are deciding on a speech topic. What kind of audience would be interested in each of the following topics: fleas, the junior astronaut program, world hunger, drug abuse.

Activities

In-Class

1. Work as a class or in small groups. Write two general topics such as *pets* and *sports*. Under each topic write at least three specific subtopics that relate to each one. Finally, give the purpose of each subtopic. Discuss your choices in class.

2. Everyone knows enough about certain topics to use them as topics for speeches. What topics are you personally familiar with? Make your own list and then share it with the class. As each person's list is read and discussed, the reactions of your classmates will give you a good idea of topics that they would enjoy learning about.

3. Choose a problem that your community faces. It may be a problem like traffic congestion or air, noise, or water pollution. Discuss the problem in class. Identify ways in which the members of the class could become actively involved in the solution to the problem. Decide whether or not the problem and its solution would make a good topic for a speech.

Out-of-Class

1. Review the list of sources for topics of speeches presented in this chapter. In your speech notebook, write as many topics as you can think of for each source. For some sources, you may have only a single topic. For others you may have five or six. In each category, choose topics that you yourself would be interested in learning about.

2. Assume that you will have to find topics for three ten-minute speeches that will be presented in class. Review the topics that you wrote in your speech notebook during the previous activity. Identify the three topics that you would use. Keep the time limit and the audience in mind as you review the topics.

Chapter Project

Take an informal poll to see what speech topics interest people. Ask at least seven people what topics they might be interested in learning more about. Ask students your age, some older, and some younger. Ask teachers, your brothers and sisters, parents, or neighbors.

Record all the answers you get. Then see if there is much overlap in what interests people. Were students interested in the same things as teachers? Did teachers and parents have the same interests?

Identify the three topics that most people are interested in. Discuss with your classmates why these would or would not make good speech topics.

CHAPTER 12

Researching and Organizing Speeches

Tom's arms are full of the books he plans to use to research his speech. As he gathers them, he thinks . . .

"How will I ever sort out all the facts I need for my speech?

I think I have enough books, at least.

But where are the recent magazine articles?

How will I pull all this research together?"

What do *you* already know about doing library research? How can you plan your research?

In this chapter, you will read about:

- the five steps in preparing a speech
- the card catalog and the *Readers' Guide to Periodical Literature*
- outlining a speech
- different ways to arrange the information in a speech
- introductions and conclusions for speeches
- transitions in a speech

You have chosen a topic for your speech. You have decided exactly what purpose the speech will serve. The next step is to gather all the information you will need and to plan exactly what you will say.

Once they know their topic, some people are tempted to plunge right in and begin writing a speech. But that's a little like building a house without a floorplan. It takes time to plan a speech that flows easily from one point to the next, is clear and organized, and leaves nothing important out. First, prepare your speech by obtaining all the information you need. Use the library to fill in gaps in your knowledge. Next, outline what you want to say. This chapter shows you how.

FIVE STEPS IN PREPARING SPEECHES

Following are five steps. If you follow them, you will save yourself time and effort when you prepare a speech.

Survey Known Information

What do you already know about your topic? You can find out very easily. First divide a piece of paper into two columns. Then label the two columns "Things I Know about (your topic)" and "Things I Don't Know about (your topic)." Write down all you know and don't know about your topic. By doing this, you will find out if you need more information. If you do need more information, you will have a list of what you need to find out.

The most frequently used sources of information are books and other printed materials.

Use Different Sources of Information

If you need more information, be sure to use more than one source when you are looking for it. Here are some sources to use.

Books and Other Printed Material   Students use this source more than any other. Besides books, printed material includes newspapers, magazines, and pamphlets. All these sources, of course, are in school libraries and town libraries. (The next section of this chapter will discuss how to use the library.)

Nonprint Media   Many libraries have videotapes or videodiscs; audiotapes or records; movies, filmstrips, and slides; and photographs, diagrams, paintings, and graphs. All of these can be used as sources of information. They can also be used as a part of your speech.

Interviews and Surveys   A good source of firsthand information is your family, friends, relatives, and neighbors. If you want to interview someone, set up an appointment. Before the interview, write a list of questions you want to ask. If you want to quote someone, write down the person's exact words.

During your speech, you will want to tell your audience something about the person you interviewed. During the interview, explore the connection between the person and your topic. For example, be sure to find out in what way the person is an authority on your topic. If you tape-record your interview, you could even play parts of it during your speech. If you want to do this, get the person's permission first. (Review Chapter 8 for suggestions for conducting an interview.)

You also might want to take a survey or poll and report your results. Before you begin, write out a form for everyone to fill in. To keep the results manageable, write the poll so that the answer to any question is "yes" or "no" or multiple-choice. For example, you might ask, "Which of the following best describes the food in the school cafeteria? Excellent, Good, Average, Poor, Uneatable."

Personal Visits   Suppose you have been asked to give a speech about your town's need for a new senior citizen's center. The best way to get first-hand information is probably to go to the present center. While you are there, take short, descriptive notes to remind you of any important details. You will be even more convincing if you also take pictures and show them during your speech.

Personal Experiences   Your own personal experiences can also be sources of firsthand information. For example, do you scuba dive, oil paint, or do any other interesting activity? If you do, you can explain any needed training, problems, and rewards of the activity. You might even demonstrate all or part of such an activity as part of your speech.

Use Note Cards

As you find information for your speech, write it down. Most students use 3″ × 5″ or 4″ × 6″ cards because they are easy to organize later. When you take notes, don't write down every sentence word by word. Instead, write the main points in your own words. Usually you should write only one piece of information on each card.

To make your note-taking faster, you should use your own form of shorthand. You can abbreviate words and drop unimportant words like the articles *a, an,* and *the.*

The library card catalog is a very important source of information in preparing for a speech.

Most of your note cards, of course, will be filled with facts. However, you can also include a set of figures, a chart, or a graph that will support a point you want to make. In your speech, you might explain such information, or you could write it on the board.

You should also write some direct quotations on your note cards. If you do, copy them exactly as they are written. To remind you that they are quotations, put quotation marks around them. Direct quotations can be very useful in speeches. They can support a point you are making, and they can add interest to your speech.

After you give your speech, keep your note cards. Perhaps you will be able to use some of the information in a future speech.

Organize Information

Once you have your information on note cards, you must organize it. Following is one way that is easy to use.

- Write the general topic or subject of a note on the top right-hand corner of a card. (Example: hobbies, pets)

- Below the general topic, write the specific topic. (Example: stamp collecting, rabbits)

- Skip a couple of spaces. Then write one piece of information. (Example: a fact, a direct quotation) If you run out of space, use the back of the card. It is a good idea to check your information before you put away your source.

- Write the details about your source at the bottom of the card. Usually you should include the author, title, publisher, date of publication, and the pages on which you found the information. You should include this information so that you could find your source again if you needed to.

The next step is to arrange your information in outline form. An outline is a summary of your information—in the order in which you will present it. You can arrange your information easily if you group your cards using the general and specific topics you wrote on them. (The last section of this chapter will deal with outlines.)

Practice Aloud

Even though this is one of the most important steps, students often skip it. However, just having a lot of good information is no guarantee that you will give a good speech. A speech is more than a report. A speech is an oral presentation, and it must be practiced aloud—just like a part in a play. (Chapter 13 gives many suggestions for delivering a speech. You can use these suggestions when you practice your speech.)

USING THE LIBRARY

The library is the most complete source of information for most speeches you write. It includes not only books, but also newspapers, magazines, and journals on specialized subjects. To use a library's resources successfully, you need to know about the two systems of card catalogs—the Dewey Decimal System and the Library of Congress System—and the source of information about magazines and journals, the *Readers' Guide to Periodical Literature.*

Dewey Decimal System

The **Dewey Decimal System** is used most often in school libraries. In this system, each book is given a number according to its subject. Following are the ten main subject groups in this system.

000–099　General Works (reference books)
100–199　Philosophy
200–299　Religion
300–399　Social Science (law, education, economics)
400–499　Language
500–599　Science (mathematics, biology, chemistry)
600–699　Technology (medicine, inventions)
700–799　Fine Arts (painting, music, theater)
800–899　Literature
900–999　History (biography, geography, travel)

Library of Congress System

The **Library of Congress System** is used by the United States Library of Congress and by most large city and college libraries. This system is based on a combination of letters and numbers. The Language and Literature books, for example, begin with a *P*. If you want to find public speaking books, you would look under *PN* and then under a number from 4000 to 4321.

When you go to a library, the first thing you should do is to look in the card catalog. The card catalog indexes information according to author, title, and subject. Therefore, if you only remember the author's name and not the title, you can still find the book. You can also look under a subject and find all the books in the library that are about that subject. For example, if you looked under *astronomy,* you would find *Cosmos* by Carl Sagan and many other books.

Each card includes the author's full name, the title of the book, the publisher, and the date of publication. It also includes the number of pages and a brief description of the book's contents.

Once you have found the card you want, look at the top left corner. There you will find the **call number** for the book. This number will be based on one of the two systems just described. Write the call number down so that you don't forget it. Then look for a diagram of the library near the entrance. It will show you where to go to find the book you want.

The Readers' Guide

Another helpful source of information in the library is the *Readers' Guide to Periodical Literature.* This source indexes all the articles in magazines and journals by subject and author. Other information included in each entry is the magazine volume, the

The local library has copies of newspapers, both old and new, that can be used in gathering information for speeches.

pages, and the date of publication. A key to the abbreviations used in the entries can be found at the beginning of each volume. The *Readers' Guide to Periodical Literature* can be a very helpful source because magazines usually have more recent information than books have.

Following is a list of other general reference books that you might find helpful.

Barlett's *Familiar Quotations*
Bibliographic Index
Biographical Index
Book Review Digest
Current Biography
Dictionary of American Biography
Facts on File
International Index to Periodicals
Kenyon and Knott's *A Pronouncing Dictionary of American English*
Mencken's *A New Dictionary of Quotations*
Roget's Thesaurus
Who's Who? series
The World Almanac and Book of Facts

1. The first step in preparing a speech is to decide what you already know and what you need to know about the topic. Divide two pieces of paper into two parts. Write the heading "Things I Know" on one side of each piece and the heading "Things I Don't Know" on the other side of each piece. Then choose two of the following topics and fill out each piece of paper.

    a. Jogging   **d.** The *Titanic*

    b. Hurricanes   **e.** Olympic Medals in *1979*

    c. Raising horses   **f.** Cats as pets

2. Choose one "Things I Don't Know" column in Exercise 1. Then decide what sources you could go to to look for information for that topic. Be prepared to share your answers with the rest of the class at the end of the period.

OUTLINING SPEECHES

Once you have all the information you need, the next step is putting your speech together or outlining it. Because an outline helps you organize your information, using one will make your speech better. When one idea logically follows another, an audience can follow a speech and understand it more easily.

Outlining information helps you see exactly what the most important points are. Writing an outline based on your index cards will also help you find any missing information.

When you give your speech, an outline can be a helpful memory tool. At a glance, you can see all your major points. Seeing them will help you remember what it is you want to say.

Basic Parts of an Outline

Students usually use either a topic outline or a sentence outline. **Topic outlines** are summaries of ideas that are written in words and phrases. **Sentence outlines** are summaries of ideas that are written in complete sentences. Both kinds of outlines have the same basic parts.

Major Points or Heads   These parts follow Roman numerals and state the main ideas of a speech. For example, following is the same basic outline for a speech about becoming a teacher, first presented topically, then in sentence form.

Topical Outline
    I. Graduation from high school
   II. Acceptance to college
  III. Entrance to department of education
  IV. Certification by state

Sentence Outline
    I. The first requirement is to graduate from high school with above-average grades.
  II. The second requirement is to get accepted by a college with a teacher-education program.
  III. The third requirement is to enter a department of education.
  IV. The fourth requirement is to get a certificate from the state you want to teach in.

The main points in both outlines have the same meaning to the central idea of the speech. The only thing that is different about the outlines is the form in which they are presented.

Minor Points or Subpoints   These parts follow capital letters and are indented under the main points. They explain or prove the main points. You should never have only *one* minor point. If you have only one, make it a part of the main head. Following is more of the outline above, showing subpoints A and B for one of the major points.

Topical Outline
III.   Entrance to department of education
    A. Good grades needed
    B. Standardized test scores needed

Sentence Outline
III.   The third requirement is to enter a department of education.
    A. Grades of at least a *B* are usually required.
    B. One or more standardized test scores may also be required.

Sub-Subpoints   These parts follow Arabic numerals and are indented under the minor points. They show greater divisions or examples of the minor points. They may be facts, quotations, or any other important evidence to support the minor ideas. Even greater divisions follow lower-case letters or Arabic numbers in parentheses. You should use these if you need even more detail. Following is an example of an outline.

I. _____
  A. _____
    1. _____
      a. _____
      b. _____
    2. _____
      a. _____
      b. _____
  B. _____

II. _____
  A. _____
  B. _____
    1. _____
      a. _____
        (1) _____
        (2) _____
      b. _____
    2. _____

It is very important to get and keep the attention of your audience.

PARTS OF A SPEECH

Speeches have three basic parts: an introduction, a body, and a conclusion. In addition, speeches include transitions, ways to move smoothly from one idea to the next. Many speech writers write the body of a speech first, then the introduction and conclusion. However, the following sections introduce you to speech parts in the order in which a speech is presented.

Introduction

The main purpose of an **introduction** is to get the attention of your audience. Some of the ways to do this are listed below. As you read the following ideas, keep one thing in mind. Whatever you use, it must relate to the topic of your speech. An introduction is an attention-getter, but it is also *part* of your speech.

- Use a quotation.

- Ask one or more questions that people in the audience will answer silently to themselves. Then the purpose of your speech will be to answer those questions.

- Use some kind of audio-visual material like a picture or a record.

- Tell a serious or funny story. The story can be true or made up, and it can be about you or someone else.

- Give some interesting background on your topic.

- Mention people in the audience.

- Use an illustration or an example.

- Use a series of actions or gestures before saying anything.

Avoid beginning a speech with "I'm going to talk about ____" or "The subject of my speech is _____." Instead, use one of the methods suggested above. After getting the attention of the audience, it is also important to motivate them to listen by showing why the subject is important to them. Tell the audience how this subject affects them. After the audience knows why it is important to listen, you should state clearly the specific purpose of the speech. A good introduction captures the audience's attention, motivates them to listen, and states the specific purpose of the speech. Now the audience is ready to listen to the body of the speech. Spend time on your introduction. It is important because it is the audience's first impression of you and your speech.

Body

The **body of a speech** contains all the main ideas and their supporting points. Since the body is the heart of a speech, it uses almost all of the time. Depending on what kind of speech you give, the body may contain the following.

statements	explanations	testimonies
propositions	examples	contentions
definitions	illustrations	statistics

You can organize the main ideas in your speech in any one of the following ways.

Chronological   The most common way to use chronological order is to begin with a past event and move to a more recent one. For example, a speech on the changes in pop music might include the 1950s, the 1960s, the 1970s, and the 1980s. Most histories and narrative stories are arranged in this order.

WHAT DO YOU THINK?

Human beings are curious creatures. People ask their friends, "What do you think about . . .?" "How do you feel about . . .?" Many people like to compare what they think with what others think. For this reason, people are often interested in speeches that include the opinions of others. However, to use opinions in a speech, you must know how to collect them. Public opinion polls or surveys were invented to see what large numbers of people think.

To construct a survey, you must first decide what you want to know. Maybe you want to know what people think about protecting wildlife, or how students feel about girls playing football. As you develop your questions, think about how people will answer them. Some questions are designed to get a certain answer. For example, few people would answer *no* to "Don't you think it's sad that eagles are becoming extinct?" It would be more fair to ask, "Do you think eagles should be protected?"

After you know what you want to ask, you must target the group you want to question. For example: people over sixty-five, under twelve, black men, eighth-grade students, or teenagers.

Next, you must decide how you will conduct your survey. You may design a questionnaire that will be mailed or passed out in school. Or you may use it for personal interviews. Your questionnaire should ask for identifying information as well as answers to your questions. See the following.

QUESTIONNAIRE

Male _____   Female _____
Age: _____   Grade: _____

Do you think girls should be allowed to play football?
Yes ____   No ____

When you have completed your survey, analyze the results by dividing the questionnaires into groups. You might divide the questionnaires by age, grade, or male/female. Then tabulate answers and compare your results. Report your results accurately, and add your own opinion!

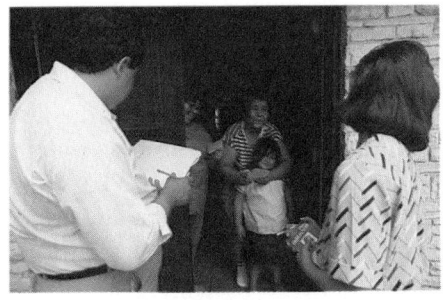

Order of Importance Some speeches begin with the most important detail first and work down to the least important detail. For example, a speech about the United Nations could begin with the General Assembly and Security Council and move to the various committees. Of course, speeches could also begin with the least important detail and work up to the most important detail.

Cause-Effect In this order, you would explain certain causes or conditions first. Then you would discuss the effects or results that they bring about. For example, in a speech on the Revolutionary War, you could explain some of the causes, such as heavy taxation, that led up to the war with England. Many historical and political speeches are arranged this way.

Spatial Order A speech may be arranged by the location of things in relation to other things. You might start with an object or a building and then describe the other things around it. Descriptions of a park or museum or building or of a trip across the country might use this order. For example, a speech on the White House might cover the rooms open to the public, the areas used by the staff, and the President's private quarters.

Problem-Solution In this organization, you state a problem and include its symptoms. You could even trace the symptoms back to their causes. Then you suggest and explain one or more solutions. If you give more than one solution, you should tell your audience which one you think is the best. For example, suppose you are giving a speech on the problem of increased traffic accidents near your school. You might begin by stating the number of people and cars that have been involved in accidents. Then you should suggest a solution. It might be to change the location of the school exit to an area that fewer cars use.

Conclusion

A **conclusion** concludes, or ends, a speech. A conclusion usually summarizes or emphasizes the purpose of the speech. Although a conclusion is short, it is very important. It ties a speech together and reminds the audience of the main idea of the speech. Because a conclusion is so important, many students write out the conclusion and memorize it.

Transitions

Transitions are the words or groups of words that relate one idea in your speech to the next idea. These are important because they help your audience understand that a new or different idea is about to be discussed. They help your audience understand how what you are saying and what you are about to say are connected. For example, the words "in addition" show you are about to give out more information. Transitions tie a speech together. Following are examples of some transitions.

- Some transitions show sequence *(first, second, next, later,* and *finally).*
- Others compare things that are similar *(and, also,* and *similarly).*
- Transitions also show that things are different *(but, however, on the other hand,* and *above all).*
- Some link what was just said to the next idea *(not only, but also,* and *in addition).*
- Others point toward results of previous statements or actions *(therefore, finally,* and *as a result).*

YOUR TURN ///////////////

1. Work together as a class to develop a sample outline. The sample outline should include subpoints. Be sure all of the outline parts are in the correct order.

2. Go to your school library and find the answers to the following questions. Report in class the steps that you followed to locate the information.
    a. What is the difference between cumulus and cirrus clouds?
    b. In what city and state is the Johns Hopkins University located? Is it coeducational?
    c. A North American songbird is called the bobolink. What is the longer form of its name?
    d. On what date did the first man walk on the moon? What was that man's name?

12 CHAPTER REVIEW

Chapter Summary

When preparing a speech, you should follow these steps.

1. Survey what information you already know.
2. Use different sources of information.
3. Write the information on note cards.
4. Organize your information in an outline.
5. Practice your speech aloud.

Although there are many sources of information, the library is the most valuable one. Don't forget to look in reference guides, journals, and magazines, as well as in books.

A speech has three parts: an introduction, a body, and a conclusion. The introduction should get the attention of the audience and relate to the topic of your speech. The body contains the main ideas and supporting details. The information in the body may be arranged in one of the following orders: chronological, order of importance, cause-effect, spatial, or problem-solution. The conclusion should summarize the purpose and main idea of the speech. Good speeches also include transitions which help listeners see the relationship of ideas. Transitions tie a speech together and give it unity.

Checklist

Mastering Research and Structuring Skills

1. Take a survey of what you know and don't know about your topic.
2. Use more than one source of information.
3. Become familiar with the information resources of your library.
4. Write the information for your speech on note cards.

5. Organize your information by outlining it.
6. Practice your speech aloud.

Vocabulary

Define each term in a complete sentence.

body of a speech	Library of Congress System
call number	sentence outline
conclusion	topic outline
Dewey Decimal System	transitions
introduction	

Review Questions

1. Name the five steps in preparing a speech.

2. List four sources of information for a speech. What source is used more than the others?

3. Identify what should go at the top right-hand corner of a note card, and at the bottom of the card. Why are these two pieces of information important?

4. Explain the three ways to look for a book in the card catalog.

5. Identify the information you will find in the *Readers' Guide to Periodical Literature.*

6. Explain why making an outline is helpful.

7. Name the three basic parts of most speeches.

8. Name five ways you can begin a speech.

9. Explain the difference between chronological order and order of importance.

10. Explain the importance of transitions.

Discuss with Your Classmates

1. Following are introductions to speeches. Explain how each one gets attention.

   a. Did you know that President Woodrow Wilson was once the coach of a college football team?

   b. *Veni, Vidi, Vici.* Translated into English, this means "I came, I saw, I conquered."

   c. It's the little things that bother
   And put us on the rack;
   You can sit upon a mountain,
   But not upon a tack.

   d. An old miner was very smart, but very lazy. The new deputy asked him how he learned so much. The miner replied, "I just heard it—here and there—but was always too lazy to forget it."

2. Which form of outline would you rather use when preparing a speech—topic or sentence outlining? Why? Can you think of reasons why one might be more helpful than the other?

3. Discuss how you would go about gathering information for each of the following speech topics.

   a. Our new police chief
   b. Recent advances in automobile safety
   c. The best Saturday ever
   d. Crocodiles and alligators
   e. How an airplane flies

4. Look again at the speech introductions in the first exercise. What is the likely purpose of each speech? Discuss possible conclusions for each speech.

 # Critical Thinking

1. Comprehension: Recall the four general purposes of speeches: to inform, to persuade, to inspire, to entertain. Which of these purposes would probably demand the most research time? Which would require the least amount of time? Explain your answers.

2. Application: What information would probably go in the introduction, body, and conclusion of a speech on the following topics? Would you need to go to the library to find more information?
    a. Abolishing the Student Dress Code
    b. The Effects of Rock Music on Teens Today
    c. If I Were President

 # Activities

In-Class

1. Read Booker T. Washington's speech at the end of this text. Work with your classmates to make an outline of it by dividing it into its introduction, body, and conclusion. Be sure to include enough information to explain the methods used to support each major point in the speech.

2. Work together in groups of three or four. For each of the following causes, list at least two effects. How might each one be used in a speech?
    a. One-fourth of the adults in our state don't have jobs.
    b. The price of school lunches has doubled in one year.
    c. Only two students made the honor roll after the first grading period.
    d. The records of five musical groups are played for more than half of a local disc jockey's program for over a week.

3. As a class, work together to create unusual attention-getting ideas for the introduction of a speech on these topics. Use your imagination and any source that is available to you. Look for quotations, funny stories, startling facts, etc.

    a. exercising   **c.** watches

    b. video games   **d.** spring

Out-of-Class

1. Choose a specific topic for a speech that provides information about people who work in local government. You will gather information about your topic by interviewing a government worker. You might want to interview a police officer, a firefighter, a highway worker, etc. Write a set of questions in your speech notebook that you will use during the interview. Get an appointment with the person you choose to interview and conduct the interview. Be prepared to give a ten or fifteen minute speech on your topic in class.

2. Choose a topic for a two-minute speech to inform or persuade. Go to the library and take notes on note cards. Then write an outline that shows the major divisions of your speech.

3. Write an introduction and a conclusion to the speech you outlined in Exercise 2. Be prepared to give your speech in class.

Chapter Project

Practice your outlining and speech skills for this Chapter Project. Think of a school subject that you enjoy or a nonfiction book that you have read recently. Choose one chapter from either one of these books. Make sure the chapter is at least ten pages long. Do a careful, complete outline, using the outlining format you prefer. Take a few minutes to think about a suitable introduction and conclusion. Then practice presenting the information in the chapter in the form of a speech. Your teacher may ask you to present your speech in class.

CHAPTER 13 · Delivery and Evaluation

Brian is practicing his speech after school in the auditorium.
As he begins, he thinks . . .

"I'll put my outline on the podium instead of holding it.

I have to remember to look at the audience.

I wonder how loud I should speak."

Do *you* practice before giving a speech? How do you practice?

In this chapter, you will read about:

- improving your delivery by practicing orally
- good eye contact with an audience
- a good sense of time
- distracting nonverbal messages
- handling nervousness better
- first and final impressions
- unexpected situations
- audience feedback during a speech
- evaluating others with critique forms and benefiting from the evaluation of others

For a very long time, people have known that practicing speeches is helpful. Early American politicians practiced their speeches as they plowed their fields or fed their cows. In ancient Greece there was a man named Demosthenes who wanted to improve his volume and diction. To do this, he practiced his speeches while climbing up hillsides with pebbles in his mouth. These people were practicing their deliveries. **Delivery** is the giving of a speech to an audience.

PRACTICING DELIVERY

How do I practice a speech? How many times should I practice it aloud? What can I do to keep the interest of the audience while I give my speech? These are very normal, logical questions that many people ask before they give their first speech. Following are some suggestions that will help you when you practice your speech. These suggestions will also answer the previous questions.

Practice in a Similar Place

If possible, practice in the room you will give your speech in or a room that is about the same size. By being in the same room or a similar one, you will be able to test what volume you should use. Your volume is very important. If people have to strain to hear you, they will quickly lose interest.

Practicing your speech is a very important aspect of preparation. Try to rehearse in the same room where you will give your speech.

You should also decide if you want to use a lectern, or speaker's stand, when you give your speech. If you do, practice your speech using one. For example, practice walking out from behind it once in a while. If you don't practice, you might simply hang onto the lectern throughout your speech and never move at all.

If you will be using a microphone, either imagine one is present or use a broomstick or similar object to suggest one. Better still, if you have a small tape recorder, use the microphone from it to practice. Keep in mind the following pointers when you use a microphone.

- Keep the same distance between you and the microphone throughout the speech.

- Avoid quick volume changes.

- Avoid making distracting noises that the microphone will pick up. (These include sounds such as rattling papers, coughing, or bumping the speaker's stand or the microphone.)

As you practice, use one or two chairs to represent the first row of your audience. They will help you remember to move around. In your actual speech, you would not want to stand in front of one person the whole time.

Use Only a Few Notes

When you give your speech, you should have only a very brief outline of it with you. You should never have all your note cards or your complete outline. If you have too much information with you, you might be tempted to *read* your speech. An audience often loses interest in a speech that is read or recited from memory. With only a brief outline, you will *talk* about your topic—and be more likely to keep the interest of your audience.

If your outline is on cards, use the cards as you practice your speech. Following are some tips about using cards.

- Write only on one side. Turning cards over can distract your audience.

- Hold the cards in only one hand. Then you can gesture with the other hand.

- Hold the cards still. Don't shuffle, twist, or bend them nervously.

Practice enough so that you don't have to use any notes during your introduction. If you don't use any, you will appear more self-confident and create a good first impression. You also will be able to look directly at your audience during your introduction.

Be Active

Practice beginning your speech with an equal amount of weight on each foot. Keep your posture comfortably straight, but not stiff. This position will then allow you to move or gesture easily.

Practice the actual movements and gestures you will make during your speech. You might begin by exaggerating them. At first these large movements and gestures might seem awkward. However, they will gradually become a natural part of what you are saying. Of course, all movements and gestures should emphasize what you are saying. They should support your message, not distract from it.

When you move or walk, take your time. Quick movements or pacing back and forth will make you seem nervous. You can also move longer distances than you probably are used to. Rather than just moving a few inches away from the center of the room, try moving a few feet. Just remember to move *slowly*.

As you practice, keep most of your weight forward on the balls and toes of your feet. This position gives the impression that you are

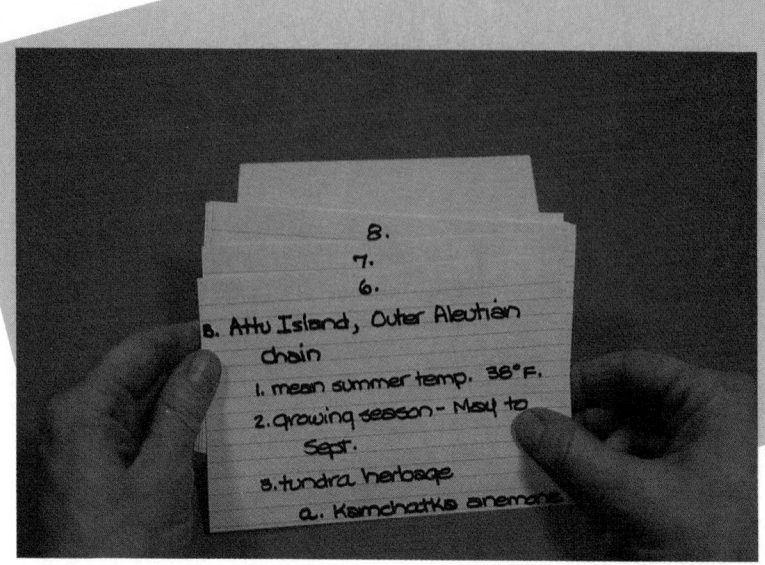

If you use notecards, be sure that your outline is brief.

ready for action. Be careful that you do not put all your weight on only one foot or cross one foot in front of the other. People sometimes do these things when they are nervous. However, if you are aware of these movements when you practice, you can avoid them during your actual speech.

Practice Good Eye Contact

Because they are nervous, many beginning speakers don't look at the people in the audience. Instead, they look at their notes, look out the window, or look over people's heads. To avoid this, always pretend that there is an audience in front of you when you practice. By doing this, you can practice eye contact. **Eye contact,** looking directly at the people you are talking to, is an important part of your delivery. Eye contact is one sign of your self-confidence and your interest in the audience.

One way to practice eye contact is to use a figure 8 pattern. To do this, start by looking at your notes. Next, move your eyes to the people closest to the right of the room. Then your eyes should move left in a curve through the center of the audience to the left rear. Finally, they should curve back to the right, across the room. This continuous motion forms a figure 8. As you become experienced in public speaking, you may find that other patterns of eye contact work just as well for you.

One big advantage of eye contact is instant feedback. By looking at the faces of the people in the audience, you will be able to see their reactions. Do they look interested? Are they smiling? Do they look bored or tired? These reactions can give you direction for the rest of your speech.

Vary Your Vocal Messages

Give yourself enough time to practice different inflections, pitches, rates, and volumes. For example, as you practice, you should see that some words need to be stressed and others de-emphasized. Practicing gives you a chance to "play with sounds" to see which ones best support your verbal messages.

When you give your speech, watch the people in the back row. If some lean forward, they probably can't hear you very well. You also might watch other people who are sitting near an open door or open windows. If they don't seem to be able to hear you either, move closer to them or speak louder.

Develop a Sense of Time

Since most of your speeches will be timed, you need to develop a sense of time. The best way to do this is to keep a watch or a clock with a second hand nearby as you practice. Find out how much you can say in one minute. If some ideas take too long to express, make them shorter. Don't, however, speed up your rate to fit them in.

Another way to time yourself is to go through your *whole* speech out loud many times. Don't stop in the middle and begin again. By completing the whole speech each time, you soon will be able to see whether you meet the time limit.

Avoid Distracting Nonverbal Messages

Many small gestures and facial expressions that would go unnoticed in a conversation will become quite visible in front of an audience. The following are three common, but distracting, nonverbal and vocal messages. Once you are aware of them, you can work to avoid them.

First, some speakers sway from side to side, or backward and forward, without moving their feet. To an audience it appears that the speaker wants to move, but can't. To avoid this, walk and move around during your practice periods.

Second, some speakers make repeated vocal sounds, such as clearing their throats or smacking their lips. People usually make these sounds because they are nervous. To avoid these, practice as much as you can. The more you practice, the more confident you will become, and self-confidence will drive away the nervousness.

Third, some speakers fill pauses with meaningless sounds such as *um, uh,* or *ahhh.* At other times, words such as *well* and *you know* are used between ideas. These vocalized pauses can be very distracting. An audience might think that the speaker didn't prepare very well. To avoid this, try to practice on a tape recorder. Listen to find out if and where you include any of these sounds or words. Then work to eliminate them. Always keep in mind that a silent pause is better than a meaningless, vocalized pause. The following are some other distracting nonverbal messages to avoid.

- wringing the hands, cracking knuckles, or clenching and relaxing the hands frequently

- scratching, patting, or smoothing the hair, rubbing or touching the face

- biting or licking the lips

- rolling, tapping, and playing with pencils, pens, or note cards (A good idea is never to take a pen or pencil to the front of the room with you.)

Practice as Long and as Often as Necessary

There is no magical number of the times each person should practice each speech. The number and length of practice periods will depend on factors such as the following.

- difficulty of the subject

- familiarity with the subject

- the time limit of the speech

- self-confidence

- past experience giving speeches

In general, however, you should have a *minimum* of three separate practice periods for each speech. You will get the most out of these periods if you spread them out over several days. For each practice period, you should spend at least five minutes for each minute of your speech. For example, a three- to four-minute speech would need at least three practice periods of 15 to 20 minutes each. Remember, though, this would just be the *minimum*. More practice will give you greater confidence and, therefore, probably more success.

YOUR TURN /////////////

1. Check your sense of time by sitting where you can see a clock or watch. Try to estimate the passing of 30 seconds, a minute, and two minutes without counting to yourself. Check the clock at the end of each experiment and see how close you were. Then try the same thing while someone is speaking. Did your estimate of time improve? Keep practicing off and on until you can determine time within five to ten seconds.

2. Class members should give unrehearsed one-minute speeches. Your teacher may assign the topics, or you may choose your own. During the speeches, listeners should write down any distracting nonverbal mesages that the speakers use. After five speeches, discuss some of them. Five more speeches should then be given. Were there fewer distracting gestures in the second group? Do you think there were fewer because students were more aware of these movements and gestures? Discuss this idea as a class.

NERVOUSNESS

One of the early astronauts was dropped from the space program because he got too nervous when he had to make a speech. This man had something in common with almost every speaker: nervousness. Nervousness has both physical and mental causes. Physically, it is caused by tension in the muscles and the increased flow of adrenalin. Mentally, it comes as a result of everyone's wish to do well in front of others. Other terms for this kind of nervousness are **anxiety** or **stage fright.** Even the most experienced speakers get stage fright. However, experienced speakers know something that beginning speakers don't. They know that some tension is both normal and desirable.

Adrenalin gives people energy and makes them ready for action. In emergencies, adrenalin gives people strength to do things they couldn't do under normal circumstances. That's why you should stop worrying about your nervousness. Instead, you should learn to use it to your advantage. The following are some helpful hints in dealing with nervousness.

- Understand that you are not the only nervous person. The other students in your class are probably just as nervous as you are.

- Keep in mind that you *never* look as nervous as you feel.

- Your nervousness will lessen as you get into your speech.

- The best way to keep your nervousness under control is to be as well prepared as possible. This will give you the greatest amount of self-confidence—one of the best conquerors of nervousness.

The best way to keep nervousness under control is to be as well prepared as possible. Is anyone in this photo nervous? Is one person too early or is one person late getting ready?

FIRST IMPRESSIONS

You learned in an earlier chapter that even before you say your first word, you are making an impression on your audience. This is true in a conversation; it is also true when you give a speech. For example, if you yawn and stretch, your audience may think you are bored. If you fidget with a pencil or note cards, your audience may think you are nervous. If an audience's first impression of you is negative, it may not be willing to listen closely to your speech.

Another part of your first impression comes as you walk to the front of the room. You should take quiet, deep breaths, gather your notes, get up, and walk confidently to the front of the room. When you get there, look at the audience before you begin to speak. Finally, take a deep breath and begin. This is the point when direct eye contact should begin. By doing all of this, you will create a positive first impression.

HANDLING THE UNEXPECTED

In spite of all your planning, unexpected things can happen to distract you. The following are suggestions for handling some unexpected situations.

- You accidentally drop your note cards. If you know your speech well enough, go on without picking up the cards.

- You are interrupted by an announcement on the PA system. Wait for it to end, smile, and then go on.

- You are distracted by an outside noise or a knock on the door. Pause for the noise to stop and then go on.

- You discover that you have left part of the notes for your speech at home. Continue with what you can remember.

- There is a fire drill. After the drill, begin your speech again if you had just started. However, if you were almost finished, remind your audience of your last point and then finish.

- For a minute, you can't remember what comes next in your speech. You could (1) admit you forgot, pause until you can think of the next idea, and then go on; (2) summarize what you have already said and then find the next point; or (3) finish your speech without the part you forgot.

It's impossible to cover everything that might happen. However, if you are well prepared and have confidence, you will usually be able to handle even difficult situations.

Be Prepared for the Unexpected

THE FINAL IMPRESSION

Your speech ends with your last word. Your impression, however, doesn't end until the next speaker begins. It is easy to spot the students who feel that their speeches were good. They walk back to their seats straight and tall, still looking confidently at the audience. A first impression is important, but the final impression is equally important.

YOUR TURN

1. In groups of three to five students, discuss the following idea. *Most public speakers—experienced and inexperienced—are nervous before they begin to speak.* Do you believe this? Why or why not? Discuss some of the physical signs of nervousness. Does everyone have the same signs? Discuss how these signs might be hidden or eliminated.

2. What would be your first impression of each of the following speakers?
   a. A girl stands behind a lectern and never moves away from it. She is short and can hardly be seen behind it.
   b. A woman will speak about fund raising for schools. She walks to the podium in the auditorium. She takes some notes out of a briefcase and puts them on the lectern. Then she looks up, smiles at the audience, and begins.
   c. A boy walks to the front of the room. As he passes his friends, he makes funny remarks under his breath.

EVALUATION OF SPEECHES

Your speech is over and you have taken your seat. How did you do? Was your speech good? Was it the best speech you have ever given? Before you sat down, you probably had some idea of how you did. You have your own reactions and your comparison of this speech with the last one you gave. However, the following are some specific ways by which speeches are often evaluated.

A DREAM THAT CONTINUES

More than 200,000 people had gathered in Washington, D.C., on that hot, steamy day of August 28, 1963. The huge crowd had been standing under a broiling sun since nine o'clock that morning. The speeches were running long, and by 3:30 in the afternoon many people were beginning to walk away. It was finally time for the last speech of the day. Mr. Philip Randolph introduced Martin Luther King, Jr.

The speech that Dr. King was about to give was more carefully planned than any he had ever made before. During the previous two days, he had written and re-written his speech many times. Mostly he had used his own words, but he also had borrowed from such sources as the Declaration of Independence and "My Country 'Tis of Thee."

The night before the rally, Dr. King never went to sleep. He continued to work on his speech. His speech also had to be condensed to eight minutes, but it still had to say something important. After everyone else had gone to bed, he practiced the speech he would give the next day.

As Dr. King stepped to the podium, the crowd applauded thunderously. Dr. King smiled and waited and then began. Once the round, deep tones of his voice spilled out and its slow cadence reached the ears of the people, there was almost instant silence.

As he spoke, his tone and volume changed, depending on what he was saying. He spoke about his dream for his four little children in a husky whisper as the audience leaned forward to hear him. When he repeated the words from an old spiritual, his voice rang out loudly. "Free at last! Free at last! Thank God almighty, we are free at last!"

It was a short, simple speech, said in ordinary words to people he knew. Nevertheless, Dr. King's "I Have a Dream" speech stands out as one of the most moving speeches of modern times. Even today, whenever his speech is read, it continues to inspire. It is a speech of lasting effect.

The earliest form of evaluation comes from audience reaction to a speech.

Audience Reaction

The earliest form of evaluation comes while you are still giving your speech. Vocal and nonverbal responses from the audience are a good source of information. They form the **audience reaction.** As a speaker, you need to learn to interpret smiles and other facial expressions. Are they suggesting interest, boredom, doubt, or agreement? For example, if members of the audience shift a lot in their seats, they probably are not listening very closely to your speech. On the other hand, if they move or lean forward, they might be expressing great interest in your speech. By watching these movements, you can usually find out if most of your audience is positive, negative, or neutral.

Another way to analyze an audience's reaction is to have each person fill out an evaluation form. After each speech, classmates rate the speaker in several categories. The following is a sample evaluation form. (You will learn more about these specific evaluation forms in Chapter 15.)

Audience Evaluation Sheet

NAME _____ DATE _____

TOPIC _____

Rating Scale: 1: inadequate 2: poor 3: fair 4: good 5: excellent

Approach	1	2	3	4	5
Poise	1	2	3	4	5
Eye Contact	1	2	3	4	5
Physical Delivery	1	2	3	4	5
Vocal Delivery	1	2	3	4	5
Introduction	1	2	3	4	5
Use of Language	1	2	3	4	5
Content of Body	1	2	3	4	5
Organization	1	2	3	4	5
Conclusion	1	2	3	4	5

Grade: _____

Comments:

Critiques

A **critique** is a special type of evaluation which is made by one or more members of an audience. The writer of a critique describes some of the things a speaker did. Then that person makes value judgments. A critique also points out areas of strengths and weaknesses. Finally, the critique writer always includes suggestions for improvement.

Senator Bentsen, an experienced speaker, would have nothing to fear from a critique of his speech.

Oral Critiques   The purpose of an oral critique is to give a speaker immediate feedback. The person giving the critique usually does the following.

- Briefly describes a few things that were done well in the speech. (Example: "I was pleased that Joe used several pieces of information from recent publications.")

- Describes specific problems and gives examples of those problems. (Example: "Mary's introduction was weak. The story she told about the dog should have been related more to her speech. I couldn't understand the connection.")

- Chooses one problem that needs the most work. Then suggest a way of working on it for the next speech. (Example: If a speaker didn't move during his or her speech, someone might say, "Kevin never moved away from the lectern today. He should practice his next speech while walking around. By doing this, he can get used to moving and speaking at the same time. Also, he should hold his note cards in one hand, rather than putting them on the lectern. This would allow him to get away from the lectern more easily.")

Oral critiques should never be used to attack or flatter people. They should give practical suggestions that will help speakers improve. Comments such as "It was a good speech" or "I liked it" are not very helpful. These remarks can only be helpful if they are backed up with examples.

Written Critiques   Most written critiques are checklists about the speaker and his or her speech. Critics circle numbers that indicate their feelings about items on the form. The following are two sample critique forms.

Critique of the Speaker

NAME _____ DATE _____

TOPIC _____

Rating Scale: 1: inadequate   2: poor   3: fair   4: good   5: excellent

1. How was the speaker's preparation   1   2   3   4   5
   (research, organization, and evidence
   of practice)?

2. Did the speaker stay within the time limit?   1   2   3   4   5

3. How did the speaker handle vocal   1   2   3   4   5
   messages (volume, rate, emphasis, and
   vocalized pauses)?

4. How did the speaker handle nonverbal   1   2   3   4   5
   messages (eye contact, gestures,
   movement)?

5. How did the speaker handle verbal   1   2   3   4   5
   messages (word choice, figurative
   language, sentence and phrase
   structure)?

6. Did the speaker appear self-confident?   1   2   3   4   5

7. How did the speaker respond to the   1   2   3   4   5
   audience?

Grade _____

Suggestions for improvement:

Critique of the Speech

NAME _____ DATE _____

TOPIC _____

Rating Scale: 1: inadequate   2: poor   3: fair   4: good   5: excellent

1. Was the purpose of the speech clear?	1	2	3	4	5
2. Was the speech well organized? Did it contain an introduction, a body, and a conclusion?	1	2	3	4	5
3. Did the introduction get attention?	1	2	3	4	5
4. Was the purpose of the speech supported with enough facts, quotations, and/or examples?	1	2	3	4	5
5. Was the speech suitable for the audience?	1	2	3	4	5

If you get written critiques from all your classmates, you will be able to compare the results. For example, if most students rate you very high on certain items, you probably are successful in those areas. Keep your critique forms. Then you can look them over before you prepare your next speech. The forms should reinforce your strengths and remind you to work on your weaknesses.

YOUR TURN /////////////////

1. Make a speech critique form that would be useful to your class.

2. Your teacher will divide the class into groups of three to four students. Each group should then discuss the critique forms made for Exercise 1. Take the results of this discussion and make one critique form that includes all the best items. Then use this critique form during the next series of class speeches. Afterwards discuss how well it worked. Could it be used while class members were listening? Was it helpful to the speakers?

13 CHAPTER REVIEW

Chapter Summary

There are many ways you can practice the delivery of your speech. For example, you should practice using only a few notes. You should also practice your movements and gestures, as well as eye contact. The minimum amount of practice is three times for each speech. The more you practice, the greater your confidence will grow.

Some nervousness is good. It will give you more energy during your speech. It is also important to remember that everyone is nervous, but no one looks as nervous as they really are. In spite of any nervousness, you should remember to create a good first impression and a good final impression.

Some evaluation of your speech will come during your speech. By watching the nonverbal messages of people in the audience, you should get a sense for how your speech is going. After you finish, your classmates might evaluate you with either an oral or a written critique. This kind of evaluation should point out strengths and weaknesses and offer suggestions for improvement.

Checklist

Improving Delivery and Evaluation

1. Practice in the room where you will deliver the speech, or in a similar one, using the same equipment.
2. Use as few notes as possible.
3. Move around and use appropriate gestures.
4. Practice good eye contact, moving your gaze in a figure 8.
5. Vary your tone, inflection, pitch, volume, and speaking rate.
6. Develop a sense of time.
7. Avoid distracting nonverbal messages.

Vocabulary

Define each term in a complete sentence.

anxiety

audience reaction

critique

delivery

eye contact

stage fright

Review Questions

1. Identify the best place to practice a speech. What are the advantages of this place?

2. Explain why you should have only a few notes with you when you give a speech.

3. Explain why good eye contact is important when speaking.

4. Describe how the figure 8 pattern for eye contact works.

5. Explain how to eliminate some distracting nonverbal gestures.

6. Identify the minimum number of times you should practice a speech out loud.

7. Describe the advice you could give someone who is nervous before giving a speech.

8. Explain how you can create positive first and final impressions.

9. Explain how oral and written critiques can be helpful.

Discuss with Your Classmates

1. What sort of message do you receive when a speaker reads a speech to you? Is it ever appropriate to read during a speech?

2. Have you ever experienced stage fright? In what situation? What did you do to deal with it?

3. What can a speaker do to create a good first impression? How can a speaker maintain that impression throughout the speech? What can a speaker do to create a good final impression?

Critical Thinking

1. Analysis: Imagine that you have spent a great deal of time preparing for a speech. Just as you get to an important place in the body of your speech, your mind goes completely blank. You cannot think of what to say next. Analyze this situation and suggest various strategies to bring your speech to a successful conclusion.

2. Evaluation: Watch your area's television listings for an announced speech by a government official. Watch the speech and complete an audience evaluation chart. To what extent did the speaker observe this chapter's suggestions for good delivery?

Activities

In-Class

1. See how many students in your class can speak for 30 seconds—on any topic—without using any vocalized pauses. What kind of pauses are used most often? See if students become better at avoiding vocalized pauses once they are aware of them.

2. Your teacher will assign you and another student to work together as listener-observer. You should practice your next speeches together at least twice. After the second session, each of you should write a one-page summary of what happened. Include the problems and the progress you noticed in the other student's practice sessions.

3. After presenting your next speech, fill out a written critique form about it, and compare it with those of your classmates.

Out-of-Class

1. Carefully watch and listen to people in the next few days. Notice the kinds of vocalized pauses most of them use. Then, without using any names, discuss these with your class.

2. In your speech notebook, keep a written record of your oral practice periods for your next speech. After each session, write the time and place where you practiced. Also include the number of minutes you practiced and any problems you had.

3. After presenting your next speech, write in your speech notebook one page that describes what you felt, heard, and saw while you were speaking. List any audience feedback that you noticed during your speech. Explain in what ways you knew how your speech was going because of the audience feedback.

 # Chapter Project

You have a speech to give approximately three weeks from now. Decide upon your speech's general purpose and select a specific topic. Develop a schedule that lists all of the tasks that you must complete between now and the time that you will deliver your speech. Indicate the days on which you will complete each task. Be sure to allow enough time for gathering information and structuring your speech and for practicing its delivery.

Keep an accurate log of the time you spent on each task in your speech notebook. Be prepared to share this schedule with your classmates.

Your classmates will complete an audience evaluation form after your speech. Study these forms to identify areas where your performance was weakest. Check your log to see if you gave enough time to those areas during the preparation of your speech. Think about how you can improve your performance. In your speech notebook, list some things that you can do as you prepare for future speeches.

14 The Informative Speech

Lorraine is giving a speech about using a telescope. These are some of her thoughts as she begins.

"I've used my telescope a lot.

I practiced my speech with it.

I should be able to explain how to use it."

Have *you* ever given a demonstration speech? What did you demonstrate?

In this chapter you will read about:

- an appropriate introduction, body, and conclusion for an informative speech
- presentation of an informative speech
- identifying and using visual aids in an informative speech
- methods of evaluating an informative speech
- demonstration speeches
- evaluating a demonstration speech

A zookeeper with a baby snake wrapped around her waist tells some visitors to the zoo all about the anaconda, the largest snake in the world. A high school senior leads a group of freshman on a tour of their new high school, explaining the rules and mentioning all the after-school activities. At the town meeting, one of your neighbors explains why he is against building a new library. At dinner, your sister tells the family about the class paper drive. All these talks have something in common. They are all forms of informative speeches.

An **informative speech** is any talk whose main purpose is giving information to people. An informative speech offers useful or interesting facts. It can be short or long, formal or informal. It can be based on personal experience or on research. The goal of an informative speech is to explain a subject so clearly that listeners will easily understand.

More informative speeches are given than any other kind. You will probably have to give a number of them yourself: answering questions in class, reporting to a club, explaining things at home, reporting to a boss, or perhaps explaining things to the public. This chapter covers the development of an informative speech and describes a special kind of informative talk, the demonstration speech.

THE INTRODUCTION: BEGINNING AN INFORMATIVE SPEECH

You know that the introduction to your speech accomplishes many purposes. It sets the tone of your speech. It introduces you and your subject. It also prepares your listeners for the main points. A strong

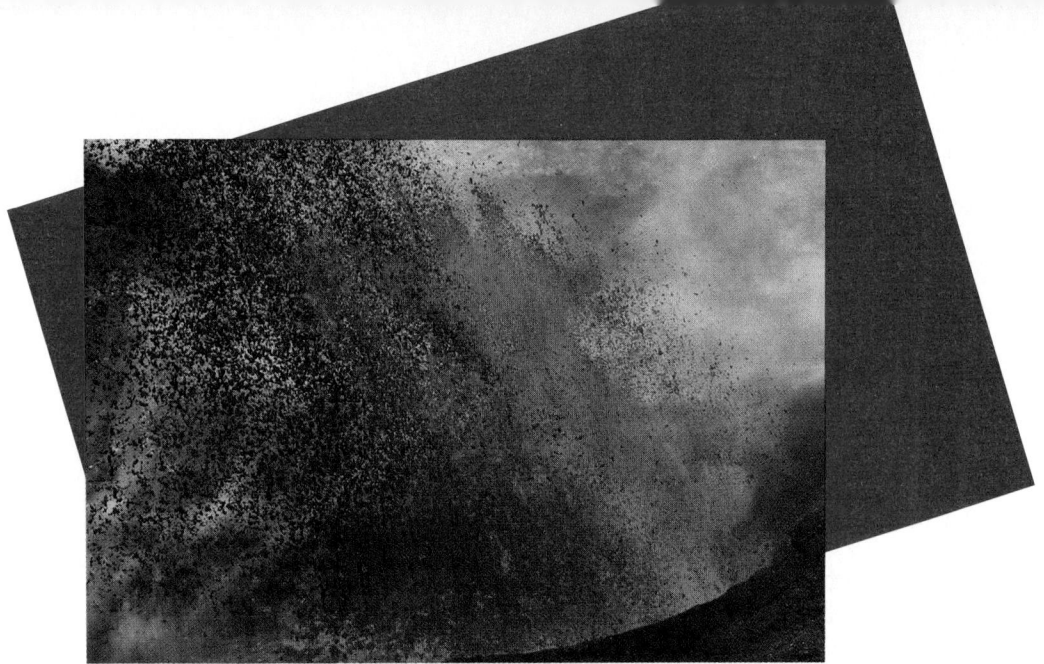

A good introduction contains an attention-getting device. If you were to talk about a volcanic eruption, how would you begin your speech?

introduction will make your listeners eager to hear more. When you prepare the introduction to an informative speech, follow the suggestions below.

Use an Attention-Getting Device

Did you ever plan to turn off the television and then become so involved in the first few scenes of a show that you ended up watching the whole show? A bright, interesting start is also important to a good speech. All of the following are good attention-getters.

Humor   One of the best ways to get the attention of your audience is by telling a joke or a funny story. For example, Mai used humor to start her speech about intelligence in dogs. Notice that the joke she told relates directly to her subject.

"A man once lost his dog and felt very worried. A friend said, 'If you lost your dog, why not put an ad in the paper?' The anxious pet owner replied, 'Oh, there's no point in that. My dog can't read!'"

Some very serious topics are not suitable for humor. Lighter subjects are off to a good start with a laugh.

Narrative   Starting your speech with a story, or **narrative,** is another good way to get the audience's attention. The story might show how you became interested in your subject. It might also show why your subject is important to the audience. For example, Paulo started his speech on bicycle safety with the following narrative.

"Last fall I was riding my bike home from school. I was riding right alongside some old railroad tracks. I decided to cross them, and my front tire got caught in the groove of the tracks. Down I went, landing heavily on my right side. Ever since then, I've taken bicycling seriously. And I've learned a lot about bicycle safety, too."

Shock or Startling Statement   With the following lines Maria began her speech about solar eclipses. She painted such a clear picture that her classmates listened carefully. A dramatic scene or surprising statement almost always puts listeners at the edge of their seats.

"An eerie darkness began to cover the land. Farmers stopped working in the fields, birds took to their nests, dogs crawled to safety. The darkness was soon complete. The hour was still daytime. But the sky was as black as night."

"Can you imagine Yellowstone Park without bears? The bears are almost a symbol of the park."

Quotation   Many speakers like to begin with a *quotation,* or a famous saying. Notice how Angelo, for example, used a quotation to start his speech.

> "Pearl S. Buck wrote, 'Truth is always exciting. Speak it, then. Life is dull without it.' Truth is sometimes missing from public affairs. New laws, however, help keep public officials honest. These laws are taking the 'dullness' out of political campaigns."

You can find quotations in the library in such books as *Bartlett's Familiar Quotations* and *The Home Book of Quotations.* Look for sayings you have not seen before. They make a better impact than tired, overused quotations.

Rhetorical Question   A **rhetorical question** is a question you ask to start people thinking. You do not really expect an answer to it. For example, Jeannine began a speech about grizzly bears with a rhetorical question to get her listeners thinking.

"Can you imagine Yellowstone National Park without bears? The bears are almost a symbol of the park. And yet there are so few bears remaining that the park may well be without them before too long."

Build Interest in the Topic

Before giving your speech, think about the interest level of your topic. Do most of the audience members already find it interesting? Or might some of your listeners be bored?

For example, Suzanne gave a speech about Beethoven, her favorite composer. She realized, though, that some of her listeners might not be as interested as she was in her topic. Therefore, early in her talk she told about Beethoven's deafness. Her listeners were touched by this great man's struggle with this handicap. They listened carefully to her whole speech because of the interest she built in the introduction.

Preview the Topic

Listeners like to know what to expect. In the introduction, tell your audience the main points you intend to cover. When listeners know what to expect, they can more easily absorb ideas.

Suzanne, for example, previewed the main points she would cover about Beethoven. She said that she would talk about three different periods in Beethoven's life. In each period the music he wrote reflected his inner feelings. When she began the body of her speech, Suzanne's listeners were prepared to hear about three different styles of music.

Tell How the Topic Relates to Your Audience

Some speakers make the mistake of writing a speech without knowing anything about their audience. That can be a big mistake! Imagine it: you decide to talk about how to skateboard; then you find out the average age of people in the audience is 45. Or you decide to tell why, once you are old enough to vote, you will always vote for Democrats. Then you discover every single person you are talking to is a Republican.

Find out about what the people in the audience are like before you write your speech. Then prepare a speech that will hold their interest.

You can find out about an audience in a number of ways. You can ask the person who invited you to speak or you can talk to people who have given speeches to this group in the past. You can attend one of the group's meetings, read its newsletters, or even distribute questionnaires. The following list includes some things you may want to ask about your audience.

- How old are they?
- How much education have they had?
- Do they all belong to one group? What are its goals and interests?
- What are their interests and hobbies?
- Where do they live?

Once you know a little about your audience, you can make your speech more interesting for them.

When listeners feel you are talking directly to them, or that they can benefit from information in a speech, they pay close attention. In your introduction, link your topic to the interests and concerns of your listeners. Notice how simply Suzanne showed the importance of learning about Beethoven.

"We can all learn from Beethoven. We can try to overcome, as he did, the handicaps we have. More than that, we can be inspired by his music to be the best we can be."

Call for Questions After the Speech

If you are speaking outside of class, or if your teacher allows it, tell your audience they can ask questions after your speech. Often, careful listeners will think of questions while you are speaking. If they know they can ask them later, they will remember them until the end of the speech. For this reason, tell your audience during the introduction that you will answer questions after your speech.

Project Confidence and Enthusiasm

One of a speaker's most important jobs is to establish a good feeling with the audience. A confident, sincere presentation will make your listeners want to pay attention.

THE INFORMATIVE SPEECH
Time Well Spent

Raoul was worried about his assignment in science class: an informative speech about an endangered species of animal. The teacher expected Raoul to choose the animal he wished to speak on, do research, and deliver the speech in class. Raoul remembered seeing a television program about the humpback whale, so he chose the whale as his topic.

Raoul was still worried about the assignment. He knew very little about whales, so he decided his first stop should be the local library. There the librarian helped him locate books and recent magazine articles about the whale. Raoul learned about the whales' habits of migration, the kinds of foods they eat, and how they reproduce and care for their young. He also learned how they were being endangered as a species by whale hunters. The more Raoul read, the more interested he became in whales. He visited the local aquarium, and found pictures of the whale and a tape recording of whale sounds, which he was able to borrow.

By the time Raoul was ready to give his speech, he had learned a lot about whales. Also, he had learned to like whales and had become concerned about their survival as a species. When Raoul gave his speech to the class, he had become so interested in his subject that he forgot all about being nervous. To get the attention of his listeners, he started his speech with a description of the great whaling ships of the past century and the dangers of hunting the whale with harpoons. He used statistics on the estimated number of whales in the past century and the estimated number of whales today. He showed pictures of the humpback whale and played the tape-recorded whale calls. He succeeded in making his classmates as enthusiastic about whales as he was.

Show Interest   When Terry started his speech about motorcycles, Lee was prepared to be bored. She wasn't interested in motorcycles. Before long, however, she was listening carefully. Terry was so interested *himself* in what he was talking about that his interest caught on. When you give your speech, let your enthusiasm show. In your words, voice, and gestures, show that your subject is worth hearing about.

Be Well Prepared   Listeners also respond well to speakers who appear confident. The best way to project confidence is to prepare as well as you can. Take the time you need to gather your facts. Organize them effectively into a clear presentation. And practice your delivery so that you can relax. Remember that you probably know more about your subject than any of your listeners do.

YOUR TURN

1. Think about the people in your speech class. What sorts of information should a good speaker keep in mind about them when preparing a speech? Make a list of topics that you think would be of interest to your classmates. Discuss them in class.

2. Prepare a speech introduction for one of the topics below. Assume you will be giving the speech to your speech class.

Working in outer space	How world records are determined
Search and rescue dogs	What an archeology dig is like

THE BODY: DELIVERING THE MESSAGE OF AN INFORMATIVE SPEECH

The body is the core of your informative speech. In it you fulfill your purpose of informing or explaining. If your introduction was successful, your listeners are ready now to hear what you have to say.

Identify Main Points Clearly

In the introduction to your speech, you previewed the main points you were going to cover. As you proceed to the body, remind your listeners of each main point. When possible, use the same words you used in your introduction to refer to each main point. This will help your listeners understand.

Also, try to express your main ideas in similar, or parallel, phrasing. Your listeners will be able to recognize your second main idea if it is phrased in the same form as your first main idea. For example, Dennis included the following main ideas in the outline for his speech. All of the main ideas are expressed in parallel form.

Unidentified Flying Objects

I. *Most common:* explainable after investigation
II. *Less common:* admitted hoaxes
III. *Rarest:* unexplainable even after investigation

Use Supporting Materials to Maintain Attention

The main points you identify for your listeners need to be backed up with solid information. As you develop your supporting materials, keep your informative purpose in mind. Ask yourself, "What information will help my listeners understand?" Then choose lively supporting material to keep the attention of your audience.

Facts and Statistics   In informative speeches, much of the information you give will be facts and statistics. A fact is a statement that can be proved true. Which of the following is a fact?

- The radar picked up an unknown blip on the screen.

- The radar picked up a flying saucer on the screen.

The first statement is a fact, since it can be checked by studying the radar records. The second statement is a theory, or guess, since it cannot be proved true.

A **statistic** is a fact expressed in numbers. See the following.

- Yosemite Falls, the highest waterfall in the United States, is 2,425 feet high.

- Texas became a state in 1845.

- Between 1980 and 1986, computer jobs increased by 75%.

Showing a slide of the State House at Austin would be an excellent way to introduce a speech about Texas.

Carefully researched facts and statistics will provide the information you need to explain your subject well. For easy reference, be sure to jot the information down on notecards.

Audio-Visual Aids   **Audio-visual aids** are pictures or objects that help to explain a point. Notice how the following common types of audio-visual aids can be used to help listeners understand or listen to the information presented.

- In his speech on UFO's, Ramon used a chart to define the three types of close encounters.

- Nina used a graph showing the rising cost of doctor bills in her speech about medicine today.

- To help explain the workings of a motorcycle engine, Terry drew a diagram with all the parts labeled.

- Sophia used a map of southern California to show the earthquake zone along the San Andreas fault.

- A large poster from the last Olympic games helped Bruce explain the meaning of the Olympic symbol.

- Esteban used an enlarged political cartoon to show how people felt about the last election.

- Marcy brought in pictures of guide dogs being trained. She could also have used slides or videotapes.

- Raoul used a model to show the design of a DC10 airplane.

- Tony passed out handouts during his speech on football plays. They contained diagrams that would have taken too long to write on the board.

- Ling struck a Chinese gong to show what it sounds like.

To be effective, audio-visual aids should be neat and attractive. They should also be large enough for your whole audience to see. If you are going to use audio-visual aids, practice with them ahead of time. Make notes on your cards to remind you when to use them.

React to Audience Feedback

As you deliver your speech, watch for reactions from your listeners. If people in the back are leaning forward and craning their necks, you may need to speak louder. If you notice knit eyebrows, chances are your audience is confused. Learn how to read "body language." Then adjust your presentation as needed.

Make Smooth Transitions

Another way you can help your listeners understand is to use smooth transitions between points. Remember, a transition is a word or phrase that shows how ideas are related. Such common ones as *first, second,* and *third* keep your listeners aware of your progress. Transitions like *but* and *however* point out contrasts.

THE CONCLUSION: ENDING AN INFORMATIVE SPEECH

Although brief, the conclusion to your speech is very important. As the last words your listeners hear from you, the ideas in your conclusion are likely to be remembered well. Use your conclusion to strengthen your main points.

Summarize Main Points Briefly

Someone once gave the following rules for speaking to an audience. 1. Tell them what you are going to say. 2. Say it. 3. Tell them what you just said. Although overly simple, these rules do have some merit. In your conclusion, briefly summarize your main points. This repetition helps your listeners learn.

Remind the Audience of Your Purpose

In your conclusion, remind your listeners of your purpose. For example, Jeannine included the following comments in her conclusion.

"Earlier I asked you to imagine what Yellowstone Park might be like without bears. I hope I have shown you today that bears are in danger of dying out. . . ."

Make a Final Statement

The very end of your speech will probably need special thought. Try one of the following ways to end an informative speech. 1. Restate the importance of your subject. 2. Try to stir the feelings of your listeners. 3. Drive home a single, most important idea. Remember that your last words will leave a strong impression, so make them count.

Hold a Question-and-Answer Period

When you have finished giving your prepared speech, if it is appropriate, invite questions from the audience. Listen carefully to each question and answer briefly and respectfully. If you do not know the answer to a question, say you do not know.

EVALUATION OF AN INFORMATIVE SPEECH

The more you speak in public, the easier your job as a speaker will seem. Practice builds confidence. You can learn from each experience before an audience. Evaluate each speech after you have given it. Note strengths as well as areas in which you need improvement.

Self-Evaluation

After your speech, ask yourself, "Was the audience interested?" The body language of the audience can give you a good indication. Also ask, "Could I answer most of their questions?" The answer to this question will give you a good idea of how well-prepared you were.

Evaluation by the Audience

Following is a form that your teachers and classmates might use to evaluate your speech.

Informative Speech: Evaluation Sheet

NAME _____ DATE _____

TOPIC _____

Rating Scale: 1: inadequate   2: poor   3: fair   4: good   5: excellent

Approach to platform	1	2	3	4	5
Poise and confidence	1	2	3	4	5
Eye contact	1	2	3	4	5
Volume	1	2	3	4	5
Rate	1	2	3	4	5
Gestures	1	2	3	4	5
Vocal emphasis	1	2	3	4	5
Introduction:	1	2	3	4	5
Attention-getter	1	2	3	4	5
Statement of purpose	1	2	3	4	5
Body:	1	2	3	4	5
Clear identification of main points	1	2	3	4	5
Adequate use of supporting material	1	2	3	4	5
Clear transitions	1	2	3	4	5
Conclusion:	1	2	3	4	5
Final statement	1	2	3	4	5

Grade _____ Comments:

1. Discuss each of the following statements in class. Decide whether each is a fact or a theory or guess.
    a. This is the safest car available today.
    b. The battleship *New Jersey* is 888 feet long.
    c. Angel Falls in Venezuela has a total drop of 3,212 feet.
    d. Jobs in medicine are more important than other kinds of jobs.
    e. The highest speed ever achieved on land is 650 m.p.h.

2. Discuss each of the following speech topics. Suggest visual aids that might be useful to the speaker.
    a. Eliminating fire hazards in the home.
    b. Fun with a birdfeeder
    c. America's aging population
    d. Gifts that you can make yourself
    e. Local hiking and backpacking trails

THE DEMONSTRATION SPEECH

A special kind of informative speech is the **demonstration speech.** The purpose of the demonstration speech is to show the members of your audience how to make, do, or use something. In a demonstration speech you will teach your listeners. You might explain to them how to make a fantastic paper airplane. You might show them how to tie a number of useful knots. You might teach them how to use a compass.

Choosing a Topic

In choosing a topic for a demonstration speech you must keep in mind the needs of your audience. Don't try to explain to your listeners how to do something that has taken you years to learn. And don't try to teach them how to make something that is very complicated or that demands expensive equipment or tools. Remember that people are always interested in learning a useful skill and in learning how to make something that they can benefit from and enjoy. Most people will respond to a speech that explains how to dry flowers or how to sharpen a dull knife or how to build a birdhouse with easily found materials. Each of these topics teaches a useful skill and does not demand a lot of the listener's time.

Introducing the Speech

Although you can use one of the attention-getting openings identified earlier in this chapter, the most useful opening for a demonstration speech is a simple explanation of what the listener will learn. You should also explain the benefit that will come to the audience by learning the skill. If you have chosen your topic with your listeners in mind, they will already be interested in what you have to say. Juan opened his speech in this way: "Today I am going to show you how to build an attractive birdfeeder. All you will need is a few items that won't cost more than three dollars and about two hours of your time. But when you're finished, you'll have something worthwhile that will bring you weeks and months of enjoyment."

List All of the Needed Materials

If you are going to show your audience how to do something or make something, begin the body of your speech by listing and showing all of the materials your audience will need. Juan began the body of his speech by identifying what materials and tools would be necessary. As he mentioned each item, he held it up for the audience to see. "You will need a piece of pine three feet long, three inches wide, and one-half inch thick and a piece of plywood one foot square and one-quarter inch thick. You will also need ten one-inch brass screws, a screwdriver, an awl, a small handsaw, a sheet of medium sandpaper, a half pint of bright paint, and a small brush."

Practice Handling the Demonstration Object

Kiri decided to give a demonstration speech on how to groom a dog. Since she could not bring her own dog to class, she decided to use a lifelike toy animal. Also needed were a grooming brush and comb and a set of dog nail clippers. When she practiced her speech, she also practiced handling all the different pieces together so her movements would appear coordinated. Practice until you are comfortable with the item(s) you are going to demonstrate.

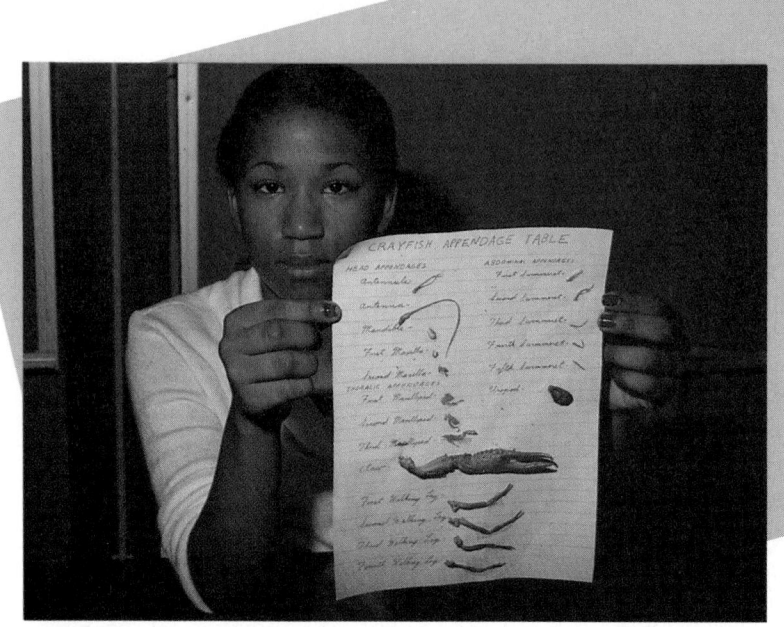

Visual aids are a very important part of a demonstration speech.

Point Out Errors, and Give Helpful Hints

Since you are an "expert" in your subject, include, in the body of your speech, possible pitfalls that your audience might encounter. Kiri, for example, warned her listeners about pulling too hard on a snag and hurting the dog. She suggested using a de-tangler.

Show Results

To emphasize the importance of her method, Kiri borrowed two pictures from the neighborhood groomer. They were "before" and "after" pictures of an Irish Setter. When an audience can see results, your demonstration will have a lasting impact.

Conclude with a Review and an Evaluation

As in all speeches, be sure to review the main steps or procedures in the conclusion of your speech. If you can summarize them in an easy-to-remember way, your listeners will be able to apply what you have taught them. You might want to distribute a written list of the steps that you described in your speech. The farm on the next page will help you polish your speech and evaluate those of your class-mates.

Demonstration Speech: Evaluation Sheet

NAME _____ DATE _____

TOPIC _____

Rating Scale: 1: inadequate   2: poor   3: fair   4: good   5: excellent

Analysis of audience in choice of topic	1	2	3	4	5
Approach	1	2	3	4	5
Poise and confidence	1	2	3	4	5
Handling of object(s)	1	2	3	4	5
Eye contact	1	2	3	4	5
Volume	1	2	3	4	5
Rate	1	2	3	4	5
Gestures	1	2	3	4	5
Vocal emphasis	1	2	3	4	5
Introduction	1	2	3	4	5
Use of supporting material	1	2	3	4	5
Conclusion:	1	2	3	4	5

Grade _____   Comments:

YOUR TURN ///////////////////

1. Discuss each of the following topics for a demonstration speech. Decide how suitable each would be for an audience of classmates.
   - **a.** How to build your own computer
   - **b.** How to make a box kite
   - **c.** How to perform difficult magic tricks
   - **d.** How to use a camera
   - **e.** How to make a terrarium
   - **f.** How to use a word processor
   - **g.** How to put together a crossword puzzle
   - **h.** How to assemble a stamp collection

2. Discuss with your classmates the things that they would like to learn to do, use, or make. Develop a list of topics for demonstration speeches that your classmates would like to listen to.

14 CHAPTER REVIEW

 ## Chapter Summary

The purpose of an informative speech is to explain a subject clearly so your listeners can easily understand. The introduction should capture attention and prepare listeners for the main points in your speech. The body should present those points in a clear order with facts and statistics for support. Audio-visual aids are often useful in conveying information through pictures. The conclusion of an informative speech should briefly summarize the main points and bring the speech to an end. Throughout an informative speech, a sincere and enthusiastic delivery will keep listeners "tuned in."

One special kind of informative speech is the demonstration speech. Its purpose is to show how to make, do, or use something. Good demonstration speeches include a list of needed materials, clear instructions, and helpful hints. Practicing your speech with the object(s) you are demonstrating is very important.

Checklist:

Mastering the Informative Speech

1. Find out who your audience members are, prepare the speech with them in mind, and tell them how your topic relates to them.

2. In the beginning of the speech, use an attention-getting device, such as humor, a narrative, a startling statement, a quotation, or a rhetorical question.

3. Project confidence and enthusiasm for your subject.

4. When appropriate, call for questions from the audience, and tell them ahead of time you will do so.

5. Identify your main points clearly.

6. Use supporting materials, such as statistics or audio-visual aids, to gain attention.

7. Make smooth transitions.

8. React to audience feedback.

9. In a demonstration speech, find a good topic, be comfortable handling the thing you are demonstrating, prepare your audience for a demonstration, list all the materials needed, include helpful hints, show results, and conclude with a review.

10. In your conclusion, summarize your main points, remind your audience of your purpose, and make a final statement.

 ## Vocabulary

Define each term in a complete sentence.

audio-visual aid	narrative
demonstration speech	rhetorical question
informative speech	statistic

 ## Review Questions

1. Name five attention-getting devices.

2. Identify three purposes of an introduction.

3. Explain the difference between a fact and a theory.

4. Name six visual aids you could use in a speech about baseball.

5. Explain why a speaker should read the "body language" of the audience.

6. Describe how transitions help make points clear.

7. Name three effective ways to conclude a speech.
8. Define a demonstration speech.
9. Explain how you choose a topic for a demonstration speech.
10. Explain how you should practice for a demonstration speech.

Discuss with Your Classmates

1. Make a list on the board of at least ten speech topics people in the class have used in the past. Then brainstorm interesting attention-getting devices that could introduce the speeches.

2. If you are in the middle of a speech and see that the attention of the audience is wandering, what should you do? Think of at least four ways to get the speech back on track.

3. Discuss the question-and-answer period that occurs at the end of a Presidential news conference. If there is anyone in the room who has not seen such a question-and-answer period, have someone in the class give a description of it. What purpose do you think the questions serve? Do they usually add any new information? What rules of behavior do you think the President and reporters are following?

4. Discuss audience expectations in a demonstration speech. What do listeners expect? How do the expectations of the audience influence the choice of topics?

Critical Thinking

1. **Synthesis:** Discuss how you would give a demonstration speech about riding a bicycle to an audience of people who had never seen a bike before. What special problems might a demonstration speech pose? How would you overcome them in this particular case?

2. Analysis: The sales talk is partly an informative speech and often a demonstration speech. In what ways is the sales talk an informative speech? How is it frequently a demonstration speech? How does a sales talk differ from a purely informative speech?

 # Activities

In-Class

1. Imagine that a spacecraft from a distant galaxy lands in your backyard. The passengers come into your garage and point in wonder at your bicycle. Give a two-minute demonstration speech explaining how to ride it.

2. You have been asked to represent the United States at a conference of foreign-exchange students. As guest speaker, you are to explain the educational system in the United States. Follow the steps for planning and delivering an informative speech. Limit your speech to seven minutes. Be prepared to deliver your speech in class.

3. After preparing your speech for number 2 above, try to think of any questions people in the audience might ask. List the questions on a piece of paper, along with your answers.

Out-of-Class

1. Take a few minutes to think of the subjects that interest you. When you are with friends, what do you talk about? What subjects in television shows, books, and movies hold your attention? What is your favorite section of the library? In your speech notebook, jot down a list of all your interests. Choose one subject from your list that you think would make a good five-minute informative speech. Use the library to gather information. After you have gathered the facts and statistics you need to explain your subject, think about visual aids. Make a list of three or four visual aids that would help your presentation. Then select the two best ones and make them to use when you give your speech. Be prepared to give your speech in class.

2. Choose something you have just learned in another class. Review any notes you took. Then think about how to introduce your subject. Practice a short informative speech on the subject in front of a mirror at home. Ask some friends or family members to listen to your speech. Have them use the evaluation form on page 281 to offer comments. Be prepared to give your speech in class.

3. In your speech notebook, plan a review of a book you have read or a play or movie you have attended. Keep in mind that your purpose is to report rather than evaluate. Give *information* about the book, play, or movie, not your opinion of it. Be prepared to give your review in class as a brief informative speech.

4. Choose a book that you especially enjoyed reading. Find a quotation from your book that would serve as an introduction to a speech about the book. Try out the quotation on several of your classmates. Watch their expressions to see whether you have captured their attention with your quote. Save your quote in case you have a chance to speak to the class about this favorite book.

Chapter Project

Using this chapter as a guide, write up a checklist of steps for preparing a demonstration speech. Choose a topic. Choose something fairly simple to demonstrate, so that your speech can be limited to five minutes. Prepare the speech, assuming that your speech class is the audience, and using your checklist every step of the way.

Present your speech to the class. Be sure to accept questions at the end. Have the class fill out the evaluation sheet on page 285.

CHAPTER 15 The Persuasive Speech

Jim and Elizabeth are listening to a barker at the fair. As Jim listens, he thinks . . .

"He sure makes the show sound exciting.

He's very persuasive; a lot of people are going in to see the show.

Maybe I can use some of the same techniques in my speech next week."

Have *you* ever persuaded someone to do something? What techniques did you use?

In this chapter, you will read about:

- choosing topics for persuasive speeches
- types of audiences
- preparing a persuasive speech
- evidence and reasoning in a persuasive speech
- presenting and evaluating a persuasive speech

Think of all the ways people persuade you every day. A friend may persuade you to walk home instead of taking the bus. A teacher may persuade you to complete your homework assignment before tomorrow. Your brother may persuade you to change your mind about which football player your favorite team should draft. A salesperson may persuade you to buy a new outfit.

People who give speeches to persuade know that persuasion is a powerful force. A **persuasive speech** is a speech that tries to influence the attitudes, beliefs, or behavior of an audience. The power of persuasion comes from the ability to change people's minds and move them to take some action.

PREPARING FOR A PERSUASIVE SPEECH

In an informative speech, you are asking your audience to listen and learn. In a persuasive speech, however, you are asking your listeners to rethink their beliefs and actions. To accomplish this task, you must be well prepared and ready for a challenge. Some audience members may be very willing to keep an open mind about your subject. Others, however, may not want to change their minds. Careful thinking and planning will help you persuade your listeners in the end.

Choose a Suitable Topic

The basis of a persuasive speech is an opinion, or a judgment, that can vary from person to person. When you give a persuasive speech, you are presenting an opinion for your audience to examine. Some audience members may have a sharply different opinion. They will examine yours carefully, looking for flaws. Only a carefully chosen, carefully researched opinion will stand up under this test.

Choose an Issue You Believe in and Can Argue

The most important thing to consider in choosing a subject is finding an opinion you truly support. Danitra, for example, thought about speaking on the subject of avoiding foods with added chemicals. She knew, however, that many foods would spoil without them. So she did not feel she could argue the point with complete sincerity. Instead she chose to speak on the need for clear and accurate food labeling.

Another factor to consider when choosing a subject is the kind of supporting material you can use to prove your point. Daniel, for example, wanted to persuade the film club members that foreign films were not as good as American films. He realized, however, that the issue was really one of taste. He could not prove his opinion. So instead he decided to talk about changing the way Academy Awards are given. He knew he could gather facts and statistics about how the winning movies were chosen. With these he could argue his opinion with strength and logic.

Consider Your Audience

Knowing the attitudes of your audience ahead of time will help you choose a topic effectively. Most audience attitudes can be grouped into one of the following four categories.

The **supportive audience** already shares your views. You do not need to use all your persuasive tools to change the viewpoint of these listeners. Your main goal is to make them feel more strongly about your position.

The **uncommitted audience,** in contrast, has not yet made up its mind. These listeners do not know much about your subject. They are waiting to learn more before taking a stand. These people need information—facts and other supporting details—to form an opinion. Your job is to provide this information in a logical way.

The **apathetic audience** simply doesn't care about your subject. Audience members may already have some basic information, but they do not see the subject's importance. Your job with this group is to show how your subject affects their lives and why they should care about it. You need to awaken the concerns of these audience members before they will be open to sharing your opinion.

During a staff meeting, each person has a turn at addressing an audience. Participants share ideas and opinions.

The final group is the most difficult to reach. It is the **opposed audience.** Listeners in this group have already made up their minds on the subject—in just the opposite way from yours. You can, however, expect them to listen carefully and at least test their opinions against the evidence and proof you provide. The stronger the evidence you give, the more likely you are to weaken opposing points of view.

Very few audiences are made up of only one type; most contain a mix. As you prepare your speech, take the time to learn about the mix in your audience. Will you have more supportive listeners, or will most of your audience be opposed? How many people will you need to inspire with the importance of your subject?

One simple way to gauge your audience is to take an informal opinion poll before your speech. If you can reach them directly, ask your audience members for their views. If you cannot talk to them ahead of time, ask others about them. Keep track of how many listeners from each of the four groups will be in your audience. If most of your listeners are opposed, you will need to gear your speech to them. Plan your speech for the largest group in your audience.

Set a Specific Goal

Once you have a sense of your audience, you should refine your speaking purpose. Although your main purpose will be to persuade, a

What is the specific purpose of a speech that is meant to convince people that air pollution is not yet under control?

more specific purpose will keep you focused. For example, do you want to influence your listeners' attitudes? Or do you want to persuade them to take some action? What is the specific purpose in each of the following speech topics?

- Rosita wants people to appreciate the need for wheelchair ramps in all public places.

- Milton wants to get people to adopt a homeless animal from the shelter.

- Marsha wants to convince people that air pollution is not yet under control.

The first and last speeches are attempting to persuade people to adjust their attitudes and beliefs. The second speech, in contrast, is trying to move people to action. If your listeners are mostly opposed to your viewpoint, you may want to limit your specific goal to influencing their beliefs and attitudes. If, on the other hand, your listeners are supportive, you might well succeed in persuading them to act on their beliefs. Plan your speech with a specific goal in mind.

1. Suppose your persuasive speech topic is: The 55 mile per hour speed limit should be strictly enforced. Think about how you would treat this topic with each of the following audience types. Be prepared to discuss your answers.

    a. supportive   **c.** apathetic

    b. uncommitted   **d.** opposed

2. Think about some issues that you really believe in and that you could argue for persuasively. Try to identify four or five topics. They may be issues currently being discussed in your community, or they may be your own personal views. Share your topics with your classmates. See how many agree or disagree with your views.

DELIVERING A PERSUASIVE SPEECH

Persuasive speeches, like other speeches, have an introduction, a body, and a conclusion. But as you have learned, persuading is a more complex task than informing. The following suggestions will help you accomplish the task of delivering a persuasive speech.

Use an Attention-Getter in the Introduction

No matter what kind of audience you have, you need to capture its attention early. Some of the attention-getting devices you might use, as you know, are humor, a narrative, a startling statement, a quotation, or a rhetorical question. Mario, for example, used a startling statement to grab the attention of his audience.

"Picture this scene. He was about to leave for the long day's hunt. The arctic wind was beginning to howl—winter would soon be upon the land. She knew he would be leaving soon, so she stayed close to him until that hour. With a soft touch he reassured her that he would return. She watched him go and hung her head at the separation.

A man and a woman in the arctic wild? No. This scene accurately reflects the behavior of two wolves, animals thought to be vicious and bloody. They are, in fact, much like humans in their strong social ties and displays of affection. They deserve to be treated with respect."

The audience was surprised at this beginning. It held the listeners' attention and made them interested in what Mario had to say. It also made them sympathize with wolves right from the start.

Establish Credibility

"You must have the tooth pulled right away!" If your dentist said that, you would probably agree. If your younger sister said that, though, you might doubt her judgment. Your younger sister lacks credibility. **Credibility** means authority or believability.

If you are going to persuade people, you need to convince them of your credibility first. In some cases, your credibility may be established by the person introducing you. In the introduction, the audience would learn how you became an expert in your subject. If you are not introduced, you must establish your own credibility. Let your listeners know what kind of research you have done on your subject, or what kind of experience you have with it. Mario continued his speech about wolves.

"I've always been fascinated by wolves. Ever since I was a small boy I have been reading books about wolves. I've spent hours watching them at the zoo. I've even been in a wolf study program at the zoo. The more I have learned about wolves, the more I realize how wrong popular opinion about them is."

It is important to show your credibility throughout your entire speech. If you have done your research carefully, you will present valid evidence. **Evidence** is the information you provide to back up your opinion. The most effective kinds of evidence include facts, examples, and the opinions of experts. Thus, although Mario studied wolves himself, he also relied on the work of knowledgeable scientists to support his point of view.

If you have thought carefully about what the evidence means, you will also use clear reasoning. In other words, you will be able to draw convincing conclusions from the evidence. Mario, for example, presented evidence that healthy wolves have never attacked humans. From this he concluded logically that wolves do not deserve

Mario established credibility in his persuasive speech about wolves by telling his audience about the hours he had spent watching wolves at the zoo.

their reputation as dangerous killers. Together, valid evidence and clear reasoning will give you the credibility you need.

Use Special Approaches as Needed

You have already learned that certain techniques of delivery can be effective ways to reach an audience. The following aids are especially helpful in a persuasive speech.

Literary Excerpts   Like a simple quote, a literary excerpt can be an effective way to make a point. Mario found the following story about wolves from a collection of Aesop's fables. He used it because it showed exactly the point he was trying to make.

The Wolf and the Shepherds

One evening a wolf passed near a sheep fold and smelled mutton cooking. He drew close and peered through the bushes. A lamb was roasting over the fire and the shepherds were discussing the good quality of the meat. If it were I who had done this, thought the Wolf, they would be after me with sticks and stones and curses.

Description   If you can make your listeners see, hear, and feel a scene or event, you can make a deep impression on them. In her speech about the need for tougher clean air laws, Alexis painted the following picture.

> "Just south of Chicago along Lake Michigan, giant steel factories form an eerie skyline. Fingers of flame shoot from their smokestacks, bright orange against the twilight sky. But the sky is not blue, or purple, as a twilight sky should be. It is thick and brown with the waste that bellows out of the factories. The smell is so strong that drivers roll up their car windows as they pass."

This description made the audience vividly aware of the problem of air pollution.

Emotional Appeal   The description you just read appealed to the emotions of the listeners. It awakened their feelings of concern and even horror at the possibility of losing clean air.

Emotional appeals are appropriate for many persuasive topics. They must not, however, be used *instead of* appeals to reason and logic. Thoughtful listeners will demand solid reasoning before they can be persuaded. But an appeal to their emotions may make them more willing to hear the solid evidence you present.

Present Facts Your Audience Can Understand

Sometimes the evidence you present to your listeners will have little meaning for them. Leonardo, for example, spoke about the possibility of intelligent life in space. In his speech, he gave information about the vast distances in space. But he tried to make the numbers mean something by relating them to familiar, everyday matters.

> "The sun's nearest neighbor is Alpha Centauri. It is about 24 trillion miles away. That distance is hard to picture unless you try to think on a smaller scale. If you think of the sun as a grapefruit, and Alpha Centauri as another grapefruit, there would be 1300 miles between them, the distance between Chicago and Miami."

Whenever possible, turn the numbers and statistics in your speech into easy-to-understand examples. In this way your evidence will mean more to your audience.

WHY BUY BLUE JEANS?

Eighty years ago, denim trousers were the clothes of men who worked outdoors. Cowpokes and sodbusters wore these durable work clothes, but changed into traditional clothing for encounters with "polite society." Today, however, denim trousers—now known as blue jeans—*are* traditional clothing, to be worn almost anywhere by anyone. Many are willing to pay a high price for them.

How did lowly denim trousers become expensive, designer jeans? Comfort and practicality are two major reasons. Even more important is our changed view of blue jeans. Advertising, a highly persuasive force, has had much to do with that new view.

Advertising uses many different devices to persuade us to buy products. One subtle way advertisers may promote a product is to create an uncertainty about self-image. Then the advertisers claim that their product is the answer. Suppose, for example, we read a shampoo advertisement. It makes us worry that our hair is dull. We are likely to buy the shampoo that promises to make our hair shiny.

A still more subtle approach causes us to associate a product with something desirable. A photograph of people wearing jeans shows that they are attractive, happy, and admired by those around them. If the message is strong enough, we may pay a high price for Brand X jeans and all the good things that seem to come with them.

How does an advertiser know what will persuade us to buy a particular brand of jeans? A good advertiser conducts thorough market research first, using surveys, interviews, and mail-in cards from consumers. The research tells what kind of people are likely to buy. The advertiser then plans an ad campaign using persuasive devices intended to reach them.

During the past 80 years, advertisers have zeroed in on the right market for blue jeans. Today, blue jeans are high fashion and big business.

Using positive reinforcement in a speech about adopting a cat from a shelter is a good way to convince people of the validity of your point of view.

Use Reinforcement

If you want your listeners to change their minds, you will have to show them the benefit of doing so. Using **reinforcement** is one way to show them the value of your opinion.

Milton, for example, was trying to persuade his listeners to adopt a homeless animal. He appealed to his audience's sense of duty. Several times during his speech he said, "The caring person who adopts from a shelter . . . ." Milton used **positive reinforcement;** he offered praise to the listeners for doing what he wanted them to do. He rewarded them by calling them "caring."

Alexis, arguing about air pollution, used **negative reinforcement.** She kept referring to "short-sighted people who think only of profits . . . ." Audience members who did not agree with her would, by extension, be grouped in this category. Nobody wants to think that he or she is "short-sighted." This negative reinforcement, or blame, might make people rethink their views.

Use Parallelism

When you give a speech, you cannot expect your audience to remember everything you say. If you phrase the important points in a memorable way, however, your message will have more meaning. One way to phrase a point effectively is to use parallel structure. One of the most memorable speeches of our times used parallelism to make its most important point.

"Ask not what your country can do for you; ask what you can do for your country."—*President John F. Kennedy*

Match Your Tone to the Speech Topic

Kenneth chose the subject of prison reform for his speech. He felt the subject demanded a serious tone. **Tone** is the attitude a speaker sets toward the subject. Mai Li, on the other hand, spoke about terrible television commercials. Her subject called for a much lighter tone. She even began with humor.

Think carefully about the tone you want to set with your speech. Do you want to be serious, urgent, upbeat, light, or sad? These are just a few of the possible tones you could establish. Your choice of topic and the occasion of your speech will help you decide on an appropriate tone.

Be Sincere and Use Logic

An audience can quickly tell when you are not interested in your subject. In every way—with words, gestures, vocal inflection—show your sincerity and interest.

An audience can also tell when a speaker is relying too much on emotions and not enough on logic. Remember that your credibility is strengthened through the use of valid evidence and careful reasoning. Before your speech, test your logic. Try to develop an argument for an opposing position. Can your original logic answer all the opposing points you can think of? If not, keep working on your logic until you can overcome all possible objections.

Adapt to Audience Reaction During the Speech

Watch your audience for reactions to your speech. If you notice some people looking confused, clarify your points. If some people look bored, adjust your speech by including vivid description or startling

An audience can tell when a speaker is relying too much on emotions and not enough on logic.

statements that will regain their attention. Watch carefully for cues from your listeners and adjust your speech accordingly.

Avoid Faulty Content

Sometimes speakers stretch a point to change their listeners' minds. As you develop your persuasive speech, watch for the following common faults.

Hasty or Sweeping Generalization Roberto made the mistake of drawing a general conclusion based on only a few specific examples. In his speech on animal training, he said that food rewards are the only way to get animals to learn. He was basing his conclusion on his experience with only two dogs. Several class members had had success training with other methods. They knew Roberto had not considered enough animals before forming his opinion. He lost credibility this way. Be sure you consider as many examples as possible before drawing a conclusion.

Omitted Facts   Sometimes speakers leave out important facts because those facts might hurt their argument. By doing this, they are actually weakening their position. If you know an opposing fact that should be included in your speech, include it. Then explain why it has failed to convince you. You will probably be able to find a good reason.

"Stacked Deck"   Few opinions are so simple that they are either right or wrong. Some speakers, however, feel they need to "stack the deck" entirely in favor of their position. (In card playing, a stacked deck is one in which all the winning cards go to one player.) Good listeners know that every position has some drawbacks. Instead of denying the drawbacks in your position, address them honestly. Show how they fail to outweigh the benefits of your position.

False Assumptions   When Mario was preparing his speech on wolves, he double-checked all of his assumptions. He was tempted, for example, to assume that because wolves were like dogs in *some* ways, they were like them in *all* ways. Careful thought showed this was not necessarily true.

Similarly, Mario was tempted to assume that since wolves are social, the idea of a lone wolf must be myth. However, while *most* wolves are social, a few do fall away from the pack. What is true in general is not necessarily true in each individual case.

EVALUATING THE PERSUASIVE SPEECH

Politicians can evaluate their speeches by counting votes. Salespersons can evaluate their success by counting customers. You can use a follow-up poll and help from your classmates to evaluate your persuasive speech.

Have You Changed the Audience's Mind?

Take a follow-up poll after your speech by asking audience members their current opinions on your subject. Compare the answers with those you received before your speech. Did you strengthen the feelings of the supportive members of your audience? Did you win some new supporters from the uncommitted group? Did the uninterested members of the audience become interested? Did the opposed audience members change their positions at all? If you did any of these things, your speech succeeded.

How Do They Rate Your Speech?

The following sheet is typical of a form your classmates and teachers might use to evaluate your speech. When you are rehearsing your speech, you can also use this form yourself. How would you rate your work?

Persuasive Speech: Evaluation Sheet

NAME _____ DATE _____

TOPIC _____

Rating Scale: 1: inadequate   2: poor   3: fair   4: good   5: excellent

Approach to platform	1	2	3	4	5
Poise and confidence	1	2	3	4	5
Eye contact	1	2	3	4	5
Volume	1	2	3	4	5
Gestures and movement	1	2	3	4	5
Vocal projection and variety	1	2	3	4	5
Introduction:	1	2	3	4	5
Attention-getter	1	2	3	4	5
Tone	1	2	3	4	5
Subject statement	1	2	3	4	5
Body:	1	2	3	4	5
Organization	1	2	3	4	5
Evidence and reasoning	1	2	3	4	5
Clarity	1	2	3	4	5
Conclusion:	1	2	3	4	5
Summary of main points or	1	2	3	4	5
Final appeal	1	2	3	4	5

Grade _____   Comments:

Politicians can evaluate their speeches by counting votes. A good speech should strengthen the feelings of supportive members of an audience and win some new supporters from the uncommitted.

1. Assume you are speaking on the 55-mile-per-hour speed limit.
   a. How might you establish credibility?
   b. What rhetorical aids might you use with this subject? Explain in detail.
   c. How might a careless thinker "stack the deck" in favor of enforcing the 55-mile-per-hour speed limit?

2. Identify each of the following thinking faults.
   a. That team won't give us a problem. They lost 9-0 last month.
   b. I checked and guarantee that there is not a single opposing fact.
   c. There are a couple of facts that disturb me, but there is no reason to bring those up.
   d. Bats have sharp teeth, so they must attack humans often.

15 CHAPTER REVIEW

Chapter Summary

The purpose of a persuasive speech is to influence the attitudes, beliefs, or behavior of an audience. When preparing a persuasive speech, choose a subject you sincerely believe in and can argue well. If possible, find out the attitudes of your audience. Set a specific goal with your audience in mind.

In the delivery of your speech, capture attention early and establish your credibility and the proper tone. Use any rhetorical aids that will help you reach your audience. Be sure that your logic is free from faulty thinking. Watch your listeners and adjust your presentation to their nonverbal messages. Evaluate your speech by taking a follow-up poll and using the evaluation sheet on page 306.

Checklist

Understanding Persuasive Speaking Skills

1. Choose a topic you believe in and can argue for.
2. Take into consideration the kind of audience you will address.
3. Set a specific goal for your speech.
4. Use an attention-getter in the introduction.
5. Establish your credibility by showing how you are an authority, by presenting solid evidence, and by using clear reasoning.
6. Use special approaches as necessary. These might include literary excerpts, descriptions, or emotional appeals.
7. Present facts and statistics in a form your audience can understand.
8. Use reinforcement.

9. Use parallel presentation.
10. Match your tone to your speech topic.
11. Adapt to audience reaction during the speech.
12. Avoid faulty reasoning.
13. Use a follow-up poll and evaluation sheet to evaluate your speech.

 Vocabulary

Define each term in a complete sentence.

apathetic audience

credibility

evidence

negative reinforcement

opposed audience

persuasive speech

positive reinforcement

reinforcement

supportive audience

tone

uncommitted audience

Review Questions

1. Identify the general purpose of a persuasive speech.
2. Briefly describe the four types of audience members.
3. Explain how you should adjust your speech for each of the four audience types.
4. Describe how you should establish credibility.
5. Define evidence.
6. Explain the relationship between evidence and reasoning.
7. Name and briefly describe five special approaches you could use in a persuasive speech.

8. Define tone.
9. Name three possible tones you could establish.
10. Explain the meaning of each of the following:
   a. hasty or sweeping generalization
   b. omitted facts
   c. stacked deck
   d. false assumptions

Discuss with Your Classmates

1. What sorts of speech devices do salespeople use to persuade you to buy? Do they persuade you? What do you think is the most effective approach they use?

2. How can a speaker compliment his or her audience? Can you think of five ways? How might this help when presenting a persuasive speech?

3. Your school supports the building of a new pool for students. If your class was asked to give three persuasive speeches on this topic—one to the students, one to teachers, and one to parents—how would your speeches be the same? How would they differ?

4. Discuss how a stacked deck and omitted facts weaken an argument. Even if an audience does not know about these faults, how do they affect the speaker?

Critical Thinking

1. **Comprehension:** In what ways is a persuasive speech more difficult than an informative one? Is a persuasive speech always more difficult?

2. Evaluation: Television commercials are really miniature persuasive speeches. Pay close attention to three or four commercials. What persuasive devices do they use that are mentioned in this chapter? How persuasive do you think they are?

 Activities

In-Class

1. Each of the following opinions can form the basis of a persuasive speech. Read each one. Then decide what kind of audience member you would be for each topic (supportive, uncommitted, apathetic, opposed). Finally, explain what would convince you if you do not already agree. Share your answers with your classmates and discuss in class.

     a. Dog racing should be made illegal throughout the nation.
     b. Cars should be banned from national parks.
     c. Hospital workers should not be allowed to go on strike.
     d. Television shows containing violence should not be allowed on the air.

2. Imagine that your class would like to persuade the local school board to add a month to the summer vacation. Discuss how you might go about it. What kind of audience do you think you would be persuading? How could you establish credibility? What could you do to show the school board that learning would not suffer? List at least three persuasive arguments that you could make.

3. Imagine that you want to convince your older brother or sister to take you on a trip to visit a relative in another state. You know that your brother or sister would not be very interested in taking you along. Prepare a list of objections that your brother or sister might raise. Then develop a strategy for answering each objection. Share the objections and your persuasive strategy with your classmates.

Out-of-Class

1. You have been named student spokesperson for a "Feed the Hungry" project in your community. You will be speaking before a neighborhood council meeting. Your purpose is to convince people to volunteer to work in the neighborhood shelter on Thanksgiving Day. Prepare a seven-minute speech to accomplish this purpose.

2. Check the editorial page of your local paper for opinions and letters to the editor. Find an opinion that you disagree with. Prepare a two-minute speech expressing your point of view. Pretend that you are going to deliver your speech face-to-face to the person who wrote the letter or editorial. Be prepared to present your speech in class.

3. Find a product that your family really believes in and uses. Learn as much as possible about the product by talking with other family members or friends who use it. Think about the way it is advertised. Read the instructions that come with it. Practice demonstrating it. Prepare an outline for a short speech in which you will demonstrate and sell the product in class. Be sure to include the price and the place where it can be purchased.

Chapter Project

Prepare a persuasive speech on one of the topics below. Assume the speech is to be ten minutes long and presented to all the teachers in your school.

- Grades should be abolished.
- Field trips are more important than tests.
- After-school activities are learning experiences.
- Students should evaluate teachers at the end of the year.
- Our school needs better science labs.
- Our teachers are the best in the state.
- The school day should be shorter.
- Teachers should be active in local politics.
- Everyone should be involved in a team sport.

When you are preparing your speech, be sure to use at least one of the special approaches listed in this chapter, and be prepared to explain why you chose the one you did.

Be prepared to present your speech in class. Survey the members of the audience to see if you changed anyone's mind.

INTERPRETIVE SPEAKING

Terry and Pedro help in a first grade class each week. These are some of Terry's thoughts as she listens to Pedro telling a story.

"He really holds their interest.

They're all listening and watching so closely.

He makes the story come alive."

Have *you* ever presented a story or a poem? Did your audience pay attention?

In this chapter, you will read about:

- choosing a selection for an oral interpretation presentation
- the organization, mood, and characterization in selections
- the point of view of a selection
- the rhythm and repetition of poetry
- writing an introduction for a presentation
- giving an oral interpretation presentation

Oral interpretation is a form of public speaking. It is, however, very different from a public speech. The main difference is that speakers do not use their own words. Instead, they read literature, that is, the words of someone else. Oral interpretation, though, is not simply reading literature aloud. This is called oral reading or sight reading.

Oral interpretation is a public presentation of literature. The purpose of the presentation is to share feelings and images with the audience. Oral interpreters, however, are not like actors in a play. They do not act out movements. Instead, they depend on vocal messages and facial expressions to express the author's ideas. Their main emphasis is on the words of the author.

Oral interpretation began with storytelling—long before literature was written down. When stories and histories were finally recorded, oral interpretation remained a means of communication. For hundreds of years, oral interpretation brought news and entertainment to many people. This was especially true in places outside of big cities.

In the early part of the nineteenth century, oral interpretation was very popular in the United States. In fact, it was the most popular form of public entertainment. When radio was developed, oral interpretation became the basis for its programs. Today it is still used on radio and TV. It is also used by people who narrate films and records, or who read to the blind.

CHOOSING A SELECTION

You can choose from prose, poetry, or drama—as long as your selection is interesting to your audience. It does not have to be a new or unusual selection. In fact, many classics and fairy tales are told

When radio was developed, oral interpretation became the basis for its programs. This photo shows the cast of the Radio Theatre Guild.

over and over again. People never seem to lose interest in them because they tell exciting stories. Following are some other things to think about when choosing a selection.

Time

How much time do you have to prepare your selection? Too often, people spend too much time looking for a selection. Then they don't have enough time to practice it.

You also must think about how much time you have for the presentation. Never choose a long selection that you will have to say too fast. Instead, look for one that can be said correctly within the time limit.

Understanding and Interest

Do you understand your selection? If you don't, you can be sure that the audience won't. How you read your selection can also have an effect on audience comprehension.

Will the audience be interested in your selection? Some literature can be enjoyed equally by young people and adults. Other literature, however, is written for certain age groups. Make sure your selection suits your audience.

UNDERSTANDING LITERATURE

Before you present a selection, you must understand it. You need to know what the author has done to communicate the meaning of the selection. Following are some things you need to think about for each presentation.

Total Meaning

Before you do anything else, read the whole piece of literature. You especially need to do this if you are using only a small part of it. You need to know how your selection fits into the total piece. You would need to know, for example, the answers to the following questions. What happens to whom? How and why does it happen? What is the result? If you don't understand the whole piece, you probably won't be able to present your selection correctly.

Mood

Reading the whole piece of literature has many advantages. For example, you will understand the mood of the whole piece. Then you can decide if that mood changes in your selection or remains the same. For example, the mood could start out as a happy one, but by the time it reaches your selection, it could turn to one of sadness. It is also helpful if you understand why a mood changes.

Characterization

Usually writers give two kinds of information about most characters: external and internal. External characteristics can be seen or heard. They include such things as height, age, and color of hair. Internal characteristics can't be seen or heard. They include such things as thoughts, emotions, and attitudes. Readers learn this information by what the narrator or other characters say about someone. Readers also learn this information by what the characters say about themselves.

Organization

Most writers follow a pattern when they tell the events of a story. First, they tell readers something about the main conflict of the story. A **conflict** places the main character up against an opposing force. Next, writers tell some of the problems the character has. These problems try to stop the character from finding an answer to the conflict. This is called **rising action.**

Suspense continues to build until the climax. The **climax** is the turning point of the story. This is the moment when the main character wins or loses the struggle. Loose ends are tied up in the **falling action.** Finally, the story ends with some kind of conclusion. When you read your selection, you need to know how it fits into this pattern. Also, always remember that you know the whole story, but your audience doesn't.

Dialogue

Dialogue consists of the words spoken by characters. Since stories and plays have so much dialogue, it is very important that you understand it. Who is speaking? What is that person saying? How is it being said? To whom is it being said? If you know the answers to these questions, you will understand the characters better. You will be better able to understand the reasons why the characters do and say the things they do and say.

Word Choices

Writers usually spend a lot of time looking for exactly the right words to use. That's why it is important that you understand all of them. If you don't know the meaning of a word, look it up in the dictionary. You should also remember that words have both connotative and denotative meanings. For example, a millionaire might refer to his mansion as a "little home." People in an audience could miss this point if you didn't read the words right. They might think he was referring to a small cottage.

Within each sentence or paragraph, some words are more important than the other words. Often these words are nouns or verbs. Because these words are important, you need to emphasize them with your voice. Your *voice* says, "This is an important word!"

Punctuation

With your voice, you must express the written punctuation in your selection. Following is a chart that shows you how to translate some punctuation marks into speech.

Translating Punctuation Marks Into Speech

Written	Oral
1. Periods; colons; commas; semi-colons; dashes; spaces between words, sentences, stanzas, or paragraphs	1. Pauses of different lengths to show finished thoughts; breathing pauses; someone thinking; or changes in speakers
2. Underscored or italicized material (except titles of published material and foreign terms), words printed in capital letters, or exclamation points	2. Increased volume; to add stress on certain words to show importance; to prolong words to show their value
3. Hyphens in words not usually hyphenated, such as *s-l-o-w-l-y*	3. Prolonging words or holding onto sounds; increasing the sound; using a drawl or slower speech pattern
4. Hyphens between words, such as *never-to-be-forgotten*	4. Pauses after the hyphenated word —but not between the individual words —to show a close relationship between the words
5. Quotation marks	5. Changes in speakers by using a different voice or shifts from the narrator to a character
6. Question marks	6. Raising the voice to show a distinction from statements ending with periods

YOUR TURN ////////////////

1. Make a list of your favorite selections from literature. If possible, include at least one story, one poem, and one play. Your teacher will take a survey to find out which selections are best known. Which of the most popular selections would you want to read or hear again? Why?

2. Pick a favorite story. Describe the main character. Then outline the rising action, the climax, the falling action, and the conclusion.

PRESENTING DIFFERENT KINDS OF LITERATURE

Most literature has the same basic ingredients. Still, each kind of literature has its own special features. You need to think about a few different things, for example, when presenting a poem or a play. Following are some of those special features.

Prose

Students often choose prose for their oral interpretation presentations. There are many selections to choose from, and often they include real-life people. If you choose prose, consider the following.

Point of View   **Point of view** is the position or stand from which a narrator is presented. In other words, it is the voice through which the writer tells the story. Point of view is very important in an oral presentation. Following are the most common points of views that writers use.

Main Character   The main character is the storyteller when the pronouns *I, me,* and *we* are used in the story. Following is an example. The lines are taken from the short story "The Third Level" by Jack Finney.

> The corridor I was in began angling left and slanting downward. I thought I was wrong, but I kept on walking. All I could hear was the empty sound of my own footsteps, and I didn't pass a soul. Then I heard that sort of hollow roar ahead.

Minor Character   A minor character can be the storyteller or narrator. Still, however, readers see the other characters only through one person's eyes. Following is an example. The lines are taken from the short story "The Redheaded League" by Sir Arthur Conan Doyle. The story is *not* told by Sherlock Holmes, the main character. Rather, it is told by Watson, a minor character.

> I had called upon my friend, Mr. Sherlock Holmes, one day in the autumn of last year and found him in deep conversation with a very stout, florid-faced, elderly gentleman with fiery red hair. With an apology for my intrusion, I was about to withdraw when Holmes pulled me abruptly into the room.

A meeting of the Redheaded League.

Objective Observer   In stories told from this point of view, the storyteller is *not* a character in the story. However, the storyteller sees and knows everything about all the characters. Sometimes the storyteller tells only what the characters say and do. At other times, the storyteller also tells what they are thinking. Following is an example. It is from the short story "The Street of the Cañon" by Josephina Niggli.

The man in the doorway, while trying to appear at ease, was carefully examining every smiling face. If just one person recognized him, the room would turn on him like a den of snarling mountain cats, but so far all the laughter-dancing eyes were friendly.

When you make a presentation, you need to understand its point of view. For example, suppose your story is told from an objective point of view. Then you would use your own voice and talk directly to the audience. However, you would not do that if it were told from a character's point of view. In that case, you would have to suggest that character's age, sex, and emotional state.

Use of a Narrator   In some stories, the point of view changes. The first part is told from the point of view of one character, and the second part from the point of view of another character. If this happens, you can avoid any confusion if you use a narrator.

For example, some directors use two people for one character. One reads the lines of the character in the story. The other, the narrator, describes the people and events in the story. Two people can also be used when a story is told many years after it happened. The narrator tells the story, but another person reads the lines of the character as a child.

The narrator usually stands to one side and watches the action. Then from time to time that person makes comments. For example, the narrator explains things or adds descriptions.

YOUR TURN ///////////////

1. From whose point of view is each of the following selections told?
   a. Benjamin Banneker went up to his cabin early that night of August 11, 1799, because there was some disturbance in the heavens and he wanted to watch it. Odd things had been happening for several weeks. But he had predicted unsettled weather for this week. He didn't expect what really happened.

   from I WILL LIFT UP MINE EYES, *by Shirley Graham*

   b. America was all around us, in and out of the *barrio*. Abruptly we had to forget the ways of shopping in a *mercado* and learn those of shopping in a corner grocery or in a department store. The Americans paid no attention to the Sixteenth of September, but they made a great commotion about the Fourth of July.

   from BARRIO BOY, *by Ernesto Galarza*

2. Prepare and deliver an oral interpretation of either of the passages above or of a prose selection of your own choice.

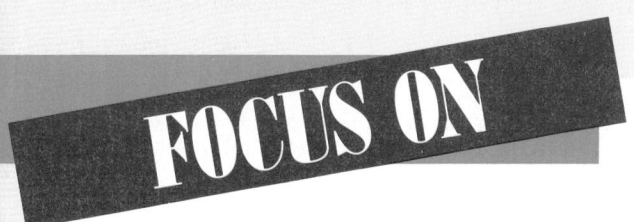
A STORY IS MORE THAN THE WORDS

by Shirley Schoonover

Shirley Schoonover is the author of both novels and short stories. The story she discusses below, "Old and Country Tale," was first published in The Atlantic Monthly *and received an O. Henry Award.*

"He had run away."

That's the first sentence of one of my short stories. It captures the reader's attention. When I prepare my work to read aloud, I want to capture the listener's attention.

The next part of the story tells how the man, Asher, ran away, where he went, and why he ran away. I pay close attention to this part of the story. I ask the story questions. What is Asher's character? How do I read his lines to show him to the listener? He's gentle, shy, not sure of himself. So I read his lines carefully, the way a shy person would speak.

How do I convey the details of the story? As the narrator of the story, I read with a matter-of-fact voice, emphasizing certain verbs and nouns to highlight those details. Is the action exciting enough to keep the audience interested? Asher runs and stumbles through a night-blackened cornfield. He is hunted by a car full of people with a spotlight. The language is simple and clear. I read the short sentences quickly.

The rising action of the story is Asher's flight. The suspense, too, is in his flight and whether or not he will be caught. As the narrator, I am calm. But when I read Asher, I put myself in his situation. He is out of breath at times, so I read only fragments of some of his words as he runs. When the mood changes, the language changes. As the story develops, I slow the pace of reading to build the suspense. For the climax I speed up to intensify the drama.

When I prepare a story to read aloud, I use all of these techniques. I listen as I read. And I watch the members of the audience as they hear it, fitting my presentation to them.

Poetry

You need to understand a few special things about poetry. Then you will have no problem presenting a poem.

Rhythm and Repetition   One of poetry's special features is rhythm. This is the pattern created by stressed and unstressed syllables. In other words, a poem's rhythm is its beat. To understand the beat, read the poem aloud and tap your foot or clap your hands. Finding the beat of a poem is almost the same as finding the beat of a song.

Another special feature of poetry is the repetition of sounds, words, and images. The most common example of repetition of sounds in a poem is its **rhyme scheme.** A rhyme scheme is a pattern created by the rhyming words at the ends of lines. One way to find a poem's rhyme scheme is to give each line a letter. You place a new letter after each line that ends with a different sound. However, the letters are repeated each time the final sound is repeated. The rhyme scheme for the following stanzas follows the pattern a–a–b–b. The stanzas are from the poem "Casey at the Bat" by Ernest Thayer.

The outlook wasn't brilliant for the Mudville nine that day;	*a*
The score stood four to two, with but one inning more to play;	*a*
And so, when Cooney died at first, and Barrows did the same,	*b*
A sickly silence fell upon the patrons of the game.	*b*

A straggling few got up to go in deep despair. The rest	*c*
Clung to the hope which springs eternal in the human breast;	*c*
They thought, if only Casey could but get a whack; at that,	*d*
They'd put up even money now, with Casey at the bat.	*d*

Frequently, images also are repeated throughout a poem to remind the reader or listener of the importance of certain ideas. If a poet wants to emphasize patriotism, for example, he or she might include images of the flag, the Statue of Liberty, the Liberty Bell, and the Declaration of Independence throughout the poem. Only if you recognize these repeated images can you give them their proper interpretation in your presentation.

Emphasis   Some people stop at the end of every line of poetry. It's true that poetry is often written in sentences—like prose. However, the ends of sentences do not always come at the ends of the

lines. When you read poetry, look for the punctuation at the end of a line. If there isn't any, keep reading without a pause. Pause only if there is a period, a comma, or a semicolon.

For example, read the following stanza from a poem by Roberto Félix Salazar twice. When you read it the first time, do not follow the punctuation. Instead, pause at the end of each line. When you read it the second time, follow the punctuation carefully. Notice how the meaning, flow, and rhythm change between the two readings.

Now I must write
Of those of mine who rode these plains
Long years before the Saxon and the Irish came.
Of those who plowed the land and built the towns
And gave the towns soft-woven Spanish names.
Of those who moved across the Rio Grande
Toward the hiss of Texas snake and Indian yell.
Of men who from the earth made thick-walled homes
And from the earth raised churches to their God.
And of the wives who bore them sons
And smiled with knowing joy.
                    "The Other Pioneers"

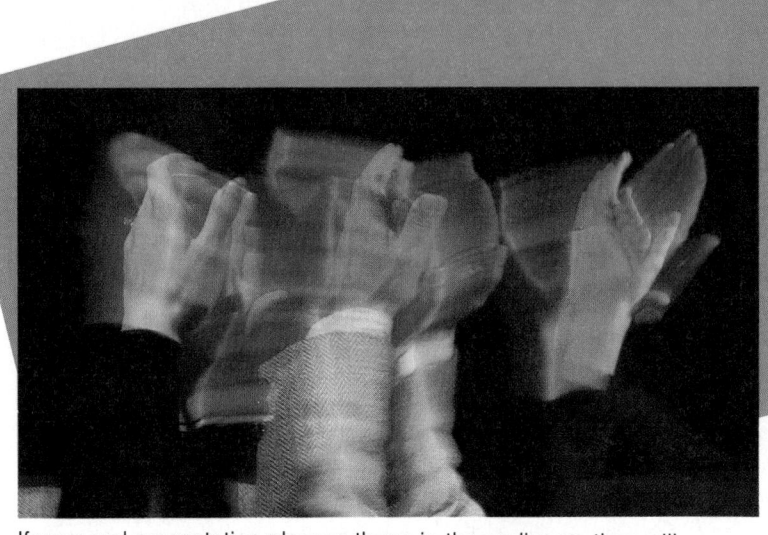

If your oral presentation pleases those in the audience, they will respond.

Drama

Like prose and poetry, drama also has some special features. The following are some of them.

Eliminating Action   In a theater, the characters' actions help to keep the audience interested. What happens when there is no action in an oral interpretation presentation? One solution is to describe the action in an introduction. Another solution is to look for a selection that does not have any important action in it. Just remember one very important thing. Once you start reading, do not stop to act out or describe any action. This also means, of course, that you should not read stage directions aloud.

Distinguishing Among Characters   Making changes in your voice to indicate many different characters is very hard. That's why it's best, at the beginning, to choose scenes with only one, two, or three characters. To indicate different characters, you can make slight changes in the pitch of your voice. You also can change your rate of speaking or use different inflections for different characters.

For example, a child's pitch might be higher than an adult's. Just make sure that the changes you make in your voice for each character remain the same throughout the whole scene. Also, be careful not to exaggerate vocal sounds. For example, a male reader with a deep voice shouldn't use a falsetto, or high-pitched, voice to read something said by a female speaker.

Another way to distinguish between characters is to use slight nonverbal cues. For example, you could make facial changes for different characters. You also could identify different characters by looking at different spots in the audience. If you do this, keep the positions of your characters fairly close. Otherwise, you will have to turn your head too quickly from side to side.

PREPARING ORAL PRESENTATIONS

In many ways, preparing an oral presentation is similar to preparing for any other public speech. If you are giving your own speech, you must write it, then practice it. When you are giving an oral presentation you must first select the material you want to present. Then you must thoroughly practice your presentation.

Condensing Selections

Sometimes you may find that a selection you want to use is too long to read in the assigned period of time. You may want to **cut,** or shorten, the selection if you can do so without changing the author's mood or meaning. Cutting prose and drama generally is easier than cutting poetry. However, long poetry sometimes can be cut without destroying the poet's rhythm or rhyme scheme.

As you decide what to cut from the selection, keep in mind that your presentation should end with the words in the selection—not with an explanation or comments. After you have finished cutting, read the selection aloud. Can it stand alone once the introduction is given? Do you need any **transitional,** or bridging, words or sentences to connect major ideas?

Writing an Introduction

An important part of all oral presentations is the introduction. The following are some things you might include in an introduction.

- Your reasons for choosing the selection.

- Why the selection will interest the audience.

- Background information on the author or the selection. This might include the author's reasons for writing it and/or information about the people or events in the selection.

Thorough preparation is a very important part of oral interpretation.

- What happened just before your scene and/or what will happen right after your scene.

- Helpful information about the characters in the scene, for example, who speaks first, to whom that person speaks, and/or reasons for the conversation.

- Definitions of terms that the audience might not know but which are important for understanding the scene.

- How the scene is similar to or different from a familiar event.

Practicing for Oral Interpretations

Practicing for oral interpretations is very much like practicing for any public speaking event. The most important thing, of course, is to practice aloud. Only then can you hear how you will sound to others. The following are some important points.

- Stay within the time limit.
- Have good eye contact with the audience.
- Maintain good volume.
- Think about what you're saying.
- Use a variety of vocal and nonverbal messages.
- Speak at a normal rate.
- Speak clearly and pronounce words correctly.

YOUR TURN

1. Study the following poem carefully. Pay particular attention to the punctuation. Practice reading the poem according to the punctuation.

A Narrow Fellow in the Grass

A narrow fellow in the grass
Occasionally rides.
You may have met him—did you not?
His notice sudden is.

The grass divides as with a comb—
A spotted shaft is seen,
And then it closes at your feet
And opens further on.

He likes a boggy acre,
A floor too cool for corn.
Yet when a child, and barefoot,
I more than once at noon

Have passed, I thought, a whiplash
Unbraiding in the sun—
When stooping to secure it
It wrinkled, and was gone.

Several of nature's people
I know, and they know me.
I feel for them a transport
Of cordiality,

But never met this fellow
Attended or alone
Without a tighter breathing,
And zero at the bone.

Emily Dickinson

2. Prepare and deliver an oral interpretation of this poem in class, or choose a favorite poem of your own.

16 CHAPTER REVIEW

Chapter Summary

Oral interpretation is a dramatic public presentation of literature. The meaning of a selection is communicated through verbal and vocal messages, not through any action. Oral interpretation, which began with storytelling, has become a form of modern communication.

You need to consider several things when choosing a selection. First, you must decide whether to read from prose, poetry, or drama. Then you should think about the time you have to prepare and present your selection. You also need to decide whether your selection will interest your audience. The next step is to understand the selection yourself. You need to consider the total meaning, mood, characterization, organization, dialogue, the author's word choices, and the use of punctuation.

There are also some special features to consider about each type of literature. Prose, for example, is told from a particular point of view. Rhythm and repetition are important to poetry. Eliminating action and distinguishing among characters are important when interpreting drama.

You may find that a selection you like is too long for the time limit. You can cut it, if doing so doesn't change the author's mood or meaning. Cutting prose and drama is generally easier than cutting poetry. After you finish cutting, read the selection aloud.

Pay attention to such things as the time limit, eye contact, and volume when you practice. When preparing an introduction, you might include such things as background information, events occurring before and after your scene, and definitions of new terms.

 **Checklist**

Practicing Oral Interpretation Skills

1. Communicate the meaning of a selection through verbal and vocal messages.

2. Choose your selection carefully.

3. Consider the interests of your audience when choosing a selection.

4. Allow enough time to prepare and present your selection.

5. Know from whose point of view a prose selection is told.

6. Study the rhythm and repetition of a poem.

7. Eliminate action and distinguish among characters for a drama selection.

8. Retain the author's mood and meaning when you cut a selection.

9. Practice reading your selection aloud before the presentation.

10. Prepare a careful introduction for the selection.

 **Vocabulary**

Define each term in a complete sentence.

climax	oral interpretation
conflict	point of view
cut	rhyme scheme
dialogue	rising action
falling action	transitional

 # Review Questions

1. Explain how an oral interpretation presentation is different from a public speech.

2. Describe how oral interpretation began.

3. Identify some things you should think about when you choose a selection for a presentation.

4. Identify the parts that make up the pattern that relates the events of a story.

5. Define dialogue. Why is dialogue important to a presentation.

6. Give two examples of ways in which punctuation can help you present a selection.

7. Define point of view. What are the most common points of view?

8. Describe how you find the rhyme scheme of a poem.

9. Tell how you can make distinctions among the voices of different characters.

10. Explain why an introduction is important in a presentation.

 # Discuss with Your Classmates

1. Discuss why it is important to know the time limit for an oral presentation *before* you begin searching for a literary selection. What else should you know before you begin your search?

2. Discuss the kinds of stories that you enjoy reading. What makes a story interesting to you? Is it a story with plenty of action? Is it a story filled with mystery and suspense? Is it a story that takes place in a faraway or unusual place? After the discussion make a list of the kinds of stories that interest the class and that could be used for oral interpretation.

3. Discuss what it is that makes poetry difficult for many readers. Identify individual poems that you like and enjoy. Why do you enjoy

these poems? How could the oral interpretation of poetry make it more enjoyable for many people?

4. Knowing what you know about life during the earliest times, discuss the role that oral interpretation played long before stories were written down. What kinds of stories do you think listeners were most interested in?

Critical Thinking

1. Analysis: Think of a story that you have read recently or think of a television show that told a story. Identify the conflict, rising action, climax, and falling action in the story.

2. Evaluation: Think of a time when you read a story to a young child or heard a story read to a young child. What oral interpretation skills did you or the reader use? How did the child react?

Activities

In-Class

1. Each student will choose a poem and prepare an oral presentation to give to the class. After each presentation, the class should discuss the mood of the poem, its rhyme scheme, and the use of repetition throughout the poem.

2. Your teacher will assign you a partner. Read the following selection. Then, with your partner, discuss how the selection can best be presented orally. Practice an oral presentation. React to each other's presentation. Each should be prepared to interpret the selection orally in class.

> I don't want to dance with him. I don't want to dance with anybody. And even if I did, it wouldn't be with him. He'd be well down among the last ten. I've seen the way he dances; it looks

like something you do on Saint Walpurgis Night. Just think, not a quarter of an hour ago, here I was sitting, feeling so sorry for the poor girl he was dancing with. And now *I'm* going to be the poor girl.

from THE WALTZ, *by Dorothy Parker*

3. Your teacher will divide the class into groups of three to five students. Within each group, each student should read aloud for one minute at his or her normal rate of speed. How many words could each student read? Then do an experiment. See if this time changes when prose, poetry, and plays are read.

Out-of-Class

1. Use your literature book or another anthology to find a story, a poem, or a play that would make a good oral presentation. Be prepared to explain why your choices would make good presentations. Also, be prepared to present your selection in class.

2. In your speech notebook write a short, short story of your own. Decide on a particular point of view and include some dialogue. Then write an introduction for your story and prepare it for an oral presentation of three to five minutes.

3. Find a prose selection or narrative poem that is told from an objective point of view. You have only two minutes to present the selection. Cut the selection to make it fit the time limit. Then prepare an introduction for it. Present your introduction and selection in class.

Chapter Project

During a class discussion, talk about scenes in plays that you have read that would be suitable for an oral interpretation. As a class, decide upon the scene and choose an excerpt from it that you believe would be most suitable for an oral presentation.

Your teacher will divide the class into groups of three or four. Using the information on pages 329-331, each group should decide how to prepare this excerpt for an oral presentation. How could you distinguish between the two characters? What will you do about the stage directions?

After each group has decided on the best way to present the selection orally, one member should be selected to present the selection. After all groups have made an oral presentation, you will discuss in class the different approaches and techniques that were used.

CHAPTER 17 Group Interpretation

David, Leslie, and Sarah are presenting part of a novel. As they begin, David thinks . . .

"I've got the right scene in my script.

I'll stoop over a little to show that my character is sick.

Then I'll lower my head to show that he is sad."

Have *you* ever presented a story or any other kind of literature with a group? How did you dramatize your part?

In this chapter, you will read about:

- the differences among various forms of group interpretation
- how to prepare for and perform in a composite recital
- how to prepare and perform choral speaking
- how to prepare for and perform in a Readers' Theater presentation

In the last chapter you learned how one person can present a piece of literature. Much literature, however, can't be handled this way. It's too complex. For example, how can one person make clear distinctions among the voices of several characters? There's a simple solution. Several people may present this kind of literature. Such a presentation, when two or more people present the same or different selections, is called **group interpretation.**

ADVANTAGES OF GROUP INTERPRETATION

The following are the four main advantages of group interpretation.

- Often people can understand a piece of literature more easily when it's read aloud.
- The readers learn to work together. They must work closely like the various instruments in an orchestra.
- Group interpretation is practical. It emphasizes voices and movement. Scenery and costumes are not necessary. As a result, presentations can be given almost anywhere.
- Group interpretation is very flexible. It has various forms. Also, there is limitless material for group interpretation.

COMPOSITE RECITAL

Composite recital is a form of group interpretation in which two or more people read various pieces of literature. All pieces, however, must be based on a theme, an author, or an event. For example, a

A composite recital might feature works by the American author Langston Hughes.

presentation might feature works of the American author Langston Hughes. The recital might include material from his various works. It might include his autobiography *The Big Sea* and his novel *Not without Laughter*. It might also include one or more of his poems. The readers could present different selections or parts of only one selection. Or, they could present some of both.

Usually someone gives an introduction before or after the first reading. The introduction tells the audience the subject of the presentation. Then someone states the title and author of each new reading. This has two purposes. It identifies each selection and shows when a new piece begins. Once in a while, a narrator also says something between the readings to link them together.

The readers usually perform on a stage and face the audience. They can stand, or sit on chairs or high stools. Each reader holds a script throughout the recital. The scripts should be held low so that the audience can see the readers' faces.

CHORAL SPEAKING

The oldest form of group interpretation is **choral speaking.** For centuries it has been used in religious ceremonies. In ancient Greece, it grew into an art form. Later modern drama developed out of it.

In choral speaking, the readers' goal is to blend their voices together to produce a **group voice.** Because of this, only certain literature can be used. It must have a very regular beat. Poetry, for example, is often used because people can follow its rhythm.

Variations of Choral Speaking

The following are some of the ways choral speaking can be presented.

1. Each person reads a different line.
2. One person reads a line. Then another reader joins in for the next line. This continues until everyone has joined in.
3. One person or one group reads a line. Then another person or group responds to that line. This statement-response pattern continues for the whole reading. This variation is used in two situations. It is used when the reading includes two people talking. It is also used when the reading includes questions and answers. The following is an example.

Group 1: What is wrong if no one sings again?
Group 2: Surely you must know. The world would end.

4. One person has solo parts. The rest of the group supports the soloist. The whole group may be broken up into smaller groups. These groups are similar to duets, trios, or quartets in music. These smaller groups read by themselves, or they might be joined by other groups. The following is an example.

Solo: The Sky is low—The Clouds are mean.
Group 1: A Travelling Flake of Snow
Group 2: Across a Barn or through a Rut
Groups 1 & 2: Debates if it will go—
Solo: A Narrow Wind complains all Day
Solo: How some one treated him
Groups 1 & 2: Nature, like Us is sometimes caught
Groups 1 & 2: Without her Diadem.

"The Sky Is Low" *by Emily Dickinson*

5. Small groups support each other or single readers. A director, therefore, can use single voices or combinations of voices. No set format is followed. This variation gives the greatest flexibility.

6. Everyone speaks together at the same time.

Use of Scripts

Every reader has a copy of all the literature in a presentation. The scripts should be kept in notebooks. They are easier to use than sheets of paper. Notebooks also keep the selections in order —especially if they are dropped.

Scripts should be printed or typed double spaced—line by line. Each line should be numbered on the left side of the page. When lines are assigned, readers should circle those line numbers. Sometimes only parts of lines are assigned. In such cases, those partial lines should be underlined. Once in a while, a director gives some special instructions on how to read a line. These instructions should be written in the right margin near the line.

Here are four poems that are suitable for choral speaking. Each is presented in script form with the lines numbered consecutively to the left.

In this poem, Deborah Austin describes a war. It is a serious war that is always going on between humans and dandelions. Who do you think will win?

DANDELIONS

1   under cover of night and rain
2   the troops took over.
3   waking to total war in beleaguered houses
4   over breakfast we faced the batteries
5   marshalled by wall and stone, deployed
6   with a master strategy no one had suspected
7   and now all
8   firing

9   pow

10   all day, all yesterday
11   and all today
12   the barrage continued
13   deafening sight.
14   reeling now, eyes ringing from noise, from walking
15   gingerly over the mined lawns

Who will win the battle between humans and dandelions?

16 exploded at every second
17 rocked back by the starshellfire
18 concussion of gold on green
19 bringing battle-fatigue
20 pow by lionface firefur pow by
21 goldburst shellshock pow by
22 whoosh splat splinteryellow pow by
23 pow by pow
24 tomorrow smoke drifts up
25 from the wrecked battalions,
26 all the ammunition, firegold fury, gone.

27 smoke
28 drifts
29 thistle-brown
30 over the war-zone, only
31 here and there, in the shade by the

32 peartree
33 pow in the crack by the
34 curbstone pow and back of the
35 ashcan, lonely

36   guerrilla snipers, hoarding
37   their fire shrewdly

38   never

39   pow

40   surrender

In the next poem, the author Langston Hughes has two dreams. How are they different? There is faster action in the second dream. What do you think this means?

DREAM VARIATIONS

1   To fling my arms wide
2   In some place of the sun,
3   To whirl and to dance
4   Till the white day is done.
5   Then rest at cool evening
6   Beneath a tall tree
7   While night comes on gently,
8   Dark like me—
9   That is my dream!

10   To fling my arms wide
11   In the face of the sun,
12   Dance! Whirl! Whirl!
13   Till the quick day is done.
14   Rest at pale evening . . .
15   A tall, slim tree . . .
16   Night coming tenderly
17   Black like me.

The following is a Tewa Indian prayer.

SONG OF THE SKY LOOM

1   Oh our Mother the Earth, oh our Father the Sky,
2   Your children are we, and with tired backs
3   We bring you the gifts that you love.

4   Then weave for us a garment of brightness;

5   May the warp be the white light of morning,
6   May the weft be the red light of evening.
7   May the fringes be the falling rain,
8   May the border be the standing rainbow.

WHEN VOICES CREATED A WORLD OF ENTERTAINMENT

Unlike any form of communication before, radio made it possible for news and entertainment to flash across the country instantly. The voice alone created this form of entertainment that attracted millions of listeners nationwide.

From about 1925 to 1950, radio was the center of family listening. People gathered around their Atwater Kent and other vintage radios to tune in to a Burns and Allen comedy, an action-packed adventure with *The Shadow,* or music by Duke Ellington, Benny Goodman, Glenn Miller, or the Dorsey Brothers. There were many other programs to choose from as well.

What attracted the listeners? Some think interest was due to a perfect sense of timing. The audience couldn't watch the performers or announcers. But, through the voices of the performers, the listeners were able to imagine characters and events. This imagination, combined with the talent and skill of the performers, created a perfect match. Both speaker and listener truly wanted to believe in the unseen situation.

Not only did every household have a wide range of shows to enjoy, but listeners also were so caught up in programs that unbelievable events occurred. Consider the *War of the Worlds* broadcast. On October 30, 1938, Orson Welles presented a program about an invasion from Mars. Though cautioned that the show was fiction, many listeners panicked.

Possibly the most tell-tale example of the power of the voice during that special quarter of a century is the *Amos and Andy* show. It captured the heart of all America. The serial was so popular that movie theaters often stopped the film from 7:00 to 7:15 P.M. so patrons could listen to the latest episode.

Through voices alone, radio involved the listeners in the broadcasts almost as much as the professionals.

Where is the speaker in the following poem by Philip Booth?
How does he make you feel that the train is gaining speed?

CROSSING

1   STOP   LOOK   LISTEN
2   as gate stripes swing down,
3   count the cars hauling distance
4   upgrade through town:
5   warning whistle, bellclang,
6   engine eating steam,
7   engineer waving
8   a fast-freight dream:
9   B&M boxcar,
10   boxcar again,
11   Frisco gondola,
12 **eight, nine, ten,**
13   Erie and Wabash,
14   Seaboard, U.P.,
15   Pennsy tankcar,
16 **twenty-two, three**
17   Phoebe Snow, B&O,
18 **thirty-four, five**
19   Santa Fe cattle
20   shipped alive
21   red cars, yellow cars,
22   orange cars, black,

23   Youngstown steel
24   down to Mobile
25   on Rock Island track,
26 **fifty-nine, sixty**
27 hoppers of coke,
28   Anaconda copper,
29   hotbox smoke,
30 **eighty-eight,**
31 red-ball freight,
32   Rio Grande,
33   Nickel Plate,
34   Hiawatha,
35   Lackawanna,
36   rolling fast
37   and loose,
38 **ninety-seven,**
39 coal car,
40   boxcar,
41   CABOOSE!

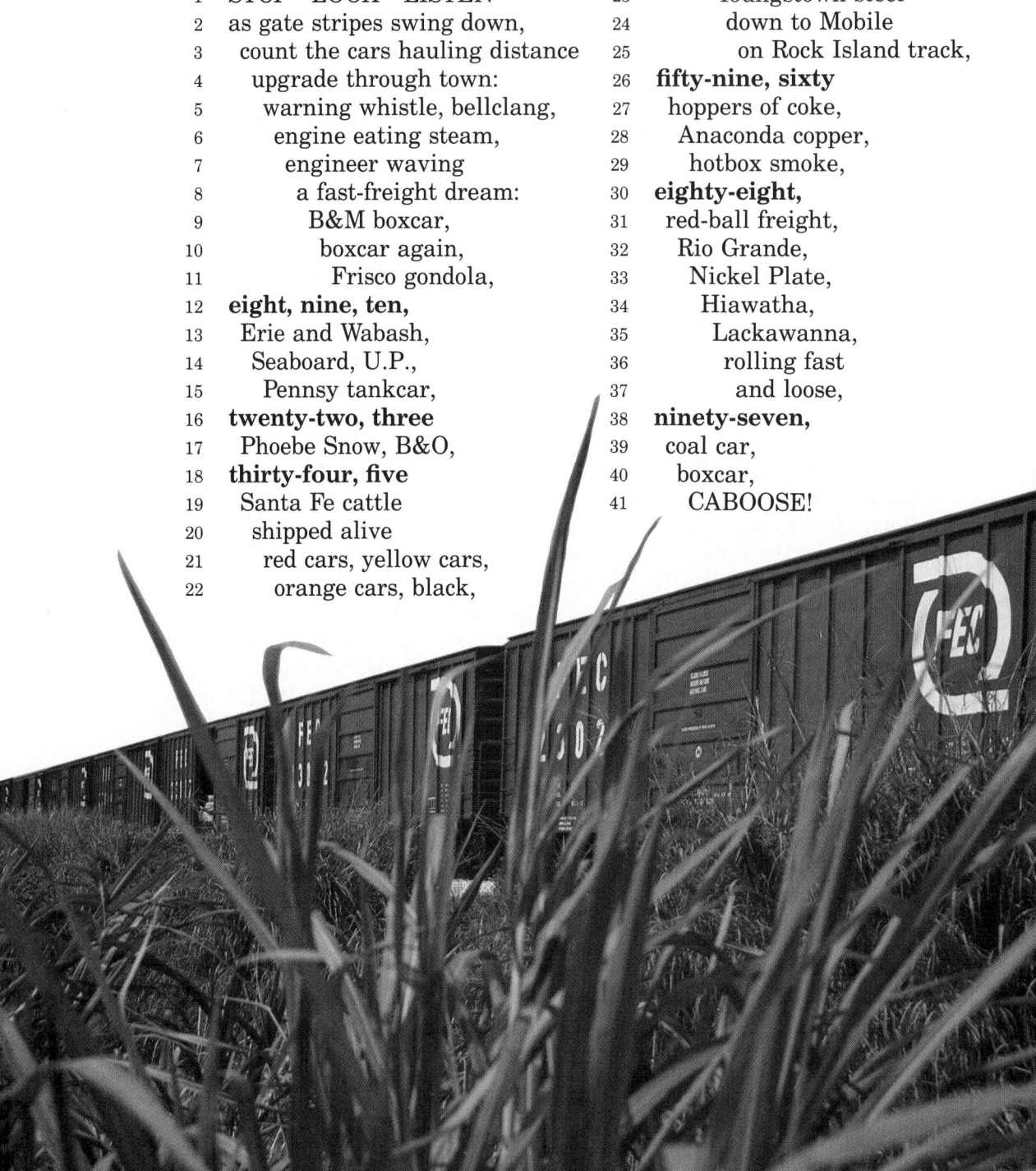

Special Features

The following are some special features that are important to choral speaking.

Precision   Choral speaking requires great precision. Readers must start and stop at the same time. To do this, they must practice often. If poetry is used, readers can get some help from the rhythm of the poem. Sometimes readers follow the beat by tapping their feet or clapping their hands. Readers must also speak clearly and accurately. Otherwise, their voices will sound blurred or fuzzy.

Movement   There is little movement during choral speaking. Most of the time readers just stand in groups. However, there may be some movement that applies to the selection. This movement is usually done by all the readers together. The following are some examples.

- jumping together
- bending from the waist
- taking a step
- raising one hand
- turning the head in different directions
- swaying from side to side
- turning completely around

Placement   Where readers stand is very important. Sometimes groups are arranged by pitch, vocal quality, or volume. For example, people with strong voices stand in the back. People with soft voices stand near the front. Soloists usually stand on the edge of their group. Then when their turn comes, they can step forward. All the groups are usually fairly close together. This is necessary so that they can hear each other.

Return to the poems on pages 342-347. Read each poem carefully, and think about the structure and meaning of each. Then prepare to read each poem aloud in groups. Your teacher will work with you to assign parts. As you prepare each poem, keep the following in mind.

1. "Dandelions" Notice how the poet uses word-sounds like *pow, whoosh,* and *splat.* How can you emphasize these words in your reading?

2. "Dream Variations" How could you read the second stanza to show the faster action it contains?

3. "Song of the Sky Loom" Since this is a prayer, would you read it differently than if it were a poem?

4. "Crossing" How can you express the speed that the train is gaining?

READERS' THEATER

Readers' Theater is another form of group interpretation. In this form two or more readers present literature in a dramatic way. It is similar to a play, but there is little action and no scenery or costumes. All the meaning comes from the words and the way the words are said.

Use of Suggestion

When you go to the theater, you see real scenery and props. In Readers' Theater these things are only suggested. People in the audience must picture these things in their minds.

Suppose, for example, that a scene from a Readers' Theater presentation includes a girl petting her dog. There is no dog on the stage. Through pantomime and the girl's words, however, everyone "sees" a dog. Of course, different people in the audience will picture different dogs. One might see a collie; another might see a terrier.

Actors in a reader's theater often need to use pantomime to help the audience "see" the scene.

Therefore, everyone does not see exactly the same thing during a Readers' Theater presentation.

Movement   In some Readers' Theater presentations, readers do some of the same things regular actors do. They look at each other, interact, and walk about the stage. At other times, however, the readers sit or stand in one place. Any gestures they use are stylized. For example, suppose a script called for two characters to turn cartwheels. To suggest this, the readers would simply move their arms as if they were turning cartwheels. Their hands, of course, would never touch the floor.

Leaving or entering might also be suggested. Characters leaving the stage, for example, could turn their backs to the audience. Characters entering the stage could turn around and face the audience.

Emotion   Emotions can also be suggested. To show disgust, for example, characters could put their hands on their hips. Anger could be suggested by shaking clenched fists. Characters could suggest horror by covering their eyes. This is one of the hardest parts of Readers' Theater. What expressions and movements can you use to suggest what is really happening? Just remember that no movement should ever distract the audience from the words.

Costumes   Usually characters do not wear costumes or make-up. An older character, however, could be given some gray hair or a few facial lines to suggest age. Sometimes a single piece of clothing can also suggest a whole outfit. For example, a reader might wear a hat, a white shirt and a necktie, or a pair of cowboy boots. From these clues, then, the people in the audience must imagine the other parts of the costume.

Use of Plays

Whole plays or parts of plays are often used for Readers' Theater. Plays work well because thoughts and feelings are often explained by the characters. This makes it easy for audiences to understand what is happening.

There is, however, one disadvantage to plays. An action or a movement might be an important clue to the meaning of the play. Without it, the audience won't understand the play. Readers can solve this problem in one of two ways. They can pantomime the action, or they can add words to the script. Suppose, for example, that a script calls for Paul to stand in a doorway. While he is standing there, he is listening to a radio. The following is the original script for this scene.

Paul: That's my favorite song.
Karen: I know.
Paul: Too bad Cindy isn't here. She likes it too.
Karen: Come and sit down. She won't get here any faster if you watch for her.

With only these words, people in the audience wouldn't know whether Paul is listening to a record or a radio. They also would have no idea where Paul is standing. However, with just a few words added to Karen's part, the audience would be able to picture the scene clearly. The following is the revised script.

Paul: That's my favorite song.
Karen: I know. *I can hear your radio.*
Paul: Too bad Cindy isn't here. She likes it too.
Karen: Come *away from the door* and sit down. She won't get here any faster if you watch for her.

In Readers' Theater two or more readers present literature in a dramatic way.

In class presentations, someone should introduce a scene, describe the setting, and name the characters. Some background information might be given. In a formal presentation, all this information would be printed in a program.

MATERIAL FOR READERS' THEATER

Finding material for Readers' Theater is easy. You can use most poems, myths, legends, and folktales. Parts of many short stories, plays, and novels also work well. Following are some helpful suggestions when you're looking for a selection for Readers' Theater.

- Does it build to a climax?
- How much dialogue does it have? Is there enough to keep the presentation interesting?
- Can the background be explained easily?
- Are all the speaking parts about equal?
- Can it be presented within the time limit?
- Will the audience understand it?

Here are two examples of selections that are suitable for Readers' Theater. As you read each, think about how you would stage a formal presentation of the selection.

The following is part of a short story by O. Henry. Sam and Bill have kidnapped a boy for ransom. Unfortunately, their plan backfires on them. The boy gives them a lot of trouble, and his parents won't pay the ransom. In fact, they make the kidnappers pay them to take the boy back!

from THE RANSOM OF RED CHIEF

I addressed this letter to Dorset, and put it in my pocket. As I was about to start, the kid comes up to me and says:

"Aw, Snake-eye, you said I could play the Black Scout while you was gone."

"Play it, of course," says I. "Mr. Bill will play it with you. What kind of a game is it?" 5

"I'm the Black Scout," says Red Chief, "and I have to ride to the stockade to warn the settlers that the Indians are coming. I'm tired of playing Indian myself. I want to be the Black Scout." 10

"All right," says I. "It sounds harmless to me. I guess Mr. Bill will help you foil the pesky savages."

"What am I to do?" asks Bill, looking at the kid suspiciously.

"You are the hoss," says Black Scout. "Get down on your 15 hands and knees. How can I ride to the stockade without a hoss?"

"You'd better keep him interested," said I, "till we get the scheme going. Loosen up."

Bill gets down on his all fours, and a look comes in his 20 eye like a rabbit's when you catch it in a trap.

"How far is it to the stockade, kid?" he asks, in a husky manner of voice.

"Ninety miles," says the Black Scout. "And you have to hump yourself to get there on time. Whoa, now!" 25

The Black Scout jumps on Bill's back and digs his heels in his sides.

"For heaven's sake," says Bill, "hurry back, Sam, as soon as you can. I wish we hadn't made the ransom more than a thousand. Say, you quit kicking me or I'll get up and warm you good."

Following is part of a play by Arthur Hailey. It takes place on a flight from Winnipeg to Vancouver. Fish and meat had been served for dinner. Anyone who ate the fish became deathly ill from food poisoning. Unfortunately, the pilot and the first officer ate the fish, and there is no one to fly the plane. Mr. Spencer eventually takes the controls even though he hasn't flown a plane for many years. With the help of Mr. Treleaven and Mr. Burdick, two men on the ground, Mr. Spencer lands the plane safely.

from FLIGHT INTO DANGER

Treleaven: All right, George. Continue to approach at two thousand feet on your present heading and wait for instructions. We'll let you know the runway to use at the last minute, because the wind is shifting. Don't forget, we want you to do at least one dummy run, and then go round again so you'll have practice in making the landing approach. Over. 5

Spencer: I'll take it, Janet. *(Into mike)* No dice, Vancouver. We're coming straight in and the first time is "it." Dr. Baird is here beside me. He reports two of the passengers 10

Would you be able to fly this plane?

and the First Officer are in critical condition, and we must land in the next few minutes. The doctor asks that you have stomach pumps and oxygen equipment ready. Over.

Burdick: He mustn't! We need time!

Treleaven: It's his decision. By all the rules he's in com-   15
mand of the airplane. *(Into mike)* 714, your message is understood. Good luck to us all. . . .

Spencer: Tell them we're at one thousand feet and level-ing off.

Stewardess: *(into mike)* Vancouver Tower. We are now at   20
one thousand feet and leveling off. Over. . . .

Treleaven: Watch your height! Don't make that turn so steep! Watch your height! More throttle! . . . He can't fly the bloody thing! Of couse he can't fly it! You're watching fifty people going to their deaths!   25

Burdick: *(shouting)* Keep talking to him! Keep talking! Tell him what to do!

Treleaven: *(urgently, into mike)* Spencer, you can't come straight in! You've got to do some circuits, and practice that approach. You've enough fuel left for three hours'   30
flying. Stay up, man! Stay up!

Spencer: Give it to me! *(Taking the mike. Then tensely)* Listen, down there! I'm coming in! Do you hear me? . . . I'm coming in. There are people up here who'll die in less than an hour, never mind three. I may bend your precious airplane a bit, but I'll get it down. Now, get on with the landing check. I'm putting the gear down now. *(To the Stewardess)* Wheels down, Janet! 35

Stewardess: *(looks out of window, then back to Spencer)* Wheels down and three green lights.

Burdick: He may not be able to fly, but he's sure got guts.

YOUR TURN ///////////

1. The class should divide itself in half. One half should work with the selection taken from "The Ransom of Red Chief." The other half should work with the selection from *Flight into Danger*. Each group should prepare a Readers' Theater presentation of the selection.

2. Your teacher will divide the class into groups of three or four students. Each group should prepare a Readers' Theater presentation. The presentation should include a 3- to 5-minute scene from a play, novel, or short story. It should have parts for everyone in the group. The readers may carry scripts as they move around. If time permits, each group present its selection to the class.

17 CHAPTER REVIEW

 ## Chapter Summary

Group interpretation is oral interpretation presented by a group. One form of group interpretation is composite recital. This form includes several pieces that are based on a theme, an author, or an event. The oldest form of group interpretation is choral speaking. This form uses various voice combinations.

Readers' Theater is another form of group interpretation. It is a dramatic presentation of literature. Very little action, however, is used. The emphasis is on the words and how they are said. The selections for Readers' Theater can be poems, myths, legends, folktales, and parts of stories, plays, and novels.

 ## Checklist

Practicing Group Interpretation Skills

1. Remember that selections for a composite recital must be based on a theme, an author, or an event.

2. Strive for a group voice during choral speaking presentations.

3. Be sure to practice often before a choral speaking presentation to achieve group precision.

4. Use movement sparingly during a choral speaking presentation.

5. Remember that in Reader's Theater there must be enough dialogue to keep the presentation interesting.

6. Be certain that your selection for Reader's Theater can be presented within the time limit.

7. Remember that in Readers' Theater the meaning of the selection comes from the words and the way the words are said.

Vocabulary

Define each term in a complete sentence.

choral speaking   group voice

composite recital   Readers' Theater

group interpretation

Review Questions

1. Name at least three advantages of group interpretation.

2. Define the term *composite recital.*

3. Describe the purposes of the introduction to a composite recital.

4. Explain what is unusual about the selections for composite recital.

5. Identify the kind of literature that is usually presented in choral speaking. Explain your answer.

6. Name three different variations of choral speaking.

7. Explain the role of movement in choral speaking.

8. Identify the main difference between choral speaking and Readers' Theater.

9. Describe how suggestion is used in Readers' Theater.

10. Describe how a reader could suggest an exit and an entrance in Readers' Theater.

11. Explain how a reader could suggest a complete costume in Readers' Theater.

12. Name some things you should think about when choosing material for Readers' Theater.

Discuss with Your Classmates

1. Discuss the role of the narrator in a composite recital.

2. Discuss the importance of a group voice in choral speaking. What is meant by a group voice? How can it be achieved?

3. Analyze the effect of precision on choral speaking? Why is it important?

4. Discuss different ways in which members of a Readers' Theater might suggest the idea of props and scenery to the audience. How might they suggest action?

Critical Thinking

1. **Comprehension:** Explain the differences between composite recital, choral speaking, and Readers' Theater. Discuss what types of literary selections are appropriate for each form of group interpretation.

2. **Synthesis:** Think of a short poem that you believe is most appropriate for choral speaking. Make a script for the poem. Determine the number of speakers needed. In the script include whatever special instructions readers will need.

Activities

In-Class

1. Your teacher will assign you a partner. With your partner, decide on a theme, an author, or an event that you think would be appropriate for a composite recital. Plan how you would present the selections, including what to say in the introduction and what role the narrator would play. Be prepared to discuss your plan in class.

2. Your teacher will divide the class into groups of four or five students. Each group should review the variations for choral speaking on page 341. Then each member of the group should choose a selection that would be appropriate for choral speaking. The group will discuss what method would be best for presenting each selection.

Out-of-Class

1. Plan a 5- to 6-minute composite recital. Select a theme, an author, or an event for your presentation that allows you to include different types of literature. You might include, for example, a poem and an excerpt from a play by Shakespeare; or a diary entry, a short story excerpt, and a poem about an historical event. Write the sentences that would link the selections. Keep your work in your speech notebook.

2. Choose an appropriate selection for a choral speaking presentation. Plan its presentation. What movement would you include? Where would you place the members? Develop your script in your speech notebook and explain your plan in class.

3. Make a list of four selections that would be good for Readers' Theater. Use your literature book or other anthologies. Make sure the selections follow the suggestions on page 351.

Chapter Project

Each class member should find two poems that take two minutes or less to read aloud. Be sure that both poems have a strong beat.

Each person will read his or her poems aloud to the class. When everyone has recited, the class will choose the three best poems. Your teacher will then divide the class into three groups and assign a poem to each group.

Each group should prepare a choral speaking presentation to give to the class. After all the presentations, the class will discuss how the presentations were similar and how they were different. What was particularly good about each one? What might the group have done to improve the presentation?

THEATER AND THE MEDIA

361

CHAPTER 18 Informal Theater

Linda and Joanne stopped in the park to watch a pantomime performance. These are some of Joanne's thoughts as she watches.

"He really looks as if he's planting flowers.

It's easy to imagine how the flowers look and smell.

All his movements are so exact."

Have *you* ever done a pantomime? How did you plan and practice your pantomime?

In this chapter, you will read about:

- developing awareness of your senses
- using your imagination to respond spontaneously with your mind, body, or voice
- pantomiming an action, character, object, emotion, or event
- improvising scenes

What does theater have to do with the study of communication? The answer is simple. Theater *is* communication. It works with verbal, vocal, and nonverbal messages. These messages communicate ideas, thoughts, and feelings to people. This definition applies to drama that is performed on a stage, or formal theater. It also applies to informal theater. Informal theater is sometimes called creative dramatics, improvisational drama, or theater games. All these names refer to using the imagination to make on-the-spot, or spontaneous, choices.

PURPOSES OF INFORMAL THEATER

One purpose of informal theater is to make people more aware of their senses. People don't always notice and respond to everything around them. Two people can observe the same people or events and describe them differently. For example, two different people get gasoline at the same station. Later, one person describes the attendant as short with dark eyes and a medium build. The other person describes the same attendant as about 5′8″, 170 pounds, with green eyes. Unfortunately, people don't always think of using their senses. They may only think about it when they encounter new or unusual people, things, or events. Informal theater, however, helps people use their senses in *all* situations.

In addition, people in informal theater use their imaginations to go beyond the details of the real world. For example, think about what happens when you watch a scary movie. A man walks down a long, dark hallway. Eerie music plays in the background. Suddenly a door opens, and a hand reaches out. The man jumps back in shock. What do you do? You probably react physically, too. You might pull away or jump. Why? You were safe; you were not in the long, dark hallway. Those things probably happened because you put yourself in the man's place. By using your imagination, you responded as if you were experiencing the same event.

In informal theater, you use your imagination to respond to different situations. You respond with your mind, body, and/or voice. For example, you might be told to imagine the following situations.

- What would happen if you could walk on clouds?

- How would people from another planet react to a big city? A football game? A rodeo?

- What would you do if you were the only survivor of a shipwreck off the coast of Alaska?

In each of these cases, you would not be able to plan all the things you would say and do. You would have to respond spontaneously, using your imagination. Informal theater helps people use their imaginations to respond creatively.

FEEDBACK

After each session of informal theater, people share their feelings, thoughts, and reactions. They do *not* decide who made the best or most creative responses. They ask questions such as the following.

- What were you thinking about as you made the sound of the plane landing in the desert?

- You didn't know what your partner was going to do. How did you know when to stop moving and start talking?

- What did the cheese you were eating smell like?

- How did it feel to be caught in a rainstorm?

During feedback sessions, people find out what others were thinking about and why they acted in certain ways. They might also apply what they saw to real situations. For example, they might make comments like the following.

- She looked exactly the way I feel when I have to clean up the kitchen and everyone else is watching television.

- You sounded just like my brother when he is caught doing something wrong. Your voice shook a little. Did you do that on purpose?

Pantomime uses only nonverbal messages. Performers use gestures, facial expressions, and movements to convey meaning.

During feedback sessions, people often ask *Why* did you do _____? and *How* did you do _____? Sometimes, performers can't answer these questions. They performed spontaneously; they didn't think about it. Or, they may not even have been aware that they did something. These sessions help everyone understand why they did or said certain things. Informal theater trains people to make genuine responses in all kinds of theater—and in life, too.

PANTOMIME

Pantomime is a dramatic form of communication that uses only nonverbal messages. Performers use only gestures, facial expressions, and movements to convey meanings. In pantomime, performers must think about the fine points of nonverbal communication. The sense of touch—weight, texture, size, shape—becomes very important. Small movements, such as a wink, and large movements, such as jumping, are also important in pantomime.

Performers of pantomime must also show emotions. For example, imagine you are pantomiming a teenager hurrying to clean up the house before his or her parents get home. You could pantomime such things as picking up magazines and dishes. However, you would also have to show nervousness or tension.

Accuracy

To make a pantomime believable, you must be careful with details. They must be correct and consistent. For example, imagine that you pantomime a scene in which you open a door, go inside, and shut the door. Then you discover that you dropped something outside. You open the door again and go out to get what you dropped. You must not forget which way the door opens and closes. You cannot open the door *into* the room when you come in, and open the door *out* onto the porch when you go out.

In pantomime, you must also show the weight of objects. For example, you must know how to suggest that a large box you are carrying is heavy. If you have trouble with this, slow down the action of your pantomime during practice. When you can imitate the action correctly, speed up the pantomime gradually.

Preparation

The best way to begin preparing a pantomime is to observe people doing what you want to imitate. Watch how they move. Notice their facial expressions and how they use their bodies. Next, do the thing yourself by imitating their actions. As you do this, think about how *your* body moves. Notice which muscles pull, how you bend, and which way you turn. Practice in front of a mirror to see what you look like. Make your movements and gestures large enough to be seen and understood.

When you know the physical movements of your pantomime, think of a situation for your action. Why are you doing this? What time of day is it? How do you feel? What are you thinking about? Can you add something to make the pantomime more interesting? For example, suppose you are pantomiming sewing a button on a shirt. You might add something such as breaking the thread again and again or pricking your finger with the needle. These actions would make your pantomime more interesting and dramatic. Finally, think about any emotions or thoughts that would affect your pantomime.

Small talk is a good way to introduce yourself informally.

Adding Characters

You may begin a pantomime by yourself or with others. If you begin alone, others may join you as the pantomime progresses. Or, others can be added even after the pantomime is over. For example, you might pantomime a teenager shooting baskets with a friend. When the pantomime is over, someone might ask, "Who was your friend?" At this point, your teacher might suggest that someone take the part of your friend. Then the two of you could "replay" the pantomime. Others can be added by having some more friends join in the game.

Pantomimed characters do not always have to be people. You can pantomime animals or objects. You might, for example, pantomime a chair that suffers every time someone sits down. Pantomiming objects helps performers learn to express the physical traits of these objects.

Mimes convey a sense of rhythm by means of gestures and facial expressions.

Adding Sounds and Rhythms

Remember, there are no spoken messages in pantomime. However, you can add sounds to pantomimes after you present them silently. For example, imagine that you want to show a huge machine with many moving parts. Each part makes its own unique noise. However, the total machine has the same rhythmical pattern once it starts. To show this, a performer might raise one arm, make a squeak, and turn. He or she could then make another turn and drop the arm with another squeak. By these actions, the performer has set the basic rhythm of the machine. Then other parts could be added— all with different motions and noises—but all must follow the same basic rhythm. Eventually, you would be showing a complicated machine in action.

At other times, performers can let a certain rhythm control their actions. For example, someone could be a bus driver. This person could use different sounds to show starts, stops, bumps, and smooth roads. Performers on the bus would respond to these sounds. For example, a woman with a basket of eggs would be alert to bumps and sudden stops. A man sleeping with his head against the window would feel many vibrations. Each person might do something different, but all their actions would be affected by the rhythm of the bus.

MAKING THE INVISIBLE VISIBLE

Walking against an unseen wind, chasing an invisible butterfly with an invisible net, tugging on an imaginary rope—these are some of the classic mime movements of the great pantomimist Marcel Marceau. He calls the art of pantomime "making the invisible visible." While pantomime is nearly 2,000 years old, Marceau has created a whole new style of modern pantomime. He uses the traditions of the past and ideas from the world around him to create his acts and characters.

One of Marceau's most famous creations is Bip, the lovable, white-faced clown. Bip is a character who wears bell-bottomed trousers, a striped sailor shirt, and a battered top hat decorated with a single flower. Marceau's ideas for Bip came from several different places. When he was starting out as a mime, Marceau had played the pantomime character known as Harlequin. (Harlequin is a character in sixteenth-century Italian comedy who runs about the stage and generally acts like a clown.) Marceau drew upon his knowledge of Harlequin when developing Bip, his twentieth-century clown.

In addition to Harlequin, another and more important influ-ence in the creation of Bip came from Charlie Chaplin, the famous comedian of silent films. Marceau had always been a fan of Chaplin's character, the baggy-trousered tramp. Much of Chaplin's tramp can be seen in Bip. Like Chaplin's character, Bip is often defeated by life, although he wins sometimes too. In either case, Marceau uses his art not just to make us laugh, but to make us see and understand how Bip feels.

Like any creative artist, Marceau uses ideas and influences from the world around him. He combines these ideas with the 2,000-year-old tradition of pantomime to create something totally new. His careful observation, practice, and creative combination of old elements are part of the reason for Marceau's success as a mime.

1. Read the following situations. Your teacher will call on different students to explain what they think would happen in each situation. Pantomime what would take place in each situation.

    a. Two trucks collide on a highway just before rush hour. No one is hurt, but their loads are scattered over the highway. One load is molasses; the other load is 2,000 live chickens.

    b. While you are walking to school, a beautiful blue moth lands on your arm. It is followed by dozens and dozens more.

2. Your teacher will divide the class into groups of five to seven students. Discuss all the actions involved in pantomiming each of the following situations. Each member of the group will practice one of these activities.

    a. breaking an egg and separating the white from the yolk

    b. stifling a sneeze while carrying a stack of dishes

    c. eating a frozen yogurt cone on a hot day

    d. trying to get a granola bar out of a broken vending machine

IMPROVISATIONS

Improvisations are pantomimes with verbal and vocal messages. They are different, however, from formal theater. Improvisations do not use scripts, even though they are based on a given event or situation. The performers choose their words and actions spontaneously. Because of this, performers must listen and watch each other carefully so that they respond correctly.

Following are three important dramatic elements that are used in improvisations. Each of these should be evaluated after an improvisation.

Conflict

A conflict is a problem between two opposing forces. In literature, for example, there are several types of conflicts. These conflicts may involve a person against self, a person against another person, or a person against nature. Drama presents conflicts and then tries to find solutions.

A conflict is a problem between two opposing forces.

Dialogue

Dialogue is the communication among characters or between the characters and the audience. Most dialogue happens onstage and is "overheard" by the audience. **Monologues** are speeches in which one character thinks aloud and is overheard by the audience. Sometimes a character may speak directly to an audience.

Informal theater does not use scripts or rules that tell characters when to speak. When you develop dialogue for an improvisation, remember that it should suit the characters. Appropriate dialogue makes characters believable.

Characterization

The element of drama that establishes the traits of each character is called **characterization.** Because an improvisation is unplanned, you cannot spend much time working out the details of characters. You must quickly find reasons for a character's feelings or actions. For example, something must happen to explain why a character is angry. Perhaps his or her car broke down or someone broke a favorite record.

Characters in informal theater must also be active. In daily life, people don't usually sit still for very long. They move in their seats, handle things, and cough or clear their throats. Likewise, characters must be active, alert, and responsive to be believable.

In both formal and informal theater, you must never "break character." In other words, you should not respond to something as yourself. For example, suppose something funny happens in the audience. *You* may feel like laughing, but you must stay in your role. While performing, you must do only what your character would do.

INFORMAL THEATER EXERCISES

There are many types of activities done in informal theater. Following are two different exercises.

Mirror Exercises

The mirror exercise is often used in informal theater. It is usually done in pantomime, but it may also include sound. One person faces the other and begins an action in slow motion. The second person duplicates the action. Both people synchronize their movements so that observers cannot tell who is the leader and who is the mirror image. The movements should be done slowly at first—until both people get used to each other.

The shadow image is similar to the mirror image. In this exercise, one person does a pantomime or improvisation. Another person stands behind or to the side of that person and imitates the movements.

Interviewing

Interviewing is another informal theater exercise. It tests each person's ability to hold a characterization beyond an improvisation. When performers finish a scene, they answer questions from the audience. However, they answer these questions as their characters, not as themselves. Members of the audience ask questions to get information that was *not* given in the improvisation. After gathering this information, the group improvises a new situation.

THE DIRECTOR OF INFORMAL THEATER

A director of informal theater helps students develop their imaginations. The director guides the students to spontaneous actions and responses. He or she probably uses questions and suggestions more than commands. A director uses the following three commands.

- *Action* means that performers begin their improvisations.

- *Freeze* means that performers stop and stay exactly where they are. A director uses this command so that observers can look at positions, space, and groupings of characters.

- *Cut* means that the improvisation is over. The director uses this command when he or she wants the performers to talk with the observers.

At any time, you may have to direct an improvisation. Because of this, you should be able to use the director's commands correctly.

YOUR TURN

1. Write a story line or basic plot for an improvisation. Include at least three characters in it. Answer the following questions in your outline: who? what? when? where? why? and how?

2. With a partner, think of at least one complication that could be added to each of the following improvisations to make them more interesting. Present your improvisation in class.

   a. Two people are in the middle of a field having a picnic lunch. A sudden rainstorm begins.

   b. Two senior citizens, a business executive, and a child with a caged bird get on an elevator. The door closes, but the elevator does not move. The door will not open.

   c. A window washer is outside the fourth floor of an office building. A secretary is giving directions from inside for getting certain spots clean. The window washer cannot hear the secretary but can see gestures and facial expressions.

18 CHAPTER REVIEW

 Chapter Summary

Informal theater is sometimes called creative dramatics, improvisational drama, or theater games. It is the process of using the imagination to make spontaneous choices. One purpose of informal theater is to make people more aware of their senses. Informal theater also helps people use their imaginations.

After each informal theater session, a group should have a feedback session. During a feedback session, everyone asks questions. They try to find out what performers were thinking and why they did certain things.

Pantomime is informal theater that uses only nonverbal messages. Performers use gestures, facial expressions, and movements. Details of movement must be correct and consistent to make the situation believable. When preparing a pantomime, you should observe others. You should also practice in front of a mirror. Pantomime may involve one or several people. You can also add sounds and rhythms to pantomimes. Improvisations are pantomimes which use vocal and verbal messages. The three elements of any improvisation are conflict, dialogue, and characterization.

This chapter also discusses some informal theater exercises. They include mirroring and interviewing. Directors in informal theater guide students to spontaneous actions and responses. *Action, freeze,* and *cut* are the commands used by a director.

Checklist

Practicing Informal Theater Skills

1. Develop an awareness of your senses.

2. Share your feelings, thoughts, and reactions after a session of informal theater. Do not make value judgments.

3. Be correct and consistent with details during a pantomime.

4. Prepare for pantomime by observing and imitating people.

5. Use only nonverbal and vocal messages during pantomime.

6. Remember that improvisations use spontaneous verbal and vocal messages.

 Vocabulary

Define each term in a complete sentence.

characterization   monologue

dialogue   pantomime

improvisation

Review Questions

1. Explain the purposes of informal theater.
2. Tell why feedback sessions are important in informal theater.
3. Define pantomime. How is it different from an improvisation?
4. Explain how you can prepare for a pantomime.
5. Explain how sound could be used in a pantomime.
6. Define *dialogue* and *monologue*.
7. Explain what it means to "break character."
8. Describe what performers do in mirror exercises.
9. Explain how interviewing can extend an improvisation.
10. Name and explain the three commands an informal theater director uses.

Discuss with Your Classmates

1. List different ways in which students can increase awareness of their environment. What techniques can help develop an awareness of the senses? What are the benefits of increased awareness?

2. Discuss the importance of developing your imagination when participating in informal theater.

3. Summarize the dramatic elements that are used in improvisations. How can they be evaluated after a performance?

4. Discuss the role that feedback plays in informal theater. How is it possible that performers cannot always answer the audience's questions?

 # Critical Thinking

1. Analysis: Distinguish between pantomime and improvisation. What aspects of informal theater do they have in common? How are they different? Discuss with classmates which one they prefer and why.

2. Comprehension: Assume that you are involved in informal theater and are told to imagine the following situation: How would you react if you suddenly discovered that you were the only person on a normally busy street? What would you gain as a performer by imagining that?

 **Activities**

In-Class

1. Imagine an object of any color, size, weight, and shape. Using only actions, gestures, and facial expressions, describe the object.

2. Work on three simple pantomimes. One should involve small, realistic movements such as buttering toast. Another should involve large, realistic movements such as chopping wood. The third should involve contrived movements such as running in slow motion. Before you present your pantomimes, write a short description of what you will do in each pantomime. When each pantomime is finished, your teacher will call on students to describe what they saw. If no one guesses correctly, your teacher will read the description aloud. Then the class should suggest ways to make the pantomime clearer and easier to understand.

3. Your teacher will divide the class into groups of three to four students. Plan and practice the movements for a machine with moving parts—similar to the one described on page 368. Each person in the group should be one of the parts.

4. Write two improvisational situations on 3″ × 5″ cards. Your teacher will collect and shuffle the cards. With two or three other performers, students should then present the situations they draw. After an improvisation, two class members should describe what they observed in the improvisation. Finally, one of the performers should read aloud the directions on the card that was drawn.

Out-of-Class

1. Plan out the plot and action of a pantomime involving each of the following. Decide how appeals to the senses could be added and shown. Write all of your work in your speech notebook.

a. peanut butter   **c.** a kitten   **e.** a balloon
b. a roller coaster   **d.** ice cubes   **f.** an umbrella

2. Use your imagination to decide what you would do, see, hear, feel, think, smell, or taste in the following situations. Be prepared to share your responses with the class.

a. Your family wins a free, two-week trip to a Mexican resort. You fly to Mexico City and take a train to the hotel. When you arrive, you discover that your luggage has been lost. Your family only has the clothes they are wearing. Few people at the resort speak English.

b. There is a huge snowstorm during a basketball game. About two hundred people cannot leave the gym because the roads are blocked. The gym is not very close to the main school building.

c. Your mother gives you $30 and a grocery list. After you have found everything, you take your cart to the checkout counter. As you unload the groceries from the cart, you discover you have lost the money.

3. Select a simple everyday activity that you do all the time at home (brushing your hair, putting on makeup, buttoning your coat). Using the real article, do what you have chosen. Concentrate on each step. Practice until you know every movement. Outline the step-by-step actions in your speech notebook. Now practice the pantomime without the real article. Present your pantomime in class.

 **Chapter Project**

Your teacher will divide the class into groups of four or five students. Each group should read the situations below. Choose one of the situations and decide how each of these characters could join in the action or add complications: a mail carrier, a robot, a photographer, a young child. Then present an improvisation to the class.

After each improvisation, the class should evaluate the performance. Remember that in informal theater feedback is an opportunity to share feelings, thoughts, and reactions. It is not intended to decide who was the best or the most creative.

The Situations

1.   A high school student is trying to teach a puppy to heel during a walk through town.

2.   A man is trying to hold his hat on his head during a windstorm while cleaning his glasses.

3.   A salesperson is trying to demonstrate how to use a new popcorn machine, but the machine is not working properly.

4.   A new homeowner is trying to nail several boards back on a fence. The nails keep bending.

CHAPTER 19 Acting

Karen is the student director of the class play. As she listens to the rehearsal of a scene, she thinks . . .

"Mark and Jason's characters just don't seem real.

They need to think about why their characters do and say things.

Maybe we should stop now and talk about that."

Have *you* ever acted? What did you do to make your character seem real?

In this chapter, you will read about:

- how to memorize a scene from a play
- the motivation for a character's actions and words
- creating a character vocally and nonverbally
- terms that deal with formal theater
- character relationships within a play
- directions for entrances, exits, and other stage movements

Why do people go to movies and plays? Why are they willing to pay money to watch people pretend to be other people? That's a good question. But there's an even more interesting question. Why do people become actors and spend most of their lives working in a world of make-believe?

There is no one answer to any of these questions. Because people are different, each person would probably have a slightly different answer. Nevertheless, most people's answers usually have something to do with an escape from reality. The theater and movies create fantasy worlds. These worlds carry people away from their cares and worries—if only for an hour or two.

The more you understand about the theater, the better you are able to appreciate it. For example, when you watch a movie, you probably don't think of the hundreds of people who worked behind the camera. You are unaware of the many scenes that had to be taken over because a dog barked at the wrong moment or someone sneezed. You see only the final film, not the effort behind it.

In this chapter, you will learn some of the things every actor must know to be successful. You also will discover a form of communication that is different from any other you have studied.

PERSONAL RESPONSIBILITIES

Acting is the process of taking on the characteristics of another person. However, acting also includes communicating those characteristics to other people in a convincing way. In Chapter 18, you learned to mimic other people after observing their behavior. You also learned to be sensitive to the people and things around you. These things are all very important to an actor.

Among the many responsibilities of an actor, memorizing lines has high priority.

An actor has many responsibilities. The following are some of the things that you, as an actor, must do before you even rehearse with other actors.

Memorizing Lines

Your first job is to memorize your lines. Not much can be done at a rehearsal until lines have been memorized. This is because actors need verbal cues to their own lines. **Cues** are the words that come right before your lines. You can imagine the problems that are created when the right cues aren't given.

Memorizing many, many lines may seem impossible to you at the beginning. There are, however, many tricks to memorizing that can help you. For example, most people memorize lines by repeating them aloud over and over again. Finally they are able to look away from their scripts and say them.

Some people memorize best by working only on the lines of a small scene in a play. They don't go on to another scene until the first one is completely memorized. Other people do better by reading through the whole play each time and memorizing parts of different speeches whenever they can. Eventually, they put all the parts together.

Exaggeration is also a good way to help you memorize. This works especially well on lines that you keep forgetting. When you study those lines, emphasize important words. Say them in an exaggerated way. This should help you remember them more easily.

Some people tape-record their cues. Then they leave empty spaces on the tape for their lines. They memorize their lines by playing the tape over and over again, each time filling in their lines. If you don't have a tape recorder, a friend or family member can give you your cues. If people help you, they can also **prompt** you. Prompting is giving you a word or part of a line when you can't remember a line. Usually people can memorize faster when someone works with them.

Finding Motivations

People have reasons for doing what they do and saying what they say. As an actor, you must find out what your character's motivations are for his or her actions and statements. No matter how short a line may be, it should have a reason for being there. In most plays, the writers state *what* is said, *to whom* it is said, and sometimes *how* it is said. But you must often find the reason *why* it is said. If you don't know why a line is said, you probably won't say it correctly. As a result, you may not create the right emotion.

Some directors ask the actors to outline the motivations for each of their speeches and actions. For example, your character might move to a table and pick up a book. You would have to give a reason for that action. Why does the character want to look at the book at that moment? Is your character trying to avoid doing something else? Is your character hunting for a hidden letter? Finding the correct motivation for each action and speech is very important. Strong motivations create clear, believable characters.

Building a Character's Background

A play can cover only a certain period of time. The action in some plays, for example, takes place within only one or two days. However, what happened before those two days is also important. What a character did then will help you understand that character's motivations. The following are some of the places you can find this background information.

- Stage directions. (Examples: "She walks with a cane." "He is slightly overweight.")

- Statements made by a character. (Examples: "I haven't been this frightened since our barn burned down when I was seven years old." "No thanks, I would rather walk.")

- Statements made by other characters. (Examples: "She is very generous to poor people." "They have been friends since grade school.")

- Relationships among the characters or with objects. (Examples: "They are constantly together." "He has collected many famous paintings."

Start to establish your character's background from the first time you read through a play. The following are other areas of a character that you might think about for additional information. Remember, the more you know about your character, the better you will understand your character's motivations.

age	fears	family
place of birth	goals	likes and dislikes
education	past residences	personality traits
hobbies	personality	moods
friends	accomplishments	strong points

Handling Vocal Messages

Voice is extremely important in the theater. It makes a writer's words understandable. It also makes a character believable. Professional actors change their own voices to match their characters. For example, sometimes young actors play old characters. These actors, however, do not use their own voices. They use the voice of an older person. Actors work especially hard on accents and different patterns of inflection.

When you get a role, learn as much as you can about your character's background. Then experiment. Read your lines aloud with many different vocal changes. Keep at it until you find the patterns that sound right for your character.

Projection is the degree of force and volume used to send a person's voice forward. It requires the constant control of the diaphragm and the abdominal muscles. It also involves precise articulation to produce distinct sounds. Obviously, projection is another

Projection is the degree of force and volume used to send a person's voice forward.

important concern for all actors. When people in an audience can't hear or don't understand the actors, they quickly lose interest.

Another feature of projection is called **pointing.** It is the emphasizing of certain words to create an emotional response. It is called *pointing* because the actor is vocally pointing to certain words to stress their importance. Pointing can be handled in the following ways.

- by pausing before and/or after an important word
- by saying it with more stress or volume
- by prolonging the sounds
- by changing the regular pattern of inflection
- by changing the voice quality

The following dialogue contains examples of pointing. As you read it, emphasize the italicized words.

Bonnie: *(pacing back and forth)* No, that couldn't be the *real* reason she left. That's much too simple.

Tim: She never told anyone she was leaving. Wouldn't she have told *at least* Sylvia? After all, Sylvia is her closest and *dearest* friend.

Bonnie: Maybe, if she wanted to involve Sylvia in her plans. And then, *only* if Sylvia would *not* be hurt.

Actors must know the gestures and expressions of each character they play.

Handling Nonverbal Messages

Your character's background should also help you understand other things. For example, how does your character move? What expressions and gestures does your character use? Sometimes it's helpful to watch people who are like your character. Then you can give your character some of those realistic movements and gestures. When you're planning your character's nonverbal communication, you should think about the following points.

- Will the messages help to make your character different from the other characters in the play?

- Will the messages be in keeping with the character's personality?

- Can you keep the messages the same throughout the play? (For example, a gesture like trembling hands may be hard to keep doing through a whole play.)

- What is the character's motivation for the messages?

- Will the messages be large enough to be seen by most of the audience? (For example, some actions that are usually quite small, such as sewing, may need to be exaggerated slightly.)

The dialogue below is from a play by Reginald Rose. As the scene opens, jurors are filing into the jury room. They must decide the guilt or innocence of a young man who has been accused of a crime. Notice that the author did not give the jurors' names. He merely numbered them. You can use this passage to examine and practice the personal acting responsibilities mentioned in this chapter.

from *TWELVE ANGRY MEN*

Seven: Chewing gum? Gum? Gum?

Nine: Thank you, but no. *(Jurors Two and Twelve shake their heads.)*

Seven: Y'know something?

Twelve: I know lots of things. I'm in advertising.

Seven: *(tugging at his collar)* Y'know, it's hot.

Twelve: *(to Two, mildly sarcastic)* I never would have known that if he hadn't told me. Would you?

Two: *(missing the sarcasm)* I suppose not. I'd kind of forgotten.

Twelve: All I've done all day is sweat.

Three: *(calling out)* I bet you aren't sweating like that kid who was tried.

Seven: You'd think they'd at least air-condition the place. I almost dropped dead in court.

Twelve: My taxes are high enough.

Seven: This should go fast, anyway. *(Moves to table, as Eight goes to window.)*

Nine: *(nodding to himself, then as he throws his paper water cup into the wastebasket)* Yes, it's hot.

Guard: Okay, gentlemen. Everybody's here. If there's anything you want, I'm right outside. Just knock. *(He goes out L, closing the door. They all look at the door, silently. The lock is turned.)*

Three: Did he lock that door?

Four: Yes, he did.

Three: What do they think we are, crooks?

Foreman: *(seated at left end of the table)* They lock us up for a little while . . .

Three: *(breaking in)* And then they lock that kid up forever and that's okay with me.

Five: *(motioning toward the door)* I never knew they did that.

Ten: *(blowing his nose)* Sure, they lock the door. What did you think?

Five: *(a bit irritated)*   I just didn't know. It never occurred to me.

Four: Shall we all admit right now that it is hot and humid and our tempers are short?

Eight: *(turning from the window)*   It's been a pretty hard week. *(Turns back and continues looking out.)*

Three: I feel just fine.

Twelve: I wonder what's been going on down at the office. You know how it is in advertising. In six days my job could be gone, and the whole company, too. They aren't going to like this. *(Jurors start to take off their suit coats and hang them over the backs of chairs.)*

Foreman: Well, figure this is our duty.

Twelve: I don't object to doing my duty. I just mentioned that I might not have a job by the time I get back. *(He and Nine move to the table and take their places. Nine sits near the right end of the table.)*

Three: *(motioning to Four)*   Ask him to hire you. He's rich. Look at the suit.

Foreman: *(to Four, as he tears off slips of paper for a ballot)*   Is it custom-tailored?

Four: Yes, it is.

Foreman: I have an uncle who's a tailor. *(Four takes his jacket off, places it carefully over the back of his chair and sits.)*

Four: How does he do?

Foreman: *(shaking his head)*   Not too well. Y'know, a friend of his, that's a friend of my uncle, the tailor—well—his friend wanted to be on this jury in my place.

Seven: Why didn't you let him? I would have done anything to miss this.

Foreman: And get caught, or something? Y'know what kind of a fine you could pay for anything like that? Anyway, this friend of my uncle's was on a jury once, about ten years ago—a case just about like this one.

Twelve: So what happened?

Foreman: They let him off. Reasonable doubt. And do y'know, about eight years later they found out that he'd actually done it, anyway. A guilty man—a murderer—was turned loose in the streets.

Three: Did they get him?

Four: They couldn't.

Three: Why not?

Four: A man can't be held in double jeopardy. Unless it's a hung jury, they can't try a man twice for the same crime.

Seven: That isn't going to happen here.

Three: Six days. They should have finished it in two. *(Slapping the back of one hand into the palm of the other.)* Talk! Talk! Talk! Did you ever hear so much talk about nothing?

Two: *(laughing nervously)* Well — I guess — they're entitled . . .

YOUR TURN ///////////

1. Based upon the dialogue and stage directions in the selection from Reginald Rose's *Twelve Angry Men,* write down what things you know about each juror. Do this in your speech notebook. Number a page from one through twelve. (The foreman of the jury is Juror One.) Discuss with your classmates the personality of each juror.

2. Choose at least ten different speeches from the selection from *Twelve Angry Men.* In your speech notebook, identify a possible motivation for each speech. Discuss the motivations with your classmates.

GROUP RESPONSIBILITIES

Many people work in and on plays. Therefore, there are always interpersonal considerations. They might involve two actors or the entire cast, including the director and stage crew.

Analyzing and Interpreting

The following literary aspects are a part of all plays.

- dialogue
- the **protagonist,** the character around whom the play revolves
- the **antagonist,** the character who threatens the protagonist's efforts

- the struggle or conflict of the major character
- the mood or atmosphere
- the structure of the play (scenes and acts)
- the climax or point of highest interest

All actors must know and understand these aspects. If they don't, the meaning of the play won't be clear. If it isn't clear to the actors, it certainly won't be clear to the audience.

Finding Rhythm and Climaxes

In Chapter 18, you learned that you must understand a whole selection before you can analyze a part of it. This is also true of plays. Every play has one major climax. This is the point at which the audience learns whether the main character wins or loses the struggle. However, plays also have minor climaxes. They are based on complicating factors in the plot. Actors must understand all of these climaxes to maintain the correct rhythm throughout the whole play.

For example, each scene is one beat in the overall rhythm of the play. As in music, each beat is important. The actors, however, must decide how or why a particular scene, or beat, is important. Does the scene help to build suspense? Does it tell more about a character? Does it provide comic relief? In other words, does it give the audience some humor after a very dramatic scene? Does it point toward the conclusion? Does the scene speed up the action of the play or slow it down? If you play a scene too quickly, for example, you may not emphasize important lines. As a result, the meaning of later lines that refer back to those lines might be lost.

Each major act and scene should have at least one minor climax. Your character may be in only a small part of one of these acts or scenes. Nevertheless, you need to know how that small part aids or disrupts movement toward the climax. If you don't, you can cause your scene to lose an important beat.

Establishing Character Relationships

There is another important thing you need to think about. What is the relationship of your character to the other characters? This does not refer only to family relationships. It also includes known and unknown friends and enemies.

THE MAN WITH A METHOD
Acting with the Inside Out

Are great actors born, or does someone teach them to act? The answer is a combination of the two. Great actors have talent. But teachers help actors develop their talent. Lee Strasberg was one such teacher.

Lee Strasberg taught and directed some of the finest actors we know today. He began his career as a director and actor in 1925, and went on to found the Group Theater in New York. In 1948, Strasberg became artistic director of Actors' Studio—a theater workshop in New York City with an extension in Los Angeles. Over the years, he lectured at such universities as Harvard, Brown, and Yale.

Strasberg based his concept of theater on the ideas of Stanislavsky, the great Russian teacher of acting. Around the turn of the century, Stanislavksy departed from the old acting style that depended mostly on external effects. Instead, he demanded inner truth.

Strasberg emphasized improvisation and gave actors an opportunity to broaden their experience through team criticism. He encouraged actors to recall incidents from earlier times in their lives—especially from childhood.

Strasberg's approach is sometimes referred to as "the Method:" A character must cry in a play. The actor remembers a sad time from childhood to enhance the scene. Actors recall all sorts of feelings to increase the power of their performances.

Many stars known for their abilities to portray complex characters worked with Actors' Studio: Karl Malden, James Dean, Paul Newman, Eva Marie Saint, and Julie Harris. Many playwrights and directors benefited from the training as well.

At times, Strasberg and his method have been criticized. Critics argue that the method emphasizes psychological insights and neglects more external skills. Still, Strasberg's method has made an original and valuable contribution to quality performances.

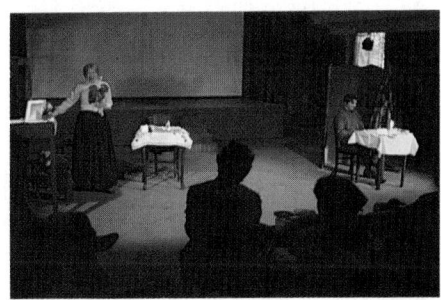

The first thing you should decide is your character's place in the whole play. Why is he or she in the play? What does your character add to the movement of the play toward the conclusion? Next, you need to decide your character's relationship to the protagonist and antagonist. Is your character friendly toward one and not the other?

In real life, you have different kinds of relationships. Some become complex because they change. For example, someone who is a casual friend this year could be your best friend next year. The same thing is true of relationships of characters in plays. As an actor, you need to know what your character's relationships are to all the other characters in the play when the play begins. Then you need to watch to see if those relationships change during the play.

The first thing you should decide is your character's place in the whole play. Why is he or she in the play?

TECHNICAL CONSIDERATIONS

To make your character "real," you need to add more than an accent and some motivation. You also need to add realistic movements. For example, how should your character make an entrance? An exit? Should your character sit or stand?

It is important for actors to *become* the characters they portray before they walk onto the stage.

Movement

All movement on a stage must have a meaning. In other words, there must be a reason why a character enters, moves about, and leaves. Also, suppose a character just climbed three flights of stairs. That character would have to enter out of breath. This entrance, of course, would be very different from that of a character entering from the next room.

As an actor, you need to become your character *before* you walk onto the stage. You must also make sure that your entrances and exits are always on time. A knock on the door that comes four seconds late could destroy the climax of a scene. Once you are on the stage, you must always be the character. Never—even for a few seconds —can you be yourself.

During a scene, actors sometimes cross the stage. These crosses can be long—especially when characters enter. However, most long crosses are broken by a short stop. During this time, a character will do something, such as taking off an overcoat or removing a pair of gloves.

If you must make a cross, you should begin to move before you speak. If you do this, the people in the audience see your movement first. Then they will be able to concentrate on what you are saying. If you speak first and then move, they might be distracted. As a result, they might miss what you are saying. For the same reason, you should never cross the stage while another character is speaking.

Most actors begin to move with the hand or foot that is farthest away from the audience. Most movement should also be at a diagonal with the audience—rather than parallel to it. When actors talk with each other, their bodies should be at a 45 degree angle with the audience so that everyone in the audience can see their faces.

The Stage

Most stages are **proscenium** stages. They are like a big picture that is framed by the arch and stage floor. Years ago all stage floors were slanted downward toward the audience. As a result, stage directions call for people to move downstage and upstage. **Downstage,** therefore, is the part of the stage that is closest to an audience. **Upstage** is the part of the stage that is farthest from an audience. These terms are still used today—even though stage floors are no longer slanted.

All other directions are given in terms of an actor facing an audience. Suppose, for example, that an actor comes in from a back

Diagram of Stage Positions

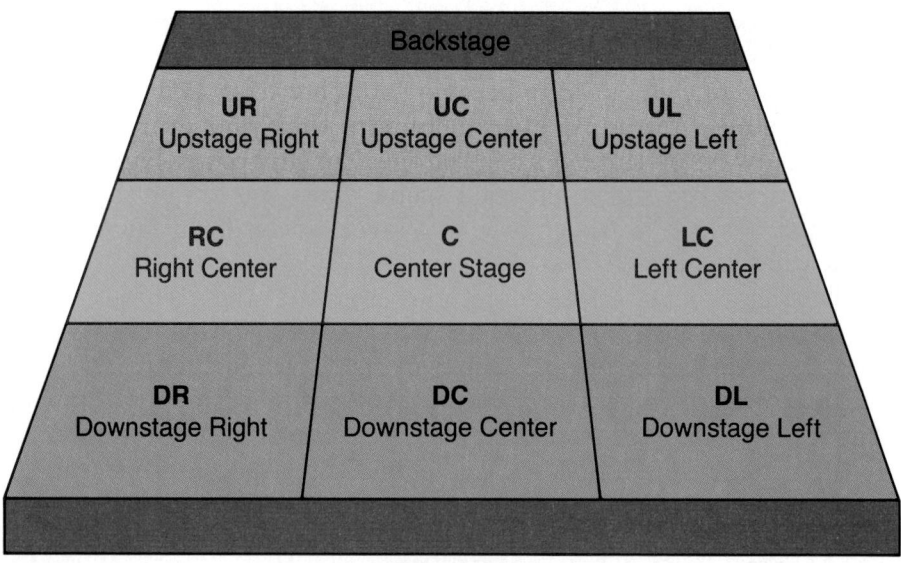

entrance in the center of the stage. The actor must cross to a seat near the right front of the stage—as the audience sees it. The stage direction for this actor would read *(moves DL),* which means "down left." The most important place on the stage is downstage center. The following diagram will help you understand stage directions more easily.

Blocking is the director's plan for the movements of all the actors. Usually a director blocks an entire play before the first rehearsal. During the first "walk through" of a play, the actors write the movement for each line in pencil on their scripts. Actors never change these movements unless the director tells them to. By rehearsing the same movements, all the actors always know where everyone is during a scene.

Here is a selection from the play "Oliver Twist Asks for More." It is based on the classic book *Oliver Twist,* written by the famous English author, Charles Dickens. You may recall that Oliver was an orphan boy who was lonely, frightened, and hungry. The play takes place at a workhouse for homeless boys. The selection will give you a good idea about the importance of movement in a play.

As the play opens, Oliver and three other poorly dressed boys, plus some extra boys, are seated behind a long, plain table. The room is bare and cheerless. The boys hungrily scrape the last bit of oatmeal from their bowls, then set them down while sighing.

First Boy: *(plaintively)* I'm still hungry.

Second Boy: *(licking spoon)* We are always still hungry. Not even a crust of bread tonight.

Third Boy: *(to Oliver)* Don't forget your promise, Oliver. *(As the Cook enters from the right, the Third Boy nudges Oliver, whispers.)* There he is. Go ahead. *(Oliver timidly hesitates as the Cook approaches table. The Cook snatches two or three bowls, grabs Oliver's.)*

Cook: *(gruffly, sourly)* Get back to your work. No time for idleness around here.

Oliver: *(holding out hand)* Please, sir, may I have my bowl back? There's a spoonful left . . . .

Cook: *(slamming bowl on table)* Finish and be off with you! *(The Cook turns away to collect other bowls.)*

First Boy: *(whispering anxiously to Oliver)* Hurry!

Oliver: *(rising, choking with fright as he speaks to Cook)* Please, sir . . . .

Cook: *(sourly)* What do you want? Speak up, boy.

The most thrilling moment of all arrives when the cast is on the stage, putting on the play at last.

Oliver: *(miserably shaking head, sitting down)* Nothing . . . nothing sir.

(The Cook growls and busies himself at a far end of the table. The boys turn hopefully toward Oliver.)

Second Boy: *(pleading with Oliver)* Oliver, please . . . you promised to ask for more supper.

(Oliver nervously fingers his bowl and spoon, finally picks them up, rises and circles to stand in back of the Cook.)

Oliver: *(stammering)* Sir . . . could you please . . . .
Cook: *(turning around, scowling, nodding, reaching for Oliver's bowl)* Through at last? All right, I'll take your bowl.
Oliver: *(holding bowl up with both hands)* Please sir, I want some more.

(The stunned Cook is speechless for a moment. He claps a hand to his forehead.)

Cook: *(exploding)* What! What did you say?
Oliver: *(trembling)* Please sir, I want some more supper.
Cook: *(staring in horror at Oliver)* What! What's that? Why, you ungrateful wretch! More indeed! I'll teach you! *(He swings*

(Mr. Bumble and Mr. Limbkins, two harsh, self-righteous charac-
ters, race in from left, glance around in alarm.)

Mr. Bumble: *(excitedly)* What's happened?
Mr. Limbkins: *(anxiously)* Are we on fire?

(The Cook takes Oliver by the ear and leads him before the two
men. Oliver cringes.)

Cook: *(slowly, emphasizing his words)* This boy . . . this miser-
able wretched, ungrateful scoundrel has dared to push his
empty bowl into my face. *(shouting)* He asked for more supper!

Mr. Limbkins: *(gasping)* After all we have done for him! I am
painfully shocked! *(shaking Oliver)* Young man, you are the
worst of scoundrels! What evil within your heart rebels
against our kindness?

Oliver: *(trembling)* I . . . I am not ungrateful for your many
kindnesses, sir . . . but . . . I am still hungry. *(gesturing to
boys)* We thought your generosity might spare another mouth-
ful to fill our emptiness.

Mr. Limbkins: *(arrogantly)* Tell me boy, how hungry would
you be if we put you out on the streets where you belong?
(painfully grimacing) How it grieves my kindly heart to
witness such rash impudence.

Mr. Bumble: *(leering)* Perhaps a few days in a dark cellar will
cleanse him of evil. *(pompously nodding)* Yes, yes, for the boy's
own good we must punish him severly.

(Mr. Bumble nods self-righteously in unison with Mr.
Limbkins.)

YOUR TURN //////////////

1. In your speech notebook, draw a diagram of a stage. Then follow
the stage directions in the selection from "Oliver Twist Asks for
More." Imagine that you are the director of this scene. Block the
movement of the characters in this scene.

2. Discuss with your classmates whether you, as director of this
play, think there is enough movement in this scene.

19 CHAPTER REVIEW

 ## Chapter Summary

The job of actors is to convince an audience that they are other people. Acting involves many personal responsibilities. They include memorizing lines, finding motivations for their characters, and building a character's background. Actors must also handle vocal and nonverbal messages effectively.

All actors also have group responsibilities. They include play analysis and interpretation. As a part of these activities, actors must find a play's rhythm and climaxes and establish character relationships. There are also technical considerations which include things such as movement and blocking.

 ## Checklist

Understanding Acting Skills

1. Decide what is the best method to help you memorize lines. Practice the technique you choose.

2. Understand the motivation of the character you are playing.

3. Develop and understand your character's background.

4. Experiment with several different vocal presentations for your character.

5. Project your voice so the audience can hear and understand your words.

6. Plan your character's nonverbal communication.

7. Analyze the play before you begin practicing your role.

8. Remain in character while you are on stage.

 **Vocabulary**

Define each term in a complete sentence.

acting   projection

antagonist   prompt

blocking   proscenium

cues   protagonist

downstage   upstage

pointing

 Review Questions

1.   Describe why it is important for an actor to memorize lines even before the first rehearsal.

2.   Explain why you should understand a character's motivations for saying and doing certain things.

3.   Tell how you can find out about a character's background.

4.   Define the term *pointing*. Explain some ways you can do it.

5.   Identify some things you should think about when deciding on a character's nonverbal communication.

6.   Explain the difference between the protagonist and antagonist.

7.   Explain why an actor should start to move before saying a line.

8.   Explain why characters who are talking to each other usually stand at 45 degree angles, rather than face each other directly.

9.   Define the term *blocking*.

10.   Explain the difference between *downstage* and *upstage*. Identify the most important position on the stage.

Discuss with Your Classmates

1. Discuss the historical background of the technical terms *down-stage* and *upstage*. Why do you think these terms are still used in modern theater?

2. Explain why it is important for actors to understand the background and motivation of characters whom they play. What are some techniques for determining background and motivation.

3. Summarize the technical considerations that must be taken into account when acting.

4. Discuss how a character's age, health, and position or job can affect his or her posture and movements. Why is it important for an actor to understand these things?

Critical Thinking

1. **Synthesis:** Summarize the responsibilities of individual actors and the responsibilities of the group. In what ways do these responsibilities overlap? How would an individual's actions affect the group as a whole?

2. **Evaluation:** Watch a dramatic presentation on television. How well did the actors perform their roles? Did they observe all of the acting responsibilities presented in this chapter?

Activities

In-Class

1. Working with a partner, choose a 2- to 3-minute scene from a play in which two characters talk to each other. Memorize the lines. Present the selection in class.

2. Your teacher will divide the class into groups of four or five students. Each group should write its own 3- to 4-minute dramatic scene. Before you begin, you should review the important literary aspects of a play on page 389. Be sure to create a character for each group member.

Out-of-Class

1. Memorize Oliver's speech on pages 395-397. How long did it take? Which method of memorization did you use? Be prepared to recite the speech in class.

2. With another class member, prepare a 4- to 5-minute scene from a play. Memorize the scene and block it together. Be sure to include gestures and movements that have motivations. Be prepared to present the scene in class.

3. Your teacher will give you a list of plays. Select a play from the list and write a short analysis of the protagonist. Describe that character's interactions with the other characters. Explain the character's possible motivations for specific words and actions. Support your opinions with quotations from the play. Also, prepare a major speech of the character to present in class.

Chapter Project

Your teacher will assign you a partner. With your partner, select a two-person scene from a play.

Independently, analyze both of the characters in the play. You and your partner should then compare your analyses.

Present the selection in class, with each of you playing a different character. You may memorize the lines or you may read from a script.

After each presentation, the class will discuss both characters, their apparent motivations and backgrounds, and how they interacted together. Did the class know as much about the characters as you and your partner did?

20 Producing Plays

Andrea is the stage manager for the class play. These are some of her thoughts as she prepares for dress rehearsal . . .

"Those lights aren't working correctly.

I'll check the props next.

Then I'll see if the sets are ready."

Have *you* ever helped produce a play? What did you do?

In this chapter, you will read about:

- choosing a play that suits a particular group
- terms related to theater arts
- the duties of various production people

In Chapter 19, you learned that actors must do many things before they appear before an audience. For example, they do not just walk around the stage without any reason. Each movement has a motivation, and each movement is well planned and rehearsed.

The same principle applies to the production of a play. Much goes on behind the scenes that an audience never sees. Why was one play chosen instead of another? Where did the costumes come from? Who turned on the spotlight? These are just a few of the questions involved in any play production.

GETTING READY

There are many questions you must answer before you choose a play. For example, are there enough people to produce the play? Suppose a play has four characters in it. You will still need about 20 people to produce it because there are so many jobs besides acting involved in a production. (These jobs will be discussed later in this chapter.) Do you want to put on a musical? Then you have to decide whether you can find enough singers and musicians.

Another important consideration is finances. Do you have enough money to put on the play? Is there a school drama budget? If there is no budget, is there any other way to raise money? For example, how much money could be raised through ticket sales? Who would come to the play? If you work hard on a play, you want people to see it. Do many people from your school and community attend school plays?

Finally, you have to think about space and equipment. Does your school have an auditorium? Would it be free for rehearsals, or is it often used for other purposes? If your school doesn't have an auditorium, what else could you use? Could you use a gym or a large room? Is there a place to store scenery and costumes?

What were your answers to these questions? Could you find solutions to all these problems? If you could, you just might be on the doorstep of a very exciting experience—producing a play.

CHOOSING A SCRIPT

What makes a good play? Think about the following standards.

- Will the play keep the interest of the audience?

- Is it suitable to your particular audience?

- Does it have true-to-life characters rather than stereotypes?

Sources

To find a play that meets the standards listed above, first check anthologies in the city and school libraries. The next thing to do is to read play catalogs put out by publishers. These catalogs, however, give only brief descriptions of plays. Therefore, you might have to order and read single copies of the plays you think might be good.

One good source of information about plays is the publication *Dramatics*. Since it annually reviews high school plays, you can see what other schools have done. The following are three lists of plays. They have been produced most often in the past several years in schools in the United States.

Drama
Our Town
The Crucible
The Miracle Worker
The Diary of Anne Frank
Flowers for Algernon

David and Lisa
Spoon River Anthology
The Night of January 16th
Ten Little Indians

Comedy
You Can't Take It with You
Harvey
Arsenic and Old Lace
The Curious Savage

Up the Down Staircase
The Star-Spangled Girl
The Man Who Came to Dinner

Musical
Oklahoma!
Music Man
Fiddler on the Roof
Guys and Dolls
Bye, Bye Birdie
Sound of Music

Hello Dolly
Godspell
You're a Good Man, Charlie Brown
West Side Story
Porgy and Bess
The Wizard of Oz

Professional productions publish playbills for the audience.

Playbooks

Once a play is chosen, copies of it must be bought for most of the cast members. The only cast members who don't need copies are those who have small parts with only a few lines. One playbook can be cut up and given to the people playing those parts. Always remember, however, that it is against the law to make copies of plays. If you copy a play, your school could receive a heavy fine.

Royalties

Part of your budget must go toward paying **royalties,** the fee charged for the right to perform the play. The amounts are usually set by the publishers and printed in their catalogs. Sometimes the fee is a percentage of the total amount of the ticket sales. At other times it is a set amount for the first performance and a lower amount for other performances: Giving a play without paying royalties is also against the law, although there are some exceptions. Some older plays no longer charge royalties. Although once in a while a playwright does not ask for royalties, you must still ask permission to produce the play.

HOLDING AUDITIONS

After a play is chosen, students must **audition** for parts. This means that they must perform before one or more judges. These judges can be a casting committee or the director. The judges decide who should have the various parts in the play. Anyone can go to **open auditions.** However, only certain people can go to **closed auditions.** If closed auditions are held, usually the conditions for trying out are announced earlier. Following are some of the possible conditions:

- special talents such as dancing or playing an instrument
- previous acting experience
- age or grade in school
- minimum grade average
- previous classes in chorus or drama
- certain physical factors, such as height or hair color, if they are important to a certain part

"I think someone didn't read the audition notice carefully."

THE PLAYWRIGHT COLLIDES WITH THE CAST AND CREW . . . ACTION!

by Nancy Lenau

Nancy Lenau is a writer, poet, and playwright. Three of her plays were finalists at the National Playwrights Conference.

When beginning playwrights write "The End" on the final page of a play, they often have no idea that the play has just begun. Everyone else involved in a play understands the play differently. Here are some examples.

- In my first play, I described a handsome hero of about 30. But a short actor, about 20, weighing 200 pounds came to rehearsal. After a few moments, I realized the fellow was good. His appearance became a plus for my comedy.
- In another play, I called for three sets. We only had the space and budget for one, so we'd change the mood with lighting.
- One of my scripts alternated between a dream world and reality. The company asked: "Is any of this real, or is it all in the character's mind?" They questioned every word

of the play. A playwright must justify directions and add insights into motivations.

Everyone involved brings unique experiences and insights to a show. Unexpected incidents can change a play. Examples? The lady rings for her butler. He misses his cue. She adlibs and creates a little "stage business." Another ring, no butler, more business. Again. Finally, the butler enters. "You rang, madam?"

She glares, "No, I was tolling. I thought you died!"

That improvisation earned a laugh and kept the show going. For the playwright, those moments mean changes. The situation is simply communication between actor and audience—the playwright can only hope, standing in the wings.

Audition Forms

Everyone who comes to an audition fills out an **audition form,** a form that asks for certain information that will be helpful to the director. It includes such things as your name, address, telephone number, and grade in school. It might ask you to list any conflicts you might have with rehearsals. For example, do you watch your younger brother after school or do you have a part-time job? Usually you are also asked to list any previous acting experiences. Then you are usually asked to write the name of the part you want in the play. You might also be asked if you are willing to work on the stage crew if you don't get a part.

Audition Procedures

Basically, two kinds of auditions are held: script readings and improvisations. During a script reading, you would read the part of the character in the play. Therefore, you should be familiar with the script. Sometimes you can check out one of the playbooks from the library before the audition. During the audition, include as many of the vocal and nonverbal characteristics of the character as you can.

You learned about improvisations in Chapter 18. During an audition, the improvisations might relate to the play, or they might be original. You might be asked to talk to an imaginary person, or you might work with other students. Sometimes the director will give you specific instructions. At other times, you will have to make up your own character or action.

During both kinds of auditions, the director will be looking for several things. Do you project your voice well? Do you speak clearly and pronounce words correctly? Do you move easily? How flexible are your voice and expressions? After these things, a director also looks to see how well you fit the physical descriptions of the characters in the play.

Sometimes you must wait to find out whether you got a part. You might even be asked to attend a second audition, or a **call-back.** This happens when two or more people were good in one part. The director asks to see each person once again before making a final decision.

Casting Decisions

The **cast,** or the people who actually perform, is chosen in different ways. Probably the most common way is for the director to

The director must watch and listen carefully during auditions.

make the final decisions. These decisions may be based on talent, experience, or dependability.

The cast may also be selected by a casting committee. Experienced students or teachers are usually on such a committee. Often the committee will vote by secret ballot after the auditions. There is also a third way. All the students who attended the auditions vote. They choose the people they think have the most talent.

REHEARSING PLAYS

School plays are rehearsed mainly after school. There also might be several evening rehearsals just before the play opens. If you have responsibilities after school, you should tell the director at the very beginning. If you are going to miss too many rehearsals, you may have to drop out of the play.

Rehearsal Feedback

One of the most helpful parts of a rehearsal is the **feedback,** or the information the director gives to the cast and crew. For example, the director might point out that an actor was talking too fast or entering too late. The director also might suggest some special techniques that should be tried at the next rehearsal.

Sometimes a rehearsal is filmed so that the director and cast can see whether the performance is up to their standards.

These feedback sessions might come during a scene, at the end of a scene, or at the end of the rehearsal. Sometimes the director talks to the group as a whole. At other times, the director might hand out written comments. The purpose of feedback sessions is *not* to criticize. Rather, its purpose is constantly to improve the play.

Dress Rehearsal

At least one dress rehearsal is usually held before the first public performance. At this time all the actors rehearse in their costumes and use all their props. The entire play is rehearsed without any stops or interruptions. If any problems come up, the actors go on—just as if it were an actual performance. All lighting and scenery is used to be sure scene changes can be done quickly and correctly.

Curtain Call

The director decides whether there will be a curtain call. If there is a curtain call, it should also be rehearsed. Usually minor characters are on the stage when the curtain is raised for the curtain call.

They should bow together and then turn toward upstage center. This is where the major characters usually appear to take their individual bows. When everyone is on the stage, the entire cast bows together. Then the curtain comes down. If the applause continues, the actors may take a second—and even a third—curtain call.

YOUR TURN

1. Think of a play you would like to present at your school. What are some problems you might have producing it? Various choices should be discussed with the class.

2. Pretend you are on a casting committee for a school play. Write out an audition form. It should contain the information you would want to know about anyone trying out for a part.

PRODUCTION PEOPLE

Some people don't want to perform in front of an audience. They still can work on plays. Following are some of the important non-acting jobs needed to produce a play.

Assistant Director or Student Director

The assistant director works closely with the director. Usually the assistant director sits near the director and writes down the comments for the feedback session. The assistant director is also responsible for the **promptbook.** This is a copy of the play's script that contains all the director's notes and blocking. The pages of the script are usually pasted onto large sheets of paper and are kept in a notebook. Instructions for lighting, sound effects, and costumes are also kept in the book. At performances, the assistant director may also be the backstage prompter.

Stage Manager

The stage manager is responsible for the stage crew. Together they are responsible for the following duties:

- building the set
- changing scenes
- handling furniture and props
- positioning and operating all lights
- handling special effects and sound effects
- managing the curtain
- taking the set down after each performance or after the final performance

A stage manager must also know all the light and curtain cues, as well as the cues for sound effects and special effects. This person must also check to be sure that everything is onstage and in place before the curtain goes up on each scene. The stage manager must also know how to handle emergencies, such as a burned out light.

Business Manager

With the help of the director, the business manager handles all financial matters. The business manager keeps a record of all income and costs. This means that he or she is also responsible for keeping track of all ticket sales.

In many schools, the business manager also supervises the publicity. For example, this person might have some students make posters and hang them around the school or community. Some business managers even run publicity campaigns in the school. They might give away free tickets for such things as the best program cover or the best poster.

House Manager

The house manager is in charge of seating. This person must find ushers for each performance. Then at each performance, the house manager must make sure that the ushers have programs to hand out.

The house manager should get to each performance before any of the audience arrives. He or she should make sure the house lights and air-conditioning or heating systems are working. If they aren't, that person must get someone to fix them. Then the house manager should make sure the restrooms are unlocked and lighted. Finally, the house manager should close the doors leading to the auditorium

The business manager is responsible for keeping track of all ticket sales.

when the play begins. After each performance, the house manager checks the auditorium for any items left behind by mistake.

Makeup Committee

In addition to the production staff just discussed, several committees are needed. For example, stage makeup is very different from regular makeup. Therefore, several people are needed to help the actors put on their makeup.

There are several purposes for stage makeup. It compensates for the bright lights and changes facial characteristics. It also exaggerates some features so that the audience can see them from a distance.

Members of the makeup committee usually start to work about an hour before the play begins. They make up the actors who appear first on the stage. It is a good idea for the same people to make up the same actors for each performance. Once they learn the proper makeup for these actors, they will be able to apply it more quickly. Once the makeup is applied, it should be powdered to prevent it from running. After their makeup is on, the actors should then put on their costumes.

Costume Committee

Unless special or unusual costumes are needed, actors are asked to get their own. The members of the costume committee merely check to see if the costumes are clean and ready for each performance. After each performance, they are also responsible for storing the costumes in a safe place.

If costumes are rented, the costume committee must measure the actors. With the director's permission, the head of the costume committee orders the costumes. Names of rental stores are listed in the yellow pages of most telephone books.

Prop Committee

Props (short for *properties*) are all the movable items that actors use during a performance. They can range from a piece of string to a portable TV set. Members of the prop committee must find all the props. Then they must go onstage after each scene and remove any props that will not be used in the next scene and add any new props to the upcoming scene. Changing furniture is usually another responsibility of the prop committee. The prop committee must store all the props in a safe place until the next performance, and after the final performance they should return all borrowed props to their owners.

The business manager supervises publicity.

Publicity Committee

The **publicity** committee advertises the play by preparing news stories for school and local newspapers. These stories should be approved by the director. They should include the play's title and author, the time and place of performance, and the names of the leading actors and director. With the director's permission, the committee may also use other methods of advertising, such as the making and placing of posters and the writing of letters of invitation to other schools and organizations. If the committee has enough members, it may also design and prepare the program.

YOUR TURN ///////////

1. What production job would you find most challenging? Why does this job interest you?

2. Look at the excerpt from *Twelve Angry Men* on page 387. What costumes would be needed for this scene? What props would be needed? If you were the director, what notes might you write in the promptbook about this scene?

20 CHAPTER REVIEW

Chapter Summary

Play production includes all the things that go on "behind the scenes." Production begins by determining the number of people needed for a play. It also includes deciding how much money can be raised and what space is available.

Selecting a good script is also important. It should be one that will suit and interest the audience. It should have true-to-life characters. The next step is to set up auditions and select actors for the play. Once the actors are chosen, rehearsals should begin.

Some of the major production people include an assistant director, a stage manager, a business manager, and a house manager. There should also be committees to handle makeup, costumes, props, and publicity.

Checklist

Play Production Skills

1. Choose a play with true-to-life characters that will interest the audience.
2. Find out what royalties, if any, must be paid for permission to produce the play.
3. Be familiar with the play before you go to auditions.
4. Listen carefully when the director gives rehearsal feedback.
5. Know what your responsibilities as a crew member are.
6. Be aware of the importance of good publicity for your play.

 **Vocabulary**

Define each term in a complete sentence.

audition	open audition
audition form	promptbook
call-back	props
cast	publicity
closed audition	royalties
feedback	

 Review Questions

1. Identify some things you should think about before you choose a play.

2. Define royalties. Why must they be paid?

3. Explain the difference between open and closed auditions.

4. Describe the kind of information that is usually asked for on an audition form.

5. Define *call-back*.

6. Identify the two different ways that are used at auditions to judge acting ability.

7. Name three ways that a cast can be chosen.

8. Name three duties of each of the following production people.
   a. an assistant director   **c.** a business manager
   b. a stage manager   **d.** a house manager

9. Explain why actors wear stage makeup.

10. Define the term *props*.

Discuss with Your Classmates

1. Consider what places in your school would be suitable for a play. Discuss the advantages and disadvantages of each one.

2. Discuss the importance of the assistant director. How do the assistant director's responsibilities compare with those of the stage manager?

3. Often a school chooses a play because a movie or TV show created or renewed interest in it. List on the board some stories that have been popular over a number of years. State whether they became successful movies or TV shows in the past five years. What are the basic conflicts or themes of these plays? Why do you think they continue to create interest?

 # Critical Thinking

1. Evaluation: Think of the plays that you are familiar with and select one that you believe your school could perform. In making your choice, consider everything about the play, including the level of acting required and all of the production needs. Be prepared to discuss your choice.

2. Synthesis: Explain why a director might decide to hold closed auditions. What might the advantages be? What might be the disadvantages?

Activities

In-Class

1. With a partner, look at the list of plays on page 404. In an anthology or other resource book, find one of the plays. Make a list of the costumes and props you would need. Discuss in class.

2. Divide into two or three large groups. Within each group, one person should be the director. The other group members will be cast and crew. Role-play a rehearsal feedback session.

3. Your teacher will call on various students to improvise the following situations. Assume that you are a director. Be prepared to comment on each performance.
  a. A teenager meets a visitor from outer space. This creature can read minds and control actions.
  b. A girl receives a million dollars on a phone-in game show.
  c. A boy's alarm didn't go off. He wakes up and finds that he has only ten minutes until the school bus arrives.

Out-of-Class

1. Review the different ways that a cast can be chosen (page 406). Which way do you think is best? In your speech notebook, write a brief paper explaining why you prefer that way. Be prepared to discuss your decision in class.

2. Prepare a checklist of duties for the assistant director, the stage manager, the business manager, and the house manager in your speech notebook. Compare your list with those of other students.

Chapter Project

Your teacher will divide the class into groups of three or four students to present a plan for producing a play at your school.

Each group should first decide on a play to produce, then consider how to finance it and what other decisions would have to be made. Would special costumes be required? Would the play require special talents, such as singing and dancing? Where would the play be held? Who might attend it? The group should review the questions on page 403 to be sure they have addressed all the issues of producing a play.

After each group presents its plan, the class should discuss whether all the issues were adequately addressed. If not, the class should make suggestions for resolving those issues.

CHAPTER 21 Mass Media

These are some of Amado's thoughts as he watches television with his family.

"I wonder what people did before they had television.

I learn a lot about what's happening in the world from television.

I'm sure glad somebody invented it."

Do *you* enjoy watching television and listening to the radio? What do you know about the beginnings of both television and radio?

In this chapter, you will read about:

- the growth and popularity of early radio
- the development of radio networks
- the early history of motion pictures
- the development of Hollywood studios
- the influence of movies and why they are sometimes used for propaganda
- careers in the movie industry
- the growth of television into a major system of mass communication
- the influence of television on viewers' lives

By 1900, the world was well on its way to becoming a modern, electronic society. So many inventions and discoveries were being made that one could hardly keep track of them. Each new invention seemed to make people's lives easier and more enjoyable.

At the turn of the century, electricity greatly changed people's lives. It was adapted to things such as sewing machines, phonographs, and ice boxes. Electricity was also used to create new things. One of the most amazing creations was the radio.

In 1906, Lee DeForest discovered the vacuum tube. With this discovery, modern radio became possible. By Christmas Eve 1906, a Canadian, Reginald Aubrey Fessenden, made the first broadcast from Brant Rock, Massachusetts. The broadcast consisted of only a couple of songs. Nevertheless, it marked the beginning of a medium that would change people's lives around the world.

RADIO

Surprisingly, radio got off to a slow start. Radio receivers and broadcasting equipment had to be made. What's more, they had to be made at a cost people could afford. Also, there were no trained announcers or technicians.

Eventually, however—through trial and error—an industry began to grow. Several small stations sprang up in the East. At first most of them only played records for short periods of time each day.

Radio was the most important means of mass communication of its day. Families gathered around the radio to listen to their favorite programs.

The first daily broadcast began at KCBS in San Jose, California, in 1910. The first commercial radio station was KDKA in Pittsburgh, Pennsylvania. It began broadcasting on November 2, 1920. On its first broadcast, it carried the returns for that year's Presidential election.

For the next 20 years, radio continued to improve. Home radios became smaller, lighter, and less expensive. Portable sending units were developed. This made on-the-scene broadcasts possible. Eventually radios could be found everywhere. They were placed in cars, and battery-operated radios could be carried anywhere. By 1941, the first FM station began. For the first time people in the United States got static-free radio reception.

Radio Compared with Other Mass Media

From its very beginning, radio became the most important means of mass communication of its day. It was faster than telegraph messages since it didn't have to be coded and decoded. What's more, radio messages could be sent and received as an event happened. As a result, radio messages could be sent to—and received by—masses of people faster than any other existing medium.

Radio also had other advantages. Its messages were more realistic than those of other mass media. They could include music and sound effects as well as spoken messages. Radio messages also sounded more personal and direct—like daily conversations. Radio soon became a friend of the masses—from childhood to old age.

Development of Networks

The popularity of radio grew quickly. All big cities had stations. All of these stations turned to local businesses to support them through commercials. **Commercials** are on-the-air advertising of a product or a service. If a company was the only advertiser for the same program each week, it was known as the program's **sponsor.**

Soon small cities and towns had their own radio stations. These smaller stations couldn't charge as much for commercials as the larger stations. As a result, they had fewer employees and smaller budgets to produce programs. Some way had to be found to keep them on the air. The most practical solution seemed to be to form **networks.** By joining together, the stations could use each other's programs. Eventually many of the most popular programs were made at a network's headquarters.

Within time, four large radio networks were created. They were the American Broadcasting Company (ABC), the Columbia Broadcasting Company (CBS), the Mutual Broadcasting Company, and the National Broadcasting Company (NBC). As these networks grew, large companies eagerly advertised on their many stations. They also agreed to sponsor daily or weekly programs that were too expensive for local stations to produce. By doing this, they were able to keep the names of their products always in the minds of the listeners.

The forming of networks had another important benefit. The high production standards of the networks were picked up and followed at the local stations. In addition to the network programs, all local stations kept some time to carry programs of local interest. These included local weather and news, local sports events, local disc jockey shows, and educational shows. The announcers and technicians on these shows copied the example of the networks. As a result, all of broadcasting improved.

1. When radio was invented, it affected nearly everyone in the world. Can you think of any recent mass communication invention that has had the same effect? What benefits have been gained from these changes?

2. Most radio stations have limited programming. Why do you think most of it is music and news? In your area, are there any popular radio programs that are not music or news?

MOVIES

Probably the first real moving pictures were created by Thomas A. Edison and his assistant William K.L. Dickson in 1893. At the time, they were working in their studio in West Orange, New Jersey. Edison called his moving pictures *kinetoscope*. At first he didn't think his invention had any commercial value.

Nevertheless, he set up a Kinetoscope Parlor on April 12, 1894, in New York City. It was nothing more than two rows of coin-operated machines. People looked into them and saw 50 feet of film that revolved on two spools. By 1896, Edison gave the first American showing of projected pictures. It included moving pictures of a prize fight, a dancer, and rolling waves.

Immediately, motion pictures became popular. Almost over-night, stores were turned into **nickelodeons,** places where people could see several short films for a nickel. Those early silent films were in black and white and didn't have a plot. By 1900, people could see films in traveling fairs, vaudeville theaters, and arcades.

The Great Train Robbery was the first important film made in this country. It was directed by Edwin S. Porter in 1903. It was only eleven minutes long, but it was the first film that told a story. After that, all films had plots. This created a new interest in films. By 1907, there were over 5000 nickelodeons in the United States.

Development of Hollywood Studios

Today everyone thinks of Hollywood as the film capital of the world. This reputation began in 1907 when the first movie was made

The movie industry attracted a wide audience by presenting a great variety of films.

in Los Angeles, California. Until then, most movies had been made in New Jersey and New York City. However, for year-round filming the weather in California was much better.

In 1911, the Nestor Company built a studio in the Hollywood section of Los Angeles. Eventually all film producers moved to California. In fact, by the mid-1920s, most of the major Hollywood studios were already operating there. These included Columbia, Fox, MGM, Paramount, United Artists, Universal, and Warner Brothers.

By 1912, movies moved out of stores and into actual theaters. The industry attracted a wider audience by filming popular novels. Several Broadway theater actors and actresses made their first appearances in films. During World War I (1914-1918), American movies were in great demand throughout the world. Because of the fighting in Europe, most European studios were closed. However, foreign countries still wanted to see films. The American studios tried to fill this need.

One producer, Thomas H. Ince, began mass-producing films. When he found he couldn't direct all the films in his studio, he hired other directors. Eventually he stopped directing entirely. Instead, he made sure that the films were completed on time and didn't go over their budgets. By doing this, he established a method of production that lasted for about 25 years.

Development of Talking Pictures

The first "sound" pictures were nothing more than a phonograph playing along with a movie. Usually the sound wasn't anything more than musical background to create a mood. In many theaters this music simply replaced the person who played the piano.

By the mid-1920s, the Bell Telephone Laboratories found a way to coordinate recorded sound with a movie projector. It was first used by Warner Brothers in 1926 to create sound effects and background music for the film *Don Juan.* Warner Brothers used it again in 1927 to make *The Jazz Singer,* starring Al Jolson. This film is usually considered the first talking film because Al Jolson spoke a few lines on the recording. By 1929, the American people no longer wanted to watch silent films. They demanded to see and *hear* "talkies."

The Influence of Movies

During the 1930s, the United States was working its way out of the worst depression in its history. These tough times, however, did not affect the movie industry. People continued to go to the movies because they were a means of escape. Movies reminded everyone of the good times. They were filled with examples of wealth, glamour, and luxury. In fact, by the end of the decade, the highest grossing film of all time, *Gone with the Wind,* was in theaters across the country. Running 220 minutes, it was the longest film ever produced in Hollywood. It was also in color, a rather recent invention.

By the end of the 1930s, motion pictures had become a respected medium. Furthermore, their influence was felt throughout the world. This was especially noticeable when World War II began. For the first time, people watched newsreels and saw the horrors of war that they had only read about before. Many countries also made propaganda movies. Governments realized that movies were one of the best means of mass communication.

Careers in the Film Industry

Have you ever watched the Academy Awards presentations? If you have, you know that there are hundreds of people who work on a single movie. Most of them work behind the scenes. Their work, nevertheless, is essential for a successful movie. The following are a few examples of some of those behind-the-scenes workers.

- *producers:* make all the business decisions from setting up the budget to making sure the filming finishes on time

- *directors:* control the artistic aspects of the film

- *writers:* prepare the script (Sometimes more than one writer works on a script.)

- *cinematographers:* run the cameras

- *designers:* create scenery, costumes, makeup, special effects, sound effects, and lighting

- *composers:* write original music or adapt existing music

- *choreographers:* plan and direct the dancing

- *editors (cutters):* cut films and put them together

YOUR TURN //////////////

1. Think of a story or novel you have read that would make a good movie. If you were the director, whom would you cast in the various leading roles? Why would you choose these people?

2. Have you ever seen a silent movie? If you have, explain your reaction to it. Did you understand it? What did you enjoy most about it? What didn't you like about it?

TELEVISION

NBC began the first regular telecasts in the United States in 1939. However, during the years of World War II, nothing much was done to develop television. There was a simple reason for this. The

Television Got Off to a Small Start

Most of the first television sets had very small screens.

production of all luxuries, including radio and television sets, had been stopped until the end of the war.

As a result, most Americans never saw television until the late 1940s or early 1950s. They got their first view of television through the windows of stores that had sets for sale. At first, people thought they were seeing poor quality black and white movies on some kind of lighted screen. Needless to say, everyone was amazed.

Radio was at its peak of popularity in the late 1940s. People were used to hearing their favorite programs at certain times. As a result, few were interested in television. They were not willing to spend a lot of money on a new gadget that they could use for only a few hours.

Early television sets were also not very attractive. Most of the first sets had very small screens. People had to sit close to them to see anything. Sets with larger screens were large, bulky, and heavy. There was also another disadvantage. People had to put up outside antennas on their houses to receive the television signals. Eventually, however, some people did buy television sets. People who did not have sets began to visit friends who had them. Television started to catch on.

Television Programming

Early television benefited from both radio and movies. The industry hired actors and technicians from both sources. As a result, the best ideas and methods from both industries were adopted by television. For example, getting businesses to sponsor programs was carried over directly from radio. Often, in fact, the sponsor of a radio series would continue to sponsor the same program when it moved to television.

During the early days of television, programs didn't begin until the afternoon, and they all ended at midnight. The best programs were shown during **prime time**—from 7 to 10 P.M. This was the time when entire families usually were at home. Because late night programs had small budgets, they were usually talk shows and sports events.

As the number of viewers increased, the number of broadcasting hours increased. Talk shows, news programs, and variety shows were added to the morning schedule. The early afternoon dramatic programs were followed by children's shows, comedies, and news.

At first, all programs were live telecasts. Home viewers saw the actors as they were performing. If a performer forgot a line, the entire home audience saw it. There were no retakes. Most programs were 30 or 60 minutes long, including commercial breaks.

Most programs were produced on the East Coast at the network studios. Because programs were live, this meant that prime time programs were seen in California in the middle of the afternoon! Delayed telecasting became possible after videotape was invented. Then most television production was relocated to the movie studios on the West Coast. There the television networks used the equipment and the talent of the movie studios. Like movie producers, television producers also began to use portable equipment for location shots. Television got better and better.

Television requires skilled technicians behind the scenes at all times.

The Influence of Television

Color telecasting began in 1953. At about the same time, television producers began to make movies just for their home viewers. When these two things happened, television suddenly became a strong rival of other mass media. In spite of the small screens, television movies drew larger audiences. Movie theaters felt this competition as people began to stay home.

The number of television stations also began to grow throughout the world. Each new station brought a wider choice of programs. The radio industry began to suffer as a result. Major sponsors preferred to advertise on television rather than on radio. The budgets of radio stations were suddenly cut. As a result, radio became a medium for news, weather, music, local interest programs, and talk shows only. Most of the quiz shows, soap operas, variety shows, and radio dramas disappeared. Radio could no longer make these costly shows.

The influence of television took another leap with the invention of the Early Bird satellite. It was used to telecast the first direct program to Europe in 1965. In 1969, television telecast its first program in outer space. People throughout the world watched live pictures of the American astronauts landing on the moon. Then in the 1980s, television showed that it was truly a medium for mass communication. In 1984, over a billion people watched the summer

Olympic Games in Los Angeles. These viewers were located in 40 different countries!

TELEVISION'S IMPACT ON YOUR LIFE

How many hours a day do you watch television? A recent survey showed that the average person watches over six hours a day. That's almost as long as you spend in school each day. Because you spend so many hours in front of the television, you should stop once in a while and think about what you are seeing. For example, how many times have you watched the *same* rerun of a show? Why did you watch it the second time or the third time? It is also important for you to think about the influence television might be having on you.

Television as a Source of News

There is no question that the general public is more informed today than it has ever been before. Most of the credit for this accomplishment belongs to television. Today news of the world is as easy to get as turning on the set. Many local stations have news programs three times a day, and all the major networks have 30 minutes of world news each evening. Some of these news programs are on while families sit around the dinner table.

Meet the Press, the longest-running television show still on the air, was first seen on November 20, 1947. This program laid the groundwork for other news features. As a result, today some viewers faithfully watch news magazines such as *60 Minutes* and *20/20.* Occasionally the networks also present **documentaries.** These are in-depth reports on important subjects. If these sources of news are not enough, the American public has another choice. There is now a cable channel that shows nothing but news all day long.

Television as a Source of Entertainment

Many people get most of their news from watching television. Nevertheless, people turn to their television sets more often for entertainment. Comedy programs are probably at the top of most people's entertainment list.

Because of television, the news of the world is as easy to get as turning to a favorite channel.

In the early days of television, Sid Caesar, the host of "Your Show of Shows," introduced the variety show to television audiences. Lucille Ball, the star of "I Love Lucy," introduced the situation comedy. Both shows became very popular. When any type of program becomes popular, other networks try to imitate it. Often, however, these imitations are unsuccessful.

Drama is another source of television entertainment. One of the oldest forms of drama on television is the soap opera. **Soap operas** began on radio, as dramatic afternoon shows for women. Usually, these shows were sponsored by companies that made soap. Soap operas made a quick and easy transition to television during its earliest days. Over the years, soap opera fans have increased. In fact, some dramatic evening programs are called prime-time soap operas.

A recent development in drama has been the **mini-series.** These programs take from four to sixteen hours to air. Many are based on novels or historical characters or events. Even though some programs are shown four or five nights in a row, they still attract huge audiences.

Today television viewers also have **spin-offs.** Characters on popular comedy and drama programs become stars of their own programs. Programmers hope that the interest of the first show or the interest in the stars of the first show will make the viewers watch the new show.

LIVE, FROM THE NEWSROOM, ON SATURDAY NIGHT

by Susan Ballard

Susan Ballard was a reporter and part-time anchorperson at WXII in Winston-Salem, North Carolina. This article describes a typical day.

I was the anchorperson. Twice each Saturday evening, I mounted the news set, clipped a microphone to my lapel, and sat under banks of hot, bright lights. The cameraperson held up five fingers, four, three, two, and pointed at me. A red light shone atop the camera. I was on the air.

Viewers often asked, "Do you write what you read on the news?"

"Yes," I answered, "and no." Television is never a one-person production, but our Saturday evening newscasts came close. We had a skeleton staff on weekends.

I was always in the newsroom by 3:00 P.M. I made sure the Associated Press wire service machine had plenty of paper. I sorted the tangle of world, national, and state news that the machine spewed onto the floor and selected the most important stories. Then I found a humorous one to place at the end of the newscast. I sat at my typewriter and began rewriting.

A reporter and cameraperson usually burst into the newsroom around 3:30 P.M. After a few minutes of typing, the reporter handed two or three lead-ins to me. A lead-in is what anchors use to introduce reporters' stories.

The newsroom had a large collection of 35mm slides. If I mentioned the governor, for example, a slide of him was used. I wrote bold notes on my script, telling myself when to turn from one of the three huge studio cameras to another. Then the station's technical director reviewed the newscast with me. After that, I taped a set of scripts together to feed the Tele-PrompTer. I was ready to anchor the six o'clock news. I could worry about the eleven o'clock news later.

Connie Chung, anchorperson

Television as a Business

As you watch each news show, each comedy, and each drama, remember that network television is a business. Stations air programs to make money. These stations sell air time for advertising. The cost of each show is then subtracted from the money raised through commercials. What is left is profit.

How much influence does an advertiser who pays the bills for a television show have? The answer is simple: an advertiser has tremendous influence. Advertisers can threaten to stop advertising on a program if changes are made. Without the financial support of advertisers, stations and networks usually would not have enough money to produce the program.

How do advertisers decide whether to support a show? They use a program's **ratings.** These are the results from a survey of selected homes to find out which programs are being watched at certain times. The number of people watching a show in these homes may decide its future. The quality of the show may not be the most important thing to advertisers. Even news shows are expected to have high ratings.

If ratings for a show are low, the producers will have fewer advertisers. They will also have to charge lower advertising fees than they charge for a show with higher ratings. The ratings can affect the type of programs available on television, from comedy to news to drama.

Viewers of commercial television pay *indirectly* for the programs they watch. They buy the products that are advertised on television. Then the makers of those products take some of that money and turn it back into advertising. Viewers can also pay *directly* for the programs they watch by subscribing to cable television.

Cable television began in the 1950s. At first, it was most popular in areas where television reception was poor. Now, more than one in every five homes in the United States subscribes to cable television. With this system, most people pay a monthly fee to have their television attached by a cable to large antennas. These large antennas are able to pick up stations across the United States. Cable television greatly increased the number of stations a home can receive.

YOU AS A CONSUMER

As you learned earlier in this course, you and a friend may have very different perceptions of the same event. As a consumer of electronic media messages, you need to learn the difference between actuality and make-believe. You also need to know when you are hearing and seeing programs or films that were created deliberately to make you feel, believe, or do a particular thing.

Many critics of radio, television, and film believe people are influenced too much by the messages they see and hear through the electronic media. As an educated consumer, you should remember that you always have control over your own listening and viewing habits. Suppose you find yourself watching something that presents incorrect, unpleasant, or biased ideas. You have a choice to make. You can continue receiving the message, or you can stop receiving it. If you continue to receive the message, you can decide to watch and listen critically rather than uncritically. If you decide to stop receiving the message, you may change the radio station, turn off the television set, or walk out of the movie. Just because the message is being transmitted does not mean you must receive it.

YOUR TURN ///////////////

1.   Think about the television programs you watched when you were about six years old. Then answer the following questions. Have there been any major technical advances since then? How has television programming changed since then? Do you prefer the television back then or now? Explain your answer.

2.   Think of some television shows that were once very popular but are no longer on the air. What do you think caused their loss of popularity?

21 CHAPTER REVIEW

Chapter Summary

Radio developed quickly after its beginning in the early 1900s. Soon many stations sprang up across the country. After more and more small towns got radio stations, networks were formed to share the cost of producing programs. Networks provided more programming and raised the standards of all broadcasting.

Thomas Edison and his assistant William K.L. Dickson created the first moving pictures. Soon, short movies with plots were being shown in nickelodeons across the country. To meet the demand for films, studios were built in California because of its good year-round weather. The industry got another boost when "talkies" were introduced in the 1920s. Throughout the history of motion pictures, movies have often been used for propaganda.

Television began in 1939, but it didn't become popular until the late 1940s or early 1950s. In its early days, television borrowed the best techniques and talent from radio and movies. However, as the interest in television increased, the interest in radio and movies decreased. Today, television has great influence because it is watched by so many people. Much of what is seen on television is controlled by advertisers and ratings.

As an educated consumer, you have the responsibility to decide what messages you want to receive through the electronic media.

Checklist

Electronic Media Skills

1. Understand the historical significance and influence of radio, movies, and television.

2. Distinguish between actuality and make-believe when listening to electronic media.

3. Listen critically to messages that are intended to persuade or convince.

4. Recognize the influence of television in your life.

5. Make careful judgments about which messages you choose to receive and which you choose not to receive.

 Vocabulary

Define each term in a complete sentence.

commercials	prime time
documentaries	ratings
mini-series	soap operas
networks	spin-offs
nickelodeons	sponsor

 Review Questions

1. Explain why radio became so popular shortly after it was invented.

2. Explain why sponsors and commercials are important to radio and television.

3. Explain why networks were first formed.

4. Explain the significance of the film *The Great Train Robbery*.

5. Identify Thomas H. Ince? How did he affect the film industry?

6. Name and describe four possible careers in the film industry.

7. Explain what was happening in radio about the time television first began in the United States.

8. Explain how the increased popularity of television hurt the radio industry.

9. Define *documentary*.

10. Explain how the success or failure of a television program is decided.

Discuss with Your Classmates

1. Discuss the beginnings of radio. What kinds of activities do you think radio replaced? Why did radio get off to a slow start?

2. Point out some possible advantages of working in the film industry. Then discuss some possible disadvantages.

3. Compare seeing a movie in a theater with seeing a movie on television. Discuss reasons why people prefer one or the other. Which do you prefer?

4. Different people react differently to television. Some prefer one kind of show over another. Some people rarely watch anything. Discuss your viewing habits. How do they compare with the viewing habits of those who live with you?

Critical Thinking

1. **Evaluation:** Explain the United States government's use of radio and movies to distribute propaganda during World War II. Discuss whether the use of propaganda is ever justified.

2. **Analysis:** Listen to a local radio station for one hour. How many kinds of services or programs are provided? How many minutes are devoted to each? How well does the station serve local needs?

 **Activities**

In-Class

1. Early sound effects for radio programs were made during live broadcasts, without using recorded sound. Your teacher will divide the class into two or three large groups. Each group should consider what objects could be used in a radio studio to make the following sounds:

a. footsteps on earth
b. footsteps on a tile floor
c. a doorbell chime
d. a creaking door

e. thunder
f. rain falling on pine needles
g. a galloping horse
h. a crackling bonfire

2. Write a 30-second TV commercial for a product you use. The class will choose the five best commercials by secret ballot. Your teacher will then divide the class into five groups. Each group should produce one of the commercials. The writers of the winning commercials will be the directors of each commercial.

3. Saturday morning television programs offer entertainment for young children. Watch television on Saturday morning. Pay particular attention to the commercials. What kinds of products are advertised? How are these products presented? Discuss your findings in class. With your classmates, develop a list of advertising techniques used in commercials aimed at young people.

Out-of-Class

1. Your teacher will tell you to watch a particular television show. Afterwards, write a report in your speech notebook that answers the following questions:

a. What was the major conflict?
b. How was the conflict solved?
c. Which character had the most speaking lines?
d. Was the program performed before a live audience?
e. Was the program videotaped and rebroadcast?
f. Who produced and directed the show?

2. Choose three television shows that you would send to other countries as representative of American life. Identify your choices and list your reasons in your speech notebook. Be ready to explain your choices in class.

3. What is your opinion of the ratings system? Do you think there should be another way to judge the success of a program? Think of a substitute for the present ratings system, and explain it in your speech notebook. Be prepared to discuss your plan in class.

4. Use reference books to find information on each of the following people. In your speech notebook identify each person and explain his or her contribution to the mass media.

a. Rudy Vallee   **g.** Dorothy Kilgallen

b. Ted Mack   **h.** Jimmy Durante

c. Gabriel Heater   **i.** Clara Bow

d. Charlie Chaplin   **j.** James Cagney

e. Shirley Temple   **k.** Sarah Bernhardt

f. Fred Astaire   **l.** Edward R. Murrow

Chapter Project

Take a survey of five people, one in each of the following age groups: 8–12, 13–20, 21–30, 31–40, over 40. Ask each person the following questions; then tabulate the answers. The class will then compare the results of each student's survey, discuss the findings in class, and prepare a summary of the survey results.

Questions

1. Which one of the following sources of news do you trust most?
   a. radio   **b.** newspapers   **c.** television   **d.** magazines

2. What one movie has made the most lasting impression on you? Was the impression favorable, or unfavorable? How old were you when you saw it? Do you know why it made such an impression?

3. What two movie or television personalities do you admire most? What do you find admirable about them?

4. How many hours a day do you usually spend listening to the radio? What is your main reason for listening to the radio?

5. What is your favorite television program? Why do you like it? Is there anything about it you would like to see changed?

UNIT 7

DEBATE AND PARLIAMENTARY PROCEDURE

CHAPTER 22 Debate

Sam and Melody have just finished their debate before the elections for class president. As the audience's questions begin, Sam thinks . . .

"Louis is asking the first question.

He always asks questions that really make you think.

I'll have to answer carefully."

Have *you* ever participated in a debate? How did you prepare?

In this chapter, you will read about:

- terms that apply to a debate
- the different kinds of propositions
- the different kinds of evidence
- the purpose of rebuttal and refutation
- three kinds of debate
- the duties of each speaker in a debate

Where does a discussion end and a debate begin? A discussion goes on as long as people do not take opposite sides on an issue. When people take sides, a discussion stops and a debate begins.

WHAT IS A DEBATE?

A **debate** is an orderly communication process. During a debate, two or more opposing speakers try to prove or disprove a statement. In a formal debate, speakers for the **affirmative side** support the statement. Speakers for the **negative side** oppose it. Debaters do not try to change the minds of the other team. Instead, each side presents a **case** to a judge. A case includes all the evidence and reasoning that supports its side. At the end of the debate, the judge makes a decision.

Throughout your life you will take part in formal and informal debates. From time to time, everyone becomes a judge. A parent decides whether a child should or should not take a trip. A jury decides whether someone is innocent or guilty. Voters decide which candidate will best serve the people. If two sides can be presented to any question, that question can be stated as a formal debate proposition. A **proposition** is the subject of a debate. Most propositions propose a change from something that already exists.

A formal debate always has set conditions. These may include how many people may speak and when they will speak. They also might include which side of the problem each person will defend. As a result, a debate is very different from a discussion. In a debate, people get to present their side of a problem without any interruptions. A debate also gives each side equal time.

The first step in preparing for a debate is to do research to find a suitable debate proposition.

DEBATE PROPOSITIONS

Finding a good debate proposition is the first—and often the hardest—part of a debate. There are a number of kinds of propositions, but they are all judged by the same characteristics.

Characteristics of a Good Proposition

Debate propositions can be judged according to the following characteristics.

They must be debatable. This means that the two sides must be evenly balanced. This gives both teams the same chance to prove their sides and win their cases. If a debate used a proposition in which one side was a lot easier to argue, one debate side would have a better chance to win, and the debate wouldn't be a fair contest. For example, no one would want to argue for the idea that people should be licensed drivers at age 9.

They should be phrased affirmatively. "Affirmatively" means the same as "positively." The words *no* or *not* should not appear in the proposition. This allows the affirmative side to propose a change and take the offensive. The negative side opposes the proposition.

They should deal with only one question.   This limits the scope of a debate. Each side, therefore, can concentrate on just one part of a problem.

They should be stated simply and clearly.   Long, complex propositions are confusing to both the debaters and the audience. Simple, concrete words should be used. Then many terms do not have to be defined.

They should deal with important and timely problems.   Audiences should be able to see how a proposition can affect their lives now and in the future. If they do, they are usually eager to listen to the debate.

Kinds of Propositions

Formal debate propositions are written as **resolutions.** They begin with the words "Resolved That" and go on to state the proposed change. The following are three kinds of propositions.

Value   In propositions of value, people or ideas are examined for their fairness or usefulness. Following are some examples.

- Resolved, That the separation of male and female students in United States schools is desirable.

- Resolved, That courses in typing are more helpful than courses in history for students who plan to go to college.

- Resolved, That this school's tardy rules are unfair to students who take public transportation to school.

Judgment or Fact   These deal with questions of truth. They try to show that something really happened or that something exists. The following are some examples.

- Resolved, That the United States has a higher rate of literacy than Canada.

- Resolved, That William Shakespeare was the sole author of all his plays.

- Resolved, That female drivers in the United States are cited for fewer traffic accidents each year than male drivers.

Policy   These deal with various courses of action that should or should not be taken. These propositions are used most in school debates. Following are some examples. Notice that they all use the word *should* or *ought*.

- Resolved, That this school's baseball team should help in fund raising to increase the school's athletic budget for all sports.

- Resolved, That this school should allow students to choose whether or not they will attend assemblies.

- Resolved, That the state constitution ought to be amended to require a balanced budget at the end of each fiscal year.

THE FIRST STEPS OF A DEBATE

Following are the first steps of a debate, finding issues and defining terms. All debates follow these steps.

Finding Issues

The most important step in organizing a case is to choose the issues that will be debated. An issue is a matter on which the two sides disagree. The affirmative side always has the **burden of proof.** In other words, it must win every issue that it introduces. The negative side, on the other hand, must win only one issue. If it can do this, it can prove that the proposition should be rejected.

In propositions of policy, for example, there are always the following three **stock issues.** These are called stock issues because they are questions that will be supported and attacked in most debates.

- Is there a need for a change?

- Is there a plan that meets the need to change?

- Is the proposed plan the best, most practical one available?

The affirmative answers "yes" to each of these questions. However, the negative may argue "no" to one, two, or all three.

THE POLITICS BEHIND DEBATES

She lugged an eight pound briefing book everywhere. A special debate staff coached her in domestic and foreign affairs. Finally, they rented a television studio and duplicated the one in Philadelphia where she would meet her opponent. For two more days, Congresswoman Geraldine Ferraro practiced, debating an aide who'd taught himself to look and sound like Vice President George Bush.

In political debates, there is no set format. A sponsor helps opponents set the ground rules in advance. Here are some of the issues settled prior to the 1984 debates:

- Whether the candidates should sit or stand. Sitting at a table with the President of the United States, Mondale would appear as his equal. Reagan would seem more presidential and imposing if allowed to stand apart, behind a podium. Reagan won this issue.
- Whether Ferraro could become taller. Her advisers didn't want her looking up to him, so they built a special ramp behind her podium.
- Whether a panel would ask questions. The League of Women Voters, which sponsored the debates, wanted the candidates to address each other. The politicians wished to avoid arguments, and asked the journalists to buffer their exchanges.
- Who would sit on the panel. Negotiations turned ugly when sponsors tried to assemble the panel. The two sides vetoed dozens of names in a snowballing battle to top each other. Finally, they agreed.

If voters judge political debates, Reagan and Bush won. Observers gave one of the three debates to Reagan, one to Mondale, and the vice presidential debate, to Bush. Still, Geraldine Ferraro was a tough competitor. If she didn't win, it wasn't from lack of trying.

In addition to stock issues, there are **basic** or **fighting issues.** These are the major points of disagreement between the affirmative and negative sides. For example, suppose a debate is held on getting rid of grading systems in high schools. One of the basic or fighting issues might be the effect this would have on students trying to get into college. Even though the third stock issue deals with whether or not the proposed change is the best plan, the real or basic issue in this debate would be getting into college.

Of course, it is not always easy to pick out the most important issues in a debate. The following are some factors that will help you locate these issues.

- a good understanding of the historical background of the problem

- a clear understanding of current and developing trends

- clear definition of terms

- an understanding of value statements or premises

Sometimes, a judge will point out the basic issue or issues in a debate. He or she may say, "Although all the other points are important, the one point that both sides kept disagreeing on was _____." Then the judge decides which side wins, based on the attack or defense of this issue.

Debaters often find the most important issues in a debate by writing all their arguments for or against the proposition on one side of a sheet of paper. Then they try to predict all the arguments that will be used by the other side. If a team predicts correctly, it can find the evidence and reasoning it needs even *before* a debate takes place.

Defining Terms

Before a debate can occur, unclear or abstract terms in the proposition must be defined. The first speaker in a debate usually does this. If terms are not agreed upon in the beginning, debaters may spend too much time arguing over meanings of terms. For example, the term *majority* can mean a majority of those voting or a majority of the total membership. Think about the following proposition. "Resolved, That all class officers in this school should be elected by a majority vote." If the term *majority* were not defined, each side might develop its case, using a different definition.

Where does discussion end and informal debate begin?

CONSTRUCTING DEBATE CASES

If debaters can outline, they have no trouble constructing debate cases. Cases follow the same format that is used in sentence outlines. The only exception is that each item that must be proved will have either *for* or *because* at the end of the line. When debate cases are outlined this way, they are called **debate briefs.** Debaters use these briefs to organize their ideas before a debate. They also use the same system during a debate to outline the other team's case. Sometimes these briefs are called **flow sheets.**

To understand how debate cases are constructed, look at the following example. Notice that the ideas follow the order that will be used during the debate.

I. The introduction, which could include the following:

    A. Reasons why the topic is currently important.

    B. Information on the history and background of the question.

    C. Definitions of terms used in the proposition.

    D. A statement about any matters that will be omitted or admitted in advance.

    E. A summary of the main issues faced by the debaters.

II. Basic issues that will be proved and their supporting arguments and proof.

    A. There is a need for a change from the present situation because:

        1. Contention #1 because:
          a. Proof A.   b. Proof B.
        2. Contention #2 because:
          a. Proof A.   b. Proof B.
        3. Contention #3 because:
          a. Proof A.   b. Proof B.

    B. The proposed plan will meet the existing need because:

        1. Contention #1 because:
          a. Proof A.   b. Proof B.
        2. Contention #2 because:
          a. Proof A.   b. Proof B.
        3. Contention #3 because:
          a. Proof A.   b. Proof B.

YOUR TURN

1. Decide whether the following resolutions are propositions of value, fact, or policy.

    a. Resolved, That the eight-hour work day is too long.

    b. Resolved, That the government should adopt a sales tax.

    c. Resolved, That the ninth grade in this school has a higher cumulative grade average than any other class.

    d. Resolved, That single-family homes are superior to condominiums for raising children.

    e. Resolved, That this class should meet in the library during the debate unit.

2. Use one of the resolutions in Exercise 1 to construct an affirmative outline for the first major issue in a debate. Refer back to the outline given on pages 451–452.

FINDING PROOF

Each contention on a debate brief is supported by proof. This proof generally comes from evidence and reasoning. **Evidence** consists of factual information. Inferences, or conclusions, that are drawn from these facts make up the **reasoning.**

Evidence

Debaters spend a lot of time gathering evidence and recording it on note cards. Usually they separate the cards into two groups: constructive speech and rebuttal speech. The **constructive speech** is the debater's first speech. It develops the case that the team supports. The **rebuttal speech** is the shorter, final speech which is given by each debater. This speech argues against the statements made by the other side. Usually debaters mark these two kinds of cards to make them easier to find during a debate.

The following is a list of the information that should be included on evidence cards.

- the side of the proposition the card supports—affirmative or negative

- the specific issue the card supports or rejects

- the piece of evidence or reasoning

- the source of evidence

- comments about the qualifications of the source

General Tests of Evidence   The answers to the following four questions usually will tell you how strong your evidence is.

- *Is it relevant to the point being made?* This is the most important question. Evidence that is indirectly related is weak and usually useless.

- *Is the evidence consistent?* Sometimes a statement from one source is different in another source because authorities disagree. This type of evidence has little value—except in a rebuttal.

- *Is the evidence recent?* In debates, evidence a year or two old may not be recent enough to use. In this modern world, things change very fast.

Verification of evidence is a most important factor in a court trial.

- *Can the evidence be verified, or checked?* Debaters should
  have several sources to support their information. If
  evidence cannot be checked, it should not be used.

Kinds of Evidence   Generally, debaters are judged on two
things. They are judged on the kinds of evidence they use and the
amount they use. As a result, debaters should know all the following
kinds of evidence.

- *Accepted or known facts.* This evidence doesn't need any
  further proof. The facts are so well known that everyone
  accepts them. For example, if outlawing the use of nuclear
  weapons were being debated, no one would have to prove
  that nuclear weapons exist. Everyone knows they do.

- *Documented statistics and facts.* This evidence is figures and
  information that anyone could check in books or other
  publications. This evidence may even be objects that can be
  observed and/or analyzed. For example, two price tags could
  be compared.

- *Examples or samples.* This evidence can be illustrations,
  comparisons, or situations that help to explain a statement.
  A debater, for example, might name schools in the area that

are in session for only a half day every Wednesday. The debater could explain how this system decreases vandalism. All examples should be clearly and easily understood.

- *Testimonies or opinions of authorities.* This evidence presents objective viewpoints. Debaters, however, must make sure that their authorities have good qualifications. Opinions of authorities, of course, do not prove a contention. They do, however, give a reasonable basis for believing it.

Reasoning

Reasoning is often classified as inductive and deductive. It is used to show how you intend to prove a contention. The contentions used in reasoning may be based on any of the kinds of evidence just covered.

Inductive Reasoning **Inductive reasoning** begins with a group of facts, cases, or examples. Then it moves to a generalization made from them.

For example, suppose you were debating the following proposition. "Resolved, That officers in all school organizations must have an overall grade average of at least a *B* at the beginning of each grading period to stay in office." You want to prove that this proposition would not change anything. Most officers already have this grade average. You could test this idea inductively. You could get the grade average of each officer. If you did, you might get the following results.

	Senior Class	Junior Class	Sophomore Class	Freshman Class
Drama Club	B+	A−	B	B+
Athletic Boosters	B	B+	B+	A
Student Council	A−	B	C−	B+
Musicians Unlimited	B	C+	A	A−

Only two of the sixteen officers would be affected by the policy change. Therefore, you would be safe to argue that *most* officers already meet the proposed standard.

Deductive Reasoning **Deductive reasoning** moves from a large, general rule to a specific one. It is, therefore, the opposite of inductive reasoning. Deductive reasoning depends on the three parts of a **syllogism.**

"Most teenagers watch television at least two hours each night."

1. *The major premise.* This is a generalization.

All students at Kennedy School must take final exams.
All dog owners in this county must register their dogs each year.
Members of the French Club must pay annual dues of one dollar.

2. *The minor premise.* This is an example of the generalization.

Carrie is a student at Kennedy School.
Mrs. Kim owns a dog in this county.
Mitchell is a member of the French Club.

3. *The conclusion or contention.* If the major and minor premises are accepted, this is the result.

Therefore, Carrie must take final exams.
Therefore, Mrs. Kim must register her dog each year.
Therefore, Mitchell must pay annual dues of one dollar.

Of course, some syllogisms can be faulty in their reasoning. For example, the major premise of the following syllogism is not true. Since it isn't true, then the conclusion would not be true either.

All Texans are rich.
Ted Franklin is a Texan.
Therefore, Ted Franklin is rich.

If debaters accept the major and minor premises, they must also accept the conclusion. Therefore, most debates will be over the truth of the premises.

1. What kind of evidence is each of the following statements?
   a. Tomorrow the sun will appear in the east in the morning.
   b. According to *The People's Almanac,* the third modern Olympic Games were held in 1904 in St. Louis, Missouri.
   c. An example of a calculated risk: depending on a car that has stalled twice in ten minutes to get you to the airport on time.
   d. My grandfather says a thermometer must be used to make excellent fudge. He has won three first-place State Fair ribbons for his fudge.
   e. Lake Superior consists of 31,800 square miles of fresh water.

2. Your teacher will divide the class into groups of three to five students. Each group should then discuss the inductive reasoning that could be used to prove or disprove the following statements.
   a. The apple is the favorite fruit of people in this community.
   b. Most teenagers in this community watch television at least two hours each night.
   c. In this community homeowners have more maple trees in their yards than any other tree.
   d. Men prefer sandwiches over salads for lunch.
   e. Preschool children are afraid of doctors.

REFUTATION AND REBUTTAL

Refutation is the process of attacking the opposing side's case. This is done by disproving or weakening its major arguments. **Rebuttal,** on the other hand, is the process of rebuilding an argument after it has been attacked by the other side.

Refutation

Refutation can occur any time throughout the debate. When it does, it usually follows five steps.

1. The argument that is to be refuted is pointed out. If possible, a debater states the exact words that the other side used.

2. The importance of this argument to the opposite side's position is explained.

3. The position of, or counterpoint to, the contention is stated.

4. Evidence is given to support the position.

5. The refutation is summarized. Its relationship to the proposition is shown. A debater, for example, may show through reasoning that his or her contention is more probable than the other side's.

Judges usually remember major arguments presented in a speech. Therefore, it is smart to refute arguments as quickly as possible. If debaters wait, time may run out before they can respond. Debaters also might forget to refute an argument if too much time passes. The following are some of the common ways to handle refutation.

- Present an argument that is stronger than the other side's.

- Show that their argument doesn't apply to the proposition and should be ignored.

- Admit that the argument is correct. Nevertheless, show that it is so unimportant that it shouldn't even be considered.

- Point out any errors in the other side's reasoning, evidence, or organization.

Rebuttal

Rebuttal is not just a summary of arguments. New evidence may be used, but new arguments may not be introduced. During rebuttal, five steps are followed:

1. The speaker restates the arguments exactly as they were said earlier.

2. The speaker restates the other side's refutation.

3. The speaker shows weaknesses in the other side's arguments. Then the debater repeats his or her own position.

4. The speaker gives additional evidence to support the original point made just before the other side spoke.

5. The speaker summarizes by restating the original argument. This includes all of the additional evidence that was given.

Rebuttal is the process of rebuilding an argument after it has been attacked.

FORMS OF DEBATE

There are many forms of debate. Those used most often in schools are described in this section.

Traditional or Standard Debate

Traditional debate consists of two teams of two people each. One team is the affirmative, and the other team is the negative. This kind of debate usually lasts for about one hour. The time is divided equally among the speakers. The following is the order of speakers and their time limits.

Constructive Speeches		Rebuttal Speeches	
First affirmative	10 minutes	First negative	5 minutes
First negative	10 minutes	First affirmative	5 minutes
Second affirmative	10 minutes	Second negative	5 minutes
Second negative	10 minutes	Second affirmative	5 minutes

Cross-Examination Debate

This form of debate also has two teams of two people each. However, after speakers finish their constructive speeches, they are questioned, or cross-examined, by a member of the other team. The purpose of the questions is to point out weaknesses in the other team's arguments. Following is one variation of the cross-examination debate. It takes a total of 60 minutes.

First affirmative constructive speech	8 minutes
Second negative questions first speaker	3 minutes
First negative constructive speech	8 minutes
First affirmative questions second speaker	3 minutes
Second affirmative constructive speech	8 minutes
First negative questions third speaker	3 minutes
Second negative constructive speech	8 minutes
Second affirmative questions fourth speaker	3 minutes
First negative rebuttal speech	4 minutes
First affirmative rebuttal speech	4 minutes
Second negative rebuttal speech	4 minutes
Second affirmative rebuttal speech	4 minutes

The Lincoln-Douglas Debate

Lincoln-Douglas or Two-Person Debate

This form of debate is named after Abraham Lincoln and Stephen A. Douglas. They held a series of debates in 1858 and made this form popular in the United States.

This form is a variation of the cross-examination debate. One difference, however, is that each side has only one speaker. Both speakers have equal time. However, the time may be set up differently for each speaker. Before the debate, both speakers must agree to any changes.

At the beginning of the debate, a moderator introduces the topic and explains the rules. After the debate, the moderator accepts questions from the audience, and the speakers answer them. Usually the proposition debated in this form is one of value rather than policy. Variations of this form are often used in political debates. The following are two variations of this form.

First Variation		Second Variation	
Affirmative	10 minutes	Affirmative constructive	6 minutes
Negative	15 minutes	Negative cross-examination	3 minutes
Affirmative	5 minutes	Negative constructive	7 minutes
Audience		Affirmative cross-examination	3 minutes
Questions	15 minutes	Affirmative rebuttal	4 minutes
		Negative rebuttal	6 minutes
		Affirmative rebuttal	3 minutes
		Audience	
		Questions	15 minutes

CONSTRUCTIVE AND REBUTTAL SPEECHES FOR TRADITIONAL DEBATE

You know that debate is an orderly communication process. The duties of the various speakers in a traditional debate are listed below in the order in which the speeches are given.

First Affirmative Constructive Speech

This speaker is the only one who knows exactly what he or she will say for an entire speech. The main purposes of this speech are to inform and to persuade. The speaker opens with a friendly greeting and states the proposition. Following are other duties of this speaker.

- Creates interest in the topic by showing its importance.

- Defines any unclear words.

- Gives background information on the question.

- States the affirmative position, accepts the burden of proof, and presents a ***prima facie case*** (one that is strong enough to win if it is not answered).

- Points out what the major points of argument will be between the two sides.

- Outlines the affirmative case.

- Tries to defend the affirmative case in the remaining time.

- Summarizes what has been said and says that the next affirmative speaker will continue to support the proposition.

First Negative Constructive Speaker

This speaker sets the tone for his or her team. First this person responds to the greeting. Then he or she accepts or rejects the words that were defined by the first speaker. Following are other duties of this speaker.

- Recognizes and summarizes the affirmative position.

- Refutes the most important arguments immediately.

- Makes the negative position clear. This may be
  a. to keep the present system *(status quo)*.
  b. to improve the existing plan by making a few changes.
  c. to present an entirely different plan (counterplan). If this is the plan, little more is said about the need for a change since both sides accept the idea. The main concern is: *Which is the better plan?*

A two-person, or Lincoln-Douglas, debate is an orderly communication process with definite rules for the participants.

    d. to refute all affirmative arguments without presenting any constructive or defensive positions (straight or running refutation). The *status quo* is not defended or denied.

    e. to compare the advantages of the affirmative plan and the current plan (comparative advantages).

- Attacks the weak arguments of the affirmative side and insists that the affirmative side defend each issue.

Second Affirmative Constructive Speech

This speaker responds immediately to the arguments raised by the previous speaker. He or she also answers any questions that were asked about the first affirmative's position. Then this speaker presents the rest of the affirmative case. This will be the last affirmative speech for at least 15 minutes. As a result, this speaker summarizes the affirmative case and ends with a strong conclusion.

A debater presenting his side of an issue.

Second Negative Constructive Speech

This speaker briefly reviews the debate. He or she does this by concentrating on the major issues. Next, this speaker attacks the arguments of the second affirmative. Finally, he or she summarizes the negative case. In the conclusion, this person then makes a major attack on the affirmative case.

First Negative Rebuttal Speech

A negative speaker begins the rebuttal. This person reminds the audience of what the affirmative side has not yet answered. He or she also restates the major negative objections. Then this speaker calls attention to any weaknesses in the affirmative case.

First Affirmative Rebuttal Speech

This speaker reviews the affirmative case quickly. Next this person refutes any important arguments that the previous speaker made. He or she then responds to the second negative's constructive speech, which has not yet been refuted. If there is any time left, this speaker summarizes the affirmative position.

Second Negative Rebuttal Speech

This is the last speech by the negative team. As a result, this speaker must make a strong conclusion. He or she does this by answering any important questions raised by the affirmative side that still remain unanswered. Finally, this speaker asks for acceptance of the negative side.

Second Affirmative Rebuttal Speech

This speaker responds to the previous speaker. Then he or she gives a balanced summary that answers the major negative objections. Finally, this speaker restates the affirmative side and asks for its acceptance.

YOUR TURN /////////

1. Your teacher will divide the class into groups of three to four students. Then each group should think of effective ways to refute the following arguments.

   a. The United States has never elected a woman president even though 50 percent of the population always has been female. In the future, even women will not support a female for this high office.

   b. The walls and ceilings of rooms around the band room have cracked. As a result, large pieces of plaster have fallen down. Noise from the band is so great that the whole school is falling apart. Band should not be offered until a new band room can be built.

   c. Many healthy, important people in this town are jogging at least once a day. Some examples are Dr. Farcia, Mayor Lee, Mrs. Rubenstein, and Eva Schmidt, the Student Council president. Jogging can help you be healthy and successful.

2. Your teacher will divide the class into pairs. Each pair should think of a proposition that could be debated in a Lincoln-Douglas debate. Make sure the proposition is well balanced. You can check this by listing the arguments for and against it.

Chapter Summary

A debate is a formal, orderly communication process. During a debate, two or more opposing speakers try to prove or disprove a statement with evidence and reasoning. The affirmative side supports the debate proposition. The negative side opposes it.

Good debate propositions must have certain qualities. They must be debatable and phrased affirmatively. They must deal with one question and be simply stated. They must also deal with important, timely problems. There are propositions of value, judgment or fact, and policy. First a team must have a proposition. Then it must define its terms and select the issues to be debated.

Debate briefs are the outlines used in constructing a debate case. A brief has an introduction. Then it lists the main issues and offers a plan to solve the problem. Each contention must be supported by proof. Proof generally comes from evidence and reasoning.

Refutation is the process of attacking the other side's case. This can be done by disproving or weakening its major arguments. Rebuttal is the process of rebuilding an argument after it has been attacked by the other side.

The three most common debate forms are traditional debate, cross-examination debate, and Lincoln-Douglas (two-person) debate. Traditional debates proceed in a set order, alternating between constructive and rebuttal speeches.

Checklist

Reviewing Debating Skills

1. Three main kinds of propositions are propositions of value, propositions of judgment, and propositions of policy.
2. To prepare for a debate, find the issues and then define the terms.

3. To construct a case brief, construct a sentence outline, following the traditional debate format.

4. Support each contention in a debate by proof in the form of evidence and reasoning.

5. Present arguments in a debate in the form of refutation and rebuttal.

6. Three forms of debate are traditional, cross-examination, and Lincoln-Douglas (or Two-Person).

7. Present speeches in a debate in a set order that alternates between constructive and rebuttal speeches.

 ## Vocabulary

Define each term in a complete sentence.

affirmative side	inductive reasoning
basic issues	negative side
burden of proof	*prima facie* case
case	proposition
constructive speech	reasoning
debate	rebuttal
debate briefs	refutation
deductive reasoning	resolutions
evidence	stock issues
flow sheets	syllogism

Review Questions

1. Define the following terms as they apply to debate.

   a. affirmative side   **f.** evidence
   b. negative side   **g.** burden of proof
   c. case   **h.** stock issues
   d. proposition   **i.** debate brief
   e. *status quo*   **j.** reasoning

2. Explain how debate differs from discussion.

3. Identify the things to keep in mind when choosing a debate proposition.

4. Name and briefly describe the three kinds of debate propositions. Give an example of each one.

5. Identify the three stock issues for any debate.

6. Explain the difference between constructive and rebuttal speeches.

7. Explain the difference between inductive and deductive reasoning.

8. Explain the difference between refutation and rebuttal.

9. Explain the major differences among the three kinds of debate.

10. Identify the only speaker in a debate who can plan exactly what he or she will say.

Discuss with Your Classmates

1. Have you ever watched a debate between two political candidates? What did you learn during the debate? Did it make the stands of the candidates clearer? Did it help you decide which candidate you liked more? Why?

2. Discuss ways in which delivery in a debate can help or harm your argument. How is debating like delivering a speech? How is it different?

3. Discuss the importance of refuting the opposing side's arguments in a debate as soon as possible. Why should refutation take place quickly?

4. Discuss the two types of reasoning that may be used in a debate. Which type do you think would be used most often? Which type do you use most often when you try to prove a point in a discussion?

Critical Thinking

1. Analysis: Resolved: The United States should impose heavy taxes on imported products. What type of evidence would you want to gather if you were arguing this proposition on the affirmative side? What type of evidence would you want to stay away from?

2. Application: Resolved: Girls should be allowed to play on our football team. Is this a usable resolution? How would you construct a positive argument for it? A negative one?

Activities

In-Class

1. Your teacher will assign you a debate topic and a side of the question for a Lincoln-Douglas debate. Work with a partner. When you get your assignment, write one issue for the debate and support it in two ways. Write out evidence cards, as described on page 453. Be ready to read your support material aloud at the next class session.

2. Your teacher will assign you a debate proposition. Work with a partner. Write two arguments that you think could be used against the proposition. Outline arguments that refute one of these arguments. Then support your arguments with documented evidence cards.

3. Your teacher will assign you a debate partner and a proposition to attack or defend. You should then jointly write a debate brief for your constructive speeches. Then practice your speeches together. Be ready to present your debate after one week of research.

Out-of-Class

1. First think about the things that make a good debate resolution. In your speech notebook list five topics that would cover all those things. Finally, properly word at least two resolutions.

2. Listen to an editorial on a news show. Then choose one argument and prepare a refutation of that argument in your speech notebook. Use the five-step process explained on pages 457–458.

3. Find an issue that is important to your school. Outline and support the arguments you could use for or against the issue in your speech notebook. Be ready to present your arguments aloud in a two-minute presentation to the class. You should use at least two different forms of support.

 Chapter Project

Resolved: That learning computer skills is more important than learning math.

Is this a good proposition? If not, revise it so that it meets the rules for a debatable proposition.

Next, choose to support the affirmative or negative side of the argument. Then construct a flow sheet that covers the points of your argument in proper order.

Arrange to have a formal debate in class. Follow the rules for setting up a debate that are presented in this chapter.

CHAPTER 23 Parliamentary Procedure

Cassie has just joined a special student planning committee. The committee is making graduation plans. These are some of Cassie's thoughts as she attends her first meeting.

"I think the committee uses parliamentary procedure in its meetings.

I don't know all the rules, but it seems to help the meeting run smoothly.

I guess I'll need to learn how parliamentary procedure works."

Have *you* ever used parliamentary procedure? Why do people use it?

In this chapter, you will read about:

- the purposes of parliamentary procedure
- certain terms that apply to parliamentary procedure
- the basic principles of parliamentary procedure
- the order of business for a meeting
- different kinds of votes
- five general types of motions
- the Table of Motions

Throughout their lives, people join organizations. They may belong to social or professional clubs, church groups, or political organizations. Some people get elected to an office in an organization. Unfortunately, many people don't make good officers or good club members for one simple reason. They don't understand parliamentary procedure.

UNDERSTANDING PARLIAMENTARY PROCEDURE

Parliamentary procedure is a set of rules for keeping order during meetings. These rules help people avoid wasting time when they work together in a group. The rules are also useful for deciding future actions of the group. They set up procedures to follow for such things as electing officers and conducting business meetings.

Purposes

Basically, parliamentary procedure has two purposes.

1. *To provide a way to conduct business in an orderly, efficient manner.* Parliamentary procedure allows people to conduct the most amount of business in the shortest amount of time—with the least amount of confusion.

2. *To ensure each member's right to make proposals, discuss issues, and vote on them.* This purpose is the basis for each member's freedom of speech.

Terminology

Following are some important terms that relate to parliamentary procedure. If you know these terms, you will more easily understand the rest of this chapter.

abstain: to decide not to vote.

amend: to change the words in a proposal.

chair: the presiding officer or chairperson.

floor: the right to speak. For example, when one person has the *floor,* no one else can talk.

minutes: the report of what happened at the previous meeting.

motion: a proposal put before a group for its consideration. A motion is made by saying, "I move that . . . ."

pending: action that is being considered.

second a motion: to show approval of a motion. A second may be stated as "Seconded" or "I second the motion." Motions are seconded so that they can be discussed.

table: to put a motion aside until later.

Principles

Parliamentary procedure is based on the following principles. These principles apply to both officers and members.

The majority rules. In parliamentary procedure, the minority agrees to accept the decisions of the majority. The simple majority usually consists of one more than half of those voting. For example, if a club has 50 members at a meeting, the simple majority is 26. In some cases, however, a two-thirds majority is needed to pass a vote.

The minority will be heard. Voting on the minority side of an issue does not mean voting wrong. It only means that the majority voted on the other side. Parliamentary procedure protects the rights of the minority. It allows the minority side to continue to be heard. As a result, the minority has a chance to change the minds of the majority.

All members have equal rights and equal responsibilities. All members have the right to vote and the right to speak. On the other hand, all members have a responsibility to vote and take part in the discussions.

President Reagan addresses the Senate and House of Representatives. Our government follows the rules of parliamentary procedure.

Only one matter may be debated at one time. To avoid confusion, discussion of one matter stops when discussion of another begins. Parliamentary procedure has a priority system. By using this system, the chair tries to be efficient, dealing with only one matter at a time.

Members speak only about issues on the floor. The rules of parliamentary procedure require all motions that are seconded to be discussed. Motions to limit or cut off discussion need a two-thirds vote to pass. This protects the freedom of debate. Members are expected to talk to the presiding officer rather than to other members. Also, they are required to speak about the issue on the floor—not about other members or other issues.

The chair must remain objective on all matters. People recognize that leaders—by virtue of their position—could sway opinions during debate. Therefore, the presiding officer must remain neutral. This neutrality should be demonstrated in a presiding officer's discussion of a topic and in the order in which he or she calls on people to speak. An impartial chair gives equal time to all viewpoints.

THE ORDER OF BUSINESS

Before a meeting can begin, a quorum must be present. This is the minimum number of members that must be present before any business can be discussed. The quorum is stated in the bylaws. Usually it is a simple majority of the members.

If a quorum is present, a meeting usually follows this order of business.

Call to Order, and Reading of the Minutes

The chair says, "This meeting will come to order." At this time the meeting may begin.

The chair says, "The secretary will read the minutes of the last meeting. After the minutes are read, the chair asks, "Are there any additions or corrections?" If there are no changes, the chair says, "The minutes are approved as read."

Treasurer's Report, and Reports of Other Officers and Committees

This is handled the same way as the reading of the minutes. Then, other officers may have reports to give. These are followed by reports from chairs of standing committees. The duties and terms of standing committees are stated in the bylaws. Special committees give their reports next. These committees are appointed for special jobs.

Unfinished Business, and New Business

The chair asks, "Is there any unfinished business?" This allows members to discuss matters that were not settled at the previous meeting. If no comments are made, the chair goes to the next area immediately.

The chair says, "The floor is now open to new business." At this point, the chair may inform the group about matters that need to be discussed (the agenda). The chair also may ask if anyone has other new business that should be discussed. A member may raise his or her hand. The chair calls on that person. The person either indicates a topic that should be discussed or proposes a motion.

Following the order of business, the chair calls the meeting to order.

Elections for new officers are also held during this time. The chair says, "The floor is now open for nominations for (office)." As nominations are made, the chair writes the names on the board. A motion is made and seconded to close nominations. The chair takes a vote and says, "The motion passes and nominations are closed." After this, no more nominations may be made. The chair conducts an election of the people who were nominated.

Announcements and Adjournment

The chair may make an announcement or ask, "Are there any announcements that should be made?"

When there is no more business, the chair says, "Is there a motion to adjourn?" A member may say, "I so move." If the motion is seconded, a vote is taken.

Voting

During the normal order of business, many votes will be taken.

Voice Votes   This is the most common way to vote. The chair may say, "All those in favor say 'aye.' Opposed say 'no.'"

Standing Up or Raising Hands   A voice vote might be close, or a motion might need a two-thirds vote. In both cases, the chair may ask members to stand up or raise their hands. Then someone counts the people or their hands. The chair calls for this vote as if it were a voice vote.

Roll-Call Votes   When their names are called, members call out their votes. This kind of vote is often needed when there are many visitors in the group.

Secret Ballots   This kind of vote is usually required when a group is voting for officers. It is also used for important issues. The chair must make sure that each member has a ballot and understands the vote.

YOUR TURN ///////////////////

1.   Your teacher will take a survey of class members who belong to different organizations. Then these organizations should be discussed. How many use parliamentary procedure? How many do not? Can students see any difference in the effectiveness of the groups that follow parliamentary procedure?

2.   Your teacher will divide the class into groups of five to eight students. Each group should discuss the six principles of parliamentary procedure on pages 474–475. Members of each group should discuss why each one is important. They should also discuss which of the principles is most often ignored by organizations.

TYPES OF MOTIONS

There are many things to remember in parliamentary procedure. However, one is probably harder to remember than all the others. This is the order in which different motions and types of motions must be considered when they are introduced. This becomes easier, however, if you can remember the following general types of motions.

PLAYING BY THE RULES

Rules designed to keep people with opposing points of view from resorting to fists or bullets to settle their differences were developed centuries ago. In the eleventh century in England, King Edward the Confessor drew his knights around him and outlined a plan for a parliament. This parliament would be an orderly assembly of men (no women were allowed for hundreds of years) who would make laws and settle grievances.

As Parliament became an institution in England, so too did "parliamentary procedure." This procedure gave each speaker a chance to present a point of view without monopolizing the time and attention of the assembly. Anyone who tried to push an idea through without using the correct procedure could easily be stopped by calling for a "point of order" or "the previous question" or any of a dozen other rules.

The system proved to be so democratic—and so successful —that it was exported to America with the colonists. The Continental Congress used parliamentary procedure in 1776, and the Constitutional Convention used it in 1786. In fact, there were so many different points of view about what should be in the Constitution that it probably would never have been written without parliamentary procedure.

In 1876, a U.S. Army general named Henry M. Robert wrote down the basic rules of parliamentary procedure in a book that came to be known as *Robert's Rules of Order.*

General Robert's rules continue to keep government operating smoothly and fairly. The United States Senate and the United States House of Representatives use these rules. They are also used by all of the state legislatures and by the thousands of county and local governments. What began over a thousand years ago continues to guide our democracy of today. The rules of parliamentary procedure are still used because they still work.

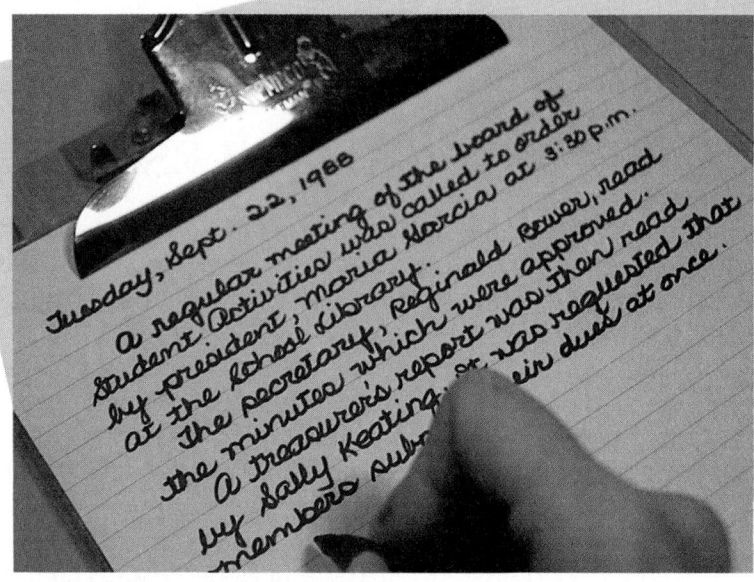

It is important to remember the order of motions.

Main Motions

These motions introduce topics members want to discuss. For example, a member might suggest a membership drive or a contest. When a main motion is seconded, it is discussed. Then a majority vote is needed to pass it. Since main motions are often changed by other motions, main motions have the lowest priority in any discussion.

Subsidiary Motions

These motions change or do away with other motions. For example, these include such motions as the motion to table, to end debate, to postpone, or to amend. These motions are always proposed after the main motions that they apply to. Members must discuss these motions and vote on them before they return to the original main motion.

Privileged Motions

These motions are concerned with the needs and duties of the members. For example, they could include motions to set time to meet again, to adjourn, or to recess. These motions are made and considered before any of the other types of motions.

Incidental Motions

These motions deal with procedures involved with conducting parliamentary business. For example, they could include motions to withdraw a motion, to rise to a point of order, and to object to consideration. These motions may interrupt other business. They take precedence over motions that they relate to.

A specific main motion brings matters back to the floor that were previously tabled or dropped.

Specific Main (Unclassified) Motions

These motions bring matters that were previously tabled or dropped back to the floor. For example, they could include motions to remove a motion from the table or to reconsider a motion. These motions may be made when other motions are not on the table.

Following is a Table of Motions. It is a handy reference tool when parliamentary procedure is being used. For example, it can quickly show a chair which motions need to be seconded and which do not.

Table of Motions Used in Parliamentary Procedure
(listed in order of precedence)

Type	Precedence or Priority	Motion	May Interrupt a Speaker?	Requires a Second?	Debatable?	Amendable?	Vote Needed?
Privileged	1	To fix time to reassemble	No	Yes	No	Yes	Maj.
	2	To adjourn	No	Yes	No	No	Maj.
	3	To recess	No	Yes	Yes[3]	Yes[3]	Maj.
	4	To rise to a question of privilege	Yes	No	No	No	Chair Decides
	5	To call for orders of the day	Yes	No	No	No	Chair Decides
Incidental	6	To appeal a decision from the chair	Yes	Yes	Yes	No	Maj.
	7	To rise to a point of order	Yes	No	No	No	Chair Decides
	8	To call for a division of the assembly (or house)	Yes	No	No	No	Maj.
	9	To object to consideration of a question	Yes	No	No	No	2/3
	10	To ask permission to withdraw a motion	No	No	No	No	Maj.[4]
	11	To suspend a rule	No	Yes	No	No	2/3
Subsidiary	12	To table a matter	No	Yes	No	No	Maj.
	13	To move the previous question	No	Yes	No	No	2/3
	14	To limit or extend debate	No	Yes	Yes[3]	Yes[3]	2/3
	15	To postpone to a definite time	No	Yes	Yes[3]	Yes[3]	Maj.[1]
	16	To refer to a committee	No	Yes	Yes[3]	Yes[3]	Maj.
	17	To amend	No	Yes	Yes	Yes	Maj.

Type	Precedence or Priority	Motion	May Interrupt a Speaker?	Requires a Second?	Debatable?	Amendable?	Vote Needed?
Subsidiary (continued)	18	To postpone indefinitely	No	Yes	Yes	No	Maj.
Main	19	Any main motion	No	Yes	Yes	Yes	Maj.[2]
Specific or Unclassified Main Motions		To consider tabled main motions (resume consideration)	No	Yes	No	No	Maj.
		To rescind (reverse previous action)	No	Yes	Yes	No	Maj.[5]
		To reconsider	Yes	Yes	Yes	No	Maj.

1. A majority vote is required for general order; a two-thirds vote is required for special order.
2. A constitution and bylaws may require more than a majority for certain matters such as amending the constitution.
3. Restricted (check a parliamentary authority such as Robert's or Sturgis's).
4. If no one objects to withdrawal of motion, no vote is required.
5. If announced at a previous meeting; otherwise, usually two thirds is needed.

Understanding the Table of Motions

Following is a closer look at the motions on the Table of Motions.

1. To Fix Time to Reassemble (Privileged Motion)   This motion takes precedence over *all* other motions. Usually this motion is made right after a motion to adjourn has been seconded. However, it is made before a vote is taken to adjourn. (Example: "I move that we set the time for our next meeting at 4:00 P.M., Friday, April 22.")

2. To Adjourn (Privileged Motion)   This motion legally ends a meeting. (Example: "I move that we adjourn.") Sometimes members use adjournment as a means of stopping a debate. They might want to stop the debate so that a pending vote will not go against them. If the motion is seconded, all discussion must stop. Then a vote is taken right away. If the majority votes for the motion, the meeting ends. Of course, the motion that was being debated will be brought up at the next meeting.

3. To Recess (Privileged Motion)   A member might make a motion to recess. This stops the meeting for a short period of time but doesn't end it. (Example: "I move to recess for two hours for lunch and to reconvene at 1:30 P.M.") This motion is made if a meeting has gone on too long. It also is made if more information is needed. It can be amended only to change the amount of time. A recess often saves a lot of time. If a meeting were adjourned, then the regular order of business would have to be repeated.

4. To Rise to a Question of Privilege (Privileged Motion) This is called a motion, but it is really a request. It can be made by any member at any time—even if someone else is speaking. This motion can be about anything that concerns the safety, comfort, rights, or convenience of one or all of the members. (Example: "I rise to a question of privilege." The chair may answer, "State your question." Then the member may say, "This room is very hot. May we have some windows opened?" The chair then decides what should be done.)

5. To Call for the Orders of the Day (Privileged Motion) Sometimes a previous motion has stated the date and time when something must be discussed by the group. If someone is speaking and that time arrives, a member may call for the orders of the day. (Example: "I call for the orders of the day.") The chair must then decide if it is the right time for the prearranged order to be followed. Orders of the day may also be called if the chair forgets to ask for the minutes to be read or if a committee has not been asked to report.

6. To Appeal a Decision (Incidental Motion)   A member might disagree with a ruling by the chair. In such a case, the member could turn to the group and ask the group to vote on it. By doing this, the member would be taking the decision-making power away from the chair and giving it to the whole group. (Example: "I appeal the decision from the chair." If someone seconds the motion, the chair may say, "The decision of the chair has been appealed. All those who support the chair's decision, say 'aye.' Opposed, the same. The chair's decision is (or is not) sustained, or upheld.") Before the vote is taken, however, both sides can state the reasons for their beliefs.

7. To Rise to a Point of Order (Incidental Motion)   A member uses this motion to show the chair and the other members that an error is being made. (Example: I rise to a point of order." The

A town meeting, during which voters meet to discuss town business, follows the rules of parliamentary procedure.

chair may answer, "State your point." The member may say, "The speaker is not speaking on the motion that was seconded. She is talking about an entirely different topic." If the chair agrees, he or she may say, "Your point is correct. The speaker will limit all remarks to the motion which was seconded." If the chair disagrees, he or she may say, "Your point is not correct.")

8. To Call for a Division of the Assembly (Incidental Motion)   A voice vote is the fastest vote. At times, though, a voice vote may be too close. In such a case, a member may ask for a more exact count. (Example: "I call for a division of the assembly.") If the chair agrees, he or she asks members to raise their hands or stand up. If the chair disagrees, he or she asks the group if they want a standing (or hand) vote. If the majority is in favor of this, the chair must take a more exact count.

9. To Object to Consideration of a Question (Incidental Motion)   A member uses this motion when he or she wants to stop the discussion. There are many reasons to stop a discussion. The issue may be too personal or simply not worth everyone's time. The member can make this motion even when someone else is speaking. (Example: "I object to consideration of _____." Without any more discussion, the chair would take a voice vote. The chair may say, "An objection to consideration of ⎯⎯ has been made. All those in favor of discussing this matter say 'aye.' Opposed, the same. The motion is carried (or lost), and the subject will (or will not) be discussed.") Since this motion can prevent discussion, a two-thirds vote is needed for it to pass.

10. To Ask Permission to Withdraw a Motion (Incidental Motion)   A member makes a motion, and the group discusses it. It soon may become clear that the motion is no longer a good motion. In such a case, the member who made the motion can ask to withdraw it. (Example: I wish to withdraw my motion to ⎯⎯." The chair may ask, "Is there any objection to allowing (name) to withdraw this motion?" If there is no objection, the chair may say, "Hearing no objections, permission is granted to withdraw this motion.") If it is seconded, the motion is voted on without any discussion.

11. To Suspend a Rule (Incidental Motion)   Once in a while, a group may want to get around a certain rule. For example, the order of business calls for the minutes to be read before the treasurer's report. However, a member might want to hear the treasurer's report before the minutes. In such a case, the member could ask for the rule to be suspended. (Example: "I move that we temporarily suspend the rule that requires the secretary to read the minutes next in order to hear the treasurer's report first.") If the motion is passed, the rules are suspended for only the time needed to do what the motion calls for.

12. To Table a Motion (Subsidiary Motion)   During a discussion, members might find that they need more information before a vote is taken. If this happens, a member may ask that the motion be tabled. This motion isn't meant to stop discussion. It is merely meant to postpone it. Because this motion is so important, it has the highest precedence of any of the subsidiary motions. (Example: "I move to table the motion to donate 50 dollars to the Y.M.C.A. Since we don't have an up-to-date treasurer's report, we don't know what bills we have. We need that information in order to tell us how much money we have.")

13. To Move the Previous Question (Subsidiary Motion)   This motion is used to close discussion on a topic. This is not a formal motion, but it reminds the chair and the group that some arguments are being repeated. (Example: "I move the previous question." The

A government committee meeting, such as this one in Washington,
D.C., follows the rules of parliamentary procedure.

chair may say, "Unless there are further new arguments to be made,
a vote will be taken soon.") This does not mean, however, that the
chair can end the discussion. If other members still want to speak,
the chair must recognize them. He or she can, however, tell them to
limit their comments to new or relevant information.

14. To Limit or Extend Debate (Subsidiary Motion)

Parliamentary procedure should never prevent freedom of speech.
However, sometimes time is limited. Therefore, a group can vote to
limit debate in one of following three ways.

- It may limit the number of speeches.

- It may set a time limit for each speech.

- It may limit the total amount of time given to certain
  topics.

Since these motions limit the debate, a two-thirds vote is needed to
pass them. (Example: "I move to limit debate on the matter of an
increase in dues to 15 minutes.")

If the motion passes, the chair stops the debate when the time is
up. At that point, the group votes on the issue or votes to extend the
debate. (Example: "I move to extend the debate on this matter for five
more minutes.")

15. To Postpone to a Definite Time (Subsidiary Motion)

This motion is different from the motion to table a motion. This motion sets a certain time when the motion will be taken up again. That time may be later in the meeting or at a later date. (Example: "I move to postpone further consideration of an end-of-the-year party until our meeting on February 2.")

16. To Refer to a Committee (Subsidiary Motion)   One purpose of this motion is to save time. It asks for a committee to study a complicated problem and report back to the group. This motion is also used if the group feels that a compromise is needed on a certain issue. The member who makes the motion could also include the following information in the motion.

- a certain committee to review the issue

- a certain number of people to be on the committee

- when the committee should report back

(Example: "I move that this matter be referred to a committee of three students and three teachers, and that the committee report its recommendations at our next meeting.")

17. To Amend (Subsidiary Motion)   Any motion that amends another motion changes the motion in the following ways.

- by adding words

- by taking out words

- by taking out words and substituting other words

- by substituting a completely new motion

Amendments may be made to main, subsidiary, and privileged motions. (Example: "I move to amend the motion by taking out the words *February 13 at 9 P.M.* and substituting the words *February 18 at 8 P.M.*") Motions to amend must be seconded. Then they must be discussed right away and a vote taken. If an amendment passes, then debate continues on the original motion—as it has been amended. If an amendment fails, debate continues on the original motion.

18. To Postpone Indefinitely (Subsidiary Motion)   The purpose of this motion is to stop a vote on a pending main motion. If the motion passes, the motion on the floor may not be brought up again during the meeting. If it fails, opponents know how many people favor the motion. As a result, they may modify it or try to defeat it. ("I move to postpone consideration on this motion indefinitely.")

19. Main Motions   All main motions need a majority vote. The only exception is when a change in the governing documents such as the bylaws is proposed. Main motions should be stated simply and directly. Also each motion should contain only one proposal. (Example: "I move that we hold a car wash next Saturday to make money for this club.") If this motion passes, the next motions may consider the place, assignments, or other details.

20. Specific or Unclassified Main Motions   To consider tabled main motions: When a motion was previously tabled, it may be brought back by a motion to resume consideration. (Example: "I move that we resume consideration of ____.") If the motion is seconded, a vote is taken right away. There is no discussion. The motion may not be amended. If the motion is passed, the chair says, "The floor is open for further discussion on the motion."

To rescind: This motion cannot cancel a motion that has already been carried out. It can, however, cancel a motion that was passed but not carried out. (Example: "I move that we rescind the motion passed at our November meeting to limit membership to 50 members.") If the motion is seconded, the chair opens the floor to discussion. If the members did not know that this motion would be introduced, a two-thirds vote is needed to pass it. If members knew about the motion ahead of time, only a majority is needed to pass it.

To reconsider: The purpose of this motion is to reconsider a previous question that did not pass. If the original motion was debatable, the floor is opened to discussion. If, after discussion, the motion passes, it cancels the previous action. It is just as if that motion never happened.

YOUR TURN ////////////

Discuss what the duties of the chair are when each of the following occurs.

    a. motion to recess
    b. a question of privilege
    c. call for the orders of the day
    d. a point of order
    e. call for a division of the assembly
    f. to suspend a rule
    g. motion to adjourn

23 CHAPTER REVIEW

 **Chapter Summary**

Parliamentary procedure is a set of rules for order. It provides organizations with a method of conducting business in an orderly, efficient way. Parliamentary procedure also insures each member's freedom of speech.

Parliamentary procedure has six basic principles. (1) The majority rules. (2) The minority will be heard. (3) All members have equal rights and equal responsibilities. (4) Only one matter may be debated at one time. (5) Discussions are held on all issues. (6) The chair must remain objective on all matters.

If there is a quorum, a meeting follows an order of business. That order includes a call to order, the reading of the minutes, the treasurer's report, reports of other officers and committees, unfinished business, new business, announcements, and adjournment. During a meeting the following kinds of votes can be taken: voice votes, standing up or raising hands, roll-call votes, and secret ballots.

There are five general types of motions: main, subsidiary, privileged, incidental, and specific main (unclassified). A closer look at the specific motions that fall under these general types is covered on pages 483–489.

Checklist

Understanding Parliamentary Skills

1. Use parliamentary procedure to conduct business in an orderly, efficient manner, and to ensure each member's freedom of speech.

2. Participate in discussions, and exercise your right to vote.

3. Be objective and maintain your neutrality if you are the presiding officer of an organization.

4. Accept the decisions agreed to by the majority.

5. Protect the rights of the minority.

6. Follow the usual order of business to help ensure that the group completes everything it wants to.

 Vocabulary

Define each term in a complete sentence.

abstain	motion
amend	parliamentary procedure
chair	pending
floor	second a motion
minutes	table

Review Questions

1. Name the six basic principles of parliamentary procedure.
2. Define simple majority.
3. Define the word *floor* as it relates to parliamentary procedure.
4. Describe the regular order of business for a meeting.
5. Name the four ways votes can be taken.
6. Name the five kinds of motions. Briefly explain each
7. Explain why a motion to adjourn has to be seconded. of vote is needed to pass such a motion?
8. Describe why someone might make a motion to tab
9. Explain the purpose of a motion to refer to a comr
10. Identify the two ways in which a motion can be a

Parliam

Discuss with Your Classmates

1. Discuss how parliamentary procedure protects the rights of the minority. What is the most important of those rights?

2. Discuss the requirement of needing a two-thirds vote to change the rules of a meeting. Under the circumstances, why is this better than a simple majority?

3. Evaluate the importance of requiring that a quorum be present before any business is conducted. Why do you think this rule was established?

4. Discuss the usual order of business that meetings follow. Why is it important to have a standard procedure for discussing business?

 # Critical Thinking

1. **Analysis:** It has been said that parliamentary procedure can be a two-edged sword. It can protect rights as well as destroy them. Give as many examples as you can to show that this statement is true.

2. **Comprehension:** At any kind of meeting, the chair must be especially objective concerning the rules of procedure. Explain why this objectivity is necessary to protect the rights of the minority.

 # Activities

In-Class

1. Try to get the constitutions of the Student Council and three other groups in your school. Discuss the strengths and weaknesses of each one. Which constitutions are the least complicated? Are they as effective as the others? Are the constitutions basically the same? How do the bylaws differ? Can anyone suggest any changes that would make any of them better?

2. Your teacher will divide the class into groups of three to four students. Each group should write a sample motion for each of the motions listed on the Table of Motions on pages 482–483.

3. Some people who are very knowledgeable about parliamentary procedure can use that knowledge to stall and delay action on important matters. They hope that the time spent will bring other members to their point of view. Knowing what you know about parliamentary procedure, discuss how it could be used to delay action.

Out-of-Class

1. Attend a meeting in your school or community where parliamentary procedure is followed. Then in your speech notebook write a one- to two-page summary of the major motions covered at the meeting.

2. Imagine that you are to be the chair at a meeting. A proposal is to be debated that about half of the participants support and about half oppose. In your speech notebook, put together a set of notes that will allow you to understand at a glance the various motions you are likely to hear. The notes should tell you how you ought to rule in each situation.

3. In an encyclopedia or other reference book, look up information about Henry Martyn Robert. In what way is Robert connected with parliamentary procedure? For what is he best known? Write two or three paragraphs in your speech notebook describing what you learn about Robert.

Chapter Project

Pretend that your class is a science club.

First, elect a chairperson. Then have a meeting that follows the order of business listed on pages 476–478. Include in the order of business electing officers and establishing standing committees.

GERRY SIKORSKI

Will and Vision, the Tools You Need

United States Congressman Gerry Sikorski (Minnesota) delivered this commencement speech at Breckenridge High School, Breckenridge, Minnesota, on June 1, 1986.

Graduates, parents and friends: I'm proud to be from Breckenridge and happy to be back today. And I'm really happy to see Ms. Linneman from my old days at Breckenridge High School. Did you know that she can predict the future? Time and again during my high school career, in library and study hall, Ms. Linneman would stop me in the halls and say, "SIKORSKI—I'VE BEEN WATCHING YOU. AND IF YOU DON'T CHANGE YOUR WAYS, YOU'RE GOING TO BE HERE 20 YEARS FROM NOW!" And Ms. Linneman was right. Here I am.

Writing a graduation speech is a real challenge. No graduation speaker I know has ever delivered a speech that any graduate has ever remembered 10 minutes after it ended. That's probably why so many Congressmen feel qualified to deliver them. I mentioned that to one of my colleagues in Washington last week, and she said, "Why go all the way back to Minnesota not to be listened to? Why don't you just write a letter to the President?"

Frankly, I don't remember who spoke at my graduation here 20 years ago. I don't remember a thing that he or she said. I do remember that it was hot as heck. The auditorium was packed and un-air-conditioned. And I remember thinking to myself: "HERE I AM SITTING INSIDE ON A 98 DEGREE DAY WITH A WOOL SUIT ON AND A GOWN OVER THAT. I SPENT HALF AN HOUR COMBING MY HAIR SO I COULD MESS IT UP WITH A HAT THAT LOOKS LIKE A GEOMETRY PROBLEM. AND I'M DOING ALL THIS BECAUSE TODAY'S THE DAY I'M SHOWING THE WORLD HOW SMART I AM."

Let's see. What else do I remember? I guess just that I was wearing a carnation that my Great Aunt Alice had crushed to death when she hugged me. And I remember that the kid sitting in front of me was wearing enough English Leather cologne to risk being shut down by the EPA. One of my classmates clipped his fingernails during the commencement address. Click. Click. Click.

But as I said, I don't remember the speaker. I suppose we were told that today was the first day of the rest of our lives. And I suppose we were told that we were about to enter "the golden door of opportunity." In 1966, the only door many young people were entering was the door to the draft board office—and the sign above it might just as well have said THIS WAY TO VIETNAM. It was a door from which too many did not return to finish the rest of their lives.

But you are a new generation and you don't need embroidered cliches any more than we did. I don't have to tell you that the world has changed in astounding ways during your lives. But it's amazing to think that when I went to B.H.S. we were reading the book "1984" as science fiction—while you read it as history.

The year 2000 was used as a science fiction writer's shorthand for some far-distant era. Today, the college class of 2000 is already in grade school. We are now as close to the 21st Century as we are to Vietnam . . . .

Rather than spending these few minutes talking about changes —as exciting as they are—I want to talk with you about some things that stay the same. Countries change, technologies change, leaders change, but human nature and human challenge don't really change.

So to give you something to remember 10 minutes after graduation today, I did a little research. One of the best things about being a Congressman is that I meet a lot of exciting, successful people— religious, political, business and scientific leaders. So a few months ago, I started carrying a note pad around with me and asking those folks a question that went something like this:

"TELL ME THE MOST IMPORTANT THING YOU'VE LEARNED ABOUT LIFE AND YOURSELF AND PEOPLE SINCE YOU GRADUATED FROM HIGH SCHOOL?"

I want to pass along some of the best ones. Some you may agree with. Some you may think are crazy. But I can almost guarantee you've heard every one of them from your parents. ("HEY NO GROANING THERE IN THE BACK ROWS!")

Number one is—BE ABSOLUTELY DETERMINED TO *ENJOY* WHAT YOU DO.

I've never met anybody who succeeded at something he or she hates. A news reporter interviewed Kenny O'Donnell, John Kennedy's friend and White House Chief of Staff some years ago. The interview was recorded shortly before O'Donnell's death, and you can tell by his voice that he wasn't well. But when the reporter asked him about the best part of his job with Kennedy, you could hear the energy coming back. He said:

"THE BEST PART WAS EVERY MINUTE OF EVERY DAY. I MEAN IT. I LOVED TO GO TO WORK EVERY DAY. BECAUSE I WAS DOING EXACTLY WHAT I WANTED TO DO . . . WHERE I WANTED TO BE . . . WORKING WITH WHO I WANTED TO BE WITH." Same with Kennedy.

Point number two—and almost everybody told me this in one way or another: DON'T BE AFRAID TO FAIL.

Lou Brock holds two baseball records: most stolen bases—and most times being thrown out trying to steal bases.

Babe Ruth holds two short season records: Most home runs—and most strike outs.

Columbus left Spain to find India. He failed. But he found America.

Lee Iacocca was fired by Ford Motor. Then he went to work and saved Chrysler. (Iacocca understood another great truth: Don't get mad. Get even.)

I'm not advising you to go out and fail. But when you fail at something—and you probably will—learn from it. An old saying goes: "The gifts are burdens. The burdens are gifts."

In 1972, I managed a congressional race and we lost. The next time, my candidate won.

In 1978, I ran for Congress and I lost. The next time I won.

Abe Lincoln lost five elections before he won the Presidency.

That brings me to another piece of good advice. NEVER GIVE UP ON ANYBODY. After all, Mark Twain pointed out 100 years ago that the only true and unredeemable criminal class in America is Congress.

"Never give up on anybody" was one of the favorite sayings of Minnesota's Hubert Humphrey. One of the last calls he made from his bed before he died was to Richard Nixon. They didn't agree on very much, but they shared a determination never to accept any defeat as final.

When you come back here for your 20th reunion, the success stories from this class of 1986 will amaze you. . . . Don't be surprised if the kid who got the "D" in speech class comes back earning a quarter of a million dollars as a network newscaster. And don't be surprised if you come back happily married to the girl or guy you couldn't even stand to dance with at the prom.

And I hope you come back home often, because I can tell you from personal experience that when you face the toughest times in life, you have to be able to GET BACK TO YOUR ROOTS AND REMEMBER YOUR FUNDAMENTALS. That's the fourth point and those roots begin right here with your family and your community.

I'm proud to have my parents here in the audience today. Because when I talk about successful people, people who know a lot, they're on the list. My dad was a railroad worker. And for over 40 years, he worked on the bridges and buildings of Great Northern in the blistering heat of July and the terrible cold of January.

My mom took in laundry and gutted turkeys at the Swift plant. They had 8th grade educations. And now as they approach their 50th wedding anniversary, they don't have a lot of bucks. They're not written up in Who's Who. And Dan Rather doesn't interview them on the CBS Evening News. But that doesn't diminish the importance of their lives. They raised five kids and they raised us well. They overcame their problems. And they love each other. They taught us to work hard and care deeply. To suspect people on the make and still respect people who just can't make it. In the words of the song from the country-western band "Alabama": THEY DIDN'T KNOW NOTHING ABOUT A SILVER SPOON. BUT THEY KNEW A LOT ABOUT THE GOLDEN RULE." Thanks, mom and dad, for everything.

Speaking of getting back to fundamentals, I remember a Sunday twenty years ago when Coach Vince Lombardi watched his Green Bay Packers—the best team in football in the 60s—get absolutely slaughtered by the Chicago Bears—the worst team in football. (In those days, William "The Refrigerator" Perry was just a bouncing 100 pound baby boy).

Anyway, after that disastrous game, Lombardi got on the team bus. He was angry—really angry. And he shouted: "THIS TEAM IS

GOING BACK TO FUNDAMENTALS. AND I MEAN REAL FUNDAMENTALS. AND WE'RE GOING TO START RIGHT NOW. THIS," he said holding up the ball, "IS A FOOTBALL." And from the back of the bus, player Max McGee shouted back: "HEY COACH . . . COULD YOU GO A LITTLE SLOWER? SOME OF THE GUYS AREN'T GETTING THIS ALL DOWN!"

Fifth, TRUST YOUR INSTINCTS. Your instincts come from the fundamentals. So develop good ones and depend on them.

In one of his last songs, John Lennon wrote that "life is what happens to you while you're busy making other plans." And sometimes, your instincts are all you've got to tell you you're moving in the right direction when everyone else is telling you you're going crazy.

Sometimes your instincts will tell you to break the rules. A couple of years ago, a small New York City advertising firm landed the account for NIKE shoes and sportswear. And they developed an ad campaign that everybody in the advertising industry predicted would be a total disaster. Because they broke all the rules. They produced a series of billboard and magazine ads with people wearing NIKE products. But the people didn't look like the glamorous and sophisticated sorts who lounge around. They were runners—dirty, sweaty, exhausted—finishing a race and looking like they were about to throw up. And the word NIKE appeared on the ad—not in huge letters at the top—but in tiny, almost unreadable letters at the bottom. The ad campaign failed miserably—right? Wrong! It boosted NIKE sales by 25 percent and helped make the firm one of the fastest growing, most successful advertising agencies in the world. That happened because those people trusted their instincts. But there's more to it: *Trust your instincts and never give up on yourself.* That's the sixth point. . . .

When you make the commitment never to give up on yourself, you come to understand the last bit of advice I want to leave you with today. And it's simply that in your own life, and in the life of your country—ONE PERSON—YOU—CAN MAKE A PROFOUND AND LASTING DIFFERENCE.

It's easy to diminish our own importance. The mathematicians tell us that in terms of size, our significance is infinitesimal. A map of the universe that we know of would be 80 miles long. On that map, our galaxy would take up one 8½ by 11 sheet. Our solar system would be a molecule on that sheet. And Earth would be a speck on the molecule. The astronauts tell us that as they observe Earth from outer space, they don't think about Star Wars defense systems.

Instead they see Earth as one vulnerable ship Gallactica, riding through a cold and dangerous universe as the lone outpost of humanity.

We are the stewards of human progress on this planet. Human progress is a chain, and every generation forges a little piece of it. You've heard the old expression that a chain is only as strong as its weakest link. My challenge to you today is to do what you can in your own lives to strengthen your link and thereby hand down a stronger chain to the next generation.

That's what President Kennedy had in mind when he told us that from now on, every generation will have the capacity to make theirs the best in the history of the world—or the last. For from those to whom much is given, much is expected. Now, the great unfinished tasks are being passed into your hands. And your obligation is to carry on for those who have gone before and after you. Truly: "If it is to be . . . It is up to you."

IF JUSTICE IS FINALLY TO BE GAINED FOR THE OP-PRESSED, it will be because your generation gives us people like Martin Luther King—who faced guns and police dogs because he believed that injustice *anywhere* is a threat to justice *everywhere*.

It will be because your generation gives us people like Lech Walesa—who stood before God and the world and insisted on basic human rights for Polish workers and farmers; Jacabo Timmerman—who had just toured the Argentinian jail cell where he was tortured—but this time as a free man; Cory Aquino, who with a yellow dress, tenacity and right, brought down a mighty and corrupt regime in the Philippines.

IF THE HUNGRY ARE TO BE FED, it will be because your generation gives the world people as committed as Harry Chapin, who gave the last years of his short life, not to the riches he could gain for himself as a singer, but instead to raising millions of dollars to help feed the hungry. Harry died on the way to one of those concerts. But just a few days ago, millions joined "Hands Across America" to help finish what he began.

IF OUR CHILDREN ARE TO HAVE CLEAN AIR, GREEN TREES AND CLEAN WATER, it will be because your generation gives the world more people like Lois Gibson—who risked her life to expose what the chemical companies had done at Love Canal.

AND IF WE ARE TO GET WASTEFUL SPENDING CHECKED, it will be because your generation gives us more people with the courage of Ernie Fitzgerald. He sacrificed a career at the Pentagon by telling what he knew about a $3 billion cost overrun for the C58 Transport Plane almost 20 years ago. . . .

In short, WHEN OUR TWO TRILLION DOLLAR NATIONAL DEBT IS FINALLY PAID, WHEN RURAL AMERICA IS FINALLY SAVED, WHEN THE ARMS RACE IS ENDED BEFORE THE HUMAN RACE IS ENDED, it will be because your generation and those who come after you take to heart what Robert Kennedy told students just your age in South Africa 20 years ago:

He said:

"EACH TIME A HUMAN BEING STANDS UP FOR AN IDEA . . . OR ACTS TO IMPROVE THE LOT OF OTHERS . . . OR STRIKES OUT AGAINST INJUSTICE . . . HE OR SHE SENDS OUT A TINY RIPPLE OF HOPE. IN CROSSING EACH OTHER FROM A MILLION DIFFERENT CENTERS OF ENERGY AND DARING, THOSE RIPPLES BUILD A MIGHTY CURRENT WHICH CAN SWEEP DOWN THE MOST TERRIBLE WALLS OF OPPRESSION AND INJUSTICE."

I submit that you do not represent America's last generation— but America's best generation. You will not find all the answers. The poet Carl Sandburg once wrote that as a nation, America is more the seeker than finder—ever seeking its way through storms and dreams.

And as you seek your way for yourself and America, you will have the tools you need. All the tools Americans have needed to overcome world wars, great depressions, and terrible natural disasters:

—The values of a just society.
—The strength of a revolutionary democracy.
—The power of a free economy.
—The muscle of a skilled work force.
—The talents of an educated people.

But that's not enough. As the Book of Proverbs tell us, "where there is no vision, the people perish." We need the vision of a restless people.

Our vision for ourselves and our country should be as John Steinbeck described it:

"I SEE US . . . NOT IN THE SETTING SUN OF A DARK NIGHT OF DESPAIR AHEAD. I SEE US IN THE CRIMSON LIGHT OF A RISING SUN, FRESH FROM THE BURNING, CREATIVE HAND OF GOD. I SEE GREAT DAYS AHEAD. GREAT DAYS MADE POSSIBLE BY MEN AND WOMEN OF WILL AND VISION."

You are those men and women of will and vision. So go to work and carry on.

Thank you very much.

SUSAN B. ANTHONY

Woman's Right to the Suffrage

This speech was delivered by Miss Anthony after she had been fined for voting in the Presidential election of 1872.

Friends and Fellow Citizens: I stand before you tonight under indictment for the alleged crime of having voted at the last Presidential election, without having a lawful right to vote. It shall be my work this evening to prove to you that, in thus voting, I not only committed no crime, but instead, simply exercised my citizen's rights, guaranteed to me and all United States citizens by the national Constitution, beyond the power of any state to deny.

"We, the people of the United States, in order to form a more perfect union, establish justice, insure domestic tranquillity, provide for the common defense, promote the general welfare, and secure the blessings of liberty to ourselves and our posterity, do ordain and establish this Constitution for the United States of America."

It was we, the people; not we, the white male citizens; nor yet we, the male citizens; but we, the whole people who formed the Union. And we formed it, not to give the blessings of liberty, but to secure them; not to the half of ourselves and the half of our posterity, but to the whole people, women as well as men. And it is a downright mockery to talk to women of their enjoyment of the blessings of liberty while they are denied the use of the only means of securing them provided by this democratic-republican government—the ballot.

For any state to make sex qualification that must ever result in the disfranchisement of one entire half of the people is to pass a bill of attainder, or an *ex post facto* law, and is therefore a violation of the supreme law of the land. By it the blessings of liberty are forever withheld from women and their female posterity. To them this government has no just powers derived from the consent of the governed. To them this government is not a democracy. It is not a republic. It is an odious aristocracy; a hateful oligarchy of sex; the most hateful aristocracy ever established on the face of the globe. An oligarchy of wealth, where the rich govern the poor, or an oligarchy of learning, where the educated govern the ignorant, might be endured; but this oligarchy of sex, which makes father, brothers, husband, sons, the oligarchs over the mother and sisters, the wife and daughters of every household—which ordains all men sovereigns, all women subjects, carries dissension, discord, and rebellion into every home of the nation.

Webster, Worcester, and Bouvier all define a citizen to be a person in the United States, entitled to vote and hold office.

The only question left to be settled now is: Are women persons? And I hardly believe any of our opponents will have the hardihood to say they are not. Being persons, then, women are citizens; and no State has a right to make any law, or to enforce any old law, that shall abridge their privileges or immunities. Hence, every discrimination against women in the constitutions and laws of the several States is today null and void.

INSPIRATIONAL SPEECH

SIR WINSTON CHURCHILL

"This was their finest hour."

When France was taken over by Germany in June, 1940, Winston Churchill, then Prime Minister of England, spoke to the English people—vowing to fight on alone.

During the first four years of the last war, the Allies experienced nothing but disaster and disappointment. . . . We repeatedly asked ourselves the question, "How are we going to win?" and no one was ever able to answer it with much precision, until at the end, quite suddenly, quite unexpectedly, our terrible foe collapsed before us, and we were so glutted with victory that in our folly we threw it away.

However matters may go in France or with the French government or other French governments, we in this island and in the British Empire will never lose our sense of comradeship with the French people. . . . If final victory rewards our toils they shall share the gains—aye, and freedom shall be restored to all. We abate nothing of our just demands; not one jot or tittle do we recede. . . . Czechs, Poles, Norwegians, Dutch, Belgians, have joined their causes to our own. All these shall be restored.

What General Weygand called the Battle of France is over. I expect that the Battle of Britain is about to begin. Upon this battle depends the survival of Christian civilization. Upon it depends our own British life, and the long continuity of our institutions and our Empire. The whole fury and might of the enemy must very soon be turned on us. Hitler knows that he will have to break us in this island or lose the war. If we can stand up to him, all Europe may be free and the life of the world may move forward into broad, sunlit uplands. But if we fail, then the whole world, including the United States, including all that we have known and cared for, will sink into the abyss of a new Dark Age, made more sinister, and perhaps more protracted, by the lights of perverted science. Let us therefore brace ourselves to our duties, and so bear ourselves that, if the British Empire and its Commonwealth last for a thousand years, men will say, "This was their finest hour."

ACCEPTANCE SPEECH

ROSALYN S. YALOW

Join Hands, Hearts, and Minds

Dr. Yalow is the second woman to receive a Nobel Prize in physiology or medicine and the sixth woman to win such recognition in science. She delivered the following speech to about 1200 people—many of whom were students at Stockholm University—at the banquet in honor of the 1977 laureates.

Your Majesties, Your Royal Highnesses, Ladies, Gentlemen, and you, the Students, who are the carriers of our hopes for the survival of the world and our dreams for its future. Tradition has ordained that one of the laureates represent all of us in responding to your tribute. The choice of one among the several deemed truly and equally distinguished must indeed be difficult. Perhaps I have been selected for this privilege because there is certainly one way in which I am distinguishable from the others. This difference permits me to address myself first to a very special problem.

Among you students of Stockholm and among other students, at least in the Western world, women are represented in reasonable proportion to their numbers in the community; yet among the scientists, scholars, and leaders of our world they are not. No objective testing has revealed such substantial differences in talent as to account for this discrepancy. The failure of women to have reached positions of leadership has been due in large part to social and professional discrimination. In the past, few women have tried and even fewer have succeeded. We still live in a world in which a significant fraction of people, including women, believe that a woman belongs and wants to belong exclusively in the home; that a woman should not aspire to achieve more than her male counterparts and particularly not more than her husband. Even now women with exceptional qualities for leadership sense from their parents, teachers, and peers that they must be harder-working, accomplish more and yet are less likely to receive appropriate rewards than are men. These are real problems which may never disappear or, at best, will change very slowly.

We cannot expect in the immediate future that all women who seek it will achieve full equality of opportunity. But if women are to start moving towards that goal, we must believe in ourselves or no one else will believe in us; we must match our aspirations with the competence, courage, and determination to succeed; and we must feel a personal responsibility to ease the path for those who come afterwards. The world cannot afford the loss of the talents of half its people if we are to solve the many problems which beset us.

If we are to have faith that mankind will survive and thrive on the face of the earth, we must believe that each succeeding generation will be wiser than its progenitors. We transmit to you, the next generation, the total sum of our knowledge. Yours is the responsibility to use it, add to it, and transmit it to your children.

A decade ago during the period of worldwide student uprisings there was deep concern that too many of our young people were so disillusioned as to feel that the world must be destroyed before it could be rebuilt. Even now, it is all to easy to be pessimistic if we consider our multiple problems: the possible depletion of resources faster than science can generate replacements or substitutes; hostilities between nations and between groups within nations which appear not to be resolvable; unemployment and vast inequalities among different races and different lands. Even as we envision and solve scientific problems—and put men on the moon—we appear ill-equipped to provide solutions for the social ills that beset us.

We bequeath to you, the next generation, our knowledge but also our problems. While we still live, let us join hands, hearts, and minds to work together for their solution so that your world will be better than ours and the world of your children even better.

INSPIRATIONAL / INAUGURAL SPEECH

JOHN F. KENNEDY

Inaugural Address

On January 20, 1961, John F. Kennedy became the 35th President of the United States. He was the youngest man ever to be elected President. After poet Robert Frost recited a poem, JFK took the oath of office. His inaugural address, which follows, mainly stresses foreign affairs.

My Fellow Citizens: We observe today not a victory of party but a celebration of freedom—symbolizing an end as well as a beginning—signifying renewal as well as change. For I have sworn before you and Almighty God the same solemn oath our forebears prescribed nearly a century and three-quarters ago.

The world is very different now. For man holds in his mortal hands the power to abolish all forms of human poverty and all forms of human life. And yet the same revolutionary beliefs for which our forebears fought are still at issue around the globe—the belief that the rights of man come not from the generosity of the state but from the hand of God.

We dare not forget today that we are the heirs of that first revolution. Let the word go forth from this time and place, to friend and foe alike, that the torch has been passed to a new generation of Americans—born in this century, tempered by war, disciplined by a hard and bitter peace, proud of our ancient heritage—and unwilling to witness or permit the slow undoing of those human rights to which this nation has always been committed, and to which we are committed today—at home and around the world.

Let every nation know, whether it wishes us well or ill, that we shall pay any price, bear any burden, meet any hardship, support any friend, oppose any foe to assure the survival and success of liberty.

This much we pledge—and more.

To those old allies whose cultural and spiritual origins we share, we pledge the loyalty of faithful friends. United, there is little we cannot do in a host of new co-operative ventures. Divided, there is little we can do—for we dare not meet a powerful challenge at odds and split asunder.

To those new states whom we welcome to the ranks of the free, we pledge our word that one form of colonial control shall not have passed away merely to be replaced by a far more iron tyranny. We shall not always expect to find them supporting our view. But we shall always hope to find them strongly supporting their own freedom—and to remember that, in the past, those who foolishly sought power by riding the back of the tiger ended up inside.

To those peoples in the huts and villages of half the globe struggling to break the bonds of mass misery, we pledge our best efforts to help them help themselves, for whatever period is required —not because the Communists may be doing it, not because we seek their votes, but because it is right. If a free society cannot help the many who are poor, it cannot save the few who are rich.

To our sister republics south of the border, we offer a special pledge—to convert our good words into good deeds—in a new alliance for progress—to assist free men and free governments in casting off the chains of poverty. But this peaceful revolution of hope cannot become the prey of hostile powers. Let all our neighbors know that we shall join with them to oppose aggression or subversion anywhere in the Americas. And let every other power know that this hemisphere intends to remain the master of its own house.

To that world assembly of sovereign states, the United Nations, our last best hope in an age where the instruments of war have far outpaced the instruments of peace, we renew our pledge of support— to prevent it from becoming merely a forum of invective—to strengthen its shield of the new and the weak—and to enlarge the area in which its writ may run.

Finally, to those nations who would make themselves our adversary, we offer not a pledge but a request: that both sides begin anew the quest for peace, before the dark powers of destruction unleashed by science engulf all humanity in planned or accidental self-destruction.

We dare not tempt them with weakness. For only when our arms are sufficient beyond doubt can we be certain beyond doubt that they will never be employed.

But neither can two great and powerful groups of nations take comfort from our present course—both sides overburdened by the cost of modern weapons, both rightly alarmed by the steady spread of the deadly atom, yet both racing to alter that uncertain balance of terror that stays the hand of mankind's final war.

So let us begin anew—remembering on both sides that civility is not a sign of weakness, and sincerity is always subject to proof. Let us never negotiate out of fear. But let us never fear to negotiate.

Let both sides explore what problems unite us instead of belaboring those problems which divide us.

Let both sides, for the first time, formulate serious and precise proposals for the inspection and control of arms—and bring the absolute power to destroy other nations under the absolute control of all nations.

Let both sides seek to invoke the wonders of science instead of its terrors. Together let us explore the stars, conquer the deserts, eradicate disease, tap the ocean depths, and encourage the arts and commerce.

Let both sides unite to heed in all corners of the earth the command of Isaiah—to "undo the heavy burdens . . . [and] let the oppressed go free."

And if a beachhead of a co-operation may push back the jungles of suspicion, let both sides join in the next task: creating, not a new balance of power, but a new world of law, where the strong are just and the weak secure and the peace preserved.

All this will not be finished in the first one hundred days. Nor will it be finished in the first one thousand days, nor in the life of this administration, nor even perhaps in our lifetime on this planet. But let us begin.

In your hands, my fellow citizens, more than mine, will rest the final success or failure of our course. Since this country was founded, each generation of Americans has been summoned to give testimony to its national loyalty. The graves of young Americans who answered the call to service surround the globe.

Now the trumpet summons us again—not as a call to bear arms, though arms we need—not as a call to battle, though embattled we are—but a call to bear the burden of a long twilight struggle, year in and year out, "rejoicing in hope, patient in tribulation"—a struggle against the common enemies of man: tyranny, poverty, disease, and war itself.

Can we forge against these enemies a grand and global alliance, north and south, east and west, that can assure a more fruitful life for all mankind? Will you join in that historic effort?

In the long history of the world, only a few generations have been granted the role of defending freedom in its hour of maximum danger. I do not shrink from this responsibility—I welcome it. I do not believe that any of us would exchange places with any other people or any other generation. The energy, the faith, the devotion which we bring to this endeavor will light our country and all who serve it—and the glow from that fire can truly light the world.

And so, my fellow Americans: Ask not what your country can do for you—ask what you can do for your country.

My fellow citizens of the world: Ask not what America will do for you, but what together we can do for the freedom of man.

Finally, whether you are citizens of America or citizens of the world, ask of us here the same high standards of strength and sacrifice which we ask of you.

With a good conscience our only sure reward, with history the final judge of our deeds, let us go forth to lead the land we love, asking His blessing and His help, but knowing that here on earth God's work must truly be our own.

INSPIRATIONAL SPEECH

MARTIN LUTHER KING, JR.

I Have a Dream

Following is the speech Martin Luther King, Jr., gave in front of the Lincoln Memorial in Washington, D.C., in support of civil rights. The speech was delivered before 200,000 people on August 28, 1963.

. . . Five score years ago, a great American, in whose symbolic shadow we stand, signed the Emancipation Proclamation. This momentous decree came as a great beacon light of hope to millions of Negro slaves who had been seared in the flames of withering injustice. It came as a joyous daybreak to end the long night of captivity.

But one hundred years later, we must face the tragic fact that the Negro is still not free. One hundred years later, the life of the Negro is still sadly crippled by the manacles of segregation and the chains of discrimination. One hundred years later, the Negro lives on a lonely island of poverty in the midst of a vast ocean of material prosperity. One hundred years later, the Negro is still languished in the corners of American society and finds himself an exile in his own land. So we have come here today to dramatize an appalling condition.

In a sense we have come to our Nation's Capital to cash a check. When the architects of our Republic wrote the magnificent words of the Constitution and the Declaration of Independence, they were signing a promissory note to which every American was to fall heir. This note was a promise that all men would be guaranteed the unalienable rights of life, liberty, and the pursuit of happiness.

It is obvious today that America has defaulted on this promissory note insofar as her citizens of color are concerned. Instead of honoring this sacred obligation, America has given the Negro people a bad check; a check which has come back marked "insufficient funds." But we refuse to believe that the bank of justice is bankrupt. We refuse to believe that there are insufficient funds in the great vaults of opportunity of this nation. So we have come to cash this check—a check that will give us upon demand the riches of freedom and the security of justice. We have also come to this hallowed spot to remind America of the fierce urgency of now. This is no time to engage in the luxury of cooling off or to take the tranquilizing drug of gradualism. Now is the time to make real the promises of Democracy. Now is the time to rise from the dark and desolate valley of segregation to the sunlit path of racial justice. Now is the time to open the doors of opportunity to all of God's children. Now is the time to lift our nation from the quicksands of racial injustice to the solid rock of brotherhood.

It would be fatal for the nation to overlook the urgency of the moment and to underestimate the determination of the Negro. This sweltering summer of the Negro's legitimate discontent will not pass until there is an invigorating autumn of freedom and equality. 1963 is not an end, but a beginning. Those who hope that the Negro needed to blow off steam and now will be content will have a rude awakening if the Nation returns to business as usual. There will be neither rest nor tranquility in America until the Negro is granted his citizenship rights. The whirlwinds of revolt will continue to shake the foundations of our Nation until the bright day of justice emerges.

But there is something that I must say to my people who stand on the warm threshold which leads into the palace of justice. In the process of gaining our rightful place we must not be guilty of wrongful deeds. Let us not seek to satisfy our thirst for freedom by drinking from the cup of bitterness and hatred. We must forever conduct our struggle on the high plane of dignity and discipline. We must not allow our creative protest to degenerate into physical violence. Again and again we must rise to the majestic heights of meeting physical force with soul force. The marvelous new militancy which has engulfed the Negro community must not lead us to a distrust of all white people, for many of our white brothers, as evidenced by their presence here today, have come to realize that their destiny is tied up with our destiny and their freedom is inextricably bound to our freedom. We cannot walk alone.

And as we walk, we must make the pledge that we shall march ahead. We cannot turn back. There are those who are asking the devotees of civil rights, "When will you be satisfied?" We can never be satisfied as long as the Negro is the victim of the unspeakable horrors of police brutality. We can never be satisfied as long as our bodies, heavy with the fatigue of travel, cannot gain lodging in the motels of the highways and the hotels of the cities. We cannot be satisfied as long as the Negro's basic mobility is from a smaller ghetto to a larger one. We can never be satisfied as long as a Negro in Mississippi cannot vote and a Negro in New York believes he has nothing for which to vote. No, no, we are not satisfied, and we will not be satisfied until justice rolls down like water and righteousness like a mighty stream.

I am not unmindful that some of you have come here out of great trials and tribulations. Some of you have come fresh from narrow jail cells. Some of you have come from areas where your quest for freedom left you battered by the storms of persecution and staggered by the winds of police brutality. You have been the veterans of creative suffering. Continue to work with the faith that unearned suffering is redemptive.

Go back to Mississippi, go back to Alabama, go back to South Carolina, go back to Georgia, go back to Louisiana, go back to the slums and ghettos of our northern cities, knowing that somehow this situation can and will be changed. Let us not wallow in the valley of despair.

I say to you today, my friends, that in spite of the difficulties and frustrations of the moment, I still have a dream. It is a dream deeply rooted in the American dream.

I have a dream that one day this nation will rise up and live out the true meaning of its creed: "We hold these truths to be self-evident; that all men are created equal."

I have a dream that one day on the red hills of Georgia the sons of former slaves and the sons of former slave owners will be able to sit down together at the table of brotherhood.

I have a dream that one day even the state of Mississippi, a desert state sweltering with the heat of injustice and oppression, will be transformed into an oasis of freedom and justice.

I have a dream that my four little children will one day live in a nation where they will not be judged by the color of their skin but by the content of their character.

I have a dream today.

I have a dream that one day the state of Alabama, whose governor's lips are presently dripping with the words of interposition and nullification, will be transformed into a situation where little black boys and black girls will be able to join hands with little white boys and white girls and walk together as sisters and brothers.

I have a dream today.

I have a dream that one day every valley shall be exalted, every hill and mountain shall be made low, the rough places will be made plain, and the crooked places will be made straight, and the glory of the Lord shall be revealed, and all flesh shall see it together.

This is our hope. This is the faith with which I return to the South. With this faith we will be able to hew out of the mountain of despair a stone of hope. With this faith we will be able to transform the jangling discords of our nation into a beautiful symphony of brotherhood. With this faith we will be able to work together, to pray together, to struggle together, to go to jail together, to stand up for freedom together, knowing that we will be free one day.

This will be the day when all of God's children will be able to sing with new meaning "My country 'tis of thee, sweet land of liberty, of thee I sing. Land where my fathers died, land of the pilgrim's pride, from every mountainside, let freedom ring."

And if America is to be a great nation this must become true. So let freedom ring from the prodigious hilltops of New Hampshire. Let freedom ring from the mighty mountains of New York. Let freedom ring from the heightening Alleghenies of Pennsylvania!

Let freedom ring from the snowcapped Rockies of Colorado!

Let freedom ring from the curvaceous peaks of California!

But not only that—let freedom ring from Stone Mountain of Georgia! Let freedom ring from Lookout Mountain of Tennessee!

Let freedom ring from every hill and mole hill of Mississippi. From every mountainside, let freedom ring.

When we let freedom ring, when we let it ring from every village and every hamlet, from every state and every city, we will be able to speed up that day when all of God's children, black men and white men, Jews and Gentiles, Protestants and Catholics, will be able to join hands and sing in the words of that old Negro spiritual, "Free at last! Free at last! Thank God almighty, we are free at last!"

ACCEPTANCE SPEECH

WILLIAM FAULKNER

Nobel Prize Speech

When William Faulkner went to Stockholm, Sweden, to accept the Nobel Prize for literature in 1949, he delivered the following address. It has become a classic statement of his creed. He recognized people's capacity for self-destruction, but he also put faith in people's ability to rise above their natural limitations.

I feel that this award was not made to me as a man, but to my work—a life's work in the agony and sweat of the human spirit, not for glory and least of all for profit, but to create out of the materials of the human spirit something which did not exist before. So this award is only mine in trust. It will not be difficult to find a dedication for the money part of it commensurate with the purpose and significance of its origin. But I would like to do the same with the acclaim too, by using this moment as a pinnacle from which I might be listened to by the young men and women already dedicated to the same anguish and travail, among whom is already that one who will someday stand here where I am standing.

Our tragedy today is a general and universal physical fear so long sustained by now that we can even bear it. There are no longer problems of the spirit. There is only the question: When will I be blown up? Because of this, the young man or woman writing today has forgotten the problems of the human heart in conflict with itself which alone can make good writing because only that is worth writing about, worth the agony and the sweat.

He must learn them again. He must teach himself that the basest of all things is to be afraid; and, teaching himself that, forget it forever, leaving no room in this workshop for anything but the old verities and truths of the heart, the old universal truths lacking which any story is ephemeral and doomed—love and honor and pity and pride and compassion and sacrifice. Until he does so, he labors under a curse. He writes not of love but of lust, of defeats in which nobody loses anything of value, of victories without hope, and, worst of all, without pity or compassion. His griefs grieve on no universal bones, leaving no scars. He writes not of the heart but of the glands.

Until he relearns these things, he will write as though he stood among and watched the end of man. I decline to accept the end of man. It is easy enough to say that man is immortal simply because he will endure; that when the last ding-dong of doom has clanged and faded from the last worthless rock hanging tideless in the last red and dying evening, that even then there will still be one more sound: that of his puny inexhaustible voice, still talking. I refuse to accept this. I believe that man will not merely endure: he will prevail. He is immortal, not because he alone among creatures has an inexhaustible voice, but because he has a soul, a spirit capable of compassion and sacrifice and endurance. The poet's, the writer's, duty is to write about these things. It is his privilege to help man endure by lifting his heart, by reminding him of the courage and honor and hope and pride and compassion and pity and sacrifice which have been the glory of his past. The poet's voice need not merely be the record of man; it can be one of the props, the pillars, to help him endure and prevail.

ABRAHAM LINCOLN

The Gettysburg Address

On November 19, 1863, Abraham Lincoln gave a speech at the dedication of the National Soldiers' Cemetery at Gettysburg, Pennsylvania. The ten sentences of the speech took only five minutes to deliver, but one of the newspaper reviewers of the time called it "a perfect gem; deep in feeling, compact in thought and expression, and tasteful and elegant in every word and comma."

Fourscore and seven years ago our fathers brought forth on this continent a new nation, conceived in liberty, and dedicated to the proposition that all men are created equal.

Now we are engaged in a great civil war, testing whether that nation, or any nation so conceived and so dedicated, can long endure. We are met on a great battlefield of that war. We have come to dedicate a portion of that field as a final resting-place for those who here gave their lives that that nation might live. It is altogether fitting and proper that we should do this.

But, in a larger sense, we cannot dedicate—we cannot consecrate—we cannot hallow—this ground. The brave men, living and dead, who struggled here, have consecrated it far above our poor power to add or detract. The world will little note nor long remember what we say here, but it can never forget what they did here. It is for us, the living, rather, to be dedicated here to the unfinished work which they who fought here have thus far so nobly advanced. It is rather for us to be here dedicated to the great task remaining before us—that from these honored dead we take increased devotion to that cause for which they gave the last full measure of devotion; that we here highly resolve that these dead shall not have died in vain; that this nation, under God, shall have a new birth of freedom; and that government of the people, by the people, for the people, shall not perish from the earth.

BOOKER T. WASHINGTON

The Heroes of Fort Wagner

Booker T. Washington delivered the following speech on the occasion of the unveiling of the Shaw Monument in Boston, May 31, 1897. Robert Gould Shaw was the commander of the 54th Massachusetts Regiment during the Civil War. At Fort Wagner, South Carolina, Shaw was killed when his regiment charged in the face of heavy fire.

Mr. Chairman and Fellow Citizens:—In this presence, and on this sacred and memorable day, in the deeds and death of our hero, we recall the old, old story, ever old, yet ever new, that when it was the will of the Father to lift humanity out of wretchedness and bondage, the precious task was delegated to Him who, among ten thousand, was altogether lovely, and was willing to make Himself of no reputation that He might save and lift up others.

If that heart could throb and if those lips could speak, what would be the sentiment and words that Robert Gould Shaw would have us feel and speak at this hour? He would not have us dwell long on the mistakes, the injustice, the criticisms, of the days

"Of storm and cloud, of doubt and fears,
Across the eternal sky must lower;
Before the glorious noon appears."

He would have us bind up with his own undying fame and memory and retain by the side of his monument the name of John A. Andrews, who, with prophetic vision and strong arm, helped to make the existence of the Fifty-fourth regiment possible; and that of George L. Stearns, who, with hidden generosity and a great sweet heart, helped to turn the darkest hour into day, and in doing so, freely gave service, fortune, and life itself to the cause which this day commemorates. Nor would he have us forget those brother officers, living and dead, who by their baptism in blood and fire, in defence of union and freedom, gave us an example of the highest and purest patriotism.

To you who fought so valiantly in the ranks, the scarred and scattered remnant of the Fifty-fourth regiment, who, with empty sleeve and wanting leg, have honored this occasion with your presence, to you, your commander is not dead. If Boston erected no monument and history recorded no story, in you and the loyal race which you represent, Robert Gould Shaw would have a monument which time could not wear away.

But an occasion like this is too great, too sacred for mere individual eulogy. The individual is the instrument, national virtue the end. That which was three hundred years being woven into the warp and woof of our democratic institutions, could not be effaced by a single battle, as magnificent as was that battle; that which for three centuries had bound master and slave, yea, North and South, to a body of death, could not be blotted out by four years of war, could not be atoned for by shot and sword, nor by blood and tears.

Not many days ago in the heart of the South, in a large gathering of the people of my race, there were heard from many lips praises and thanksgiving to God for His goodness in setting them free from physical slavery. In the midst of that assembly, a Southern white man arose, with grey hair and trembling hands, the former owner of many slaves, and from his quivering lips there came the words: "My friends, you forget in your rejoicing that in setting you free, God was also good to me and my race in setting us free." But there is a higher and deeper sense in which both races must be free than that represented by the bill of sale. The black man who cannot let love and sympathy go out to the white man, is but half free. The white man who would close the shop or factory against a black man seeking an opportunity to earn an honest living, is but half free. The white man who retards his own development by opposing a black man, is but half free.

The full measure of the fruit of Fort Wagner and all that this monument stands for will not be realized until every man covered with a black skin shall, by patience and natural effort, grow to the height in industry, property, intelligence, and moral responsibility, where no man in all our land will be tempted to degrade himself by withholding from his black brother any opportunity which he himself would possess.

Until that time comes this monument will stand for effort, not victory complete. What these heroic souls of the Fifty-fourth regiment began, we must complete. It must be completed not in malice, not in narrowness; nor artificial progress, nor in efforts at mere temporary political gain, nor in abuse of another section or race.

Standing as I do today in the home of Garison and Phillips and Sumner, my heart goes out to those who wore grey as well as to those clothed in blue; to those who returned defeated, to destitute homes, to face blasted hopes and shattered political and industrial systems. To them there can be no prouder reward for defeat than by a supreme effort to place the Negro on that footing where he will add material, intellectual, and civil strength to every department of State.

This work must be completed in public school, industrial school, and college. The most of it must be completed in the effort of the Negro himself, in his effort to withstand temptation, to economize, to exercise thrift, to disregard the superficial for the real—the shadow for the substances, to be great and yet small, in his effort to be patient in the laying of a firm foundation, to so grow in skill and knowledge that he shall place his services in demand by reason of his intrinsic and superior worth. This is the key that unlocks every door of opportunity, and all others fail. In this battle of peace the rich and poor, the black and white, may have a part.

What lesson has this occasion for the future? What of hope, what of encouragement, what of caution? "Watchman, tell us of the night; what the signs of promise are." If through me, a humble representative, nearly ten millions of my people might be permitted to send a message to Massachusetts, to the survivors of the Fifty-fourth regiment, to the committee whose untiring energy has made this memorial possible, to the family who gave their only boy that we might have life more abundantly, that message would be, "Tell them that the sacrifice was not in vail; that up from the depth of ignorance and poverty, we are coming, and if we come through oppression out of the struggle, we are gaining strength. By the way of the school, the well-cultivated field, the skilled hand, the Christian home, we are coming up; that we propose to invite all who will to step up and occupy this position with us.

Tell them that we are learning that standing ground for the race, as for the individual, must be laid in intelligence, industry, thrift, and property, not as an end, but as a means to the highest privileges; that we are learning that neither the conqueror's bullet nor fiat of law could make an ignorant voter an intelligent voter, could make a dependent man an independent man, could give one citizen respect for another, a bank account, nor a foot of land, nor an enlightened fireside.

Tell them that, as grateful as we are to artist and patriotism for placing the figures of Shaw and his comrades in physical form of beauty and magnificence, that after all, the real monument, the greater monument, is being slowly but safely built among the lowly in the South, in the struggles and sacrifices of a race to justify all that has been done and suffered for it.

One of the wishes that lay nearest Col. Shaw's heart was that his black troops might be permitted to fight by the side of white soldiers. Have we not lived to see that wish realized, and will it not be more so in the future? Not at Wagner, not with rifle and bayonet, but on the field of peace, in the battle of industry, in the struggle for good government, in the lifting up of the lowest to the fullest opportunities. In this we shall fight by the side of white men, North and South. And if this be true, as under God's guidance it will, that old flag, that emblem of progress and security which brave Sergeant Carney never permitted to fall on the ground, will still be borne aloft by Southern soldier and Northern soldier, and in a more potent and higher sense, we shall all realize that

"The slave's chain and the master's alike are broken;
The one curse of the race held both in tether;
They are rising; all are rising—
The black and the white together."

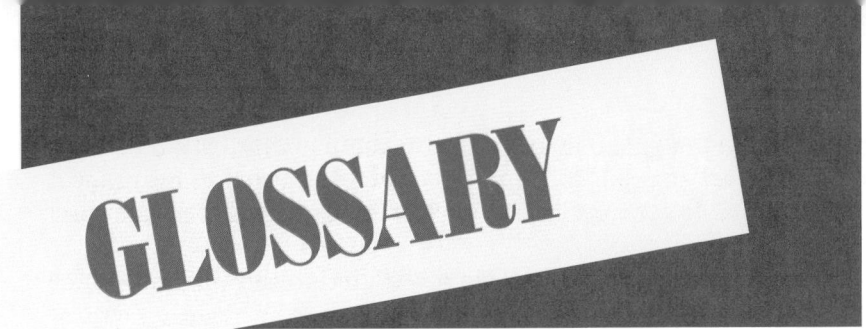
GLOSSARY

abstain: decide not to vote (23)

abstract ideas: ideas you cannot see, hear, smell, taste, or touch; ideas that mean different things to different people (11)

acting: process of taking on the characteristics of another person (19)

ad hominem **arguments:** negative remarks about a person that are used to discredit that person's ideas (4)

affirmative side: the side in a debate that favors or supports the statements (22)

amend: change the words in a proposal (23)

antagonist: character who threatens the character around whom the play revolves (19)

anxiety: nervousness (13)

apathetic audience: audience that doesn't care about the subject matter of a speech or doesn't see the subject matter's importance (15)

articulation: process of starting and stopping consonant sounds clearly (5)

audience reaction: vocal and nonverbal responses from the audience (13)

audio-visual aid: pictures or objects that help to explain a point (14)

audition: perform before judges in an attempt to secure a part in a play (20)

audition form: form that asks for certain information that will be helpful to the director and must be filled out by everyone who comes to an audition (20)

basic (fighting) issues: major points of disagreement between the affirmative and negative sides in a debate (22)

blocking: director's plan for the movements of all the actors (19)

body of a speech: part that contains all the main ideas and their supporting points; the heart of a speech (12)

burden of proof: necessity of the affirmative side in a debate to win every issue that it introduces (22)

call-back: second audition that is held to make a decision between two or more performers who had previously tried out for the same part (20)

call number: combination of numbers and letters assigned to a library book to indicate its place on the shelf (12)

case: all evidence and reasoning supporting a point of view that a debater presents to a judge (22)

cast: people who actually perform in a play (20)

cause-effect relationship: circumstance in which first event caused the second one (4)

chair: presiding officer or chairperson (23)

characterization: establishing the traits of each character (18)

choral speaking: a form of group interpretation in which voices are blended together to produce a group voice (17)

clichés: overused expressions that have lost their meaning (6)

climax: turning point of a story (16)

closed audition: kind of audition at which only people meeting certain criteria may try out for a part (20)

commercials: on-the-air advertising of a product or service (21)

communication: process of sending and receiving messages (1)

composite recital: a form of group interpretation in which two or more people read various pieces of literature (17)

concepts: things you cannot see, hear, smell, taste, or touch (11)

conclusion: the short end of a speech that usually emphasizes or summarizes the purpose of the speech (12)

concrete: things you can see, hear, smell, taste, or touch (11)

conflict: element that places the main character up against an opposing force (16)

connotation: emotional, subjective, or implied meaning of a word (6)

constructive speech: a debater's first speech that develops the case that his/her team supports (22)

context clue: any word or group of words that come before, during, or after a verbal message (4)

conversation: process in which two or more people exchange verbal, vocal, and nonverbal messages (7)

credibility: authority or believability (15)

critique: critical evaluation or judgment of a speech made by one or more members of an audience; can be oral or written (13)

cue: hint about the two people you are introducing to help them begin a conversation with each other; words that signal an actor to begin his/her lines (8) (19)

cut: shorten (16)

cybernetics: the study of machines that send messages (3)

debate: a formal, orderly communication process during which two or more opposing speakers try to prove a statement with evidence and reasoning (22)

debate brief: a debate case which is outlined; each item that must be proved will contain either "for" or "because" at the end of the line (22)

deductive reasoning: reasoning that moves from a large, general rule to a specific one (22)

delivery: giving a speech to an audience (13)

demonstration speech: an informative speech in which the speaker teaches the listeners how to make, do, or use something (14)

denotation: the direct, specific, dictionary meaning of a word (6)

descriptive gesture: body gesture that gives a visual picture of size, shape, or action (6)

Dewey Decimal System: used most often in schools, in this system each book in the library is given a number according to its subject matter (12)

dialogue: words spoken by characters in a story or play; in drama, dialogue can also occur between the characters and the audience (16) (18)

diaphragm: powerful muscle that separates the chest from the stomach area (5)

directive leader: person who takes charge by giving orders, assigning tasks, and setting guidelines for discussion (9)

discussion: an exchange of information or ideas about one subject (9)

documentaries: in-depth reports on an important subject (21)

downstage: the part of a stage that is closest to an audience (19)

etiquette: accepted ways of behaving in certain situations (7)

eulogy: speech that praises a person, generally given at a funeral or memorial service (10)

evidence: factual information to back up an opinion (15) (22)

exhaling: breathing out air (5)

extemporaneous speech: speech that has had considerable preparation time, is not written down, and normally is not committed to memory (10)

eye contact: looking directly at the people you are talking to (13)

fact: statement that can be proved (4)

falling action: action that takes place after the climax, when loose ends are tied up (16)

falling inflection: a change in pitch that begins at one note (on a musical scale) and glides downward to a lower note (5)

feedback: the receiver's response to the message or information the director gives to cast and crew after a rehearsal for the purpose of improving the play (1) (20)

figurative gesture: body gesture that suggests an idea or emotion (6)

floor: the right to speak (23)

flow sheet: a debate brief that is constructed during a debate to outline the other team's case (22)

formal usage: careful, controlled communication (6)

generalization: a statement that lumps a whole group of people or things together, then condemns all for the qualities of some (4)

group communication: communication involving three or more people (1)

group interpretation: a public presentation of literature that involves two or more interpreters presenting the same or different selections (17)

group voice: a blending together of voices (17)

half-truths: statements that tell only half the story; they are correct as far as they go but they don't go far enough (4)

impromptu speech: a speech that is given without much, if any, preparation (10)

improvisation: a pantomime with verbal and vocal messages in which the performers choose their words and actions spontaneously (18)

inductive reasoning: reasoning that begins with a group of facts, cases, or examples, and then moves to a generalization made from them (22)

inflection: the gradual change in pitch within a single breath (5) (8)

informal usage: more relaxed communication (6)

informative speech: a talk whose purpose is giving information to people; it offers useful or interesting facts (14)

inhaling: breathing in air (5)

interpersonal communication: communication on a one-to-one basis (1)

interview: a special type of communication that is planned and structured (8)

interviewee: the person being interviewed (8)

intrapersonal communication: communication with, or within, yourself (for example, thinking as well as talking aloud to yourself) (1)

introduction: the first part of a speech; its main purpose is to get the attention of the audience (12)

larynx: voice box (5)

lecture-discussion: a very formal discussion that includes periods of structured lectures by the discussion leader and generally is followed by responses by specific, predetermined individuals (9)

Library of Congress System: used by the United States Library of Congress and by most large city and college libraries, this system gives each book in the library a combination of letters and numbers to indicate its place on the shelf (12)

main idea: central thought a speaker wants to express (4)

major heads: part of an outline that follows the Roman numerals and states the main ideas of a speech (12)

manuscript speech: a speech that is written out entirely in advance of its presentation (10)

mass communication: one or more people communicating with a large audience (1)

medial inflection: change in pitch that begins at one note (on a musical scale), glides up or down to another note, and then moves back close to the original note (5)

messages: ideas, feelings, thoughts, and statements sent from one person and received by another (1)

mini-series: a program that takes from four to sixteen hours to air and is usually based on a novel or historical character or event; usually shown four or five nights in a row (21)

minutes: report of what happened at the previous meeting (23)

misleading comparison: statement that doesn't compare equal things (4)

mixed feedback: people in the audience responding in different ways to the speaker; for example, some applaud loudly, some politely, and some not at all (3)

monologue: a dramatic speech that is given by one actor as he or she thinks aloud and is overheard by the audience (18)

motion: a proposal put before a group for its consideration (23)

mutual respect: an understanding and acceptance of each other's views (2)

narrative: a story (14)

negative feedback: receiver's negative response to the sender's message; for example, no applause after a speech is delivered (3)

negative reinforcement: blame (15)

negative side: the side in a debate that opposes the statement (22)

network: several small radio stations joined together so that stations can use each other's programs (21)

neutral feedback: polite response to the speaker; for example, light or polite applause (3)

nickelodeons: places where people could see several short films for a nickel (21)

noise: anything that takes attention away from the message or the feedback (3)

nondirective leader: person who allows the group to make most of its decisions and gives very few directions (9)

nonstandard English: messages that do not follow formal rules of grammar (6)

nonverbal messages: messages that have no words or sounds; they are made up of clues such as facial expressions and body movements (1)

open forum: meeting at which people in the audience ask panel members questions about statements the panel members made (9)

open audition: audition at which anyone can try out for a part (20)

opinion: statement that has not been proven true or false (4)

opposed audience: audience that has already made up its mind on the subject-matter of a speech; its opinion is the opposite of the speaker's (15)

optimum pitch: level at which a person speaks with least strain or effort (5)

oral interpretation: formal discussion by a group of four to eight individuals; remarks are spontaneous, no pattern for participation is set (16)

panel discussion: meeting at which small groups discuss different parts of a topic at the same time, then the leaders of each group report their findings to the entire group (9)

pantomime: dramatic form of communication that uses only gestures, facial expressions, and movements to convey meanings (18)

paralanguage: changes in inflection that alter the meaning of a vocal message (3)

parliamentary procedure: set of rules for keeping order during meetings (23)

pending: describes action that is being considered (23)

personal diplomacy: ability to deal with people in a tactful way (7)

persuasive speech: speech that tries to influence the attitudes, beliefs, or behavior of an audience (15)

phonation: vibration of the vocal cords, creating sound (5)

picturesque language: descriptive language in which words and sentence patterns create an effect or atmosphere (6)

plain language: simple, straightforward language that is direct and understandable (6)

pointing: emphasizing certain words to create an emotional response (19)

point of view: voice through which the writer tells a story (16)

positive feedback: good response to a public speech; for example, loud, lengthy applause (3)

positive reinforcement: praise to listeners for doing what you want them to do (15)

prima facie **case:** a debate case that is strong enough to win if it is not answered (22)

prime time: time between 7 and 10 P.M. when the best television programs are shown because entire families are home (21)

progressive discussion: meeting at which small groups discuss different parts of a topic at the same time, then the leaders of each group report their findings to the entire group (9)

projection: degree of force and volume used to send a person's voice forward (19)

prompt: assist an actor in a play by saying a word or part of a line that the actor has forgotten (19)

promptbook: copy of a play's script in which are written all the director's notes and blocking (20)

proposition: subject of a debate that proposes a change from what currently exists (22)

props: all movable items that actors use in a play (short for **properties**) (20)

protagonist: character around whom the play revolves (19)

public communication: involves one or more speakers who present a message to a group of inactive listeners (1)

ratings: results from a survey of selected homes to find out which programs are being watched at certain times (21)

Readers' Guide to Periodical Literature: library source that indexes all articles in magazines and journals by subject and author (12)

Readers' Theater: form of group interpretation in which two or more readers present literature in a dramatic way (17)

reasoning: inferences or conclusions that are drawn from facts (22)

rebuttal: process of rebuilding an argument after it has been attacked by an opponent in a debate (22)

rebuttal speech: the shorter, final speech in a debate that argues against the statements made by the opposite side (22)

receiver: one who gets the message and interprets what it means (1)

refutation: process of attacking the opposing side's case in a debate by disproving or weakening its major arguments (22)

reinforcement: a technique used by a speaker to change the minds of the listeners by showing them the benefit of doing so (15)

resolution: the written, formal debate propositions (22)

resonance: quality of voice that is produced from solid bodies and partially enclosed cavities; these vibrate in response to sound from the larynx as it is directed upward and outward through the nose and mouth (5)

rhetorical question: a question that is asked with no answer expected; its purpose is to start someone thinking (6) (14)

rhyme scheme: pattern created by the rhyming words at the ends of lines (16)

rising action: the part of a story in which the writer tells some of the problems the character has; these problems stop the character from finding an answer to the conflict (16)

rising inflection: change in pitch that begins at one note (on a musical scale) and glides upward to a higher note (5)

royalties: fee charged for the right to perform a published work (20)

round-table discussion: form of discussion that begins with a brief report by the leader and is followed by short reports by experts who talk among themselves (9)

salutatorian speech: speech given at graduation by the second highest ranked student (10)

second a motion: show approval of a motion (23)

self-concept: things that you see and think about yourself (2)

self-confidence: belief that you have the ability to do things and do them right (2)

self-esteem: value that you place on yourself (2)

sender: the one who sends a message (1)

sentence outline: one kind of outline in which the main points or heads are summaries of ideas that are written in complete sentences (12)

slang: informal language that uses words and phrases in many different contexts; has very little meaning; or is meaningful for a short time and then disappears (6)

small talk: casual conversation about impersonal topics; for example, the weather (8)

soap opera: oldest form of drama, began on radio as a dramatic afternoon show for women; usually sponsored by companies that made soap; made an easy transition to television; some may even be seen in the evening during prime time (21)

spin-offs: popular comedy or drama programs some of whose characters become stars on their own programs (21)

sponsor: a company that is the advertiser for the same program each week (21)

stage fright: nervousness (13)

standard English: set of grammar rules taught in English classes (6)

statistic: fact expressed in numbers (14)

step: unique type of inflection that creates an abrupt change in pitch (5)

stereotypes: false generalizations or conclusions that are made from a few quick facts (2)

stock issues: standard questions that will be supported and attacked in most debates; three traditional stock issues are: Is there need for a change? Is there a plan that meets the need to change? Is the proposed plan the best, most practical one available? (22)

supporting detail: point that further explains the main idea; can be anything from fact to belief (4)

supportive audience: audience that shares the speaker's point of view (15)

supportive leader: leader who makes suggestions but doesn't give orders (9)

syllogism: deductive scheme of a formal argument consisting of a major and minor premise and a conclusion (22)

symposium: structured discussion at which several specialists deliver short addresses on a topic or on related topics; each presenter is given a time limit; the leader summarizes the presentations and draws conclusions (9)

table: put a motion aside until later (23)

tact: ability to know the right time to say or do something (7)

tangible: things you can see, hear, smell, taste, or touch (11)

thesis: central idea (10)

tone: speaker's attitude toward a subject (15)

topical outline: kind of outline in which the main points are summaries of ideas that are written in words and phrases (12)

trachea: windpipe (5)

traits: characteristics (7)

transitional: describes words or sentences that are used to connect or bridge major ideas (16)

transitions: words or groups of words that relate one idea in your speech to the next idea (12)

uncommitted audience: audience that has not yet made up its mind about the subject matter of a speech; they are waiting to learn more about the subject matter before taking a stand (15)

upstage: part of a stage that is farthest from the audience (19)

valedictorian speech: speech delivered at graduation by the top student in the class (10)

verbal messages: actual words a sender uses (1)

vocal messages: voice sounds including cries, whistles, grunts, moans and so on (1)

INDEX

ACKNOWLEDGMENTS

Grateful acknowledgment is made to the following publishers, authors, and agents for permission to use and adapt copyrighted material:

City News Publishing Company for Gerry Sikorski, "Will and Vision, the Tools You Need," in *Vital Speeches of the Day,* 1986. Reprinted by permission of City News Publishing Company.

Joan Daves for "I Have a Dream" by Martin Luther King, Jr. Reprinted by permission of Joan Daves. Copyright © 1963 by Martin Luther King, Jr.

The Dramatic Publishing Company for the excerpt from the play *Twelve Angry Men* by Reginald Rose. © Copyright MCMLV by Reginald Rose. Based upon the television show *Twelve Angry Men.* All rights Reserved. Used by permission.

Arthur Hailey for the excerpt from *Flight into Danger* by Arthur Hailey. Reprinted by permission of Seaway Authors Ltd. and Arthur Hailey.

Harper & Row, Publishers, Inc., for "Woman's Right to the Suffrage" by Susan B. Anthony from *The World's Famous Orations,* edited by W. J. Bryan and F. W. Halsey. Published by Funk and Wagnalls Company in 1906.

Harvard University Press for "A Narrow Fellow in the Grass" by Emily Dickinson. Reprinted by permission of the publishers and the Trustees of Amherst College from THE POEMS OF EMILY DICKINSON, edited by Thomas H. Johnson, Cambridge, Mass.: the Belknap Press of Harvard University Press, Copyright 1951, © 1955, 1979, 1983 by The President and Fellows of Harvard College.

Alfred A. Knopf, Inc., for "Dream Variations" by Langston Hughes. Copyright 1926 by Alfred A. Knopf, Inc. and renewed 1954 by Langston Hughes. Reprinted from SELECTED POEMS OF LANGSTON HUGHES, by Langston Hughes, by permission of the publisher.

Little, Brown and Company for poem#1075, "The Sky is low—the Clouds are mean," from *The Complete Poems of Emily Dickinson,* edited by Thomas H. Johnson; Little, Brown and Company, 1960.

The Pennsylvania State University Press for the poem "dandelions" from *The Paradise of the World* by Deborah Austin. Published in 1964 by The Pennsylvania State University Press, University Park, Pennsylvania. Used by permission.

Simon & Schuster, Inc., for speeches by Winston Churchill ("This was their finest hour") and by William Faulkner (The Nobel Prize Speech), both from *A Treasury of the World's Great Speeches,* edited by Houston Peterson. Copyright © 1954, 1965 by Simon & Schuster, Inc. Reprinted by permission of SIMON & SCHUSTER, Inc.

Viking Penguin Inc. for the poem "Crossing" from LETTER FROM A DISTANT LAND by Philip Booth. Copyright 1953, renewed © 1981 by Philip Booth. Originally published in *The New Yorker.* Reprinted by permission of Viking Penguin, Inc. Also for the excerpt from "The Waltz" in THE PORTABLE DOROTHY PARKER. Copyright 1933, renewed © 1961 by Dorothy Parker. Originally published in *The New Yorker.* Reprinted by permission of Viking Penguin Inc.

CREDITS

Senior Editor: Patricia B. Weiler
Art Director: L. Christopher Valente
Design: The Book Department, Inc.
Design Production: Richard Dalton
Preparation Services Manager: Martha E. Ballentine
Buyer: Roger E. Powers
Creative Art: Chris Demarest
Technical Art: Paul S. Foti
Photo Research: Susan Van Etten
Cover Design: Richard Hannus